The Mammoth Book of

HEROIC & OUTRAGEOUS WOMEN

The Mammoth Book of

HEROIC &
OUTRAGEOUS
WOMEN

Edited by

Gemma Alexander

Carroll & Graf Publishers, Inc.
NEW YORK

Carroll & Graf Publishers, Inc.
19 West 21st Street
New York
NY 10010–6805

First published in the UK by Robinson Publishing Ltd 1999

First Carroll & Graf edition 1999

Collection and editorial copyright © Gemma Alexander 1999

ISBN 0–7867–0695–3

Printed and bound in the EC

CONTENTS

INTRODUCTION

'Brevity is the soul of lingerie,' the American satirical writer Dorothy Parker remarked some years ago – and my introduction to this collection will be similarly brief because the heroic and eccentric women gathered together in these pages are intriguing enough not to need many words from me. In fact, they don't deserve to be kept waiting long for your attention at all; especially because while most of them were alive, they made it very plain that *no one* kept them waiting!

Although biographies of famous women have become a virtual industry in recent years, it is interesting to discover that collections of stories about notable females have actually been assembled since the days of antiquity. In the eighth century BC, for example, the Greek romantic writer Hesiod compiled a book about goddesses, queens and heroines. Later, in 1355, the Italian author Giovanni Boccaccio wrote *De Claribus Mulieribus* in which he described a number of remarkable women whose actions proved them to be every bit the equal of men. Perhaps some of my readers also remember Geoffrey Chaucer's *Canterbury Tales* and that intriguing book which the last husband of the Wife of Bath so enjoyed: *The Boke of Wikked Wyves*? And, of course, we must not forget Christine de Pisan, the medieval French intellectual who has been described as 'the first European feminist' and produced *Cité des Dames* in which she described the heroics and eccentricities of a whole assembly of women. This volume is very much in that tradition, although in the main my women are from more recent times.

If, though, this collection had a source of inspiration, I

would have to own up to Edith Sitwell's wonderful *English Eccentrics* which was published in 1933. The daughter of an upper-class eccentric herself, she became notorious with her collection, *Façade* (1923), and thereafter generated her own legend by wearing the most exotic costumes and jewellery. *The English Eccentrics* surveys the rich tradition to which she belonged, and at the same time demonstrates the part that women played in it. Her guidelines for inclusion have been very much my own, too: women who have had the courage to take on the world or, alternatively, shocked society – sometimes even changed it – by their lives, attitudes and, most of all, their achievements.

There are, of course, many other notable characters who might have found a place in this volume – names like Mistinguett and Garbo spring to mind, Christina, ex-Queen of Sweden, the adventurous Lady Hester Stanhope and the divine dancer Isadora Duncan – but I have endeavoured to be representative of both the bravest and the most outrageous of this unique sisterhood. If a favourite or two of your own is missing, do encourage the publisher to commission a second collection!

When I first began work on this volume, a male friend insisted that men had always outdone women when it came to extraordinary behaviour. On the day I put a copy of this book in his hands, I expect him to admit just how wrong he was. For if it shows one thing above all others, it is that men still have a lot to learn from women when it comes to being truly heroic and outrageously eccentric!

Gemma Alexander

One
The Bravura Ladies

A Pageant of Historical Characters

Lola Montez

Lady Godiva (c. 1040–80)

The Naked Heroine

Lady Godiva, the beautiful wife of the Earl of Mercia, is famous for her naked ride through the streets of Coventry. Her bravura performance was in answer to a challenge from her husband that it was the only thing which would make him lift the punitive taxes he had imposed on the citizens. Seriously meant or not, Godiva took the earl at his word and with only her golden tresses to cover her modesty, crossed the city on the back of a white horse. A story that one man defied the order that all households must close their shutters as she passed by gave rise to the legend of 'Peeping Tom' – as well as further enhancing her fame. **Marina Warner** examines the story of this unabashed heroine and enduring icon.

Roger of Wendover, the thirteenth-century chronicler who first tells the story of Lady Godiva's ride, does not titter or exclaim or even show any degree of surprise. He reports that in the year 1057, Leofric, Earl of Mercia, died and was buried in the monastery in Coventry which he had founded with his wife Godiva. They had endowed it so richly that 'there was not found in all England a monastery with such an abundance of gold and silver, gems and costly garments'.

In the same obituary tone, Roger then describes how the pious Godiva, a special lover ('amatrix') of the Virgin, inspired another, even greater gift.

Godiva 'longed' to lighten the toll levied on the people of Coventry, but when she pleaded with Leofric he remonstrated that she should not ask him for something so contrary to his interests. But she continued, 'with a woman's pertinacity' and he became exasperated, and challenged her to her famous ride, specifying she should go 'naked' through the market-place. Godiva took two soldiers with her, and mounted her horse. The 'hair of her head and her tresses', as Roger pleonastically puts it, veiled her whole body so that no one could see anything of her except her 'cruribus candissimus', her white, white legs.

Leofric was astonished when she returned to him, 'joyful', and he freed Coventry from the toll.

Roger of Wendover had a taste for spicy miracle stories, and Godiva's exploit did not retain him long. But it caught in the memory of his readers for ever. Like many stories that survive and grow as they pass from one writer to another, Lady Godiva's ride comes out of topsy-turvy land; it turns normal life and expectations inside-out. Leofric's challenge to his wife would seem to be rhetorical, an exasperated reaction, not a straight request. When she calls his bluff, we would expect him to feel fooled, even angry. But he is only 'astonished' (no censure, no shame).

We would also expect the kind of man who would ask such a thing to be a knave. Yet Roger presents him as a great, munificent lord, and the incident and its instigation entirely straightforward. Later writers have not been able to accept this Leofric, and he appears variously as a churl and a villain, a tyrant and an unsavoury voyeur, a second King Candaules. Tennyson's 'grim earl', in the poem *Godiva*, is a beast, surrounded by beasts.

> *And from a heart as rough as Esau's hand,*
> *He answered, 'Ride you naked through the town,*
> *And I repeal it,' and nodding, as in scorn,*
> *He parted, with great strides among his dogs.*

Godiva herself inverts the norm, too. Her public shame becomes her triumph. She takes up her husband's extraordinary challenge and cuts across the grain of everything we should expect of a virgin votary and lavish endower of monasteries. By exposing herself and defying the maidenly modesty enjoined by her religion, she significantly increases her power.

She has demonstrated that her virtue is proof against anything, even the profanity of public exhibition.

Lady Godiva certainly figures frequently as a donor to churches and religious foundations of land and gifts in various different documents. She is mentioned in the Domesday Book as the possessor of a certain village in Staffordshire.

It is possible, too, that Godiva was married before, and endowed the monastery at Ely with many possessions in 1022 during a serious illness. If this is the same woman, Godiva would have been about forty at the time of her ride.

Chroniclers introduced changes into the story of her ride. One account related how everyone was silenced by the sight of her, except for a horse that neighed. As a result, taxes continued to be levied on horses passing through the town.

Richard Grafton, who was MP for Coventry in 1562–73 and an ardent Protestant, printer of a Bible and of the Book of Common Prayer, shied from the brazenness of the medieval story, and introduced a novel element. His Godiva summons all the magistrates and officials of Coventry and the surrounding areas and orders them to make sure all windows are shuttered and all doors closed and the populace commanded to stay within 'upon a great pain'. Those fair, white legs on general view were too much for Grafton's reformed conscience.

The notion that no one witnessed her ordeal became established, but in the early seventeenth century, a new character was introduced – Peeping Tom, a tailor, who could not contain his curiosity and looked out from a window, 'But it cost him his life,' says the chronicler, sternly. Peeping Tom is probably the most genuinely popular figure in the legend, a kind of Everyman, and Coventry displays several effigies of him. The city paraded him in pride of place in the processions that began in 1678. The punished blasphemer is a stock in trade of the cautionary tales preachers used to relish.

None of this spoils the festiveness and fun of the Godiva myth; Puritan warnings had a way of being ignored. What is interesting is that the story depends on the idea that Godiva nobly accepted a kind of complete degradation, that her nudity was an act of beautiful self-sacrifice.

But while the narrative could not function without this central pin, it remains obvious that the story is also telling us that her nakedness was wonderful, that her ride was a glory to her and tremendously enjoyable, too. This ambivalence is essential, and still as powerful. Coventry could no more ask a young woman today to impersonate Lady Godiva in the buff than it could have in the Puritan seventeenth century. It would not be proper.

Streaking spontaneously is one thing, cycling nude for charity another; but institutionalized stripping for women jumbles the categories of official and unofficial rights and wrongs too subversively to be tolerated.

The city historians of Coventry stress that the processions have always been seemly (in one case the horse wore trousers, too). Lady Godiva, however much she awakens the Peeping Tom in us all, is not allowed to become an excuse for ribaldry or charivari or carnival obscenities.

Sometimes Godiva's name – which means Gift of God – is spelt 'Good-Eve'. Lady Godiva is the good Eve; her nakedness recalls the other familiar nude of premodern culture, the bad mother of us all, who led her husband to do wrong, not right.

Some historians have found traces in Godiva's story of a pagan fertility ritual, in which a young girl, a 'May Queen', was brought to the sacred Cofa-tree (after which Coventry is perhaps called) to celebrate the renewal of spring.

Ursula Sontheil (1488–1561)

The Mother
of Fortune-Tellers

'Mother Shipton' is the name by which Ursula Sontheil
is known as one of the first and still best remembered
prophets and fortune-tellers. An unfortunately ugly
and eccentric woman, stories of her psychic powers
and ability to predict the future nevertheless brought
men and women of all backgrounds to her home in
Yorkshire for consultations. Rumours that Ursula had
inherited her talent through a pact with the devil, along
with accusations that she was a witch, did nothing to
prevent the growth of her legend during her lifetime –
and beyond. Her fame was assured in 1641 with the
publication of *The Prophecies of Mother Shipton* which
has gone through countless editions and inspired numerous similar volumes of predictions, as well as the
many columns of horoscopes to be found in daily newspapers and magazines. The story of this strange and
influential women is told by **Josephine Gibney.**

Knaresborough nestles between the purple heather-clad hills and moorlands of Yorkshire, and an untold number of people journey from March until October to the picturesque town with one object in mind, to visit the birthplace of the old English prophet known as Mother Shipton.

Ursula Sontheil was born in July 1488 at Knaresborough, and when she died in 1561 she had become a legend in her own lifetime. Her mother, so history says, was Agatha Sontheil who lived in Knaresborough around 1472 and was orphaned at the age of fifteen. Legend says she met a well-dressed youth one day while walking in the woods and after several meetings he vowed eternal love.

When she told him she was to bear his child he said he could not marry her as he was not mortal. But in return for all she had bestowed upon him she would be given power to foretell the future, raise storm and tempest, and have command over man and beast. Later, because of her ability to raise storms, and other similar incidents, she was brought to trial as a witch, but was acquitted.

When her child Ursula was born never was there such an ugly creature to behold. A long crooked nose, large goggling eyes and bowed misshapen legs. Shortly after the birth Agatha entered a convent and died. The parish nurse took care of Ursula and when she began her schooling she amazed the teachers by her ability to read and write, among other things, much quicker than her classmates.

It was soon plain to see she had inherited the powers supposedly bestowed upon her mother, as when the other children began to bully and beat her because of her ugliness they were said to have been thrown to the ground by unseen hands and their hair pulled and flesh pinched until they howled for mercy. Because of this she was sent away from school and didn't attend again. At the age of twenty-four she married a man called Toby of Shipton near York, and from henceforth became known as Mother Shipton.

She set up home and quickly acquired a reputation for foretelling the future and offering advice on any problem, for a small fee. She, like her mother, was accused by some of being a witch but this didn't stop people from coming from far and wide with problems they wanted her to solve. Gradually her fame spread and many a nobleman knocked on her door seeking an answer to questions of future inheritance or knowledge of the maid they were to marry.

Part of her first historical prophecy was:

When the English Lion shall set his feet on the Gallic shore, then shall the Lilies begin to droop for fear. There shall be much weeping and wailing among the ladies of that country.

The English Lion was Henry VIII of England who with 50,000 men landed on the Gallic shore in 1513. The Lily was the national emblem of France and because of King Henry's victories the women of that country were given to great weeping and wailing.

Another prophecy read:

> A virtuous lady then shall die
> For being raised up too high
> Her death shall cause another's joy,
> Who will the kingdom much annoy.

Lady Jane Grey was the lady in question who assumed the title of queen and was later beheaded because of this. Her death, it is said, caused great joy to Queen Mary who married King Philip of Spain. This marriage, however, caused great anger among Mary's subjects.

Branching out in other directions she predicted:

Water shall come over Ouse Bridge, and a windmill shall be set upon a tower, and an elm tree shall lie at everyman's door.

Water was brought to everyman's door in the streets of York through bored elms. A windmill was built on top of the conduit house thus enabling it to draw water, and a line of pipes crossed Ouse Bridge.

She went on to say:

When there is a Lord Mayor living in Minster yard in York, let him beware of a stab.

A Lord Mayor who later took a house in Minster yard was assassinated, and his death was caused by stab wounds.

The most famous of her prophecies, however, were the ones which forecast:

> Over a wild and stormy sea shall a noble sail,
> Who to find, will not fail,
> A new and fair countree.
> From whence he shall bring, a herb and a root,
> That all men shall suit.
> And please both ploughman and King,
> And let them take no more than measure,
> Both shall have the even pleasure,
> In the belly and the brain.
> Carriages without horses will go,
> And accidents fill the world with woe.
> Around the world thoughts will fly in the
>   twinkling of an eye.
> Water shall yet more wonders do,
> How strange, yet shall be true.

Sir Walter Raleigh, on returning from his voyage to America, brought back the tobacco plant and potatoes. The coming of motor cars, road accidents, telephones, radio and steam power are described in the prophecy also.

Men shall walk over rivers and under rivers. Iron in the water float as easy as a wooden boat.

Mother Shipton without doubt had visions of bridges and tunnels spanning rivers and the modern iron and steel ships.

Readers can put their own construction on the following:

> All England's sons that plough the land,
> Shall be seen book in hand,
> Learning shall so ebb and flow,
> The poor shall most learning know.
> Waters shall flow where corn shall grow,
> Corn shall grow where water doth flow.

Young lovers, those with problems on their minds, and others just for the fun of it journey to the Wishing Well at Knaresborough mostly with an unshakeable faith that Mother Shipton's powers still flow strongly in the crystal-clear waters. There they dip their fingers, close their eyes and make a wish.

Bowler hats, shoes, boots, knitted garments, cups, saucers and a multitude of other things have been hung at the Well where the continual drip of water turns them into limestone.

A nearby cave is reputed to be the place where the seer was born and an extremely old copper sign hanging over the Mother Shipton Inn bears the inscription:

Near this Petrifying Well I first drew breath as records tell.

This extraordinary prophet is still held in high esteem by the people of Yorkshire, and even royalty has visited her birthplace.

A stroll through the magnificent avenue of beeches and along the beautiful riverside is a must for visitors, and it is not hard to believe as you wend your way among the whispering trees, rippling waters and castle ruins, that Mother Shipton wandered amidst it all, centuries ago, for the aura of mystery and folklore hangs so heavily in the atmosphere. It is almost a tangible thing, and you half expect the crooked misshapen figure to materialize before your eyes.

Mother Shipton foretold the day and even the hour she was to die. Bidding her friends goodbye she lay down on her bed and died in the year 1561 at the age of seventy-three.

Princess Pocahontas (c.1595–1617)

The Defender of Love

Pocahontas was the daughter of Powhatan, Chief of the Algonquin confederacy of Indian tribes in Virginia, and her defiant bravery has earned her a special place among American and British heroines. Although she is usually referred to by her familiar title, Pocahontas' personal name was actually Matoaka, meaning 'playful' – but her manner was anything but lighthearted in 1607 when she threw herself across the body of an English prisoner, John Smith, who was about to be executed by her tribe, and saved him from certain death. Later, she met and married another Englishman, John Rolfe, who in 1616 took her across the Atlantic to his native land where her reputation as the girl who risked all for love became a talking point everywhere. However, there are a number of mysteries surrounding the legend of Pocahontas which **Christine Baker-Carr** sets out to unravel here.

She was the first of her race to become a Christian, the first to marry an Englishman, the first to visit this country, and the first to die off the shores of England.

But no one has ever found the bones of that girl-wife who was perhaps one of the first to improve Anglo-American relations.

She was, of course, Princess Pocahontas, one of the best-loved of our schoolday heroines.

In 1595, the year that Shakespeare finished writing *A Midsummer Night's Dream*, a daughter was born into the large family of Powhatan, hereditary chief of the Red Indian tribes in Virginia.

Twelve years later, on a fine April day three ships sailed into Chesapeake Bay and headed up the James river, Virginia. On board were about 140 colonists and forty sailors sent out by the newly formed Virginia Company of London, established by James I.

They were a motley collection: aristocrats down on their luck, adventurers out for a change, and pirates in search of a rest and a liberal sprinkling of honest men.

The vessels carried a number of potential leaders for the new colony. Among them were Edward Wingfield and John Smith. Wingfield was an aristocrat, a spendthrift and an idealist, and it was he who was finally elected President of the Council. Captain John Smith was not even allowed a seat on the Council, since he had made treasonable remarks on the way over, and had been clapped in irons for the remainder of the voyage.

Jamestown took shape slowly, protected only by lopped-off tree tops; but food became short, even though the local Indians supplied an occasional deer for roasting. Disease spread and colonists sickened and died.

Smith struck out on his own in the search for food, sailing up the River James, trading as he went. Soon he ran into trouble – subsidiary chief Opechancanough and his band of warriors saw Smith who retreated into a bog which held him fast. He had to surrender.

Smith was led to the great Indian chief Powhatan. At the

end of the long march he arrived at the village and the twelve-year-old Pocahontas was among the small group of children watching.

Shortly he faced Powhatan, and he knew he was to die. But first came the customary feast, when he ate while a circle of chiefs watched. Smith finished eating and wiped his hands. Then he was seized and hurled to the ground. His head was thrust back on to a huge flat stone.

His blue eyes stared up at the two stone axes held aloft by his executioners who were awaiting the signal from Powhatan. Suddenly something crashed on to his body, something warm yet fierce. The tomahawks hovered uncertainly in the terrible silence and John Smith's rescuer spoke up: 'He is mine my man. I take him.' Pocahontas had decided to save him.

That night the traditional pipe of peace was passed solemnly between the old chief and Captain John Smith. After a short stay, Smith was sent back to Jamestown.

During the next two years the relationship between the Indians and the colonists became less strained.

Pocahontas became a frequent visitor to the village, and played with the few white children. Captain John Smith, with his forceful personality and 'no nonsense' methods, began to build up a flourishing community. To cap it all, he became President of the Council in September, 1608, but his rule lasted for a brief eighteen months.

A new 'white chief' arrived from England. Sir Thomas Dale had been appointed interim Governor of Virginia. Smith became ill, so ill, that all the Indians and most of the colonists thought he was dying. He sailed home to England, out of the life of Pocahontas – who never shed a tear. She was growing up. A strange mixture of Indian character tempered with Western ways and knowledge complicated the young girl's life.

But soon it became the turn of Pocahontas to be made prisoner – by the English. Governor Dale had been ruthless in dealing with the Indians and had angered Powhatan, who reacted violently. His daughter became a hostage, but she

was allowed the freedom of Jamestown under the care of
Bessie and Mollie Gates, girls of her own age. It was a tense
situation . . . Powhatan held a number of hostages too.

Every day Mr Buck, the preacher, gave the Indian princess
lessons in Scripture and taught her to read and write.

She was baptised into the Church of England and given the
name Rebecca. Soon afterwards she met her future husband,
a morose widower named John Rolfe, who was the first
Englishman to grow tobacco in Virginia while Pocahontas
was a minor expert herself. She grew all her father's tobacco
and had plenty of advice for the solitary, hard-working
Englishman from Heacham in Norfolk.

Slowly the friendship developed until in April, 1614, they
were married by the Rev. Richard Buck, her former teacher,
in Jamestown. They built their home further up river near to
Henricopolis, and were soon tilling the ground for a new
tobacco plantation.

Their son was born in that unique Anglo-Indian home and
they named him Tom.

In 1616 the Rolfes decided to visit England. John had
worked hard on his plantation, exporting the dried leaves to
England at a handsome profit. For Pocahontas the country
she had heard so much about lay ahead – England with its
hedges and green fields, its cities and its ships.

After arriving in London she and her husband set off with
baby Tom for Heacham.

After a short stay at Heacham Hall, where a younger
brother, Edward Rolfe, and his family were looking after
the ancestral home, John and his family went back to London
again, staying at the Bell Inn.

Visitors to the Rolfes included Dr King, the Bishop of
London, and Sir Walter Raleigh.

But Pocahontas grew ill. As soon as she recovered she
visited the Queen in Denmark House. That was the signal for
all the courtiers to come to the inn and pay their respects.
However, the illness returned. Queen Anne's own doctor
arrived to help treat her.

By the end of the year she seemed cured. The Rolfes were

invited to attend the Twelfth Night Ball given by the King and Queen in Whitehall. Rolfe, watching from the gallery (he was allowed no closer), saw Pocahontas in her court clothes attempting to dance.

In January, 1617, Pocahontas was ill again, and this time it was far more serious. They moved from Ludgate Hill to Brentford.

One of the few really welcome visitors to the house in Brentford was the old and faithful Bishop of London, Dr King. However, one morning there was a knock and in walked her first love – Captain John Smith. He was a changed man, gaunt, haggard, ragged, and the adventurer's gleam had gone from his eyes. If Pocahontas had any illusions left at all they fled at that brief meeting. From a hero he had turned into a bloated bore.

In March, 1617, their visit to England ended, John Rolfe and Pocahontas went on board the *George* at the Tower steps – she had to be carried from the coach. Her illness had worsened. Pocahontas knew she was going to die, and her life ended on board the *George* not far from Gravesend.

Little Tom had been left behind – it was the dying wish of his mother that he should be brought up an Englishman – while Rolfe sailed on to Virginia, his tobacco plantations and another wife (this time an English girl).

Pocahontas was buried in the chancel of St George's Church, Gravesend. The entry in the burial register reads:

1617, March 21st. Rebecca Wrolfe, wyffe of Thomas [sic] Wrolfe, gent, a Virginia lady borne was buried in ye chauncel

She was just twenty-two.

That church was destroyed by fire in 1727 and all the bodies were supposed to have been moved to another grave. Then, as recently as 1897, another church was built on roughly the same site and workmen came across hundreds of bones.

Thinking, incredible as it may seem, that they were animal

bones, the workmen threw them all in a huge heap. Rag-and-bone men passing through Gravesend found a ready trade.

It was too late by the time the authorities realised the bones were human. And where was the skeleton of Pocahontas?

When search parties failed to locate it it was suggested that the 'water rats' – graveyard body-snatchers who operated by barge after dark – had spirited the coffin away to London and then exhibited it at a peep show until authority intervened once more and had it reinterred in 1842 in a London church.

Whether or not the story was true, the body had still to be found.

In November, 1932, there was a startling development: a man named James Isherwood remembered being taken to the church of St John the Evangelist in Waterloo Road in 1872 by his uncle, the verger.

There he was shown a tarnished silver casket bearing a plate indicating that it had been originally interred at Gravesend.

His uncle said it was supposed to contain the body of an Indian princess, had been brought to London by 'water rats', exhibited at a peep show and then reburied some thirty years earlier. The story seemed to fit perfectly with the accepted legend.

But by 1932 the shelves in the crypt had been bricked up. The vicar and a party of research workers made a careful examination, all in vain. There was no trace of the casket.

Searching through the burial registers for that date, however, the vicar, the Rev. Charles W. Hutchinson, found one entry and the following note in the margin:

18 January, 1835; the favourite squaw of an Indian chief, who came to London, died this day at her lodgings in the Waterloo Road. She was baptised a few hours before her death by the name of 'Antoinette O Whon O Qua' and was buried in an elegant black coffin, richly ornamented, at St. John's, Waterloo Road.

Coincidence? Yes – but no more.

Yet where was that coffin anyway? Mr Hutchinson had heard past vicars mention that in 1851 all remains were removed from the church as a result of a cholera scare, and buried in Brookwood Cemetery. Maybe Pocahontas lies there for her final resting place on earth?

The Notorious Mrs Behn

Aphra Behn was one of the most extraordinary females in that great age of eccentricity, the Restoration. A talented and ingenious woman, she was the first professional writer of her sex in England and for a time worked as a spy against the Dutch. More particularly, she has been revered by Virginia Woolf and any number of feminists for 'having given women the right to speak their minds'. A friend of Nell Gwynne, John Dryden and the notorious Earl of Rochester, John Wilmot, she wrote one of the earliest novels in English, *Oroonoko*, which was published in 1688, and followed this with nineteen outspoken and satirical plays in which topics such as adultery, foreplay and impotence were combined with statements about morality and politics that gave her a notoriety second to none. To one half of the population she was 'the ingenious Mrs Behn', while to the outraged remainder she was a 'lewd harlot'. Her action-packed life is recounted by **Dorothy Hobman**.

Aphra Behn was by no means the first English woman writer, but she was the first professional author; that is to say she was the first to earn her living by her pen. She was probably illegitimate, and fancy may speculate upon her ancestry: could she have been descended from some famous poet of the past, whose blood flowing through her veins made fertile the creative gift? Her alleged father, John Amis, who is believed to have adopted her, was appointed Lieutenant-General of a group of islands in the West Indies, and it is supposed that she spent part of her childhood in the tropics. She wrote a story, *Oroonoko, The Royal Slave*, which is almost certainly based on personal observation in Surinam.

At the age of eighteen she was married to a Dutchman called Behn, a wealthy merchant whose social position enabled her to take part in the brilliant life at the Court of Charles I. A portrait of her, painted by Sir Peter Lely, shows a lovely oval face, straight nose, full mouth and chin, high forehead, brown hair, and bright almond-shaped eyes. Since she had beauty, youth, and a daring wit, one may assume that Royalty was not unamused.

There was a brief dazzling period of glitter and gaiety and then, in the plague year of 1665, came the death of her husband: the young widow was left in poverty, thrown upon her own resources to struggle along as best she could. She had, in fact, to look for a job. She was able to find one through her influence at Court and her Dutch connections, being sent to Holland as a kind of political agent, or what we should now call a spy, in order to send home secret anonymous dispatches. The undertaking was incredibly daring for a young unprotected woman, and she must have had an adventurous spirit, for she embarked upon her journey with very little money, which soon went on personal expenditure and on the payments that had to be made for information. In spite of her frantic appeals no money was sent out to her, so that, after pawning her jewels, she had to borrow the cost of her return journey in 1667. She was unable to repay the loan and was threatened with imprisonment for debt.

'I have cried myself dead,' she wrote to the King's cupbearer, 'and could find in my heart to break through all and get to the King, and never rise till he were pleased to pay this; but I am sick and weak and unfit for it or a prison; I shall go tomorrow.' And go she did. However, the money due to her was eventually forthcoming, and after a short term of imprisonment Aphra was released, free of debt, but once more faced with the necessity of earning her keep.

She now set to work to write for a living. Her first play, *The Forced Marriage or the Jealous Bridegroom*, was produced at the Duke's Theatre in 1670, where it ran for no more than a week. She was not discouraged and, with the success of her third play, *The Dutch Lover*, in 1673, her reputation was established. She continued to produce plays steadily, fifteen during her lifetime, while a few more appeared after her death. She must at times have handled large sums of money, but her careless and generous temperament made her reckless, and she seems to have been perpetually in want of funds. She was in trouble in other ways also, for she meddled with politics, and on one occasion a warrant was issued against her for abusing persons of quality: in other words, the Whigs were offended by her Tory ridicule of them. No harm, however, seems to have come to her from this threat. Apart from politics, as an established writer she stepped outside the range of rules which bound the conduct of women, nor did she see any reason why she should conform to convention.

She was accepted in masculine literary circles, and found both friends and lovers among the noted writers and wits of the day. One of them wrote the epitaph for her tomb in Westminster Abbey:

Here lies a proof that wit can never be
Defence enough against mortality

She does not appear to have had any children, either in wedlock or out of it. However, in view of the fact that her successor, the woman playwright and journalist De La Rivière Manley, employed the services of a midwife at the ominous address of 'The Coffin and Cradle,' it is obvious that without vital statistics such a matter as childbirth cannot now be established either way.

Aphra Behn's popularity is amazing when one considers the barrage of jealousy to which she was exposed from some of her less successful masculine rivals. They spared her no slanderous attacks that scandal could embellish or spite invent. Of course they insisted that her lovers helped her to write and produce her plays. That is as it may be. Her feminine intelligence seems to have been adequate in itself to the task of doing the work unaided. She was accused of stealing her plots from Marlowe, Molière, in short from any play on which she could lay her hands. If so, she was not the first playwright to have found and adapted a ready-made plot; and much may be forgiven the woman who could write to a friend of 'the garden from whence I gather'd and I hope you will not think me vain, if I say, I have weeded and improv'd it'. She was blamed because her plays were lewd and bawdy. A plague on't, what did a Restoration audience expect? Was she alone among authors to be squeamish, because she was a member of the sex?

'Had the plays I have writ come forth under any man's name, and never known to have been mine,' she once wrote, 'I appeal to all unbiased judges of sense, if they had not said that person has made as many good comedies, as any one man that has writ in our age; but a devil on't the woman damns the poet.' And here is her version of what befell on the first night of *The Dutch Lover*:

. . . that day 'twas acted first, there comes into the Pit, a long lither, phlegmatick, white, ill-favour'd, wretched Fop, an Officer in Masquerade newly transported with a Scarf and Feather out of France . . . this thing, I tell ye, opening that which serves it for a mouth, out issued such a noise as this to those that sat about it, that they were to expect a woeful play, God damn him, for it was a woman's.

It goes without saying that she was attacked for her way of life. Yet it never seemed to occur to her contemporaries or, for that matter, to her critics at a later more prudish period, that this vital and magnetic woman could have spared herself the trouble of working for her living, if she had allowed her lovers to maintain her instead. For hard and continuously she did work, all through a long and painful illness ('I humbly beg pardon for my ill writing Madam for 'tis with a lame hand scarce able to hold a pen', ran the postscript of a letter to a friend), until her death in 1689. Passionate she may have been, and romantic, but it is quite clear that she was never a light-of-love.

In a preface to *The Dutch Lover*, she addresses the 'Good, Sweet, Honey, Sugar-Candied Reader', to tell him that she considers a play as a *divertissement*, and to ask him for his shilling to judge whether she has succeeded in entertaining him. Today an audience would no longer consider that she gave him his money's worth, but women owe her more than they know, for if she was no conscious champion of their rights, she was undoubtedly a pioneer. Mrs Behn fought her way, in no rarefied impersonal atmosphere: one imagines the disorderly candle-lit room where she sat scribbling, in a loose house-gown, open a shade too low in front, undisturbed by her chattering crowd of visitors, the air thick with the smell of tallow and ale, of sweat and ink. No well-bred uplift about all this, but warmth and laughter, coarseness and zest, and through it all divine generosity and goodwill.

That was Aphra Behn. She loved pleasure and never pretended otherwise, and she loved her friends. She shoved and elbowed her way through the ranks of hostile male competitors to recognition and success. She gave rein to an imagination as luxuriant as the tropical vegetation of the West Indies, where she is believed to have spent her youth. She worked hard and she played hard, she was honest and without affectation, and she did not shrink from life. She has won a humble place in the literature of her country, and she has earned some gratitude from succeeding generations of women because she was the first to fight for that place; but

most worthy of remembrance, when her name is recalled, is
the woman herself, of whom a contemporary wrote: 'She was
of a generous and open Temper, something passionate, very
serviceable to her Friends in all that was in her Power; and
could sooner forgive an Injury than do one.'

The Adventurous Life of 'John Taylor'

Mary Anne Taylor is the first of several women in this book who lived for years as men and had the most extraordinary adventures. Believed to have been the daughter of an English lord whose mother died in childbirth, she was placed in the care of a guardian, one Mr Sucker. He, in turn, handed her over to a Captain Bowen who enlisted the little girl on his ship as 'John Taylor, footboy'. Thereafter Mary Anne served as a drummer-boy, cabin-boy, soldier and sailor during the course of a remarkable, adventure-filled odyssey which took her around the world without anyone having the slightest idea of her real identity. 'John Taylor' survived injury and imprisonment and it was not until 'he' was in danger of being press-ganged, that Mary Anne was forced to reveal her sex. Shortly before her death an authorized biography 'related by herself', *The Life and Surprising Adventures of Mary Anne Talbot in the name of John Taylor*, was published in London and caused a sensation. This account of her life – including a richly satisfying reunion with the awful Mr Sucker – is related by **Margaret Dowie.**

The extraordinary lure of the sea and a spirit of adventure led girls as well as boys at one time to brave the dangers of a sailor's life. Some of the women, however, who became both soldiers and sailors, were led by force of circumstances to conceal their sex and adopt the life of a man.

A strange case of this kind was that of Mary Anne Talbot, a woman shown by her remarkable career to have been both brave and valiant, and with a determination that would have been a credit to a member of the sex she assumed.

She is said to have been the natural daughter of Earl Talbot and the youngest of sixteen children, her mother having died in giving birth to twins. She was born in London on 2 February 1778, at a house in Lincoln's Inn Fields, and for the first five years of her life she was placed in the charge of a nurse, in a village about twelve miles from Shrewsbury. When she was older she was sent to a boarding-school kept by a Mrs Tapley in Foregate Street, Chester, where she received her early education and remained a pupil for nine years.

Her only surviving sister, who was married to a Mr Wilson of Trevalyn, in Derbyshire, lived not a great distance away, and Mary regarded her as her parent until one day when she was about ten years old, Mrs Wilson told her the truth and showed her a miniature of her mother. The face made a lasting impression on the child's memory, and she never forgot it. Her sister also told her that before her mother's marriage she was known as the Honourable Miss Dyer, the name of the family in which she had been brought up, and she had possessed a fortune of £30,000 besides a yearly income of £1500.

Mrs Wilson died soon afterwards, and within three months of her death, a Mr Sucker of Newport, Shropshire, became her guardian, and removed Mary from school and placed her with his own family. Here her life was most unhappy and she was treated with great harshness. Sucker was an arrogant and domineering man and the girl had an absolute dread of him. It was soon evident to Mary that he wished to get rid of her and his responsibility. Later, he introduced her to a Captain

Essex Bowen of the 82nd regiment-of-foot and directed her to consider him as her future guardian. The Captain declared he would arrange for her further education as he was greatly interested in her family and would take her abroad.

Early in 1792, he took her to London and arranged to stay at the Salopian Coffee-house near Charing Cross. Captain Bowen introduced Mary to the landlady as his ward, but before many days had elapsed he took advantage of her innocence and seduced her. After this his benign attitude changed and he began to treat the girl with unkindness and even cruelty. Mary had neither acquaintance nor friend to appeal to in London, and, left to the mercy of a tyrant, she was obliged to carry out his harsh commands.

Suddenly, an order came for him to rejoin his regiment, which was to embark for St Domingo, and Mary began to hope her troubles were over, but Bowen informed her that he intended to take her with him. It was impossible for him to take a girl with him on the ship, so he insisted that she should dress as a foot-boy, or servant, so that she might accompany him on the voyage to the West Indies. He called her 'John Taylor', and under that name she sailed in the transport as his servant in the ship *Captain Bishop* on 20 March 1792.

Once on board the Captain had to alter his attitude towards the girl, but he treated her with his former harshness and compelled her to live and share the mess of the ship's company.

The voyage proved a terrible one and the *Captain Bishop* encountered severe gales in the Atlantic. She sprang a leak and all hands had to be called to the pumps, while guns and provisions had to be thrown overboard. For eight days they were without water and reduced to a ration of a biscuit a day each person, but the weather moderated and at last they reached land in safety.

In spite of all the hardships and privations which Mary faced with indomitable courage, she managed to keep her secret and dressed as a boy was successful in concealing her sex.

The regiment had scarcely landed at St Domingo when

new orders were received to re-embark and return to Europe, to reinforce the troops under the Duke of York in Flanders.

Under a threat of sending her up the country to be sold as a slave, Bowen compelled Mary to enrol herself in the regiment as a drummer. There was no escape, and in that capacity she sailed again with Bowen for Europe. He continued to use her as his servant when her duties as drummer permitted.

Eventually the ship arrived at Flanders and the regiment was at once marched to a camp, where frequent engagements were taking place and the soldiers were undergoing considerable suffering. From day to day, Mary was exposed to fire, and towards the end of the siege of Valenciennes she was hit by a musket-ball between the breast and collar-bone, and was also wounded in the small of her back by a blow from the sword of an Austrian trooper.

Terrified that her sex would be discovered if she went to hospital, she carefully concealed her wounds and treated them herself with basilicon ointment, lint, and some Dutch drops she managed to obtain. Fortunately for her, Captain Bowen, who had treated her so shamefully, was killed in the attack on the town. She set out to search for him and found him among the dead on the battlefield. On examining his pockets she found several letters referring to herself, and, in his wallet, the key of a case in which he kept his papers. In this case she discovered part of a correspondence that had passed between Bowen and Sucker, and evidence that money which had been sent for her use had never been handed over to her. These documents she carefully preserved by sewing them up under the shoulders of her shirt.

She had no friends in the regiment, and sick and unhappy she determined to desert and try and reach England. She managed to obtain some sailor's clothes, and as soon as an opportunity occurred she abandoned her drummer-boy's uniform, and, dressed as a sailor, set off by night across the country. The tramp was long and arduous, but at length she reached Luxembourg.

She found the city was in the possession of the French, and as she could obtain no work, through sheer necessity she shipped on a French lugger that was just sailing. She sailed in September 1793, and it was not long before she found out that the vessel was a privateer. She underwent great hardships on the ship, which cruised about for four months until in the Channel it fell in with the British Fleet commanded by Lord Howe.

When the ships engaged, the intrepid Mary went to the French captain and told him she would not fight against her countrymen, to which he replied with a sound beating with a rope's end, but to her relief the lugger soon surrendered and a boarding party carried off the captain and crew, including Mary, to the *Queen Charlotte*, the Admiral's ship. Here Mary was fortunate enough to be able to relate her story to the Admiral himself. She told him of her service in the Army, and how owing to privation she had been forced to ship on the French lugger, but had determined to escape at the first opportunity in order to return to England.

Lord Howe, impressed by her candour and courage, believed her story and promised her she should have her desire, for he would transfer her to another ship. Mary was delighted, and especially since she had been able to keep the secret of her sex concealed.

She was soon after sent on board HMS *Brunswick*, commanded by Captain Harvey, where she was instructed to act as powder-boy on the quarter-deck. Her quickness and obedience, together with her smart appearance, at length attracted the attention of the Captain. He thought she was a lad who had run away to sea, but finding she was well-educated and had seen active service on land, he made her his principal cabin-boy.

He took a strong liking to his sharp and nimble new boy, who became a favourite with the ship's company. Mary was in many fights, and, in the action in which Captain Harvey later lost his life, she took an active part. Just before his ship was engaged by the *Ramillies* she received a severe wound in the leg by a grape-shot. She fell and lay wounded on the deck and while almost unconscious received a musket-ball in the thigh. Suffering acute pain and weak from loss of blood she was at length carried to the cockpit. The busy surgeon made but a cursory examination and decided to send her to port as soon as possible with others severely wounded.

The *Brunswick* sailed for Portsmouth and when she reached Spithead, Mary was taken to Haslar Hospital, where the bullet was extracted and she remained a patient for four months.

During this time Captain Harvey did not forget her or lose interest in his 'cabin-boy', for he sent her money and made frequent enquiries as to her progress.

When she was well enough to be discharged from Haslar, she was drafted as a midshipman to HMS *Vesuvius*, commanded by Captain Tomlinson, whose ship was attached to Sir Sydney Smith's squadron. They sailed from Spithead, and when off Dunkirk the *Vesuvius* fell in with two French privateers. Captain Tomlinson maintained a running fight for seven hours, but being outnumbered by the enemy had at length to give in. Mary, with others, was made prisoner, and with another midshipman named Richards she was taken to Dunkirk on one of the privateers and lodged in prison. Here they were treated with great harshness and kept in a damp dungeon. After a while they made a plan to escape which unfortunately miscarried and they were discovered. As punishment they were confined for eighteen months in separate cells where it was so dark they did not see daylight for eleven weeks. Mary's daily ration of bread and water was lowered down by a cord and her bed consisted of a bundle of straw which was never changed. It is little wonder that she became very ill, but while recovering she received better treatment and was allowed to mix with other prisoners. Among those with whom she came in contact was a German who was permitted to occupy his time with making trinkets with gold wire after the style of filigree work. After watching him closely Mary learned the art, which proved to be an acquisition of great use to her later when she gained her liberty and returned to England. Years afterwards, when she settled in London, she got work from a jeweller named Loyer in Denmark Street. Here she made the bracelet chains which

Queen Charlotte wore in the Royal procession to St Paul's Cathedral, to commemorate the great naval victories.

Some five weeks after recovering from her illness, Mary obtained her liberty through an exchange of prisoners. Her intention was to get a passage in a ship for England as soon as possible, but the spirit of adventure innate in her again asserted itself. Happening to hear a man inquiring for a lad willing to go to America as a ship's steward, Mary volunteered and at once struck a bargain with him. He was a Captain Field, master of the *Ariel*, an American merchantman. He agreed to give Mary fifty pounds besides what she could make as a steward from passengers on the voyage from Dunkirk to New York.

The *Ariel* sailed in August 1796, and during the voyage Mary was treated with great kindness by the Captain. He proved a real friend and when they landed insisted she should come and live with his family at his home on Rhode Island. While there his young daughter fell violently in love with the youthful steward. She even proposed they should get married and tried her utmost to get Mary to consent, but the latter was determined to put an end to this embarrassing position and she fled from the Fields' house. She had not got more than two miles away when she was overtaken by a servant who begged her to return at once as Miss Field had been seized with alarming fits. Mary returned to find the love-sick maiden prostrate, but on giving the girl a promise that she would speedily return from England, she soon recovered.

She then went with Captain Field to New York to rejoin his ship, and after a good voyage the *Ariel* arrived in the Thames in November 1796.

They soon obtained a fresh cargo and were due to sail for the Mediterranean, when Mary came in for a new adventure. While in port the Captain had engaged a couple of new hands and she, as steward, was deputed to see them and take their descriptions. She saw them in the cabin where money and bank notes were lying about on the desk. In the middle of the same night, Mary was woken by a crash at the upper cabin door. She felt alarmed and snatched at her tinder-box to get a light, when close by she noticed there lay a brace of pistols. A more violent attack was then made on the inner door behind which she was standing, and recollecting that a sword was hanging near her bunk, she seized it just as the door gave way to the attackers. She made a thrust, and although she heard neither groan nor cry, she was sure she had wounded some-one. She now struck a light, but the attackers had fled, and after making the door secure she stood on guard till the morning.

Later she learnt that one of the new hands had been found in his berth with a deep wound in his thigh which he said he had got by accident. He was in such a serious condition that he had to be taken to St Thomas's Hospital. Mary, however, had no doubt how he came by the wound.

A few days before the ship was due to sail, Mary, wearing her sailor's clothes, went on shore with the mate. Just as they landed at St Catherine's stairs they fell in with a press-gang who seized them both. As Mary obstructed them and fought for her liberty she was thrown out of the boat and received a wound on the head from a cutlass. They were held by the gang and put on board a tender near by. The mate, having his 'protection' paper in his pocket, was soon liberated, but Mary was less fortunate, for she had left hers on the ship. The mate, however, stood by her, and declared his compa-nion was an Englishman; but that did not satisfy the officer in charge and in the end she was obliged to reveal her sex in order to get free. After she returned to the ship and she imparted her secret to the astonished Captain Field. He again treated her with kindness and discretion and told her he wished her to continue on as steward and return with him to America: but Mary, disheartened, and feeling she could not continue in her role as a man, had to decline his proposal. She left the ship after thanking him for all his kindness to her and bade him good-bye.

Now, alone in London, with no friends, she debated what to do for the best. She first decided to make an application to the Navy Pay Office at Somerset House to see if she could get the money due to her for service while on board the *Brunswick* and the *Vesuvius*. Giving the name of 'John Taylor' she interviewed the clerks only to meet with repeated rebuffs and rudeness. This at length aroused her temper and she turned and abused them in violent language accompanied by personal chastisement, and as a result she was conveyed to Bow Street. When brought before the magistrate she repeated her complaints of the treatment she had received and was discharged, but several people in court who had heard the story of her sufferings came to her aid. Among them they raised a subscription sufficient to pay her twelve shillings a week until she had got her money from the Navy Pay Office. One of the gentlemen thus interested in her found her lodgings and placed her in charge of the landlord. At the same time he advised her to wear female dress and give up masculine habits. But this did not come easy to Mary, who for so long had worn trousers and assumed the manner and habits of a man, and she continued to go about in her sailor's rig-out.

As her story became known, 'John Taylor' bid fair to become famous, and now, having a little money, she used to frequent the theatres and coffee-houses in the neighbourhood of Covent Garden, where she was a popular visitor.

One night in a coffee-house she became acquainted with Haines, the notorious highwayman, although she had no idea of his criminal career. When seated at the same table one evening she happened to mention she was at the end of her money.

'Damn it, my fine fellow,' exclaimed Haines, clapping a hand on her shoulder, 'I'll put you up to the best way in the world to get the cash you stand in need of.'

Leaving the house together shortly afterwards, Haines proposed an adventure on the road and gave Mary some money to equip herself for the purpose, as he took exception to her sailor's clothes. She therefore went off and bought herself a pair of buckskin breeches and top-boots, which she at once donned. A rendezvous was fixed and she met Haines and found him accompanied by six other desperadoes. They gave her a brace of pistols and were all ready to start when for

once Mary's courage failed her and she resolved to give up
the adventure and not embark on a career of crime.

Having but little money left she sought some kind of
employment, and remembering the gold wire-work she
had learnt at Dunkirk she applied to Mr Loyer, a jeweller
in Denmark Street, who finding she was clever in making
filigree engaged her for a time, but paid her very poorly. She
wrote:

> At the time of my employ by Loyer, I put on my seaman's
> dress and accompanied the procession when their Majes-
> ties went to St Paul's, and the different colours of the
> enemy were carried to be hung up in the Cathedral as
> trophies of the victories of Howe, St Vincent, and Duncan.
> I was one of Lord Howe's attendants with his colours and
> rode on the car. The chains on the bracelets which Her
> Majesty wore on the occasion were made by me at Loyer's
> by order of Grey and Constable, the jewellers of Sackville
> Street, Piccadilly.

About this time she joined a lodge of Odd Fellows that met
at the 'Harlequin' in Drury Lane, although the fraternity
little knew their new member was a woman.

Mary remained on in the same lodgings until February
1797, when the leg which had been wounded with grape-shot
began to trouble her again. It became so bad that she sought
and obtained admission to St Bartholomew's Hospital,
where, after several pieces of shot had been removed, she
was discharged. Later on, however, the wound began to give
her further pain and she became a patient at the Middlesex
Hospital. While there she heard one day that a woman was
attempting to impersonate her and trying to pass herself off
as 'John Taylor who had fought in the *Brunswick*'. Suspected
of being an impostor she was arrested and charged at Bow
Street. Hearing that Mary was an inmate of Middlesex
Hospital, the magistrate sent for her to confront her imper-
sonator. When the woman saw her she confessed to the
imposture and was committed to the house of correction.

On her discharge from the hospital Mary again assumed woman's clothes, and one day in the street she was suddenly attacked by a man who worked as a hairdresser and who mistook her for someone else. He knocked her down, cut her head, kicked her, and so hurt her wounded leg that she had to be taken to hospital again. The man was arrested and charged at the Quarter Sessions with committing a brutal assault. He was sentenced and ordered to pay Mary ten pounds as compensation. Meanwhile she had a narrow escape of losing her leg at the hospital, where the surgeons thought it might be necessary to amputate it. Her extraordinary career and sufferings now became known to some influential visitors, who brought her case to the notice of the Royal Court with the result that to her delight she was granted a pension by Queen Charlotte, and also received help from the Duke and Duchess of York and the Duke of Norfolk.

When she was once more able to get about, her old spirit revived, and she resolved to try and ascertain what had become of the inheritance which was supposed to be coming to her. With this object she set out for Shrewsbury to see if she could find Mr Sucker, her supposed guardian, at Newport. Failing to find him, she returned to Shrewsbury, determined to make him see her, and hiring an ensign's uniform and a horse she rode back to Newport. Arriving at Sucker's home she sent in a message that a gentleman knowing the late Captain Bowen wished to see him. She was asked into a room, and shortly Sucker, whom she could hardly recognize, came in. She saw he had no idea who she was and asked him if he knew a 'Miss Talbot' or could give any information about her. Sucker replied that he had known the lady well, but that she had died in 1793.

Mary, unable to conceal her anger any longer, declared herself to the astonished man and proved her assertion by a mark on her forehead. Sucker stared at the soldierly figure confronting him in amazement, and Mary, determined to frighten the man who had treated her so badly, drew her sword and demanded he should give her an account there and then of the money of which he had defrauded her. Throwing up his arms he declared he was a ruined man and rushed from the room.

Seeing it was useless to pursue him Mary returned to Shrewsbury with the object of consulting a lawyer. Determined to gather more particulars about her family she again paid a visit to Newport, but on arrival at Sucker's house she was informed that he had suddenly left his home and had been found dead at a village nearby.

With very little money left, Mary decided to abandon her quest and return to London. On a suggestion that she should go on the stage, as she had a flair for acting, she became a member of the Thespian Society, which had a theatre in Tottenham Court Road. Here she played Juliet and Floranthe, and in low comedy took the parts of Mrs Scout and Jack Hawser. After one of her performances she was summoned for wearing hair-powder without a licence, which was an offence against the law at the time.

More trouble came to Mary, when she got into arrears with her rent and at the instance of her landlady, to whom she owed eleven pounds, she was arrested and taken to Newgate.

During the time she was in prison she used to preside at the evening convivial meetings held within the walls of the gaol in those days. Dressed as a man she would sing, smoke, and drink with the others, and so became very popular. She was eventually liberated by the 'Society for the Relief of Persons Confined for Debt', on the payment of five pounds.

Ill-fortune, however, still pursued her, for one night in September 1804, she was thrown out of a coach in Church Lane Whitechapel, and falling into a hole in the road she received a broken arm and other serious injuries. She was unable to obtain any compensation and, being without employment, she became a domestic servant in the house of a publisher, where she lived for three years.

Though still a young woman, the hard life which she had led and the sufferings she had undergone now began to tell on her health and she was seized with a great weakness which ended in a complete collapse. She died on 4 February 1808, in her thirtieth year.

Curiously enough, this remarkable woman retained much of the sensibility of her true sex during the long period in which she passed as a man, in spite of her association with the roughest type of men on land and sea, and those who knew her always testified to her generous disposition, kindness of heart, and good nature. Her courage was ever undaunted, even when she was exposed to the greatest danger, as she undoubtedly was at the siege of Valenciennes, when she saw hundreds of her friends and foes falling round her. She used to tell how 'the 11th Dragoons fought with their broadswords hand-to-hand over the heaps of dead and dying soldiers', and would recall how she was obliged to keep a continual roll on her drum to drown the cries of those who were trampled to death under the feet of the horses.

Miranda Stuart (1795–1865)

The Bizarre Career of 'Dr James Barry'

Miranda Stuart – whose real name may have been Miranda Stuart Barry – has a unique place in the history of eccentric women as the only member of her sex to have lived her *entire life* undiscovered as a man. It was not until after the death of 'Dr James Barry' who had served with distinction as a military doctor and risen to become Inspector-General of military hospitals, that the truth was revealed. Even then there was little that could be established about Miranda's life, beyond the fact she had been orphaned as a child and then admitted to Edinburgh College at the age of fifteen as a 'frail young man'. After gaining an MD in 1812, 'Dr Barry' entered the military service and practised in Malta, South Africa and the West Indies as well as several Mediterranean countries. On the Doctor's death, 'his' military funeral was cancelled when the body was found to be that of a woman. It is now believed that Miranda Stuart masqueraded as a man in order to practise medicine – an occupation then barred to women – and thereby became the first female MD in Britain. Her incredible life-long deception is recounted by **Reginald Hargreaves**.

Of the actual childhood and early years of Amanda Stuart before she took on the persona of Dr James Barry not much in the way of authentic detail can be gleaned. She is said to have been the granddaughter of a Scottish earl, but no account of her parentage exists. In fact, the first activity of Barry's to find record is her appearance in male guise as a medical student at Edinburgh College.

In that rough-and-tumble community it is hardly remarkable that the unusual appearance of Barry should have excited the universal comment of all her fellow-students. Short, angular of body, with 'a long Ciceronian nose', high cheekbones, reddish hair, and an expression of settled melancholy, even the trim surtout the new arrival always affected excited the ribald criticism of the casually garbed crowd of embryonic medicos.

However, even at that early age, Barry had schooled herself in stern self-repression and in the assumption of that mask of cold dignity that is always calculated to keep casual acquaintances from any attempt at greater intimacy. Keeping practically everyone at a frigid distance, she made a single exception in the person of a fellow-student of the name of Jobson. A certain intimacy sprang up between them, and they even discussed the plans for the future they had both hoped and dreamed. Jobson was determined to become a military surgeon, and it is certain that this resolve of his strongly influenced Barry in the choice of the army as her career.

It would seem that Jobson never for a moment entertained any doubt as to his companion's masculinity, although his attempts to teach Barry the noble art of self-defence might well have afforded him an illuminating clue. Box the unfortunate Barry simply could not. In no way deficient in physical courage, it was impossible to induce her to strike out; very naturally she preferred to keep her arms tightly folded across the chest to protect it from injury. Puzzled and exasperated as the would-be instructor must have been, the real explanation never entered his head. Perhaps it was so obvious as to be obviously preposterous!

Time moved on, and in due course both Jobson and Barry were granted their diplomas, but, being appointed to different regiments, they were not fortunate enough to meet again.

Barry had passed out brilliantly, and at a really extraordinarily early age. Influence apart, her subsequent career in medicine clearly demonstrated that her skill in healing was well above the average, and remained with her all her life. Of course, with a distinct 'pull' amongst those in whose hands the distribution of posts and appointments was entrusted, Barry harboured no intention of drudging along for any length of time as a mere medico attached to a regimental unit. Being recognized from the first as a clever doctor, and with her subtle influence over the right people, the ambitious woman was determined that, having been denied the legitimate fulfilment of her youth and sex, she would exact the fullest retribution from fate.

Whether or no the folk in high places were actually aware of her feminine sex and the circumstances of her betrayal, and were prepared to busy themselves in her advancement rather than she should retaliate for their neglect of her by a public *exposé* of her circumstances, it is impossible to determine. With such family connections as she could claim, the speedy promotion that was accorded her is perfectly understandable, whatever the guise under which she passed with those responsible for it.

Malta was the first station to which the newly fledged medico was dispatched, and, arrived there, she seems to have taken her place in the routine of garrison life without arousing more than passing comment. Her diminutive figure, high, thin voice, carefully cultivated reticence, and rather pernicketty ways may have given rise to a certain amount of not too ill-natured chaff, but then garrison towns are notoriously the hotbeds of gossip and tittle-tattle, from which no newcomer can hope to be exempted. At least no suspicion of the new doctor's female sex was aroused, and if her eccentricities occasioned a more protracted commentary than usual, their bizarre quality certainly supplied a sufficiency of reason.

To begin with, she was a rigid and fastidious vegetarian, dainty even in the choice of the non-meat dishes in which she did permit herself to indulge. To her the potato and the apple were no more than 'filthy roots', while the odour of cooking cabbage just 'turned her sick'. Then in addition, in a pretty hard drinking age, she professed a staunch teetotalism, that only suffered mild interruption in moments of ill-health. At such times she might, under pressure, consent to drink half a glass of diluted brandy, or sip a little champagne thinned down with water.

Well may the two- and three-bottle men of the period have gulped and gaped and wondered!

Malta was followed by a tour of duty in the Cape, and here Barry was fortunate enough to find the most patient of patrons in the Governor, Lord Charles Somerset. And truly the Governor bore with the petulances and eccentricities of his newly appointed medical attendant with more than exemplary patience and good nature. The Cape was considered an excellent station, and, under the kindly aegis of a friendly 'Chief,' Barry was soon very comfortably installed. From her house in Heerengracht she would sally forth daily for a promenade in Camp's Bay. The little procession consisting of Barry, mounted on her stuffed and padded saddle, astride a pony of milky whiteness, carrying a large cotton umbrella to shield her face from the rays of the sun, and accompanied by a negro servant and a little dog named Psyche, became a spectacle the familiarity of which never quite served to rob it of its peculiar quality of humour. In this particular, it is said that for many a year after her death the shade of Dr Barry was evoked as a sort of bogey – like the spectre of Napoleon before her – with which to subdue the fractious and rebellious juvenility of the neighbourhood, mammies crying to their naughty children to behave, or 'old Dr Barry's ghost will catch you!'

From the first she was *persona grata* at the Governor's residence, where, it is to be feared, her fretful humours were often as much a cause of exasperation as of amusement. For, good medico as she was, she was no less a strong individualist, and should a patient depart by so much as a hair's breadth from the curriculum she had laid down, then, so far as Barry was concerned, for the future the invalid could fend for himself; she washed her hands of the case *hec dum*, and its outcome became a matter of supreme indifference to her. Such a high and mighty disregard of the ordinary obligations of a doctor – apart altogether from the question of discipline – imposed a strain upon the Governor's sense of toleration that, at times, became well-nigh insupportable.

From a purely disciplinary point of view, there is no doubt that Barry was permitted a liberty and degree of insubordination that aroused the comment of visitors and members of the garrison alike.

Writing of this period in his reminiscences, Lord Albemarle tells us:

There was at the Cape at this time a person whose eccentricities attracted universal attention. Lord Charles described him to me as the most skilful of physicians and the most wayward of men. He had lately been in professional attendance on the Governor, who was somewhat fanciful about his health; but the æsculapius, taking umbrage at something said or done, had left his patient to prescribe for himself. I had heard so much of this capricious yet privileged gentleman that I had a great curiosity to see him. I shortly after sat next to him at dinner at one of the regimental messes. In this learned pundit I beheld a beardless lad, apparently of my own age, with an unmistakable Scottish type of countenance – reddish hair, high cheekbones. There was a certain effeminacy in his manner, which he seemed to be always striving to overcome. His style of conversation was greatly superior to that one usually heard at a mess table in those days of *non*-competitive examinations. A mystery attached to Barry's whole medical career, which extended over half a century. While at the Cape he fought a duel, and was considered to be of a most quarrelsome disposition. He was frequently guilty of flagrant breaches of discipline, and on more than one occasion was sent home under arrest, but somehow or other his offences were always condoned at headquarters.

The circumstances which led up to the duel here mentioned are certainly not without interest. For some time Barry had been simmering in a mood of more than usual insubordination, in which she permitted herself a liberty of speech and action that one day, as the riposte to a particularly impertinent remark, resulted in her being picked up bodily by the justly incensed Governor and ignominiously dumped out of the study window. Shortly after this episode, which both parties to it had allowed to drop into oblivion, it so happened that a certain local lady of somewhat buxom proportions had occasion to call upon the Governor. The twain remained closeted together for some considerable time, a fact which was not lost on the shrewish observation of Barry. Turning to Cleoté, the principal ADC, the little waspish doctor rapped out: 'I say, that's a nice Dutch filly the Governor has got hold of!' – accompanying the gibe with a sneer that was twice as offensive as the actual words employed. Firing up, Cleoté demanded that the medico should immediately retract, accompanying his insistence with a sharp tweak of that invitingly long Ciceronian nose. Whatever else she wanted, Barry did not lack courage, and a challenge was the instant result. Pistols were the weapons chosen, and the scene of the encounter was outside the walls of the old Castle, 'where Keiser's Gracht bends round towards Papendorp'.

Throughout the whole business Barry maintained her usual air of frigid self-control, and never by so much as the flicker of an eyelid betrayed the slightest qualm of fear. The seconds having placed their principals, the word to make ready was given. Turning her meagre frame so that it presented the smallest possible target to her opponent, the little doctor slowly raised her pistol arm and took steady aim. A word of command, and both weapons flashed almost simultaneously. For a moment there was absolute stillness; the figures of antagonists and seconds alike stood rigid under the hard sunlight as though carved out of stone. Then Barry was seen to take a hesitating step forward, almost to stagger. Running up quickly, the surgeon in attendance anxiously questioned if she was hurt. But this Barry most strenuously denied, and pulling herself upright with an effort, walked toward the carriage which had brought her to the ground. The next moment she had disappeared in a cloud of dust, driving furiously toward her house at Heerengracht.

It is impossible to say with any certainty if her denial of any injury was true or not. Only that momentary sway forward, and the fact that for some time she kept more closely than ever to the seclusion of her own residence, supports the belief that she actually did sustain a wound, which fear of some accidental betrayal of her sex in the process of its dressing drove her to conceal and tend herself.

Certain it is, however, that this initial experience in no way served to subdue her irascible and umbrageous temper, for not long after, taking exception to something said in conversation by Colonel Shadwell Clerke, it was only the tactful intervention of Cleoté that prevented another meeting, which might not have been visited with so fortunate a termination as the last.

In fact it was a direct outcome of her fiery and contumaceous temperament which finally drove Barry from the Cape Town garrison. Dining in mess on one occasion, high words passed between the doctor and the officer with whom she had entered into argument. The former's manner waxed so offensive that a challenge resulted, but this she scornfully refused to entertain. As a consequence, she was solemnly expelled the amenities of the mess. Furiously indignant, she then demanded a Court of Enquiry into the whole affair. Probably to her infinite anger and amazement, the proceedings of the tribunal signally failed to exonerate her from blame, and the long-suffering Governor, his patience at last exhausted, promptly sent her home to England in open arrest.

Her actual departure is described by an eyewitness as follows:

On one of those still, sultry mornings peculiar to the tropics the measured tread of the doctor's pony woke up the echoes of the valley. There came the PMO, looking faded and crestfallen. He was in plain clothes, and he had shrunk away wonderfully. His blue jacket hung loosely about him, his white trousers were a world too wide, and the veil garnishing his broad straw hat covered his face, and he carried the inevitable umbrella over his head so that it screened him from the general gaze. The street was deserted, but other eyes besides the writer's looked on the group through the venetian blinds. No sentry presented arms at the gates, and the familiar quartet proceeded unnoticed along the lines to the ship's boat in waiting.

Once back in England, however, strings were pulled and influence brought to bear, and it was not long before Surgeon-Major James Barry was offered the alternative of an appointment at home or another tour of duty abroad. Possibly there were those in high places acquainted with her private history who were not above hinting that the further she was from England the better it would prove for all concerned. However that may be, it was to the West Indies that the little doctor next took her departure, doubtless not unaccompanied by a sigh of relief from those out of whose sides this peculiarly prickly thorn was temporarily to be removed!

Arrived at her new station, Barry lost no time in stamping the impress of her peculiar individuality upon the little community that comprised the garrison. But she was far from comfortable, and applying for leave to return home 'on urgent private affairs', her application not being attended to with that celerity she expected, she calmly took 'French leave', and re-embarked for England without troubling to notify anyone in authority of her intentions.

Naturally enough, upon reporting her return to the Medical Department at the Horse Guards, her nonchalant attitude was greeted with some asperity.

'I do not understand your reporting yourself in this fashion,' boomed the Inspector-General of Medical Services by way of greeting. 'You admit that you have returned without leave of absence. May I ask how this is?'

'Well,' replied Barry, running her long white fingers through the cluster of (probably synthetic) curls that cascaded over her brow, 'I've just come home to get my hair cut.'

Whereafter 'influence' doubtless had to put in yeoman service to restore things to a harmonious equilibrium!

The next departure was to St Helena, where, we are told, but with an irritating lack of all details, she 'made things too hot for her', and she again set sail for the West Indies.

By now she had served a good four-and-twenty years, and all regimental duty was a thing of the past, staff billets coming to her, as it seemed, without question.

But time could not wither nor custom stale her infinite – consistency. It was the same prickly, boastful, secretive, fretful, vain and imperious Barry whose goings to and fro the Cape Town garrison had learned to look upon with such uneasiness. Possibly it was the abiding dread that any suspicion of the real sex that lurked behind the braided tunic should arise which drove her to the assumption of a raffish freedom of speech, a snickering, boastful implication of libertinism that even in those far from mincing days overstepped the borders of accepted licence. Indeed, so convincingly did the masquerader carry the air of gallant that on one occasion the Adjutant of one of the regiments of the garrison quite seriously preferred the request that Dr Barry would refrain from calling on his wife at the precise hour when he knew that, as Adjutant, he would be compelled to attend either parade or orderly room!

Side by side with this almost frenzied assertion of manliness lurked an equally pathetic, ineradicable femininity, which found a muted and enfeebled expression in the unhappy woman's love of weddings, her adoration of all children, and her almost passionate care of the *enceinte* and the young mother. Poor, thwarted, hungry soul, only by such second-hand means could she give expression to that urge of

Nature which is the prerogative of her sex. Unhappy, pitiful paradox, of whom her patients swore that she had 'a hand as gentle as a woman's', and of whom no contemporary would deny the possession of a tongue as rough as any man's!

It was during the period that Barry spent in Trinidad, about the year 1844, that her sex actually did suffer discovery. During a temporary indisposition of the PMO, a subaltern of the garrison suggested to the junior medico that they should pay a call on Doctor Barry at the house of a woman friend where the invalid was staying to be nursed. Making their way to this residence unobserved, the pair stole into the room where the PMO lay sunk in a slumber that almost bordered upon coma. Acting upon some indefinable impulse, the subaltern bent and pulled the clothes back from the recumbent figure. One glance was sufficient to make it clear to the twain that they were in the presence of a woman. With a startled cry the subaltern stepped quickly back, letting the clothes fall into their original position, and at that moment Barry opened her eyes. It did not take her swift intelligence more than a moment to grasp the full purport of the situation. Realizing that her sex had been surprised, with the utmost vehemence and solemnity she swore the two intruders to eternal secrecy. The oath they took to respect her wishes was most scrupulously kept until the public revelation of her sex that followed upon her death released them from its obligations.

Indifferent health and years of service in the debilitating climate of the tropics had given Barry an appearance of age beyond her years. An officer in attendance at a court-martial in Trinidad in 1844, remarking the queer figure of Barry tricked out in a cocked hat, frock coat, high-heeled boots garnished with enormous brass spurs, and great brass-scabbarded sabre, had put the little doctor's age at about sixty, though actually at that time she was considerably younger.

But still she continued to serve abroad, in the West Indies, at Corfu, and in the Mediterranean, repairing home at intervals, but always returning to her duty on some foreign station.

If her earlier promotions had been accelerated, in later days they took on a more laggard gait. Having skipped the grades of Surgeon, Assistant Inspector, and Brevet Deputy Inspector, she commenced as Hospital Assistant in 1813. She was an Assistant Surgeon in 1815, and was confirmed as a Surgeon Major in 1827. But it was not until 1851 that she was graded as Deputy Inspector of Hospitals, being further promoted to an Inspectorship in 1858.

Colonel Rogers, who later embodied, not to say embroidered, some of her adventures into a work of fiction, *A Modern Sphinx*, has left it upon record that in 1858 he shared a cabin with Dr Barry, then voyaging out to Barbados on a visit to her whilom enemy and present friend, Josias Cleoté, then commanding the troops of the garrison. He recalls how he commented at the time on the peevish and peremptory manner in which his fellow-passenger would order him out of the cabin every morning before arising from the lower berth to dress.

In the following year Barry retired on half pay, returning to England in the midsummer.

Settling in Down Street, she adopted a quiet mode of life, enlivened by dinner-parties and drives in the Park with such old friends and one-time patients as had survived to return in the winter of their days to the land of their birth. During the brief year that followed she was greatly cheered by the friendship of Lady Charles Somerset, to whom she was a frequent visitor.

It is fairly obvious that she had looked forward to the recognition of her many years of service by some official award, her hopes rising so high as to entertain thoughts of a KCB. At least it is known that, at the time of her last illness, she had ordered a new uniform in anticipation of a summons to the last levee of the season. Certainly such hopes as she entertained were not without some warranty. She had already been mentioned in dispatches, had been strongly recommended for promotion, and an appreciation of her skill and devotion during a epidemic in the West Indies had appeared in General Orders. Some personal decoration, therefore, from the hands of her Sovereign was a reward she could look forward to with some confidence.

But fate had not destined her to survive in the enjoyment of worldly recognition. Returning from a drive one sullen day in July, she complained of having taken chill. Retiring to bed, she gave orders to cancel a dinner engagement for the morrow – a Sunday. In attendance upon her was her landlady and her manservant, John, one of a succession of such, who had been in her service for upwards of three years. Giving orders not to be awakened until the following morning, the frail little creature shambled off to bed. What follows is best told in an account given by a contemporary writer.

On that Sunday the servant went into the master's room, as usual, to lay out his body-linen. Six towels were amongst the unvariable articles of his toilet, and though Black John never assisted him personally, he was aware that his master wrapped these cloths about him; whether he did so for warmth, or to conceal any personal defects in his emaciated form, was a mystery. No wonder the form was emaciated, for James had accustomed himself to periodic blood-lettings, either by leeches or lancet. On Black John's return to the room, he found his master worse, but nothing would elicit his permission to send for the medical friend who had been in attendance on him previously for bronchitis. The faithful valet was alarmed, but he and the dog were the only watchers on the sufferer throughout the sultry July day.

James lay dozing and powerless. It was after midnight when he rallied. He sat up and spoke to John, wandering at times, and expressed concern at his long attendance throughout so many hours; he would have had John take some slight stimulant, which the faithful soul declined. Suddenly James fainted on his pillow. The valet used restoratives which revived him. 'John,' gasped the invalid, 'this must be death!'

But John did not think so. 'You are only weak, sir,' he said; 'let me give you some champagne and water, or the least drop of brandy in a wineglass of water.' For James would take such stimulants only in great extremity, and he *was* now in great extremity. He sipped a little from the glass, and said, more gently than usual, 'Have some yourself, John: you need it, and you will not mind drinking after me.' They were his last distinct words. John again declined refreshment, fearing he might fall asleep, but, at his master's request, went to lie down in an adjoining room thinking that 'the General', as James chose to be designated by his valet, would get some rest.

Always considerate to his dependents, 'the General' had been almost tender to John. He had spoken to him of his lonely life. 'It was not always so, John,' he had said; 'once I had friends. I have some still, but they are not the friends of early times; they will think of me, though, and if you want help, they will remember you for my sake. Now go and lie down. I think I shall sleep.' He never woke again. At daylight John entered the sick-room. The curtains were closed, so he took the night-light and approached the bed. 'The General' had died without a struggle. His eyes were closed; the worn features were calm. There had been apparently no pain. John drew the sheet over the face, and descended to the kitchen for a charwoman. He summoned her to assist at the last toilet of the dead 'General'. As she closed the door of the room, he retreated to his own and laid himself down, tired out. He was closing his eyes when the charwoman hurried in. 'What do you mean,' she said, 'by calling me to lay out a "General", and the corpse is a woman's?' The death was reported in *The Times*, and the next day it was officially reported to the Horse Guards that the doctor was a woman.

Immediately there arrived at the lodgings a man who gave himself out to be the valet of a certain nobleman. In the absence of anyone else professing any authority, he was permitted to make all arrangements for the simple obsequies. Thereafter, he charged himself with the winding-up of the dead Doctor's affairs, taking charge of all papers, and arranging for the return of the faithful and suitably rewarded John to his own country, for the journey to which he also furnished the necessary passage money.

Thus, dying as mysteriously as she had lived, Dr Barry passed from mortal ken to find humble sepulture in the cemetery at Kensal Green.

Lola Montez (1818?–61)

The Most Outrageous Woman in the World

Lola Montez, whose real name was Maria Dolores Eliza Rosanna Gilbert, has been described as a fabulous liar, a meddler in politics, mistress to more men than she could remember, and stunningly beautiful. Small wonder this exotic woman should be remembered as one of the most outrageous members of her sex. Born in Ireland, she studied dance and then used her undoubted allure to win the hearts of admirers and lovers all over Europe, America and Australia. Later, Lola capitalized on her notoriety by undertaking lecture tours and published a best-selling book, *Arts of Beauty, or Secrets of a Lady's Toilet*, in 1858. The story of this spellbinding adventuress of whom Alexandre Dumas wrote, 'She is fatal to any man who dares to love her,' is told by **Kendall McDonald**.

She enslaved great men . . . A man died in a duel over her . . . She ruled a kingdom . . . She threw her husband out of a window.

To have written this story in the 1850s, when Lola Montez was in England, would have been dangerous. For in 1856 Lola horsewhipped the writer of an article which did not meet with her approval.

But the story of Lola Montez, dancer and adventuress, began in the Irish town of Limerick when a Miss Oliver met a dashing young man called Edward Gilbert.

Miss Oliver was thirteen, her ancestry uncertain, her blood largely Spanish. Edward Gilbert was seventeen. And it was while Miss Oliver was being educated at a convent that the couple met. And less than a year after their first meeting Edward Gilbert became an ensign in the army. He chose an old regiment of the line to which the King's Own Scottish Borderers can trace their descent. Before he was posted to India with a different regiment, Miss Oliver made it quite clear to young Gilbert that she would like to be married. Indeed, before he sailed a child was born. A marriage was arranged with suitable haste, and when Edward Gilbert set foot in India he was accompanied by his wife and the child, baptized Maria Dolores Eliza Rosanna Gilbert – a nice mixture of the Irish and Spanish in her blood. It was from Dolores that she was to take the name, Lola, one of the diminutives of this Spanish word.

But Lola, possibly because her mother did not care much for hampering her movements before the child was born, was very small. She weighed a mere four pounds and several ounces.

The child was lucky to live at all. On one occasion she was given up for dead, and doctors are said to have abandoned, on several occasions, all hope for her survival. Long after normal children are learning to fend for themselves Lola was a child in arms. It appears that Mrs Gilbert liked the life of an Indian fort. Liked it so much that there were many rumours that she did not stay as close to her husband's side as she should have done. The child-wife blossomed out into a remarkably pretty woman. Her prospects were excellent. Mr Gilbert would not remain an ensign for ever. He had a very soldierly manner, was no coward, and seemed destined soon to become a Captain.

But cholera was no respecter of military rank. In 1824 Edward Gilbert's place was vacant at the mess table. Within six months his pretty young widow had married his best friend, Captain Craigie.

It is uncharitable but probably true to say that Mrs Craigie soon found that Lola was becoming an embarrassment. Not only was the girl becoming vain of her own looks – her dark hair, large eyes and long neck were incessantly praised by subalterns with little else to do – but Mrs Craigie was finding the question of her own age difficult with a fast-growing daughter around.

Little Lola was packed off to Montrose, Scotland. There she was placed under the guardianship of Major Craigie's father, the Provost of Montrose. At school here she found things much stricter than with her stepfather's Indian regiment. She made one friend, who was later to become a Mrs Buchanan, and was to be Lola's last source of comfort before she died.

The hard, religious atmosphere in which she was being brought up caused Lola to write tearful letters to her mother in India. In 1831 her parents removed her to the care of Sir Jasper Nicolls in London. He, perhaps not wishing to have too much trouble with the girl, bustled her off to join his own daughters completing their education in Paris.

This education in Paris finished what life in India had merely started – Lola was not only beautiful but difficult, independent and seductive. She was accustomed to getting her own way, and had now found that as far as the male species were concerned she could always do what she wished.

In India Mrs Craigie was anxious to get Lola married off and well out of her way. So she considered the proposal of a judge of the Supreme Court in India, Sir Abraham Lumley, whom Lola was later to describe as a 'rich and gouty old rascal of sixty years'. Lola was now eighteen.

With this proposal firmly in her mind, Mrs Craigie set sail for home and that venue of fashion, Bath. She saw nothing wrong in engaging her young daughter to this old man. But she reckoned without Lola and a certain Mr Thomas James, Lieutenant of Native Infantry, Bengal. This English officer was travelling home on the same boat as Mrs Craigie. He had made himself very pleasant on the voyage, and when he met Lola in Bath determined to extricate her from the prospect of Sir Abraham Lumley's wintry love.

The couple eloped and, having failed to obtain Lola's mother's consent, their marriage was finally solemnised in July, 1837, in Country Neath, Ireland.

All did not go well. Lieutenant James seems to have turned to the bottle for solace from his young wife's fits of rage, and he appears to have been relieved when ordered to rejoin his regiment in India. Lola went with him, and it seems that she took full advantage of the pleasures of the voyage and the company of a great number of male passengers.

One ardent passenger is reported to have gone to a great deal of trouble to pass messages to the Lieutenant's wife by boring a hole in the bulkhead to her cabin. This state of affairs could obviously not last long, and when Lola became even more flirtatious after landing in India the Lieutenant, now Captain, could stand no more. He eloped with the wife of another officer, and did not even bother to resign his commission.

Lola was anything but heart-broken, and in 1841 joined her mother in Calcutta. Her mother was not pleased with the even more formidable competition her presence evoked and pressed her to return to Europe. This the young beauty did, and in the spring of 1842 arrived in London. On the voyage back she met another agreeable male. Her husband, who seems to have borne a charmed life, had got himself reinstated in the Army, and rather ungallantly instituted divorce proceedings against Lola in the very year that she arrived in London. Lola ignored the case, and as a result, in December, 1842, the court pronounced a judicial separation. Mrs Craigie, by now a fully fledged Army snob, put on mourning and issued notification of Lola's death.

Lola soon left the Mr Lennox whom she had met on the voyage home and, as did many a divorced woman in those days, turned to the theatre. She had some money, was beautiful, and life was very sweet.

She started to study dramatic art, but soon admitted even to herself that she was not cut out to be an actress. But dancing – that was a different thing.

She realized that to introduce herself to London theatre-goers under her real name would merely be inviting disaster. So, trading on her Spanish blood and remote family connections with that country, she left for Spain, and is said to have undergone a short but intensive course of terpsichorean training under a Spanish dancing master.

It was while in Spain that she decided on her stage name. Probably taken from the annals of bull-fighting it was – Montez.

On her return to London she was even more Spanish than the Spanish. She approached the Director of Her Majesty's Theatre for a chance to dance there.

On 3 June, 1843, Donna Lola Montez, 'of the Teatro Royal, Seville,' was announced in an original dance called El Olano.

The evening was disastrous. Among a sparkling first-night audience was a man who had wooed but not won her – Lord Ranelagh, prominent in a box to the right of the stage. He must have known beforehand that Lola Montez was the woman who had rejected his advances, for the audience was very liberally sprinkled with his friends.

Lola started to dance and almost immediately Lord Ranelagh's voice was heard to announce to the house: 'Why! It's Betty James!' This was the signal, and Lola was not allowed to finish her dance. There was a storm of boos and hisses from his lordship's friends.

Ranelagh's revenge went further. He spread stories around the town that the latest Spanish dancer was not Spanish at all, and in the newspapers of those times appeared letters from Lola vehemently denying that she was an Englishwoman. But the damage was done. There was no dancing career left for Lola in England. A week or so later her apartment was empty. Lola Montez had left for Europe.

The first man at whom she set her cap on the Continent was King Leopold of Belgium. Susceptible though he was, in Lola's own words 'the friendship lasted only two months before I left with a Polish gentleman who brought me to Paris'.

In Warsaw in 1844 she made her greatest success – for her beauty, not her dancing – at the age of twenty-six.

It was about this time that the composer Liszt fell deeply in love with her, and for a few weeks they lived together, but Lola did not stay with him long. She returned to Warsaw, and there she captivated the old Viceroy of Poland, who offered her jewels and a castle. Headstrong as usual, Lola retorted that she could not love an old man whose hair and teeth were not his own.

And here the Viceroy made a mistake. Little knowing Lola's past experience, he and his friends tried to boo her off the stage. But the boos turned into cheers when Lola Montez in a towering rage faced the audience and told them of the Viceroy's offer.

Many of the audience were revolutionaries, and the next morning all the political unrest in Poland very nearly exploded on her account. She was ordered to leave the country. In fact, the Viceroy went further, and ordered at the same time that she should be arrested. Of this in her memoirs Lola said (she was fond of writing of herself in the third person): 'When Lola Montez was appraised of the fact that her arrest was ordered, she barricaded her door; and when the police arrived she sat behind it with a pistol in her hand declaring she would certainly shoot dead the first man who should break it.

'The police were frightened, or at least they could not agree among themselves who should be the martyr, and they went off to inform their masters what a tigress they had to confront . . .'

A little later, with the pistol still in her hand, Lola unhurriedly supervised the loading of her belongings on to the coach for St Petersburg. There she was received by the Czar Nicholas, who gave her costly presents.

By now Lola Montez was far more than a Spanish dancer – she was Europe's most notorious courtesan. She returned to Paris and lived in luxury. Her dancing was still imperfect – but only one critic dared to say so. Out came the horse-whip and the critic was soon very sorry that he had 'insulted' Lola by writing: 'There was about her something provoking and voluptuous, which drew you. Her skin was white, her wavy hair like the tendrils of the wood-bine, her eyes tameless and wild, her mouth like a budding pomegranate. Add to that a dashing figure, charming feet and perfect grace. Unluckily, as a dancer, she had no talent.' The public seem to have agreed with him, for her first appearance at the Paris Opera was her last.

Alexander Dumas was the next to fall for her charms. He had just published *The Three Musketeers* and *The Count of Monte Cristo*. To her apartments flocked all the literary and society world of Paris. She had conquered everyone – except the critics. One having been horse-whipped, the others remained lukewarm. But in 1845 even these prejudices were overcome. One of the most famous editors of the time was Dujarier. He fell in love with Lola, and if the fact that he died for her and she mourned him deeply is of any significance, then this may have been the first and probably the only real love match of Lola's life.

Unfortunately, Lola met another journalist – M. Jean de Beauvallon, the dramatic critic of Dujarier's rival paper. As a result of Dujarier's objection, Lola refused to see him any more. The rivalry between Dujarier and De Beauvallon, a Creole from Guadeloupe, grew bitter.

The Creole nursed his grievance to his heart, and this, together with the scathing attacks in Dujarier's paper upon his own, finally brought about tragedy. In a game of cards some argument arose between the two over the stakes. De Beauvallon said nothing at the time, but later reminded his rival that he owed him some 84 louis. Dujarier replied very sharply, but paid the debt. There would seem to be little ground in this incident for a duel, but the next day Dujarier was visited in his office by the representatives of De Beauvallon.

The duel took place on 11 March 1845. The chosen spot was near the Madrin restaurant in the Bois de Boulogne. It was a bitterly cold day. There was a last attempt to make up the quarrel. And despite evidence that proved that one of De Beauvallon's pistols had been tried out that very day (practice of this kind was forbidden by the duelling code) the fight took place. 'Fight' is perhaps the wrong word, for no sooner had the signal been given than Dujarier, who was in a pitiful state of nerves, fired and missed by several feet. By the laws of duelling De Beauvallon should have fired immediately, instead he took careful aim – even with the pistols of those days at such short range this was murder – and Dujarier received the bullet in the nose. It shattered his skull; he crumpled to the ground, and despite the physician's assurance that the wound was trivial, died in a few seconds. His body was piled into a coach, and when Lola flung open the door, the body of her lover fell from the hands of his seconds and pitched into her arms.

But the affair was not to end here. The rigid laws of duelling had been broken, and before Dujarier was carried to his grave, with Balzac and Dumas as two of the pallbearers, it was clear that the matter was not resolved.

Lola mourned Dujarier sincerely, but only three weeks after his death she appeared on the stage of the Porte-St-Martin Theatre. The audience were not concerned with her grief. Again she was hissed and again she stood in front of the footlights and expressed her contempt for the audience in no uncertain terms.

This was the end of her career as a dancer in Paris. But she stayed on hoping to see justice take its course against the man who had slain her lover. De Beauvallon had fled the country almost immediately after the duel and was living just across the Spanish border.

In July the Royal Court of Paris exonerated his seconds of all blame, and De Beauvallon, mistakenly thinking that this also exonerated him, surrendered voluntarily to the authorities.

He was sent for trial – accused of murder – at the Assize Court of Rouen. The whole case turned on the point that a duellist is not allowed to use arms which he has already tried. And the evidence that one of the pistols had been blackened with powder by firing was considered damning.

But De Beauvallon's counsel was so eloquent that the Creole was acquitted of the charge. Damages of 20,000 francs were awarded against him, payable to the mother and sister of his victim.

Later the case was reopened with fresh evidence, which proved without doubt that De Beauvallon had tried the pistol on the morning of the duel in a garden and had fired not once but a dozen times. On 9 October 1847, he was found guilty and condemned to eight years' imprisonment. He escaped from prison during the Revolution of the following year.

But meanwhile Lola had left France, and was off again on her travels – this time to Spain where she became associated with the bandit Madras. He proposed marriage, but Lola asked too long to consider her verdict, and the next time she saw him he was standing on a scaffold within a few moments of eternity.

Her travels continued until she met King Ludwig I of Bavaria. He was sixty-one. Five days after her first appearance on the stage in Munich she was introduced at court with the words: 'Gentlemen, I present to you my best friend.' Indeed, after his first interview with Lola, the King had confided frankly to his Ministers that he was bewitched by her. Strangely enough, the Queen Therese never showed the slightest jealousy of her husband's new friend, and more than once expressed her sympathy with Lola's subsequent actions.

On 7 March, 1847, Lola was naturalized by a special Royal decree, given the title of Baronne de Rosenthal, and later, Comtesse de Lansfeld. In addition to this the King arranged for her to draw a personal income from his coffers

– it was described as a pension – of twenty thousand florins a year.

And this was not all. He built a splendid house for her, had her portrait painted by his own command and placed it in a gallery of beauties where he was said to spend hours before her picture in rapturous contemplation.

Her house in Munich was no cold great barn, in which respect it was quite different from other great houses nearby. The style was Italian, and it had but two storeys. We are told that elegant bronze balconies – Lola's own design – relieved the plainness of the exterior.

A journalist of those days made an odd comment in one of his reports – a remark which revealed that Lola nursed no hatred for England (where, it seems, the whole habit of booing her off the stage had started). He wrote: 'Any English gentleman can, on presenting his card, see the interior; but it is not a show place.'

Soon this daughter of a hasty Spanish-Irish union was ruling Bavaria behind the old king. And, strangely enough, she was ruling the kingdom well.

But many were working hard to reverse her fortune. The clergy hated her; the Austrians schemed against her; and the aristocracy resented her intrusion into politics. Money was distributed by her enemies; the seeds of discontent were sown. But it was the students who unwittingly brought about her downfall. All members of the University were not under the thumb of the clerics. Some students frequented Lola's salon which had become the meeting-place of the artists and thinkers of Munich.

One day Lola's fancy was taken by the gay colours of one of the student's caps and playfully she placed it on her own head. The students concerned in this incident were dismissed from their corps. Immediately a large number of Liberal students resigned from their respective associations and formed a new corps. The new body was at once recognized by the King in honour of his favourite, and Lola provided every member of it at her own expense with a new and ultra-smart uniform. The new corps – The Alemannia – became her personal bodyguard, escorting her everywhere. She appeared at their festivals dressed in a close-fitting copy of their uniform.

As a result, fights broke out regularly between the rival bands of students, and the King unwisely closed the University. That was the last straw. Revolution broke out – and the old King signed her banishment from the kingdom.

King Ludwig had abandoned his self-respect – he broke every promise he had ever made to Lola, and even when she returned from banishment disguised as a boy in an attempt to see the King and persuade him to change his mind, he refused to see her. At pistol point she was told again to leave the country – for ever.

On 21 March, 1848, the King abdicated, and Lola, who had been waiting just over the border in the hope that her fortune would be reversed, fled back to England. She tried a return to the stage in a dramatization of the recent events in Munich, but the Lord Chamberlain refused to license a performance 'in which living Royal personages were introduced'.

Lola's star was now on the wane. She retired into lodgings at 27 Half Moon Street – and began a fresh affair. At the age of thirty-one she married again. Her new husband, who is described as having a wispy moustache and whiskers, was a Cornet in the Second Life Guards. He was only just twenty-one, and the possessor of a considerable fortune. They were married at St George's, Hanover Square, on 19 July 1849. Lola now wished to settle down and live in peace, away from the restless echoes her incursion into international affairs had started. Her hope was in vain, for early in the morning of 6 August, as she was stepping into her carriage from her apartment in Half Moon Street, a police sergeant and inspector stepped forward and informed her that they held a warrant for her arrest on the charge of bigamy. Her lawful husband, they said, was still Captain James, and was very much alive. She was taken to Marlborough Street police court, and the case had its first and only hearing. Lola was released on bail of £2000, and we are told that she waited with her husband, Mr Heald, in the court afterwards so that the crowd could disperse.

It was a spinster aunt, the Cornet's guardian, who had caused all this trouble. She explained that she did it from a sense of duty. But Lola and her husband did not wait to investigate her motives – they fled to Paris and thence to Spain. The marriage, however, did not go well, and Heald was once stabbed with a stiletto when Lola lost her temper. This broke his spirit and several times he tried to run away from her. Each time Lola advertised – as one would for a lost dog – and each time he returned to her side. But, at last, the advertisements remained unanswered, and Heald escaped – back to his aunt's protection.

A year later, however, on holiday in Portugal, young Heald was sailing in Lisbon harbour when he got into the wake of a steamer and was drowned. This was in 1853 – and Lola turned to America for solace. She appeared first of all as a dancer and then in autobiographical melodramas with resounding titles like, 'Lola Montez in Bavaria'.

She married yet again, this time the proprietor of a San Francisco newspaper – hoping perhaps to discover a love equivalent to that of Dujarier. It did not last long, and finally Lola threw her husband out of a window. Although he survived, he not unnaturally wanted nothing more to do with the fiery Lola.

She returned to the theatre and sailed for Australia. Once there she objected strongly to an article written about her by the editor of a Melbourne paper. Out came the horse-whip and Lola flogged her critic very lustily until dragged away from him.

But Lola was getting a bit past this form of revenge. The next time she picked up her horse-whip was to thrash the owner of a theatre in which she was appearing. She had reckoned without the owner's wife. This redoubtable female tore the whip from Lola's hands and gave her a taste of her own medicine.

That was enough of Australia for Lola: she sailed back to America. Her health was failing, and her friends had almost all deserted her, when suddenly she met her old school friend from Scotland, Mrs Buchanan, now the wife of a florist in New York.

From her Lola acquired strong religious convictions, and devoted the remaining years of her life to visiting unfortunates of her own sex in New York asylums.

Paralysis suddenly struck, and after great suffering she died on 17 January, 1861, vastly penitent and confessing: 'My life has been sacrificed to my passions.'

In Greenwood Cemetery, New York, a simple tablet marks her grave. It mentions nothing of kingdoms ruled, critics horse-whipped, wealthy lovers or Spanish blood. It mentions Lola Montez not at all.

The inscription reads: 'Mrs Eliza Gilbert, died January 17, 1861.' She was forty-three.

The Queen of the Desert

Jane Digby, who spent her early life amidst the splendours of Holkham Hall in Norfolk and swapped these for a Bedouin tent in the desert, is unique among eccentric heroines. Described as an adventuress and traveller, she was still only in her teens when she had been married and divorced amid scandal. Later she was involved in an elopement, a duel and affairs with King Ludwig of Bavaria, his son, Otto, and a string of other admirers. But it was an Arab, Sheik Medjuel el Mesrab, who captured her heart and made her the queen of his tribe. In the desert, Jane's adventurous nature, excellent horsemanship and ability to adopt Bedouin customs (including smoking a hookah pipe) earned her the respect of the Sheik's people and the amazement of the world at large. This account of the life of Jane Digby el Mesrab by **Alexander Allen** is the first to cut through the myths and legends surrounding the woman and reveal an even more extraordinary figure beneath . . .

In August 1881 the funeral took place of Jane Digby, Lady
Ellenborough, also known as 'the Honourable Mrs Digby el
Mesrab'. She was a Christian married to a Bedouin, Sheik
Abdul Medjuel el Mesrab, and she was given a Christian
burial in the self-styled 'oldest city in the world' – Damascus.
There were few mourners at the funeral of this seventy-four-
year-old English lady. The life of the bazaars went on as
usual and the clergyman officiated at the graveside in the
Protestant section of the Jewish Cemetery with the customary decorum and gravity. Sheik Abdul Medjuel el Mesrab, a
devout Muslim, suffered the closed black carriage and
strange Christian rites until he could do so no longer then,
with a heart full of grief, he left the stuffy contraption and
fled in the opposite direction. Minutes later, galloping furiously along on his wife's black mare, he caught up with the
cortège and stared into the open grave, surprising the little
group of shocked and silent mourners. Then he was gone, as
quickly as he had come. On her gravestone a single cross was
carved; her name in Arabic was placed there on a stone at the
foot by Medjuel in honour of the love of his life. Those few
pregnant and silent moments encompassed a lifetime of
happiness and sorrow, a web finely spun by a tempestuous
fate to entrap many souls and to exalt and crucify those she
had especially selected.

Jane Digby el Mesrab was one of the most flamboyant,
romantic, sensual, and tantalizingly enigmatic women who
ever left England's shores for adventure and love in countries
far removed from the stuffy, conventional atmosphere of the
Victorian drawing-room. She was also one of the kindest, one
of the most cultured, one of the most generous, and one of the
sincerest women who ever bestowed the warmth of their
affection on their friends and saved quite a modicum for their
enemies, too.

There were legal loves in her life, and there were illegal
loves, and Jane Digby coped with them all; she became Lady
Ellenborough; Baroness Venningen; Countess Theotoky
and, finally 'the Honourable Mrs Digby el Mesrab', wife
of a Bedouin Sheik who loved her passionately. On the long

trail of her manifest destiny she charmed other men; a librarian from the British Museum whom she met in the very springtime of her life, and Honoré de Balzac who called her his 'Desert Swallow' and 'this creature who glows with a strange phosphorescence'. The glittering prizes fell into her hands like baubles from a Christmas tree for among her devotees she numbered other Bedouin sheiks and an Albanian brigand. She was the epitome of romantic love in an age of Byronic elegance; what she did, she did for love and never brought that love down to a mercenary level for she spent large sums of money on her lovers until the steady flame of passion burned itself out, fanned by circumstances into a thousand dancing sparks which left her, like Niobe, weeping. She did not, however, weep for long. There were geographical frontiers to cross, leading her ever eastwards until she found the love of her life in the desert with Medjuel el Mesrab, while they rode like the wind in a freedom hardly dreamt of in the minds of her prim sisters atrophied in their conventional Victorian lives.

Jane Digby was born on 3 April 1807 to Lady Andover and her husband, Captain Henry Digby, a hero of Trafalgar, at Holkham in Norfolk; her maternal grandfather was the famous Coke of Norfolk, a Whig, devoted to George Washington, an agriculturist and landowner, heir to an enormous estate, much of it marshy and unworkable. He reclaimed it, built parks and gardens and began the building of Holkham in 1734. William Kent, nearly fifty years of age at the time, designed Holkham, which was described by Mrs Lybbe Powys as 'a stone building esteemed the most elegant of its kind in England'. However, the house was not built of stone but of yellow brick. It was said that this colour was used because yellow brick was found in antiquities brought from Rome and the brick could be made in Norfolk. The whole effect was one of length and was the biggest private house that Kent designed.

The Digbys traced their ancestry back to Aelmar; in the reigns of Edward the Confessor and William the Conqueror they helds lands in Leicestershire, their descendants sometimes called Diggeby de Tilton or just plain Tilton. Sir Everard Digby was a conspirator, born in 1578 . . .

A husband was found for her in thirty-four-year-old Edward Law, Earl of Ellenborough, who was later to serve two years as Governor-General of India. Two years at Eton, St John's College ('a Tory College in a Whig University') and two years at Cambridge (where he obtained his MA as a 'nobleman' by virtue of privilege as the son of a peer) led to the usual 'Grand Tour' of Europe. He was tall and well built, with an abundance of hair, and arched eyebrows, but his acid tongue and blasé manners made him unpopular in certain circles. Harriette Wilson was not entranced with him, for she wrote in her diary:

Young Law, Lord Ellenborough's son, was a very smart, fine young gentleman, and his impatience of temper passed, I dare say, occasionally for quickness. His wig was never on straight on his head. I rather fancy he liked to show his own good head of hair under it.

In 1813 he obtained his seat in the Commons for the pocket borough of St Michael's in Cornwall and attracted the favourable attention of Lord Castlereagh, whose half-sister, Octavia Stewart, he married in December, 1815. In spite of parental opposition (Lord Londonderry, as Octavia's father, later acquiesced) there did not appear to be any visible regrets; Lady Londonderry called Ellenborough 'my youngest and most favourite son' and the couple seemed genuinely fond of each other. However, Octavia's health suffered from the effects of a severe cold and she died in 1819 from tuberculosis. Edward Law rebuilt a monastic chapel at Southam and transferred her remains there. His love went with her, for she was the one person who really understood him. Five years later, he married for a second time, encouraged by his mother-in-law, Lady Londonderry; 'You must marry', she wrote, 'a young and beautiful companion for an improved *noblesse*. You must again be happy in married life, for no other can make you so.' He found a 'young and beautiful companion' in Jane Digby, daughter of Rear-Admiral Digby and Viscountess Andover, who had made her début at the tender age of sixteen and whose charms were irresistible and whose affection for her cousin caused a relative, John Spencer Stanhope, to write that 'Jane is not true'. Count Walewski though her the 'most divinely beautiful creature he ever beheld', according to Creevey.

They were married in September 1824, and spent their honeymoon at Brighton, described by a nineteenth-century traveller as filled with 'genteel lazzaroni'. It was not a love-match; Ellenborough was almost twice her age, extremely proud of his ravishing eighteen-year-old wife, but not a man to inspire connubial bliss. Lady Anson, Jane's aunt, and her mother, Viscountess Andover (she insisted upon retaining the title of her first husband) were well pleased with the match; Jane's future was assumed to be safe with Edward Law. In London, Jane was left more and more to herself; the wealthy aristocrats spent a great deal of time in the City, plunged in work, while their bored wives disported themselves at Almack's in King Street, St James's, the *salon* which had supplanted Carlton House, as Carlton House had itself been supplanted by Buckingham Palace. 'Aurora', as Jane was called at this time, learnt quickly, so quickly indeed that Creevey described one of the parties she attended as composed of the 'most notorious and profligate women in London', and wrote of her conduct as 'impudent' and 'bare-faced'. Ellenborough allowed her much liberty, liberty which shocked Count Apponyi who visited London in July 1828, for he failed to find the great English decorum about which he had heard.

Left alone, she found pleasure in visits and on such a visit to her grandfather at Holkha, she met young Frederick Madden, a quiet, modest Librarian from Oxford and the British Museum who had come to Holkham to catalogue the Greek poets in the Long Gallery. He did his work in the daytime, played cards with the family in the long evenings, and spent much time thinking of his fiancée, Mary. He also thought about Jane, for he wrote in his diary that she was 'one of the most lovely women I ever saw' and in the spring of 1827 he recorded that 'she pretended to be very angry as to what passed last night'. Whatever passed between them, the affair petered out; the diary was later bequeathed to the Bodleian, where it was unsealed in 1920 according to Frederick Madden's instructions.

Jane returned to London and the whirl of the London season. There were Vauxhall Gardens, with their groves and pavilions (where one could spend a moment or two in dalliance), temples, grottoes and lawns, all brilliantly illuminated with lamps, resplendent with the figures of the Hon. Horatio Walpole; Lord March; Lord Granby; and that 'she-meteor', Lady Wortley Montague; the vulgar were allowed to gape at them to a late hour. There was Ranelagh up the river, of which Walpole said; 'You can't set your foot without treading on a Prince or Duke of Cumberland.' There were the new Marylebone Gardens, noted for the firework displays, for George II loved fireworks. At Ranelagh there was on olive-green ceiling painted with a rainbow, and an organ inside an arched structure which poured forth music to aid the amateur theatricals and play-readings which supplemented the professional theatre of Garrick and Sarah Siddons. The British Museum could not hope to rival these. On 15 February 1828, Jane was delivered of a child, who was christened Arthur Dudley Law; he appears to have contributed to the conjugal estrangement between Jane and Ellenborough for they moved into separate suites; Edward Law had achieved his ambitions for he had an heir and had received the post as Lord Privy Seal in the Duke of Wellington's Ministry. As usual with Jane, there had been gossip. Her cousin, George Anson, had always been close to her and since her return to London had escorted her around the London scene with many a malicious glance from the matrons. But Edward Law, happy with his heir, went about his political business. The day after the birth he wrote in his diary:

Jane has brought me a boy. I put this down as a political occurrence because I shall make him if he lives and I live a Political character. I shall ask the Duke of Wellington and Dudley to be his Godfathers, Princess Esterhazy is to be his Godmother. A good diplomatic introduction to the world.

In April 1828, Jane visited Almack's in King Street, St James. The orchestra played and the place was ablaze with light. Almack's was founded by one Almack, a Scotsman, for the edification of ladies and gentlemen of London, the 'new Babylon'. It was opened on 12 February, 1765 and was honoured by the presence of the Duke of Cumberland. The ballroom was 100 feet in length and forty feet in width and 500 wax lights in five cut-glass lustres blazed down on the magnificently-gowned scions of the nobility and their sycophants. The building was used for assemblies, concerts, musical evenings and balls, and the great actors gave readings and performances; Charles Kemble graced it with his august presence, reading from Shakespeare.

It was extremely difficult to gain admittance; five lady patronesses vetted the applications and the acceptance of any lady or gentleman depended on a personal visit of one of the patronesses. Almack's was the 'in' place in which to be seen and at one time 1,700 members danced in the elegant ballroom until early morning. Almack (the name was an anagram) left the building to his niece, Mrs Willis, and in 1890 the rooms known as 'Willis's Rooms' became a restaurant. Almack's ceased in 1863.

The beauties of London took themselves off to Almack's in St James, to see and to be seen, to bewitch and to tantalize, with all the arts they possessed, those young men upon whom their eyes chanced to alight. This was the Romantic age, the age of powder and paint and artificial aids used, not to enhance, but to cover up. The skin was whitened with mercury water and ceruse containing white-lead, and spots (these were common owing to the prevalence of small-pox) were hidden by patches. The white lead and mercury left devastation in their wake for hair could fall out and gastric ulcers kill. Complexion cleaners were eagerly sought after and an 'English rose', such as Jane Digby, was something of a rarity. She was the delicate nymph, the unstudied character who could lead men into that first innocent blossoming, which could so easily turn into a passion of frightening proportions.

The fashionable sought every sort of distraction and the wealthy found amusement in various, and devious, ways. There were spas all over England and in London there flourished such pleasure resorts as Vauxhall Gardens, Ranelagh and Spring Gardens, Kensington Gardens, Apollo Gardens, and St George's Fields. The Bayswater tea-gardens provided a degree of decorous refinement and day-time amusements succoured the appetites of the idle middle and upper classes for mild and innocuous games and fringe dalliance. The 'Temple of Flora', and the White Conduit House of Islington catered amirably for them. But, for the evenings of mystery and imagination, there was Almack's.

Jane had recovered well after the birth of her son, and Ellenborough's heir; she and Ellenborough had appeared together at a dinner and it was apparent that life would be interesting once more, especially as Ellenborough was so pleased with himself at having gained a Cabinet Post under Wellington that she would be free to live her own life. On one of the Wednesday night Balls in April 1828, Ellenborough brought Jane to the entrance of Almack's and then left to attend to his own quiet amusement in the sphere of Parliamentary politics. Jane was gorgeously clad and entrancingly captivating. Just twenty-one years of age, she soon found a partner, far more interesting and exciting than the scholarly librarian, Frederick Madden, and far, far more of a passionate Byronic figure than the Edward Law she had married. Introduced by Princess Esterhazy, Felix Schwartzenberg, newly appointed attaché at the Austrian Embassy, was the embodiment of all Jane's romantic dreams and secret longings. He was the dark, dashing, and gallant foreign aristocrat, the Ruritanian Prince to Jane's Cinderella, who swept her off her feet in that first dance at Almack's as he clasped her close to his hussar jacket. Soon they were lovers and all London society knew that Jane, Lady Ellenborough, had succumbed to this twenty-seven-year-old sophisticated intellectual, this diplomat who had travelled the world as far away as Rio de Janeiro, leaving a trail of broken hearts. Count Apponyi, a frequent visitor at Almack's, noted in his diary: 'Among all these people one lady especially attracted my attention. It was Lady Ellenborough, one of the most beautiful women I have ever seen, blond hair, magnificent complexion, big blue eyes, young, with the figure of a nymph; in fact, she is everything desirable . . . The expression of her face is as soft as the sound of her voice, and her whole personality has something of modesty and innocence which enchanted me.' Schwarzenberg's family was one of the oldest in Europe, their history being linked with that of the Holy Roman Empire and the monarchy. They had estates in Europe (the 'Schwarzenberg Kingdom') and were blue-blooded aristocrats through and through. Felix Schwarzenberg was a scholar, had a fine singing voice, and could speak several languages. To Lady Ellenborough, the bright-eyed child of country innocence, he was the Prince of Light who had taken her hand and led her patiently through the intricacies of the quadrille in a dream sequence that was to prove devastating in its effects.

They met at his house in Harley Street and in the Norfolk Hotel in Brighton; they were spied on with relish by the servants, laughed at by the grooms and the local folk and ostracized by those peeresses who were discreet enough to keep their own bedroom farces safely tucked away. They were seen together at parties on the river, at picnics in the Surrey Woods, at masked balls, and at musical evenings. Vauxhall, Ranelagh, Rotten Row were the venues for the two lovers and the receptions in Mayfair with upwards of 1,500 guests provided opportunities of close contact in public places; private contact was maintained in Schwartzenberg's rooms in Harley Street where Jane's green phaeton, accompanied by her groom, William Carpenter, could be seen almost daily. The gossip increased and became a scandal. Lord Ellenborough was timorously appraised of it at Roehampton by a hesitant Steely, and the Bishop of Bath and Wells himself took his nephew to task. A new name had been coined – 'cad'; it derived from a horse 'Cadland' which had won the Derby, beating the favourite, 'The Colonel'. This was a sly reference to George Anson, Jane's cousin.

There was a subsequent petition for divorce and, in the meantime, there were the usual meetings, with a rendezvous at the Norfolk Hotel in Brighton in February 1829 where a perceptive waiter, one Robert Hepple, listened intently outside the bedroom door. Thomas Creevey took a dim view of the guests:

> There were Mrs. F-L- and Lord Chesterfield, who came together and sat together all night, Lady E- and the Pole or Prussian or Austrian or whatever he is they call Cadland, because he beat the Colonel. Anything as impudent as she or as barefaced as the whole affair I never beheld.

The young Arthur Dudley Ellenborough had also been brought along by his nursemaids for a change of air, but the 'good, political introduction' which Lord Ellenborough had envisaged never matured, for the baby died about a year afterwards.

A shattering event now took place – the recall of Schwarzenberg and the removal of Jane to Ilfracombe by her family in the protective custody of Steely, who must have noticed, as they walked in the country, the advancing embonpoint underneath the informal pastoral clothing of Jane. It was all too much and Jane fled, throwing away at one fell swoop the embroidery, the formal tea-drinking, and the observances of the not-too-natural habits of the fauna round about, to say nothing of the early nights and the long, hours in a cold, passionless bed. 'My situation will soon become visible', she told Steely, 'God knows what will become of me! The child is not Lord Ellenborough's but Prince Schwartzenberg's!' a fact which Steely, prim governess though she were, was not unaware of.

Felix Schwartzenberg was not oblivious of his duties to Jane and his unborn child, but marriage was not possible at this stage; his family were strict Catholics and his sister, Mathilde, had advised him to end the costly liaison with Lady Ellenborough. There remained the question of the child. Several places in Europe were suggested where Jane could be quietly confined (after all, privacy at times like these was almost routine amongst the aristocracy) and finally Basle was chosen and Jane set out on the last day of August from Ramsgate, a tortured woman, fleeing without thought to a lover whose ambitions had never included her and whose strict Catholic upbringing would, in any case, have precluded marriage with a divorcee. Ellenborough had made very generous arrangements for her, pending divorce proceedings, in order that she would not be without 'those comforts and conveniences to which her rank in life entitled her'; Jane was grateful.

On a day in August 1829 Jane left the shores of England for foreign parts. She was never, except for short intervals of time, never to return. Steely was there to help, with a sad heart bundling Jane and the maid she had found for her in Brussels into a hired coach and returning home. 'Madame Einberg', as Jane wished to be known on the journey, settled herself down with relief and expectancy, anticipating that glorious reunion with Felix which would heal all wounds. Felix did not arrive in Basle until nearly two months after Jane had set her foot on Swiss soil and her thoughts of a passionate reunion were doomed to disappointment. Felix, now older and far more prosaic, saw with diplomatic shrewdness that his ambitions did not lie in the direction of marriage and children and soon after the birth of a daughter, named 'Didi' by Felix, he left for Paris. Felix had been with her for only two weeks.

Felix was Metternich's protégé and in a city beset with political intrigue and revolutionary ideas he had ambitions to fulfill. They lived in the Rue de Grenelle and the Place du Palais de Députés and Jane entered once again into the world she had always enjoyed, the world of masked balls and the endless parties. There were plenty of 'Almack's' in Paris, although the best society was closed to her.

There were other diversions, though, for Paris at this time was full of artists, writers and musicians and the Left Bank was not far from the Place du Palais. If Felix was busy in diplomatic circles, Jane could be equally concerned with those cultural and intellectual circles which best suited her temperament. She was highly intelligent, a woman of brilliance of mind, a searcher after knowledge and a person of breeding and utter refinement and unaffected charm. The literary giants were wholly immersed in the arts, for the literary side was also pictorial; Lamartine, Hugo, de Musset, Sand were all accomplished sketchers; Gautier was a painter as well as a writer. In 1830, Chateaubriand, already in his sixties, was the acknowledged father of Romanticism and Saint-Beuve, Alfred de Vigny and Prosper Merimée were soon to be well known in the 1830s. Artists came from all over the world to study in Paris and discuss for hours the nature of art in the cafés of Montmartre.

Felix finally left her, pressurized no doubt by his family and by his own desire to escape the tender trap of marriage; he removed his quarters from the house in the Place du Palais and spent less and less time with Jane. She met her mother, Lady Andover, at Dover, taking Didi with her but there does not appear to have been any attempt at a reconciliation, although Steely must have ardently desired it. London and Paris were no longer the places in which a divorceé could live and expect to be received into the best society, especially if there had been gossip and scandal! Even in that pre-Victorian age there were limits to which impropriety could be stretched. The British Ambassador at the Court of Bavaria was an old friend of the Digby family and it may well have been he who suggested Munich as a place of residence for Jane and the child; after all, Munich in the first half of the nineteenth century was a lively city, with exciting new buildings, theatres, and a University. Under Ludwig I it had entered into a golden age.

King Ludwig of Bavaria was a godchild of Marie Antoin-

ette and a protégé of Napoleon, ruling from 1825 to 1848.
With enormous enthusiasm he plunged into the rebuilding of
Munich; he copied Greek and Roman architecture, employing architects who shared his exuberance to the full, laying
foundation stones for classical arches and building for him
his new Bavarian *Griechenland*, imposing on the city a
fantasia of Romanesque, Renaissance and Athenian architectural styles. The family art treasures were housed in the
new *Pinakothek*, and the *Walhalla*, or Teuton Hall of Fame,
was an almost exact replica of the Parthenon. The rulers of
Bavaria lived in the *Residenz*, a beautiful rococo building,
restored by Ludwig in the nineteenth century. The Cuvilliés
Theatre added grace and lustre to the ageing edifice.

Ludwig was enthusiastic, stubborn, intellectual, and
charming. He could be a wild spender on the city he loved,
spending his own money on improving methods of agricul-
ture, but in the Royal Household he was parsimonious to a
fanatical degree, cutting down the kitchen budgets and
refusing to order new textbooks in his University.

The King with the slight impediment in his speech, the
wavy fair hair and the cleft chin had other interests, too; there
were nymphs of delight, very well suited to his Athenian
architecture and for love of one of them he was to lose his
throne.

Lola Montez was born in Limerick in 1818 and baptized as
Maria Dolores Eliza Rosanna Gilbert. She went to England
as a servant girl, married an ensign in the Army, obtained a
divorce, and then toddled off to Spain to become a dancer. As
a 'Spanish' ballerina she popped up again in London and
then went over to the Continent, where, no doubt, exhausted
by flamenco whirls and twirls, she came to rest in the arms of
the old King of Bavaria; the Treasury paid her and the King
made her into a Countess. She was banished from Bavaria in
1848 (The Year of Revolutions) and died in America in 1861.
She had great power over Ludwig, his Cabinet being known
as the *Lolaministerium*, but the proposal to naturalize her
came to nothing. On 20 March 1848 the King abdicated.

In the summer of 1831 Ludwig met Jane. She had decided

upon Munich as the next place of residence; it was as lively as Paris and far, far less inhibited than England, where there was no escape from the results of situations which had caused so much scandal in elevated circles and where her indiscretions were never to be forgiven or forgotten; the family turned her picture to the wall in sorrow and in a growing sensitivity which touched off the encroaching tide of Victorian prudery. Jane was never soured by events, never bitter or cynical or unkind. She toiled through her years and her loves weaving the many passionate threads into a rich canvas of sensual delights and then 'all passion spent' accepted, with almost Eastern submission, the unkind fate that lay in store for her.

Jane had been in Munich only a few days when she met Ludwig. It was probably at one of his 'walk-abouts' in the grounds of the *Residenz*, as he stopped to talk to someone in the curious crowd of people who followed his every movement, or it may have been at Tambosi's, the fashionable coffee-house at the entrance to the *Hofgarten*. Wherever it was, it is certain that the English beauty with the shining hair and unmarked skin attracted his attention and engaged him in conversation, acquainting him of her position with her usual disarming frankness. Ludwig's obsession with beautiful women was no secret; he had thirty-six of them, including Jane and Lola Montez, and their portraits, painted by Stieler, gazed down from the walls of the *Nymphenburg*, the summer palace of the Wittelsbachs, with a haughty acceptance of their order in the Kingly hierarchy. Jane and Ludwig lived an almost idyllic life and met almost every day, exchanging letters and little gifts. Her interest in classical architecture delighted him and soon they were 'Ianthe' (the Greek form of Jane) and 'Basilli' (the Greek version of his name). The Queen, Theresa of Saxe-Hildburghausen had moved to separate quarters in the *Residenz* and preferred to remain aloof from any scandal; in any case, there had been a succession of ladies taking up quarters in the King's suite. This was just the romantic interlude that Jane needed, a meeting with a kindred spirit who was also a friend and an adviser. Although everyone accepted the fact that they were lovers, it may well have been that the friendship was platonic for in many letters she addressed him as 'my best and dearest friend'. She sat for her portrait to Stieler; embroidered Ludwig a cap; and asked him to advise her about her personal affairs.

Advice was badly needed at this juncture for her little stage was fast becoming crowded. Whilst out riding in the *Hofgarten* in September, she had met Karl Venningen and, for him, it was love at first sight. The Baron Karl Theodore von Venningen Üllner was a tall, handsome man from a noble family owning estates in Baden and Upper Austria. He took her to masked balls and to the opera and offered her the most glittering prize of all – marriage. Jane was now in a situation strangely comic and yet desperately tragic and wholly complicated. She was in touch with Ludwig, who had left Munich for Italy in the spring of 1832, writing to him of the opera and the music of Bellini which she described as 'magnificent'. She had expected to meet Felix Schwartzenberg in Italy but the anticipated encounter did not take place for he was pressed for time and Jane had to make do with his sister, the Princess Schwarzenberg, who suggested that the Schwartzenbergs keep Didi with them for all time. On 27 January, 1833 Filippo Antonio Herberro (Heribert in German) was born; Jane did not tell Ludwig about the child until three years later and, in fact, he spent his infancy in Marseilles. So now here she was, enmeshed in the old, familiar *scena* – Karl Venningen returning to his duties; little Heribert in Palermo; Didi with the Princess Schwarzenberg and Jane herself in Paris for a short meeting with her mother, which proved abortive.

The Digby family was only too anxious that Jane should be married and that she should finally break with Schwartzenberg as it was evident to all concerned that her passion for him was not returned. 'May Heaven efface his image from my remembrance and help me to keep my resolution of making Karl a good and faithful wife and showing my gratitude at last for all he has done', she wrote to Ludwig. On 16 November, 1833 Jane became the wife of Karl Ven-

ningen and, with a civil ceremony in Darmstadt and the title
of Baroness Venningen, she was accepted by society at the
Munich Court.

Jane, now Baroness Venningen, was anxious that Ludwig
should act as godfather to Berthe, the little girl born after the
Venningens' return from their two years in Palermo. But the
child was not mentally whole and had to be confined in a
mental home before she attained the age of twenty years.
(Unkind persons said that it was the Wittelsbach strain of
insanity, but there was no proof that Ludwig was the father.)
In 1834, the Baron and his wife came to Weinheim, a pretty
little town, but very unlike Munich; the new Baroness,
recently elevated to Court life and royal functions by a
marriage which made her 'respectable', grew bored and
was ready for any small excitement which might come her
way. It came in the spring of 1835 in the shape of Honoré de
Balzac, 'a very ugly young man', with decaying teeth, greased
hair, untied shoelaces, short legs, and subject to awkward-
ness. His father had intended him for the law and he duly
served his apprenticeship in the offices of a notary, but later
he revolted and the 'starving garret' period lasted from 1820
to 1822. Later, he set up as a printer and publisher at No. 17,
Rue Visconti in Paris. He was flamboyant, untidy, and
sensual, with a rich imagination. His mistresses were many;
there was the Marquise de Berny (forty-five years of age and
the mother of nine children); La Duchesse d'Abrantés;
Madame Garraud; Madame de Castries, and Madame de
Hanska, whom he married in 1850. At one time, there were
two mistresses, one in Paris and one in the Ukraine. It was
probably Laure de Berny who determined the type of woman
with whom he was to fall in love; she was wise enough to
realize that he needed women who made no claims upon his
time and that he would be happiest with 'mature women
disappointed in life and love'. With perception, he wrote;
'the woman of forty will do anything for you – the woman of
twenty nothing'. To Zulma Carraud he requested that 'if she
should happen to come across a woman with a couple of
hundred thousand francs, or even a mere hundred thousand'

to let him know. His manners were atrocious and his 'tempestuous deluge of eloquence' at the dinner table of his friends infuriated Madame de Hanska.

Honoré, impecunious as usual, was on his way to Vienna to meet Eve Hanska. In a hired carriage, with a manservant, Auguste, he called at Schloss Weinheim, near Heidelberg, where his travelling companion, Prince Alfred von Schönburg, introduced him to Lady Ellenborough. There were no doubt many anecdotes to relate about the famous and the infamous Lady Ellenborough and Balzac, busy with his novel *Le Lys dans la vallée* was intrigued and fascinated. This beautiful Englishwoman (whom he was later to call his 'desert swallow') with a quiver-full of discarded lovers and an enormous capacity for loving, probably gave him the inspiration for the character of Lady Arabella Dudley whom he believed was a faithful picture of an Englishwoman in love: 'I have described the woman of that country admirably in very few words.'

This beautiful English lady, so slender, so fragile, this peaches and cream woman, so soft, so mild-mannered, with her refined brow crowned by shining chestnut hair; this creature who glows with a strange phosphorescence, has a constitution of iron.

Whether the 'peaches and cream woman' was modelled on Jane, Lady Ellenborough, Baroness von Venningen, we have no exact means of knowing. Balzac was impecunious and in debt to Baron James de Rothschild who had lent him money to visit Vienna and meet Madame Hanska; in his frantic effort to finish *Le Lys dans la vallée* he avidly tapped the 'inexhaustible mine of reality' and was undoubtedly relieved to find that the character of Lady Arabella Dudley had come alive for him at Weinheim, although another Englishwoman, the Contessa Guidoboni Visconti, may have contributed to the composite picture. Jane's scandalous behaviour in Paris, where she lived with Prince Schwarzenberg from 1829 to 1831 must have been known to Balzac at the time and his wait of two hours in the park while Prince Alfred von Schönburg visited Jane ('But this miserable prince, as genuine as a counterfeit coin, invited me to go to Weinheim and left me in the garden for five hours, which he spent with his mistress', he wrote to Eve Hanska) afforded him time to mull over his fictional character of Lady Arabella and placate Eve who was always suspicious of his out-of-town activities. There is no evidence that either Balzac or von Schönberg were Jane's lovers. Balzac, however, with his deep and almost psychic insight, clearly grasped her fundamental qualities and it is intriguing to note that he described her passions as 'African' and her desires as 'tornadoes' in a burning desert. With what peculiar extrasensory perception did he assess her future life with a Bedouin Sheik – a life yet to come at the end of a span of thirty years? If Jane felt any chagrin at all over her imagined portrait in *Le Lys dans la vallée*, she easily recovered. After all, Lady Blessington had pushed her igno-miniously into the pages of her book *The Two Friends* as Lady Walmer, much to the delight of the sisterhood at Almack's; late joys, like late scandals, could give untold pleasure long after the sun had set.

In the summer of 1835, the Venningens returned to Munich; Karl's brother was ill. A coolness had developed between Jane and Ludwig, although he still wrote to her in affectionate terms. 'Munich is the place of all others I love best', she wrote to him and, considering that this was the time of the *Oktoberfest*, with all its attendant gaiety, it was not surprising. She was not, however, to lose her identity as a German *Hausfrau* in any easy manner, for Karl whisked her away from Munich, no doubt apprehensive that a new affair might develop with the appearance on the scene of a Greek Count Spiridion Theotoky. For centuries Greece had been under the Ottoman yoke and it was not until 1829, when Russia gained a victory over the Turks at Adrianople, that the independence of Greece was guaranteed. Grudgingly, Greece was granted a 'place in the sun' but much was left out of the brave new world of the Hellenes. The Cyclades were received into the new Greece but the Ionian Islands were not and Crete, 'the worse governed province' of the Turkish Empire, was refused autonomy. Greece sought a ruler who would bring stability and order to the country; they found him in Otto, a son of Ludwig I of Bavaria, and enthroned him in 1832 as 'The King of Greece'. He landed at Nauplia on a bleak February day to claim his kingdom, delighting Ludwig who was anxious to revive the lost glories of ancient classical Greece. The new monarchy, however, was a tender blossom, for there was, according to an observer who visited Greece in 1835, 'a want of understanding between the Bavarians and the Greeks'. Many of the Greek youth, reared in the revolutionary tradition, felt that they had exchanged the yoke of Turkey for that of another foreign power. Ludwig poured money into Greece, introducing artists and sculptors and architects, laying the foundations of a new capital and welcoming Greeks to Bavaria, dashing, dark-eyed, handsome young men afire for romance with the Bavarian maidens; he was delighted with the idea of resuscitating the classical tradition.

Spiridion Theotoky, descendant of one of the most noble families in Corfu, was young, dashing, poor, and romantic. He probably met Jane at one of the Carnival Balls in Munich, impressing her with his Byronic charm which embodied the very essence of Greek romanticism. Whatever reason Karl Venningen gave his young wife, he whisked her away to Weinheim in November; Theotoky followed, visiting Heidelberg eleven miles away. It was a wonderful place for lovers, full of classical temples and alcoves just made for discreet meetings, and in the Palace of Schwetzingen the velvet darkness of night covered them with a protective mantle. It was not long before rumours of his wife's indiscretion reached Venningen; Weinheim was a small place, its citizens fully alive to the scandalous past of the Baroness and quite prepared to sympathize with the Baron, a pillar of solid Bavarian society. It is not known what happened at this juncture; there was a ball at the Schwetzingen Palace where Karl may have confronted Jane with the gossip of her love affair with Theotoky (servants at the Palace must have been

aware of the goings-on; the late autumn rides in the forest,
the not-so-discreet lovers' caresses in the chilly corridors).
Whatever ensued, Theotoky importuned Jane to flee with
him and the thought of Greek sunshine and golden isles
'where burning Sappho loved and sung' must have appealed
to her strongly in the circumstances. A post-chaise was
ordered and they fled, Karl in hot pursuit as they galloped
madly on the road out of Weinheim. The scene which
followed, though harrowing in the extreme, was reminiscent
of a third-rate romantic novelette; there was a duel with
pistols, the postilions acting as seconds and Jane in anguish as
she bent over the wounded Theotoky, evidently breathing
his last to the consternation of poor Karl Venningen.

Spiridion survived, however, and with care at Schloss
Venningen he recovered his health. Jane took up the threads
of her life with a forgiving Karl, no doubt seeking to entice
her back into the folds of respectability by visits to Paris and
Marseilles, 'to fetch Heribert', the son who would inherit
Karl's estates and titles. There were letters to Ludwig at this
period and a visit to England in 1837 with Karl and her two
children – all quite 'Bavarian' and respectable. Her grandfather, Tom Coke, had been given the title of Earl of
Leicester and her two brothers were happily married, giving
sixteen children to the nation between them. Nevertheless,
Jane's visit to her family must have awakened memories,
'England has too many painful associations for me to be sorry
to quit it', and she returned to the 'horrid, little town' of
Weinheim, correspondence between her and Ludwig evidently ceasing after 1838. In the spring of 1839 she left for
Paris to live with Theotoky – her husband, friends, and
children abandoned; the cloak of Bavarian respectability
falling lightly from her young shoulders; the road to Elysium
open. She was now 'Ianthe' in mind and spirit. Karl Venningen never once uttered a rebuke to the butterfly who loved to
alight on whichever flower that took her fancy; he never
censured or blamed her.

There were carefree years in Paris before Theotoky took
her to the ancestral home on Corfu. In Paris they had lived as

man and wife, taking up residence at 83, Place Bourbon and on 21 March 1840 Jane was delivered of a child, Jean Henry, Comte Theotoky – Leonidas to his parents. Karl Venningen had written Jane a heart-rending letter, apparently not knowing that she had borne a child in Paris: 'in cold and sad Germany a warm and faithful heart is beating for you, a heart which will *never* forget the happiness and the heavenly bliss you gave him during several years' – the 'heavenly bliss' was now given to another. Jane asked for a divorce, which was granted, with the whole question of the legitimacy of the young Jean Henry being dragged through the Courts in a legal tangle which established the paternity of the child Jane loved above all her children: Count Theotoky was the father.

Karl Venningen never remarried and remained Jane's sincere friend, anxious as to her welfare, and informing her of the progress of their children. In July 1874, humiliated, disappointed, and ever faithful to Jane, he was killed in a riding accident in Munich.

Of Jane's children, Arthur Dudley Law died at the age of two; Didi Schwartzenberg was brought up by the Schwartzenberg family and remained loyal to them for the rest of her life; Heribert, the son of Karl Venningen, born before they married, was brought up elsewhere than the family home as a young child; Berthe, his sister, was placed in an institution before the age of twenty, not mentally capable of dealing with life. Children came and went in those days with surprising rapidity, for infant mortality was high; if a child survived its first year it often died in early infancy and strange and fearsome instruments were used to facilitate a difficult birth. Children of the upper classes were looked after by nurses and governesses, seldom seeing their parents except for presentation before guests, where they bobbed and curtseyed prettily before being whisked off back to the nursery hinterlands. The children of the working-classes were world's apart; they were fodder for the fields and the machines, working up to fifteen hours a day and often dying by their looms.

Jane enjoyed her residence in Corfu, settling down to domestic bliss after her conversion to the Greek Orthodox

faith and spending a great deal of time laying out gardens and
planting trees. She imported treasures to furnish the Corfu
home at Dukades and gathered books to form an English
library. She learnt Greek and entertained in the grand
manner with balls and levées which astounded the local
upper-crust, while the long hot summers were passed on
horseback exploring the sun-warmed countryside. It all
ended in the summer of 1844, for Spiridion Theotoky was
called to serve in Athens as aide-de-camp to Otto, the
Bavarian 'King of Greece', Ludwig's son.

There were many male children with the name of Spiridion in Corcyra (Corfu). They were named after St Spiridion, who lies in a richly carved sarcophagus in the Church
of St Spiridion, his little mummified body looking quite at
ease and his little feet, encased in embroidered slippers,
peeping out of an aperture at the bottom. He did good works
and performed miracles and when he died, some years over
ninety, his relics were removed to Constantinople, and
brought back to Greece with those of another saint, Theo-
dora Augusta; the two of them were tucked cosily away in
two sacks strapped to an unsuspecting mule as it ambled into
Greece. In 1456 they were brought to Corcyra and finally
laid to rest in the chapel of Michael the Archangel. St
Spiridion is brought flowers and candles and four times a
year he sees something of the town as his casket is borne in
procession.

Since independence had been granted to Greece, there had
been much discontent, fostered by many reasons, chief of
which was the granting of positions to Bavarians, instead of
to Greeks who had fought to oust the hated Turks. Otto's
Bavarian autocracy had not been entirely a wise one for he
had immersed himself in petty details instead of applying
himself to the major issues of policy and, as his own Prime
Minister, he learnt and digested every decree submitted to
him and 'took ten days to decide who was to be a school-
master in Syra'. The bloodless coup of 15 September 1843
brought about the replacement of Bavarians by Greeks and
the king was forced to grant a constitution. The result for the

Theotokys was a call to Athens and the end of the pastoral interlude for Jane. It was also the beginning of a new love, more romantic and more passionate than she had ever known before, a love almost savage in its intensity.

Athens was at that date little more than a collection of fishermen's quarters down by the Piraeus; there was a Turkish quarter, with ramshackle 'shanty town' huts full to overflowing with children and chickens and a new *Neopolis* with residential houses built of marble plastered over, whose inhabitants considered themselves the cream of Athenian society, affecting a mode of dress they considered fashionable and speaking the French language. Lord Byron remarked of Greece at that time: ' 'Tis Greece, but *living* Greece no more.' Ruined by Turkish oppression and misrule, the cultivation of the soil and the spirit of industry was stifled by successive rulers and the Greeks, who had regarded Otto as the saviour of their country, tore their country apart by rival political intrigues, at variance in a ruined and devastated land. There were 6,000 to 8,000 troops in Greece, paid for by Greek money 'marching in hot dusty weather in the neighbourhood of Athens to the sound of fife and drum, elevating their arms and legs in the air at the word of command, and moving with conceited strut in long files'. A traveller of the time, Charles G. Addison, thought that the labour and exertions of troops marching and countermarching across the Greek plains resulted in nothing and that the money for their keep would have been better spent in fostering Greek industry and constructing canals and plantations. The countryside died and the forests shrank as the trees were felled and not replaced and goats ate up the young seedlings intended for the fields. Ludwig found Otto a bride in the young Princess Maria Frederica Amalia but the marriage was not a success and the pretty young German lady had little inclination towards responsibility. She proved to be domineering, jealous, and extravagant and, in the absence of Otto, who was painstaking to a degree, scampered through the paperwork as though she were playing at royalty.

Lavenders Blue, Diddle diddle,
Lavenders Green,
When I am King Diddle-Diddle,
You shall be Queen.

Edmond About paints us a picture of the royal pair:

The King appears older than he is. He is tall, thin, feeble and worn out with fever; his face is pale and worn, his eyes dim: his appearance is sad and suffering, and his look anxious. The use of sulphate quinine has made him deaf . . . His mind, according to all those who have worked with him, is timid, hesitating and minute. His last word in every business is always 'We will see'.

Amalia seems to have been a veritable amazon, full of a restless energy which one suspects must have contributed in no small measure to Otto's decline. Edmond About wrote:

The Queen is a woman who will not grow for a long time; her *embonpoint* will preserve her . . . In the summer she gets up at three in the morning to bathe in the sea at Faliron, where she swims for an hour without rest.

About also noticed Ianthe:

I have often met Ianthe, who used to leap the ditches on a splendid white horse. She was the best rider in town; when she went out, followed by a large company of friends, she made such a grand appearance that the little boys always ran to salute her as she passed; they thought she must be the Queen. The Queen will never forget those mistakes.

The Queen did not forget or forgive 'those mistakes'. Jane had met Otto and had evidently captivated him, although his morals were of the strictest and he was a perfect husband, Amalia was jealous of Ianthe's popularity. She herself was spoken of as 'one of the most beautiful princesses in Europe', wearing the National (Albanian) costume with grace and galloping and riding about the kingdom oblivious of the countryside through which she passed, treeless and poor. The great grievance to her was that she was childless and no amount of sliding down the Hill of the Nymphs or drinking the orange-flower water would result in a birth.

Jane and the dashing Count were now drifting apart; according to Eugènie (Jane's maid), Spiridion had indulged in several extramarital activities and only their mutual love for their little son, Leonidas, held them together. In the heat of the summer, Athenian 'society' left Greece for spas and bathing resorts in slightly cooler climes and the Theotokys also left the blistering, dusty heat of Athens to spend the summer at Bagna di Lucca, a Tuscan village at the base of the Appenines, a beautiful place of trees and cool courtyards and a flourishing colony of English writers and ex-patriots who rented luxurious villas such as that of Mrs Stisted, 'the Queen of the Baths'. The house which they rented was tall, with balconies running round three sides and shutters of dark green. It proved to be a tragic house for Jane, for little Leonidas, anxious to see the guests at one of his mother's receptions, peered over a top balcony, lost his balance and fell on to the cold marble floor far below. It was a shattering blow for Jane for she had now lost the one child she really loved and had cut herself off by her misdeeds from her family in England (only one of her brothers, who had taken Holy Orders, ever wrote to her) although she did see Lady Andover from time to time.

In 1849 Jane was once again in Athens, striking up a friendship with Sophie, the Duchess of Plaisance, whose husband had been one of Napoleon's generals and whose daughter Louise had died whilst Sophie was travelling around Europe, endeavouring to find her a suitable husband. Jane and Sophie were of similar disposition; the duchess was witty and intelligent, though slightly eccentric, and the fact that they had each lost children must have drawn them together. Jane, separated from Spiridion Theotoky, found Sophie good company and her peculiar views on religion (she thought that God was personally interested in her) were, no doubt, amusing enough, but the life at the villa in Athens was no substitute for the love that loved 'too well'. Long ago, whilst in Paris with Felix Schwartzenberg, a fortune-teller had predicted that Jane would know many lovers. Edmond About recalls the incident where Jane told him about the prophecy:

IANTHE: 'A long time ago I consulted Mlle. LeNormand; she predicted that I would turn many heads . . .'
ABOUT: 'One would not have to be a fortune teller to know that.'
IANTHE: '– and amongst others, three crowned heads. Although I've been searching, I can find only two.'
ABOUT: 'That's because the third one is in the future.'

The 'Third One' may have been a certain Cristos Hadji-Petros, wearing the red cap of the Greeks, or it may have been Otto, King of Greece.

Cristos Hadji-Petros had risen from a brigand-in-chief in the mountains of Albania to the position of aide-de-camp to King Otto of Greece. Literature had romanticized the brigands and public opinion had been inclined to look upon them as charming rascals and rollicking ruffians, using their lawlessness to protect the down-trodden peasantry and extort what ransom money and bribes they could from the wealthy and the powerful in the comic-opera age of Greek royalty and Greek politics. There was a darker side of the picture; well-authenticated stories, submitted to the government, told of torture and the use of boiling oil and thumb screws and no traveller cared to plan an expedition without first ascertaining which parts were free from brigands. After 1870, all this changed; the government troops came to grips with them and the last of the brigands was caught and hanged.

There remained the Palikars, the chieftains who had fought for Greek independence from Turkish rule and who now regarded themselves as conquerors and saviours of Greece; those who had harried the Turks for years left their mountain fastnesses and entered into a more enlightened age, striding about in their short gold-embroidered jackets and white kilts, with their hair swinging about their shoulders in long ringlets. They were foot-loose and without employment; for the most part petted by the aristocracy who were only too anxious to keep in well with these wild men of the mountains – the Palikars, whose portraits hang in the Museum of the Historical and Ethnological Society and whose name is a Greek corruption of 'Chevalier', from the days of the Frankish Dukes of Athens. They were not admitted to Athenian society but once a year they graced the Court Ball on New Year's Eve, living it up in style on money from blackmail and extortion and from sources which it was wiser not to question. The Minister for Foreign Affairs found it advisable to placate his unruly neighbours, for his beautiful house at Tatoi was vulnerable.

Cristos Hadji-Petros was a Palikar who came to Athens at sixty years of age; with his moustache and white hair and all the fire of the craggy mountains in his ageing blood, he was truly Edmond About's 'King of the Mountains', fascinating the English rose as he took his ease, surrounded by his loyal group of Palikars, in the house opposite Jane's in Athens. The pattern emerged once more as Jane's kindness to his small son, Eirini, brought them into contact and soon it was the familiar story of kindling passion and self-abnegation to a powerful lover who could still gallop with her over the wildest country and live with her the free life she desired. There were no rivals for Jane; for the most part the Palikar women were stodgy and uncomplaining, living their uneventful lives in bleak mountain retreats, servants and footstools for their lords and masters.

Her life with Cristos (he had tacked on the 'Hadji' as he had been on a pilgrimage to Mecca) began in 1852 in Athens, but before long he was assigned to the garrison at Lamia – it was a change of which Jane thoroughly approved. Now there was excitement of Homeric proportions, with Jane throwing caution to the winds, dressing as a Palikar woman, eating the

Palikar food, and sleeping rough in the pure air of the hills, giving no thought to the morrow or the loves of yesteryear. There was only Cristos.

But it was not to last – nothing lasted with Jane. Amalia had her ear to the ground and all that she missed the society gossips supplied in full measure, providing a grand opportunity for vengeance upon the English beauty who had invaded Athens and about whom Edmond About had written:

> She has great blue eyes, as deep as the sea; beautiful chestnut hair, highlighted here and there by golden tones; as for her teeth, she belongs to that elite of the English nation who have pearls in their mouths instead of piano keys.

Cristos Hadji-Petros was abruptly dismissed from his post at the Lamia garrison and the two lovers returned from the mountains to Athens to face a situation which, to Jane at least, must have seemed very familiar. Cristos petitioned the Queen in writing, explaining, with cap in hand, his motives for the liaison: 'if I am the lover of this woman, it is not for love but for profit', and explained in humble terms that he had children to bring up and that Jane's money would come in useful. The letter was published and soon all Athens knew of the affair but Jane continued loving her brigand who had such sycophantic tendencies; time passed and the situations which remained unresolved added one more year to the constant cycle of disenchantment.

Money was never any problem; her £3,000 a year was more than enough to pay her way in Greece and jewels could always fetch more. It was just as well that money was in plentiful supply, for life with Cristos had been one long outpouring of hospitality; Turks and brigands from the wild mountains, cut-throats, pillagers, and dastardly murderers who killed for ransom money – all enjoyed Cristos' lavish welcome in the mansion Jane had provided. Jane intended to marry Cristos and sought freedom from her marriage to

Theotoky who was still living on his wife's income, happily going his own way and not in the least concerned about brigands and Palikars.

The marriage was duly annulled and all Athens waited for the grand finale which would unite in holy Greek matrimony the two reckless lovers, of whom one was well over sixty and the other now forty-six. The marriage did not take place, although Jane had already put in hand the building of a mansion which would be magnificent, but there were obstacles. Eugènie, the French maid who had served her well, was now growing older and had become very tired with all the hours of devoted work she had so willingly contributed to Madame's well-being and comfort and the excitement of life with Jane, settling in to fresh homes, whirling about in coaches from one residence to another as the seasons passed, grappling with Jane's moods as each new affair loomed on the horizon and spending hours in tears and sympathy as sorrow struck, was taking its toll. Now there was another small problem to be settled. Cristos Hadji-Petros was making advances to her and, loyally, she told Jane. It may have been a lie for her own self-preservation in order that she could remain with Jane on the same footing without the benefit of rubbing shoulders with the Palikars, in what could only be described as a brigands' nest. The bodyguard of Palikars were everywhere about the house, lounging and smoking in the doorways and on the stairs, thrusting their great bodies into rooms of elegance and refinement and extending the Palikars welcome to visiting friends with little observance of decorum and behaviour except that of the mountains and the wild, uncluttered hills.

Whatever the reason, Jane believed her and the result was a total cleavage with Cristos. She had been interested for some time in the purchase of Arab bloodstock from Syria and with this as an excuse she and Eugènie slipped away from Athens with Cristos unaware of the decampment. The humiliation must have cut deeply; the fact that her wild, independent Palikar lover had turned out to be a fawning sycophant, writing an abject letter of apology to the Queen, was bad enough, but to have enjoyed her money and the prestige which association with a lady of nobility brought to him and his friends and then make covert amorous advances to a *femme de chambre* was beyond belief!

The excuse of the purchase of Arab horses presented Jane with a valid excuse for departure and gave her a much-needed breathing space; she now had an escape route, not back to Western Europe, but to unknown territory further East. In the burning vastness of the deserts she could find peace and mend a broken heart; time, no longer on her side, could be halted a little and the tempestuous past placed on one side, hostage to the 'unforgiving minute'.

Little did she know that the last adventure of her life was just beginning and that the love she had searched for in ducal mansions and on goat-skin rugs in the sunless bosom of inhospitable mountains was to be found in the black tents of the Bedouin. When she sailed from Piraeus she was forty-six years of age.

She landed in Syria, planning to visit Jerusalem, Baalbeck and Palmyra. It was the age of expansion and travel; the European 'Grand Tour' was becoming routine and the Near East beckoned to those with time and money and a strong stomach who were fascinated by songs of Araby and love under desert stars. The romantic side, spawned by writers and poets, had its enthusiastic adherents but serious exploration was also taking place. Carsten Niebuhr's expedition in 1761–4 to the Yemen fostered interest in the whole of Arabia. Joseph Halévy travelled widely in south-west Arabia, making important discoveries of Sabaean inscriptions a few years after Jane landed at Beirut. J. L. Burckhardt had already won a reputation as the discoverer of Petra and Richard Burton travelled in the Hejaz as an Afghan pilgrim and reached Medina and Mecca in disguise. There were many others who travelled in the Middle East, often in great danger and discomfort. Palgrave had an intimate knowledge of Syria and the Arabic language, though his descriptions were later challenged as being geographically incorrect. Charles Doughty described desert life in great detail, discovering the famous inscribed stone at Taima which found its way to the Louvre and Wilfrid and Lady Anne Blunt travelled on a Persian pilgrim caravan in 1878, taking with them horses which were to form the Crabbet Park stud. There were many Jane did not know, but Richard and Isabel Burton she was to know intimately in a future as yet unborn.

Burckhardt's Petra, the old capital of the Nabateans, was known to Jane for she must have been conversant with the works of Strabo and Pliny from the well-stocked library at Holkham and it is almost certain that her interest in Palmyra was aroused when she first saw the architectural sketches in *The Ruins of Palmyra*, published in 1751. Jane was a woman of culture, with a lively imagination and a thorough grasp of whatever subject she happened to be studying; in spite of all her tempestuous love-affairs she had found time to read the books which came regularly in boxes from Paris and London.

Beirut was a good setting-off place, a spring board for the whole of Syria, and Jane lost no time in visiting a bank and arranging for horses.

The horses were ready and no doubt Eugènie viewed the future with rather less apprehension now that the Palikars episode appeared to be over and done with. The identification of Jane with the Arab world and the Arab mind was about to begin; the wild life of the desert was to take the place of the unfettered life with Cristos and his brigands; Oriental splendour was to supplant Albanian crudity – and the ways of the Koran were to graft themselves on to the Christian ethic.

Once again, a new passion arose in the shape of Saleh, a young Bedouin whom she met whilst bargaining for a horse. In his book *Le Grèce Contemporaine* Edmond About wrote: 'Ianthe found in an Arab tribe the thoroughbred horse she was looking for. The animal belonged to a sheik, who was young and strikingly handsome.' The sheik had three wives but About wrote: 'The sheik found her more exciting than his three wives put together.'

The sheik appears to have been lusty and impetuous; he swept Jane off her feet and into the black tents of his tribe. Gone were the days of the 'horrid little town' of Weinheim and fast fading the colourful dream of a sedate old age with a Palikar man of over sixty in an Athenian mansion full of brigands. Jane desired marriage and forgot the difference in their ages, and the parting came, as it inevitably did, with Saleh remaining with his tribe and Jane pushing on to Damascus to start the great journey to Palmyra, fast becoming a place of great historical interest to western travellers.

Jane loved Damascus. It was cool, green, and fertile, watered by the Barada river and sheltered from the fierce winds from the Syrian desert. She was magnetized by the historical associations of which she had read and fascinated by the ancient walls, the city gates, the bazaars, and the Great Mosque. There were private houses, too, away from the inner city, with great contrasts between the outside and the inside; the entrances were by means of doors leading into narrow, winding passages while mud walls and rickety, projecting chambers hid the Outer Courts with their marble pavements. Inside there were halls and chambers, with inner courts leading to the *harim*, the doors of which were guarded by eunuchs.

Jane's attempts to get to Palmyra met with opposition and she soon found that an escort for the ten days' journey on horseback was not possible. The British Consul, Richard Wood, thought it a most foolhardy idea and disclaimed all responsibility. With voluminous luggage and a reputation for dangerous, and often bizarre modes of travel, Jane's hopes of an exciting and safe trek were doomed to disappointment. She was advised to contact the Mesrab Arabs who controlled the desert in the Palmyra area. There was brigandage amongst the various tribes as there was amongst the Greek mountain-men and wealthy travellers were fair game for ultimate ransom, their release being a pre-arranged affair, one band of Arabs scaring the life out of the weary travellers with their shouts and wild cries, the other most solemnly effecting their release.

It was all, of course, a put-up job; thanks to Allah, money and valuables could be shared. Thus a journey across the desert could be very hazardous indeed, with marauding

Arabs and internecine warfare between the tribes, especially if the wells along the route were not known in advance.

The Mesrabs were a desert tribe of the Anazeh Bedouins and their Sheik, Mohammed was a descendant of one of the noblest of the tribe of Saba. His younger brother, Medjuel, was educated; he could read and write and spoke several languages. He was no longer young, for he had sons and so was hardly the man to supplant the lusty Saleh. Lady Anne Blunt met Medjuel some years later and described him:

> A very well bred and agreeable man . . . In appearance he shews all the characteristics of good Bedouin blood. He is short and slight in stature, with exceedingly small hands and feet, a dark olive complexion, beard originally black, but now turning grey, and dark eyes and eyebrows.

Isabel Burton, whom Jane was to meet later in Damascus and with whom she was to become friendly, had her own interpretation of Medjuel whom she also knew: 'the contact with that black skin I could *not* understand. His skin is dark – darker than a Persian – much darker than an Arab generally is. All the same, he was a very intelligent charming man in any light but that of a husband. That made me shudder.'

It evidently did not make Jane shudder, for she married him and he became her fourth husband.

But that the future held; the present was enough for Jane. The two met to discuss terms for the journey; the well-bred, intellectual Arab and the much-travelled, much-loved English lady who had trailed her affairs and her enormous amount of luggage across Europe and into Syria. The fine linen and the exquisite silver were loaded and Jane, admired by the Arabs for her steady mounting of the camel, set out with a delighted heart across the desert, under the protection of the great Saba tribe and with the mental picture of the passionate Saleh ever before her eyes. It was a delightful escapade for Jane, her past frustrations and embarrassments shut away in a time-lock for which she had no key. The mornings began with a sparse breakfast and hot tea, with

Jane taking the creases from her riding dress, and in the evenings the black goat-hair tents were erected and the insides spread with oriental rugs. During the day there was hunting, and, for Jane, sketching in the desert. The evenings were the best of all, with Medjuel explaining to Jane the life and legends of his people.

The caravan pressed on to Palmyra, Jane filled with thoughts of Saleh and Medjuel teetering on the brink of declaring his love. The name Palmyra is supposed to have been given by the Greeks, but the Arabs called it Tadmor and Josephus Thadamoura. Palmyra had arisen to meet the desert-borne trade, like Jerash and Petra, and the cultures of Babylonia, Assyria, and Syria were blended in her. With prosperity came the development of the trans-desert routes; patrolled at first by Palmyrene forces and later by Roman soldiers. Wells and fortified posts were thirty miles apart and the principal road under the Roman occupation connected Palmyra with Hit, with a branch to the Euphrates. After the capture of Zenobia and the sack of the town, it was restored by the Byzantine Emperors and under the Saracens from the seventh to the fifteenth century it once again became commercially important. First visited by an Englishman in the late seventeenth century, archaeologists discovered its historical importance in 1918.

When Lady Hester Stanhope visited the antique city she claimed that the Bedouins had crowned her queen – just like another Zenobia! Monsieur de Lamartine, on his travels in Syria, interviewed this extraordinary lady and gave his personal interpretation and the *Quarterly Review* of 1835 presented its own view:

We are rather inclined to M. de Lamartine's view of the character of this singular woman. She has so long been acting a part, at first probably assumed for the purpose of obtaining interest over wild and superstitious clans among whom she has settled in her mountain palace-citadel of Lebanon, that she has begun to act it in earnest.

Jane never acted a part; she was intensely interested in all she saw and recorded meticulously every detail of the desert scenes she loved to observe and to paint.

For Jane, Palmyra was the jewel in the lotus. She had long been conversant with the story of Zenobia, the tragic queen who monopolized all the caravan trade of the Syrian desert until she attempted to establish her autonomy and flaunted her independence from the Roman Emperor, Aurelian. It was a mistake, and Zenobia threw away her kingdom for the sake of ambition and lived to see the walls and aqueducts of her city dismembered by the Roman legions. To Jane, accustomed to German forests and Greek mountains, the sight of the ruined city must have been wonderful indeed. The great caravan road which crossed the city could be conjectured and of the original 375 fluted columns of rose-red limestone 150 still stood with their bases in the wind-blown sand. There were tombs and inscriptions and votive altars and statues erected to the honour of the *synodiarchs*, or caravan leaders, who were responsible for the trade of the city in far-away ports. Gods were honoured by altars erected to Arsu and Azizu, the patron gods of caravaners and the fiscal laws of the city were made known to the inhabitants by inscriptions upon a tablet bearing the date AD 137. The great avenue led to a triumphal arch flanked by two smaller ones, leading to the Temple of the Sun. Many travellers had seen these wonders through the ages, Saracens and Seljuk Turks and Ottoman Turks, and some had written of the great city they had seen.

Some years after Jane's death, Dr William Wright gave an account of Palmyra in his book *An Account of Palmyra and Zenobia* and described the ruins in great detail. He was not impressed by the Temple 'in its present state' and the broken walls with columns standing like a 'huge lumber-yard of columns'.

Within we find the whole area of the temple filled with clay-daubed huts, so that we can only get an idea of the place by climbing over them. We pass on straight to the

Holy of Holies, which we explore with our handkerchiefs
held to our noses, for the inmost shrine is the cesspool of
the community. We hurry out to the fresh air; but it is not
fresh, for all the offal and filth of the houses are flung out
into the narrow lanes, and lie rotting in the sun. Wherever
we go among these human dens there reek filth and
squalor, and the hot pestiferous atmosphere of an ill-kept
stye. Such is now the state of that gorgeous temple which
the proud Tadmorenes raised to their gods, which were no
gods, and where they glorified one another in monuments
of perishable stone.

The tombs were the most interesting part of Palmyra. Sir
Richard Burton, when Consul in Damascus, had visited the
ruins and advised Dr Wright to take ladders and ropes and
grappling irons for the ascent of the towers 'which he had
been unable to examine for lack of such appliances'. The
tomb-towers were more than a hundred feet high, housing
grim relics of bones and skulls.

To Jane at that time it was all harmonious, different – but
harmonious; the all-embracing desert by day and the soft
sounds of the Bedouin camp by night. Jane was now more
determined than ever to marry Saleh and settle down in Syria
to a life of domestic bliss, a dutiful wife carrying out her
humble duties to her Arab overlord in compliance with
Koranic law. The status of women in Arabia did not interest
her but she would have been fascinated, no doubt, by
Doughty's account:

The woman's lot is here unequal concubinage, and in this
necessitous life a weary servitude. The possession in her of
parents and tutors has been yielded at some price (in
contempt and constraint of her weaker sex,) to an husband,
by whom she may be dismissed in what day he shall have
no more pleasure in her . . . And his heart is not hers alone;
but, if not divided already, she must look to divide her
marriage in a time to come with others. And certainly as
she withers, which is not long to come, or having no

adventure to bear male children, she will as thing unprofitable be cast off; meanwhile all the house-labour is hers,
and with his love will be lost. Love is a dovelike confidence, and thereto consents not the woman's heart that is
wronged.

The 'dove-like confidence' was already beginning to blossom between Jane and Medjuel, and Medjuel was to prove
his strength to protect her. Between Damascus and Palmyra
the caravan fell into the hands of brigands, the Arab raiders
coming at them with pointed lancers, but the story goes that
Medjuel subdued them and the caravan went on its way
without further incident. It was all highly dramatic and
raised Medjuel in Jane's esteem to the stature of a desert
hero. The story also goes that Medjuel asked her to marry
him, offering to give up his wife. In the Palmyrene ruins, lit
by intense moonlight, it was just possible. But there were
matters to see to which needed her attention; there was the
house in Athens to sell and her affairs to wind up. Only then
could she make Syria her home and live forever with Saleh.

The caravan returned to Damascus in great splendour; the
camels raced to their home base, Medjuel changing to a
magnificent Arab horse, and the crowd applauding and
shouting words of welcome. It was a heart-warming scene,
with the green background of the city and the cool courtyards
inviting Jane to stay, but it was imperative that she return to
Greece and settle her affairs. So the house was duly sold and
her jewels put into a safe place. Sophie, the Duchess of
Plaisance, evidently did not approve of the stories Jane told
her; she had been willing to lend an aristocratic ear to her
amusing tales of illicit love, but an Arab was quite another
thing. She probably felt that Jane had, this time, gone a little
too far. The friendship cooled, and Sophie died the following
year.

Cristos Hadji-Petros continued to press his suit (no doubt
thinking of the advantages of a regular income) but Jane had
finished with Greek brigands. She longed for Saleh and
returned to Syria, hot-footing it across the desert to find a

young beauty installed, a dark-eyed girl named Sabla. Jane, hostage to fortune, returned to Damascus to lick her wounds once more. Now there was nothing. Europe was finished and the *salons* closed to her, but she had attained the Eden to which each country had been a stumbling step and the prospect of buying a small house in Damascus and living out her life with the faithful Eugènie was totally inviting.

Jane loved Damascus. George Robinson, an English visitor in 1837, gives us a description of the city which, in the intervening years before Jane was resident, could not have changed much.

The Hebrew name of the city was Damasek or Demesk, by which it is still known and from which is formed the Damascus of the Greeks and Latins. Damascus does not altogether answer the expectations held out by its exterior appearance.

He found the streets narrow and irregular and 'a sort of mysterious silence prevails throughout'. The bazaars redeemed the unfavourable impression for he found the shopkeepers well-dressed 'and extremely civil to strangers'.

The bazaars were closed at night with iron gates and the streets were headed off with wooden barriers; there being no lights it was extremely difficult and dangerous to visit friends. The mosques were numerous and were formerly Christian churches; the principal one was in the centre of the city and it was unwise for a Christian to enter into the courtyard. The coffee houses were 'numerous and elegant', with climbing plants, where the ear could be soothed by running streams. The gardens surrounding the city were a mass of verdure; the damascene plum or damson shed its blossom like a carpet. There were Christian associations, too, in the heaps of gravel and earth about a mile from the city which indicated the tombs of devout Christians and the spot in the wall where Paul is said to have been let down in a basket. A low wall enclosed the town and the citadel in the centre housed the residence of the Governor. Such was the

Damascus into which Jane entered with Medjuel and in which she was to die.

The country of Syria was still to be explored and there was plenty of time to settle down. There were wonderful sights to see and sketch and many ancient ruins to roam over, in spite of an aching heart. Jane was never the one to spend 'many pleasant years unknown to fame' and the prospect of visiting other desert countries was exciting.

There were many hazards along the routes; caravan leaders chose those along which wells were known to exist, but often in the summer months the wadis would be dry and the water below only to be reached by backaching digging; tolls had to be paid and gifts made, not only to cross the Euphrates, but when a stream was forded; each city exacted a transit tax and every caravanserai had a head-tax on both man and beast. The Euphrates in flood was apt to make the lowland parts of the desert slippery with mud and the laden camels could slip and upset their loads, causing a complete breakdown. Last, but not least, there was the bitter cold at night and the scourge of the winds; in September the north-east wind; in April and May the 'glass furnace' and in summer the dreaded Shamel, the 'poison wind'. There could be snow in winter and downpours of rain, when tents became soaked and bedding saturated with water.

It was a challenge Jane loved and only one thing was missing – another Saleh or Medjuel. Fate provided one in the shape of Sheik el Barrak, Jane's escort on the caravan; in the loneliness of the desert and the comfort and warmth of the evening camp-fire the perfect atmosphere for romance was produced. Jane, at forty-six years of age, still felt that passionate and refined love was her due and with Sheik el Barrak it would seem that she had found another soul-mate. Love blossomed on the road to Aleppo but by the time the caravan had crossed the Euphrates Jane had become disillusioned, for el Barrak did not measure up to either Saleh or Medjuel. There were quarrels about his lack of consideration for the camels (Jane was always an animal-lover) and over his denigration of her painting talent. For el Barrak, it was just adventure, something to while away the time. He took his revenge on Jane by assigning some women of the tribe to her tent; this was a shocking invasion of her privacy and would never have been countenanced by Bedouins. It had all been a disaster, another love affair to rend her heart. 'But what folly!' she wrote in her diary.

On the way back to Damascus, Medjuel rode out to meet her, bringing a beautiful Arab mare as a gift. The caravan was now in Mesrab country and el Barrak wisely decided to forgo any further dalliance with Jane. Medjuel was the same, serious man whom Jane had known. True to his word he had divorced his wife by returning to her the dowry which she had brought him and had sent her back to her people. He was now a free man, ready to marry Jane. The only serious obstacle was his family, who were hostile to her and not at all in favour of their son, a member of a proud and noble Arab family of wealth and honour, entering into a marriage with a foreign lady who was not a Muslim. Jane accepted Medjuel's proposal of marriage with all the thrill and passion of a first romance and the 'dear desert that I am so fond of' was to become her last home and her final resting place. It was not, however, all plain sailing. Richard Wood, the British Consul in Damascus, thought it all the height of folly and wondered if she were not losing her mind. Gently he pointed out the position of women in Arab society and the fact that up to four wives were allowed by Islamic law. Instructions were awaited from England which might conceivably alter Jane's mind; in the meantime the marriage took place at Homs in a ceremony according to Islamic law, which must have seemed very different from those she had experienced in the Anglican, Catholic, and Greek Orthodox churches. Medjuel made a pact with Jane; he agreed that he would live in the western fashion, taking only one woman to be his lawful wife but if he so desired in the future, he would be free to take a Bedouin woman and keep the fact of so doing from Jane so that she would have no knowledge of any more youthful rival and so remain happy and content. Isabel Burton met Jane sixteen years later: 'Gossip said that he had other wives, but she assured me that he had not, and that both her brother Lord Digby and the British Consul required a legal and official statement to that effect before they were married.'

At first they set up house in Homs and by degrees Medjuel's family came to like and respect Jane; they called her Jane Digby el Mesrab and, as a token of admiration, Umn-el-Laban, Mother of Milk, as her skin was so fair. She adopted Arab ways, wearing the traditional blue robe and yashmak and her beautiful eyes were accentuated by the use of kohl. The Arabs were greatly impressed by her horsemanship and she obviously enjoyed the hunting days with Medjuel in the desert; the dromedaries were not the easiest of beasts to ride but Jane Digby el Mesrab rode them, quite nonplussed by their erratic pitching and tossing. 'Dear, useful animals', she called them. She began to speak the Arabic she had learnt, but with a guttural accent, unlike the classical Arabic spoken by Medjuel. Her life was now a part of the desert; the vast, silent spaces of heat and cold and thirst held no terrors for her and the struggle against the elements was sufficient to blot out any desire to savour the artificial life of the western city. When Medjuel went off into the desert for weeks at a time, she was heart-broken, fearful that fate would take him from her and thus punish her for her marriage to a non-believer.

Her family were shattered by this final blow of marriage to an Arab and life in a Bedouin tent; Steely, who had become companion to Lady Andover, must have been mortally stricken by Jane's plunge into the world of what she would have considered the 'Victorian novelette' and addressed a letter to her as 'Madame Theotoky', refusing to recognize the black Bedouin and the black Bedouin tents.

In the autumn of 1856 Jane embarked at Beirut for a visit to England. She had received a letter from her sister-in-law with news of the death of Lord Digby; he had died childless and Jane's brother Edward was now heir to the family fortune. There were matters to settle which concerned Jane and so she sailed once more for England. The Greek ship touched at the port of Piraeus, the port of so many memories; Hadje-Petros was there on the dockside, emotionally dis-

turbed and tearfully reproachful, unhappy and distraught as
he told her of the illness of his young son, Eirini, whom Jane
had loved as her own child. Oddie, in her book *The Odyssey
of a Loving Woman*, tells of the reunion:

> Cristodoulos struck a heroic attitude at once. Forget her?
> How could he forget her? Betray her love by making
> overtures to a common graceless creature like Eugènie?
> How could Jane believe such things of him? There was not
> a word of truth in the story. It was an infamous fabrication
> of Eugènie's own. Could any man who had loved Ianthe –
> who had been privileged to enjoy Ianthe's love and ten-
> derness give anyone like Eugènie a thought? He went on
> weeping as he assured her that she had broken his heart,
> ruined his life, at seventy, wrecked his career.

Jane was unmoved. Greece no longer appealed to her; after
the Crimean War Piraeus had been occupied by England and
France and the Palikars had begun to lose the romantic image
of brigands wild and free in the mountains. Besides, it all
seemed a long time ago.

On 19 December she stepped ashore at Folkestone and
journeyed to Tunbridge Wells in company with Jane
Steele, sister of Steely, to meet Lady Andover. Lady
Andover and Steely had both grown older – perhaps the
wrinkles on Steely's face were due to prolonged worry over
Jane's *amours*. As the days went by, there was much family
talk and a thaw in the atmosphere, but Medjuel and Syria
were never mentioned in kindness or affection; Regency
latitude had given way to Victorian formality and strict
middle-class morality and society was now profoundly
shocked. Only Jane's brother Kenelm, who had taken Holy
Orders, took a lenient view and she still remained to him
his dear sister. It was a harrowing time for Jane; melancholy of the deepest kind enveloped her; there was no letter
from Medjuel; Karl Venningen wrote to tell her that
Berthe, who suffered from mental disturbance, was growing worse; Cristos Hadji-Petros sent a tearful message that

little Eirini was dead. Surely a setting worthy of a Victorian melodrama!

Jane's fiftieth birthday, 'triste and melancholy anniversary', came but she was still youthful in mind and body; her hair was still the colour Balzac had admired and her eyes, made lustrous and magnetic by the use of eastern kohl, entranced and fascinated all who met her. April 6 saw her embarked for Calais, for the damp English weather chilled and depressed her still further; she took a great amount of luggage, stopped off in Paris to purchase a piano for Medjuel, bolts of fabric and sketching materials, and set sail for Beirut with an armoury of guns for her Bedouins. To her mother, Lady Andover, she wrote: 'I would gladly be as you are, but I cannot change my nature. I am different. How different I hardly realized.'

As the days of the journey passed, the sun began to warm her, dispelling the gloom and depression of the parting from Medjuel, and by the time the ship had reached Beirut she was more than ready for the longed-for meeting with him. Beirut was a stopping place *en route* for there was business to be done and arrangements to be made for the journey to Damascus. 'With beating heart I arrived at Damascus', she wrote and promptly set about making a home with the 'dear, the adored one'. The house was half-English, half-Arabic, with three wings enclosing a courtyard on the ground floor and furnished in the Arab style with a large courtyard and a *liwan* with divans and cushions. There were traditional wooden screens against the windows and two bedrooms over the centre wing. Jane had her own inimitable English style represented in the English garden and the drawing room, filled with her books, her writing desk and her easel. Isabel Burton recalls Jane's home as she saw it in 1890:

The house is made noticeable by its projecting balcony-like windows and coloured glass. We come to a large wooden gateway, and are received by twenty or thirty Bedawin of the tribe of Mesrab, lounging in the archway, and a large Kurdish dog, which knows his friends and will let me pass . . . On the other side is the reception-house for any of the tribe who happen to come into town; also the bath-house, the conservatory, and the house and play-ground for the fowls, amongst which we find curious snow-white geese with curling feathers, turkeys, ducks, poultry, pigeons, guinea hens, and other pets. The whole is fronted and surrounded by a choice flower-garden. Up-stairs is a suite of apartments which is elegance itself.

It does not appear, however, that Jane turned the garden into a clinic for the poor and sick of Damascus, as did Isabel Burton, her compatriot. Isabel writes: 'Our garden presented the strangest scene in the afternoon – fever patients making wry faces over quinine wine, squalling babies guggling oil, paralytic and rheumatic Bedawain being shampooed, and gouty old women having joints painted with iodine.'

Jane threw herself into Arabic life. She wore one blue garment, dyed her glorious chestnut hair jet black and wore it in two plaits and covered her head with the usual dark kerchief. She learned to milk the camels and submissively washed the hands, face, hair and feet of Medjuel, as an Arab wife should. When it came to riding, she was allowed to ride a horse, for she was as swift as the wind and a gifted horse-woman. Other Bedouin women were relegated to camels or dromedaries. She also built magnificent stables for the Arab horses and a visitor described the 'roaring and growling and groaning' which went on as eleven dromedaries were got ready for a long journey. But the greatest monument to Jane lay in her English garden of lily-ponds, herbaceous borders and flowering shrubs. Many English travellers were to re-member with pleasure the garden, although the site of the house has never been clearly defined. Apparently it was a short distance outside the city walls.

Jane rode with the tribes, fought alongside them, bought guns for them with her own money, and advised them on financial matters and the finer points of fencing with Arabs, who would do one down for a shekel. But she was always Jane Digby el Mesrab, tall, dignified, and supremely elegant.

Many people came to visit Jane Digby el Mesrab (the Hon. Jane Digby el Mesrab as she was called, for the rank of Baron's children had been conferred on her and her brothers and sisters in 1859) and all who were genuine friends, and not just curious sight-seers, were hospitably received. The house, the gardens, and the stables were tremendously admired and the hundred cats, which Eugènie was allowed to feed, had their own plates.

Jane saw her guests in the grand octagonal drawing-room where, one day, at six a.m., the Emperor of Brazil paid his respects and was graciously received. There was more to Jane's new life, however, than the reception of guests in a European drawing-room filled with family photographs and Victorian knickknacks. There was another part to be played, that of the wife who could withstand the hardship of the wilderness with a husband whose responsibilities to the tribe were many, for in November the Mesrabs headed south to find the evergreens necessary for the camels.

There were often desert skirmishes lasting for weeks at a time in which Jane joined, galloping with Medjuel at the head of his Bedouin troops and routing the invaders with that same fearless spirit which had sustained her throughout her many adventures. With her money she bought guns and carried out reprisal raids upon those tribes which had invaded their area and carried off their camels. Sometimes the *Uttfa* was in the centre of the skirmish; this was a large camel-howdah made of bamboo, decorated with ostrich feathers; inside was an Arab girl singing the slow chant which it was hoped would whip up the fervour of the fighters. Some of the Syrian tribes used the *Uttfa* and the savagery invoked in the spectacle of wild shouts, clashing spears and the banging of old pistols must have struck terror into European hearts – all, that is, except that of the Hon. Jane Digby el Mesrab. If there were no raids to avenge there was the *fantasia*, a wild charge of the Bedouin horsemen, widely practised. Isabel Burton described one which she witnessed:

When I say the men are riding *djerid*, I mean that they are galloping about violently, firing from horseback at full speed, yelling, hanging over their stirrups with their bridles in their mouth, playing with and quivering their long feathered lances in the air, throwing themselves under the horses' bellies and firing under them at full gallop, yelling and shouting their war cry . . . The wildness of the scene is very refreshing but you have to be a good rider yourself, as they simply go wild.

Jane was also becoming adept at levying ransom on unsuspecting travellers. Isabel Burton tells us about the journey to Palmyra, which European travellers were just beginning to make. It was 'an awfully difficult thing in those days . . . First of all, six thousand francs used to be charged by the El Mezrab who were the tribe who escorted for that journey . . . There was no water, that is, only two wells on the whole way, and only known to them. The difficulties and dangers were great; they travelled by day and hid by night. You may say the camels were about ten days on the road and horses about eight days.' Jane, according to Isabel Burton, was 'more Bedouin than the Bedawi' and aided the tribe in concealing the wells and levying ransom on unsuspecting and bewildered travellers.

The winter of 1859 had been bitterly cold; hunger stalked the land, bringing starvation and utter helplessness from spring floods and a disastrous plague of worms which had threatened the food crops. Violence followed. It all began with the murder of three men near the town of Sidon; the men were Druses, amongst whom Lady Hester Stanhope had lived early in the nineteenth century, queening it over them. Now she was gone and Muslim and Christian fought fiercely with each other. Four Christians were killed from a Maronite settlement and others were dragged from their homes and massacred in a blood-bath of stupendous proportions, while whole villages went up in smoke. In July, the terror spread to Damascus; Christians were put to the sword, dragged into the blood-soaked streets and left for the dogs. Medjuel was called to Homs as his first wife was dying but he would not leave Jane in Damascus, who felt the loss of his wife keenly, believing that her death 'did not mitigate my sin in having been the prime cause of Medjuel putting aside the wife of his youth'. For days the terror raged, finding a hero in Abd-el-Kadir, a true man of the hour, risking his life to help hundreds of Christians by leading them to his fortified house. Foreign diplomats did not escape the holocaust and all the Consulates of Christian countries were burned down; the American Consul reached the house of Abd-el-Kadir but the Dutch Consul was slain and the Greek Consul faced death with a certain panache, singing from the roof of his home.

Jane Digby el Mesrab was known and respected throughout Syria and she would have been in no danger if she had chosen to remain under Medjuel's roof; that she did not do so is vastly to her credit. At daybreak she ventured into the streets that were now a shambles, clad in her Bedouin garments and with a yashmak covering her fair skin, with only an Arab servant. She had no other protection, no loving Medjuel, no band of strong Bedouin followers to repel all adversaries at a single blow. She did what she could for the people left in the blood-soaked streets and when she could do no more she joined el-Kadir and helped to feed the 12,000-odd refugees sheltering in his house and courtyards by giving her own money. Jane's religion had never come between them before but the stand she had now taken on the side of the Christians had humiliated Medjuel in Muslim eyes; she was a *giaour*, an infidel who had disobeyed her husband and had spat upon the religion of Allah. Medjuel fled into the desert distressed and bewildered, with a situation which had never before arisen. Jane remained in Homs.

A new life began for Jane with the return of Medjuel and the freedom to practise her Christianity in the Missions; she made friends with the hardworking and self-sacrificing men and women of the Gospel who welcomed with open arms the *Sitt* Mesrab who sat so unostentatiously at the back of the Mission during the service, clad in Bedouin garments. She attended Divine Service and bought her grave in the Pro-testant Cemetery in Damascus, for the long years of love and adventure had taken their toll and the tempestuous life of the Bedouin camps could no longer be entered into.

But if she had to subdue her craving for excitement with Medjuel, there were compensations in other ways. She was still beautiful; her body was like that of a young girl, her skin as fair, her hair, except for a few strands of grey as tawny under the black dye as when Balzac knew her, her mind as sharp and her intellect as keen as ever. As Damascus settled down, tourism developed in a small way with the arrival of those Europeans who had the time and money to visit ancient sites (and were prepared for danger and the payment of ransom-money). Baalbeck, Petra, and Palmyra were like magnets to the intrepid traveller, bored with Europe and ready for new adventures in the mountains and deserts of the Middle East. To Jane's house many visitors came, enjoying her hospitality and admiring the furnishings and the garden. There was Barry Mitford, later Lord Redesdale, who visited Damascus in March 1871 and was received by the Hon. Jane Digby el Mesrab. He wrote:

So many stories had been told about her and her strange life as the wife of an Arab chief, I expected to see a grand and commanding figure living in a sort of tawdry barbar-ism, something like the Lady Hester Stanhope of *Eothen* and Lamartine: an imposing personage, mystic, wonder-ful, half queen, half sybil; O Semiramis and Meg Merrilies rolled into one, ruling by the force of the eye a horde of ignoble, ragged dependants, trembling but voracious.

He was impressed by her 'gracious old-world manners' and noted with a quick eye that she was a 'little old-fash-ioned, a relic of the palmy days of Almack's; dressed in quite inconspicuous Paris fashion and very nice to look upon'.

There was Count Louis de Thurhein, who told her that her daughter Mathilde (Didi) had now been married for nearly twenty years; there was the Scot, John MacGregor, who arrived in Damascus in his canoe, the *Rob Roy*, accompanied by seven men, two horses, and six mules. He had sailed down the Barada river from its source, paddled across Damascus, and finished up in a swamp in the middle of the Syrian desert. During his stay he met 'a charming Englishwoman, married to an Arab Sheik'.

Sir Edwin Pears also paid a visit to Damascus in the autumn of 1876, determined to seek out Lady Ellenborough 'an elderly lady, granddaughter of "Coke of Norfolk" '. She had married an Arab Sheik and was, 'I imagine, thirty years older than he'. It was difficult to see her but Sir Edwin's friend had to visit Damascus twice a year to pay her her private income of £3,000 a year from the bank at Beirut and he promised to obtain an interview. Jane received Sir Edwin in the *salon*, evidently resented the intrusion, but was courteous enough to allow him to stay at one end while the money business was transacted. He admired the paintings executed by Karl Haag and this led to conversation and an invitation to tea, any afternoon he would be in Damascus at five o'clock. She was, wrote Sir Edwin in his book *Forty years in Constantinople* 'an excellent talker' and had much insight and wit and spoke to him of Arab women's life in the harem.

The women of the harem, she said, had about them the delightfulness of children. Their enjoyments were simple and genuine. Their passionate love of flowers constantly appealed to her, but there was another side to their character. There was the childishness of children which became imbecility when found amongst women. They had sudden outburst of anger, swift reconciliation, passionate affection, and even hate. The worst side of their character related to their sensuality. They had no pleasures corresponding to those found in European society, no music, no literature, no social intercourse with men. The result was that even amongst the most respectable classes there was a gross sensuality, which shewed itself in the language which well-dressed harem ladies would employ. Subjects were

spoken of even in the presence of children about which all
Christian races agree to be silent.

To Sir Edwin she told many stories of her experiences and
was the only woman the Arabs would permit to ride a horse.
'I gained', wrote Sir Edwin, 'the impression that under
different circumstances she might have exerted a most valuable influence in any society into which she had been
thrown.'

Chief of all her visitors were the Burtons, Richard and
Isabel. Richard Burton had been appointed to the post of
Consul in Damascus, a position eminently suited to his
talents and his knowledge of Arabic. They settled in a house
at Salahiyyeh in the suburbs, where was light and air and
fresh water. 'In five minutes we could gallop out over the
mountains, and there was no locking us up at sunset. Here
then we pitched our tent', wrote Isabel. 'The people loved
me', she continued, 'and my chief difficulty was to pass
through the crowds that came to kiss my hand or my habit.'
The people certainly loved Richard, but Isabel's high-
handed methods in dealing with the Arabs evoked little
feelings of genuine affection.

On Wednesdays Isabel held a reception for friends and
dignitaries and after an evening meal guests relaxed on the
flat roof of the house, settling down on divans spattered with
cushions, smoking their nargilehs and eating sweetmeats
between conversations lasting well into the night. The Burtons liked her, although Isabel ignored the Arabic name and
insisted on calling her Lady Ellenborough. Burton found her
knowledge of Arabic life extremely useful and her candour in
discussing bizarre sexual practices amongst upper-class women may have contributed in no small measure to the
unexpurgated edition of *One Thousand Nights and a Night*.

In Isabel's *Life of Sir Richard Burton* we gain a glimpse of
Jane Digby el Mesrab, for Isabel wrote of the 'large reception
every Friday', which used to begin at sunrise and go on until
sunset. The two most interesting and remarkable visitors
were Abd-el-Kadir and Lady Ellenborough, although there

were others on the house roof; Charles Tyrwhitt-Drake 'an indefatigable worker in the Palestine Exploration' and E. H. Palmer, afterwards professor of Arabic at Cambridge, and in 1882 murdered by the Bedawi in Arabia. Isabel was generous enough to write of Jane:

> She was a most beautiful woman, though at the time I write she was sixty-one, tall, commanding, and queen-like. She was *grande dame au bout des doigts*, as much as if she had just left the salons of London and Paris, refined in manner and voice, nor did she ever utter a word you could wish unsaid. My husband said she was out and out the cleverest woman he ever met; there was nothing she could not do. She spoke nine languages perfectly, and could read and write in them. She painted, sculptured, was musical. Her letters were splendid; and if on business, there was never a word too much, nor a word too little. She had had a most romantic, adventurous life, and she was now, one might say, Lady Hester Stanhope's successor. She lived half the year in a romantic house she had built for herself in Damascus, and half her life she and her husband lived in his Bedawi tents, she like any other Bedawi woman, but honoured and respected as the queen of her tribe, wearing one blue garment, her beautiful hair in two long plaits down to the ground, milking the camels, serving her husband, preparing his food, giving him water to wash his hands and face, and sitting on the floor and washing his feet, giving him his coffee, his sherbet, his *narghilehs* [sic], and while he ate she stood and waited on him, and glorying in it; and when in Damascus they led semi-European lives.

Isabel also gave a picture of Jane which combined truth overlaid with a patina of Victorian smugness and upper-crust condescension:

> She was the most romantic and picturesque personality . . . She was very unhappy with Lord Ellenborough and she ran away with Prince Schwartzenberg when she was

only nineteen, and Lord Ellenborough divorced her. She lived with Prince Schwartzenberg for some years, and had two or three children by him, and then he basely deserted her. I am afraid that after that she led a life for a year or two over which it is kinder to draw a veil. She then tired of Europe, and conceived the idea of visiting the East.

Isabel's potted biography takes no account of the fact that Jane's purpose in visiting the East was to purchase Arab blood-stock from Syria to replenish her stables; it was entirely coincidental that she met Medjuel. 'At Damascus', Isabel continued, 'she blackened her eyes with kohl, and lived in a curiously untidy manner. But otherwise she was not in the least extraordinary.'

Of Medjuel, Isabel does not enthuse. She commented on his small stature and the fact that he was 'nearly black' and wrote 'I could understand her running away with Schwartzenberg, but the contact with that black skin I could not understand . . . All the same I believe he was a very intelligent and charming man.' A grudging tribute.

Adventure came with inter-tribal warfare. In 1872 the Rowala and Saba tribes were at variance over pasture rights; the Mesrabs supported the Saba but suffered losses of men and cattle before the Rowala were finally overcome. Jane found the excitement she needed fighting at Medjuel's side and alongside his Bedouin troops, for here she could truly be his wife, sharing his defeats and battle honours, forgetting the humiliation she had inflicted upon him with her Christian apostasy and the pernicious doubts that his long sojourns without her in the desert induced in her. There were rumours that the chief's wife had been killed and newspapers of the day played it up; Jane was a well-known figure in Syria and obituary notices contained the grossest misrepresentations of facts about her life. Some were scathing in the extreme and one deliberately so: 'There has just died a noble lady who greatly used, or abused marriage.' Isabel Burton dashed off letters to *The Times* and other European newspapers and proved most loyal in her defence of Jane. She went to the Protestant church 'often twice on Sundays' and 'had but one fault' (presumably Schwartzenberg was the 'one fault') the fall from grace. Tactfully, Isabel did not itemize the others: perhaps she was not aware of them.

Jane came riding back to Damascus, highly indignant and not a little amused. In a letter to the Pall Mall Gazette in March, 1873 Isabel had intimated that she possessed material relating to Jane's biography which Jane had wished her to write.

> She wished me to write her biography, and gave me an hour a day until it was accomplished. She did not spare herself dictating the bad with the same frankness as the good. I was pledged not to publish this until after her death and that of certain near relatives.

In her life of Sir Richard Burton, Isabel wrote: 'She was my most intimate friend, and dictated to me the whole of her biography, beginning 15th March, 1871, and ending 7th July.'

Jane denied all knowledge of the biography. In a letter to her sister-in-law, Theresa Digby, she referred to the newspaper reports of her death and to the controversial biography: 'I was quite overset by the dreadful paragraphs in the papers, and as you may conceive, have been most *intensely* annoyed ever since.' With regard to the biography, one can fully sympathize with her attitude; 'I trust hers may be a correct view, but I certainly always deprecated every idea of ever publishing anything relating to myself or my former existence, as you can easily believe, and I never spoke to her at all upon the subject, excepting the answering of some of her queries as to what the world of that day knew, and positively denying some other histories that people had told, and as to "*begging* her remember *promises*" after my death of justifying me, it is pure error, and she knew the *horror* and *aversion* I have to that kind of thing.'

Although Isabel conceded without jealousy the fact of Jane's beauty, 'even two years ago she was more attractive than half the young girls of our time', she was orthodox enough in her views, 'the romantic picture of becoming a Queen of the Desert and of the Bedouin tribes exactly suited her wild fancies, and was at once accepted'. She paints for us a picture of an impetuous girl who had put aside her sense of judgment in a moment of romantic passion: 'she was married according to Mohammedan law, changed her name to that of the Honourable Mrs Digby El Mesrab, and was horrified when she found that she had lost her nationality by her marriage, and had become a Turkish subject.'

The Burtons left Damascus on the 13 September 1871; Abd-el-Kadir and Jane accompanied Isabel on her night ride to the city gates, as she was 'determined to slip away quietly by night'. The farewell was 'affectionate' and the parting with Jane greatly so, 'I was the poor thing's only friend. As she wrung my hands these were her last words: "Do not forget your promise if I die and we never meet again". I replied; "*Inshallah*, I shall soon return".' A patronizing little speech.

Jane was now seventy-four, too easily tired for long desert rides with Medjuel and too concerned with the running of the Damascus home, for Eugènie had now left her employ and she found later domestics too trying; Gabrielle and Madame Marie were not of the calibre of her faithful Eugènie. Heribert, her son by Karl Venningen, had always kept in touch with her and he now had the unhappy task of sending her 'most melancholy intelligence' of the death of his father. 'My father died as he would have wished to die – in the saddle.'

But there were visitors to brighten up the long days; Admiral Sir James Robert Drummond, Commander of the Mediterranean Fleet, came to call and Jane lent him her best pony to compensate for the poor food. Then along came the Blunts, Wilfrid Scawen and Lady Anne. The meeting was secondary to the real purpose of their visit to Syria, which was to purchase horses of Anazeh stock for stud. In her book *A Pilgrimage to Nejd*, Lady Anne Blunt recalls her meeting with Jane: 'We have been spending the day with Mrs Digby and her husband, Medjuel of the Mesrab, a very well bred and agreeable man, who has given us a great deal of valuable advice about our journey.' It was evident that Anne Blunt was greatly impressed by Medjuel and that the outrageous goings-on in Jane's past were of minor importance to the knowledge which could be gained from conversations with both she and her Arab husband.

In 1880 another visitor paid his respect to Jane Digby el Mesrab. Sir Valentine Chirol was an English diplomat who left for us a record of her charm and her wit:

> When I made her acquaintance she must have been getting on for eighty, but so long as her Turkish yashmak concealed the lower part of her face, her ivory white and almost unwrinkled brow, her luminous eyes and the fine line of her aquiline nose still preserved traces of the beauty which had captured so many hearts in many lands and the highest places.

He suggested that she ought to write her memoirs but she replied that they would be 'a very naughty edition of the *Almanach de Gotha* and that a prayer-book would be more suitable for her declining years'.

In July 1881, Jane fell ill with dysentery and on 11 August 1881, she breathed her last in the beautiful house she had so lovingly kept for Medjuel on his return from the desert. Most of her friends had left the heat of the city for cooler places in the mountains and only Medjuel remained. Jane Digby el Mesrab was buried in the Protestant Cemetery where she lies, still at last, to this day.

Martha Jane Canary (c.1852–1903)

'Calamity Jane': Frontierswoman

Martha Jane Canary (or Cannary, or Canarray) known as 'Calamity Jane', was certainly the most notorious woman in American frontier history. Her boast that she could outride, outshoot and outdrink any man was often put to the test. In between times, the wild behaviour which inspired her nickname helped to create a legend that has, if anything, grown in the intervening years. Martha Jane first earned her living dressed as a man – as a mule-skinner. Later, she became a friend of Wild Bill Hickok – who she said was the father of her only child – and then joined the Buffalo Bill Wild West Show in 1893 to capitalize on her notoriety. But even fame could not curb 'Calamity Jane's' tendency to foul language, drunkenness, brawling and assaulting law officers, and she and the show eventually parted company. Her life and last, poignant days are described by **James D. Horan**.

There is no doubt that the woman most popularly associated with the western frontier is Calamity Jane. As long as books on the West are written, Jane will be a part of them. She has no middle-of-the-road critics; they are either pro-Calamity Jane or anti-Calamity Jane.

For example, Doane Robinson, South Dakota historian, says of her, 'She was a woman low down, even in her class . . .'

Dr W.A. Allen of Billings, Montana, who knew Jane, says, 'She swore, she drank, she wore men's clothing. Where can you find a woman today who doesn't do such things? She was just fifty years ahead of her time.'

There is no doubt Jane was tragically miscast by nature. She should have been a man. Her figure was definitely not feminine. She was a good rider and could handle a mule team with ease. An old cowhand once said 'she gave the finest demonstration of firearms' he had ever witnessed.

She had an impressive vocabulary of cuss words, using them senselessly, automatically as any mule-skinner. She lived to drink, and lived her short and merry life with a rowdy sort of happiness.

Her birth and birthplace are still debated. One source lists them as Princeton, Missouri, about 1848. The United States census of 1860 lists a Martha Jane Canarray, of Marion Township, and that may have been Calamity. In 1863, the family left the 200-acre farm and rolled west. There is a blank here in the known record of Jane's life, but many legends. She is supposed to have been married, lived for a while in Virginia City, and from her own story, stopped in Alder Gulch.

She drifted from town to town, once working as a laborer on the Union Pacific. By her account, she drifted to Cheyenne in 1869. She was already wearing men's pants, chewing tobacco, and drinking heavily. Two years later she was working as a mule-skinner or in a cattle-driving train.

Abilene and Hays City knew her, also Livingston, Montana. She claimed she joined the army in 1872 in its fight against the Indians. Her 'autobiography' gives a dramatic account of saving a young cavalryman's life, but that is nonsense.

However, it was about this time that Jane got her nickname. It had a special ring of doom which appealed to the crowds in the rough frontier saloons.

'Here's Calamity!' they would shout as Martha Jane would swagger toward the bar. Sometimes she fired off her six-shooter and shattered a mirror. The crowds loved it. The bartenders grinned. It was good for business.

In 1875 she joined Crook's expedition against the Sioux as a mule-skinner but was sent back after her sex was discovered. Jane had gone swimming with some of the skinners and a horrified colonel fired her on the spot.

In the 1870s Jane was roaming the Black Hills and there her legend grew bright. Bill Hickok rode into her life. It will always be debated whether Bill was her lover. It's doubtful he considered her anything more than a humorous addition to his entourage. But whatever Hickok thought of her, Jane was enjoying her most triumphant hour when she rode into Deadwood at Bill's side while the miners, gamblers, and dance-hall girls whooped and shouted as the Great Hickok rode down Main Street. They all wore creamy new Stetsons, brand-new fringed buckskins, and shiny boots. Revolver butts gleamed and the silver decorations on their saddles and rifles flashed in the sun.

Deadwood, which always loved a good show, whooped in glee. Calamity Jane shone in Hickok's reflected glory all the summer. But then Jack McCall shot Hickok in the back of the head and Calamity was bereft. She rolled from saloon to saloon, spicing her beer with bitter tears. The great days were gone. Jane was skidding downhill. But when the smallpox plague swept Deadwood, she regained some of her lost glory. Doctor Babcock, the town's only physician, told how Jane risked her life to care for some of the dying miners. One of her patients was a small boy named Robinson. Jane was an efficient if rough nurse. She was apt to growl, 'Here, drink this, you little bastard,' or 'Damn you, sit still until I can wash your face . . .'

The Robinson boy recovered and appeared again in Jane's life.

The tales of Jane in Deadwood are many. In 1930 an old man recalled how Jane dangled him on her knee when she found him weeping with loneliness. Another recalled how Jane won a fifty-dollar bet for shooting a hole in the top of a hat hanging in the rear of a saloon. The most hilarious story comes from Charles E. Chaplin, whose account is in the Montana Historical Society. In about 1880, when he was playing with the Lard Players at the East Lynne Opera House, Jane and Arkansas Tom, a notorious gunfighter, were in the audience. Jane soon grew indignant at the conduct of Lady Isobel, who, in the play, elopes with Sir Francis. At a crucial moment Jane stood up and let fly a stream of tobacco juice. Her marksmanship was good. The juice hit the actress and splattered her long pink dress. As the house went into an uproar and the actress screamed with indignation at her, Jane calmly stood up, threw a gold piece on the stage, and said in a loud voice, 'That's for your damn dress.'

Then, with Arkansas Tom gallantly offering his arm, she strode up the aisle and out into the night. Two days later Tom was killed in a raid on a small Dakota town bank.

Jane continued to drift about the West. She was now a living legend – 'White Devil of the Yellowstone', one dime novel called her. In 1885 she is said to have married a man named Burke in California. In 1887 she turned up in Gilt Edge, Montana, her hair gray, the years of dissipation showing plainly in her face. In 1889 she turned up in Rawlins, Wyoming, and the following year Ben Arnold, the Indian fighter, saw her in a small South Dakota town. She was so old and haggard he didn't recognize her at first.

In 1896 she joined the Palace Museum at Minneapolis. She toured Chicago, St Louis, and Kansas City. She was expected to play her flamboyant role and she did. But she got drunk once too often and was fired. Now she could cadge drinks by giving the bartenders a copy of her tiny 'autobiography' which sold by the thousands.

Estelline Bennett, in her *Deadwood Days*, recalled that in 1899 Jane came back for a visit to the scene of her greatest triumph. She shuffled down Main Street dragging along a girl about seven years old. According to the *New Northwest*, a newspaper of Deer Lodge, Montana, she had been married twice, 'once to a young man named Washburne who entered the Army, and also to a Lt Summers, who apparently fathered her daughter,' the young seven-year-old. Curious townspeople watched the grotesque figure and shook their heads. Was this the glamorous Calamity Jane?

A benefit was played for her and her child. But Jane forgot her child and blew the money across the bar the same night. Miss Bennett heard her coming home, howling like a wolf and offering to give battle to anyone at all in Deadwood.

In May 1900, the editor of the *Livingston Post* found Jane in a bawdy house and nursed her back to health. She was hired by the Pan-American Exposition, but she went on 'a high lonesome', wrecked a bar, blackened the eyes of two policemen, and was fired. Two years later the *Daily Yellowstone* located her in Billings, Montana, where she had shot up a bar. The next morning she was ordered out of town.

Louis Freeman, the noted American explorer, met her in 1902 in Yellowstone. He bought her several pails of beer and took some pictures of Jane smoking a cigar. As he recalls, she looked like a woman of seventy.

In July 1903, Jane appeared at the Calloway Hotel in Terry, a short distance from Deadwood. She was dying. On 2 August 1903, she opened her eyes and whispered, 'What's the date?'

When they told her, she nodded and replied, 'It's the twenty-seventh anniversary of Bill's (Hickok) death.' Then, 'Bury me next to Bill.'

At five her breathing became labored. A short time later she died. Her funeral was one of the largest in the history of ⸱

Deadwood. There was one last wonderful touch. The man
who closed the coffin was C. H. Robinson, rector of the Mt
Moriah Cemetery. He was the little boy Calamity Jane had
nursed during the smallpox plague.

Emmeline Pankhurst (1858–1928)

The Militant Suffragette

Usually referred to simply as 'Mrs Pankhurst', Emmeline was one of the driving forces behind the campaign for 'Votes For Women'. Her unflinching and often violent battles with the establishment for the rights now enjoyed – even taken for granted – by women, has given her a place at the pinnacle of twentieth-century heroines. The eldest of ten children of a successful Manchester printer, she attended her first suffrage meeting at the age of fourteen and there found her life-long mission. In the years which followed, Emmeline rallied women throughout the country, refusing to be silenced and often risking imprisonment for her views. In 1905, she moved to London in order to recruit, lead marches and deputations, and generally put the government under such pressure that 'Votes for Women' would become a reality and not just a battle cry. The crucial years between 1899 and 1907, when the lives of women began to change for ever, are here described by an eyewitness at the very heart of the events – **Sylvia Pankhurst**, Emmeline's second daughter, who was then living as an art student in London . . .

The Labour Party Emmeline Pankhurst had so ardently desired in the 1890s had come. The Trade Union Congress of 1899 had accepted Keir Hardie's scheme to run Labour candidates under the auspices of a Labour Representation Committee of affiliated Trade Unions and Socialist organizations, of which the largest and most effective was his own Independent Labour Party (ILP). The Socialists thus gained the mass backing they had lacked. The Taff Vale judgment of 1901, which was a terrible reverse to the Unions, swung almost the whole Trade Union movement into line for political action. ILP enthusiasm ran high.

Mrs Pankhurst shared in the rejoicing. As we know, she had formed her political opinions in an atmosphere of reform and liberation. Her impressionable nature was now to be influenced by a narrowly exclusive feminist school, which saw the world of Labour in terms of 'beef-steaks and butter for working men; tea and bread for working women', refusing to admit that the welfare of the working woman, either as mother or wage-earner, was in any degree involved in raising the status of the working class as a whole. The hitherto dormant political interest of her eldest daughter was suddenly aroused by contact with the North of England Society for Women's Suffrage. When the ILP propagandists came as usual to stay at Nelson Street, Christabel heckled them fiercely. Old friends, like the Bruce Glasiers, were dismayed by her insistence on what they considered a mere barren issue of bourgeois politics. They had broken out of political Liberalism burning with the hope of a Socialist Commonwealth. They did not, like the active feminists, feel the disfranchisement of women as a searing brand of inferiority. Some of the opportunist were actually opposed to votes for women, declaring they would vote Tory, being more reactionary than men. Philip Snowden, later a strong supporter, was then an anti. Mrs Pankhurst was thrown into a ferment; was it for this that she had devoted nine years of service and sacrifice to the ILP? She bitterly seconded Christabel's reproaches to her that she had allowed the cause of women to be effaced. From that time forward she often told me:

'Christabel is not like other women; not like you and me; she will never be led away by her affections!'

As was characteristic of her, once she had re-entered the franchise struggle, it became for her the only cause in the world. Moreover, this, and this only, was the critical moment to push it forward. Another Reform Act was due. If manhood suffrage went through without women, it would be impossible to get the franchise question reopened for a long period: and the difficulty of getting the vote would be enormously increased. The Labour Party, now becoming a reality, must make the freedom of women 'A Party Question'.

She resolved to form a new organization to be called the 'Women's Social and Political Union', taking as its slogan not 'Women's Suffrage', as of yore, but the more vivid battle-cry, '*Votes for Women!*' It is curious to recall that the telling phrase was so tardily coined. On 10 October 1903, she invited a few obscure women members of the ILP to her home, and with them formed the new Union.

Then Keir Hardie appeared; he cordially welcomed the new movement and approved its tactics; a single-clause Bill to abolish the sex disability, leaving other franchise reforms to be dealt with subsequently; a new organization of women to push forward their own cause. Under his urge, the National Administrative Council (NAC) of the Independent Labour Party agreed to support Dr Pankhurst's original Bill admitting women to the Parliamentary vote on the same terms as men.

The difficulty facing those who desired to make Votes for Women popular with Labour people was the complicated and backward state of the electoral law. The poor man could qualify only as a householder; or perhaps as a lodger, if he occupied unfurnished rooms, the rateable value of which was not less than £10 a year. The man of property could vote, without restriction, wherever he could prove a qualification as householder, freeholder, copy holder, £10 occupier, University graduate, and under other heads beside. If the vote were to be extended to women on the same terms, the working-class mother would not be able to qualify, for her husband, not she, would exercise the single vote open to them as householders. The ill-paid workwoman who was a lodger had seldom sticks to furnish a room even if it were rated high enough to carry a vote. On the other hand, the wives, daughters and mothers of the rich would easily provide themselves with the required qualification. To murmurs that Votes for Women on the existing terms would increase the power of wealth, Keir Hardie replied by inviting the ILP branches to take a census of the women already voting in Local Government elections. Forty branches undertook the arduous task; they recorded that out of 59,920 women voters canvassed, 82.45 per cent were of the working class. Here, it was claimed, was the evidence needed to silence opponents, who denounced what they termed the 'Ladies Bill'. The ILP Annual Conference in Cardiff, at Easter 1904, showed its friendship to the cause of women by electing Mrs Pankhurst to the NAC and instructing it to sponsor the Women's Enfranchisement Bill. Keir Hardie immediately arranged for the measure to be formally introduced by the Labour Members of Parliament.

That autumn I went to London with a National Scholarship to the Royal College of Art, and took up lodgings at 45 Park Walk, Chelsea. In February 1905, my mother came to stay with me for the opening of the new Parliamentary session. Our mission was to induce some Member of Parliament to sponsor Votes for Women on one of the Friday afternoons set apart for the Second Reading of private Members' Bills, places for which were drawn by ballot. We were alone in this quest; not even the officials of the old National Union* were there. Keir Hardie, from the first, had promised us his place, but not another Member acceded to our pleading. Daily from the assembling to the rising of the House, often past midnight, we were there. Keir Hardie

*The National Union of Women's Suffrage Societies, a federation resulting from the original Societies formed independently in various towns. Of this organization, once led by Lydia Becker, Mrs Millicent Garrett Fawcett was now the leader. It remained non-militant and opposed the militant WSPU.

drew no place; the first twelve were pledged to other measures, but Bamford Slack, the holder of the thirteenth, agreed to take the Bill.

A thrill of life ran through the whole Suffrage movement, which had sunk into an almost moribund coma of hopelessness. That fact must always be given due emphasis when the history of the movement is reviewed.

The Bill had been set down for 12 May, the best place to be had, but only as Second Order of the day; the opponents could prevent it coming on at all by prolonging discussion on the First Order, a small utility proposition to compel road vehicles to carry a light behind as well as before. Keir Hardie had pulled every string he could to get it withdrawn. Mrs Pankhurst was almost frenzied at the unimaginative folly of men who could hold this 'trumpery little measure' against the claimant need of womanhood in bonds.

On the fateful 12th, the Lobbies of Parliament were thronged with women, Suffragists from near and far, Lancashire textile workers, more than 400 from the Co-operative Women's Guild, confident of success and mustered quite unofficially by an Australian, Nellie Alma Martel, who had run for the Commonwealth Parliament. Spurred to new eagerness by this responsive crowd, Mrs Pankhurst saw through the 'peep-hole', by which visitors may look into the House, uproarious legislators rolling in laughter at the absurdities by which the debate was being prolonged.

The Bill was talked out, of course. The placid representatives of the old National Union at once withdrew, but Mrs Pankhurst would not mildly accept frustration; a meeting of protest must be held at the door of Parliament. She thrust forward Mrs Elmy, senior in age and longest worker in the cause; but the police rudely jostled her and all of us down the steps. We gathered at the statue of Richard I, beside the House of Lords. The police inspector intervened. Where could we meet then; where could poor women voice their indignation? Mrs Pankhurst demanded, with tremulant voice and blazing eyes, passionately feminine, proudly commanding. The police inspector hesitated, argued, led us to Broad Sanctuary by the Abbey Gates. Keir Hardie stepped into the ranks, taking the hand of old Mrs Elmy. The little unnoticed meeting vainly demanded Government intervention to save the talked-out Bill. Yet a new note had been struck; the Militant Suffrage movement had begun.

The days of the Tory Government were running out. On 13 October, Sir Edward Grey was coming to the historic Manchester Free Trade Hall to announce the policy of the coming Liberal Government. The WSPU was to meet him with the question: 'Will the Liberal Government give women the vote?' Unless he gave a definite undertaking in the affirmative, which was considered improbable, for he had refused to receive a deputation, a disturbance was to be made, which would cause a sensation throughout the country. Mrs Pankhurst had to consider her registrarship, but Christabel set out for the meeting with the words: 'I shall sleep in prison tonight!' She was accompanied by a new recruit, Annie Kenney, an Oldham cotton operative.

Grey refused to answer the question. The girls were thrown out, and were arrested after a struggle in the hall and an attempt to speak in the street outside. When the turmoil had subsided, Grey said: 'As far as I can understand, the trouble arose from a desire to know my opinion on Women's Suffrage. That is a question which I could not deal with here tonight, because it is not, and I do not think it is likely to be, a Party question.'

Christabel was ordered imprisonment for a week, Annie Kenney for three days, in lieu of fines which they refused to pay. Mrs Pankhurst hurried to the cells with proud congratulations, pleading in motherly solicitude: 'You have carried it far enough; now I think you ought to let me pay your fines and take you home.' 'If you pay my fine I will never go home again,' her daughter answered hotly. Mrs Pankhurst was deeply moved. Keir Hardie telegraphed: 'The thing is a dastardly outrage; but do not worry, it will do

immense good to the cause. Can I do anything?' He was the
only prominent person who uttered a word of support. The
Press was unanimous in hostility; Suffragists throughout the
country silent; but the big Manchester public gave the
prisoners a tremendous ovation. Christabel was threatened
with expulsion from Manchester University, and obliged to
pledge herself to refrain from making any further disturbance. The rest of us must continue the fight.

The Conservatives resigned on 4 December. Campbell-
Bannerman formed a Liberal Government. A General Election was called for the New Year. In town after town, where
Cabinet Ministers appeared, we raised our little white ban-
ners, uttered our cry: 'Will the Liberal Government give
women the vote?' were violently ejected, held our meetings
outside. Sometimes the people struck us with sticks and
umbrellas; they were wild to get the Tories out and thought
we were trying to help them. Twenty years of Conservative
rule had left a big crop of reforms overdue. But everywhere
we had some support. In Manchester the audiences often
prevented Winston Churchill speaking because he refused to
answer us.

Mrs Pankhurst was in Merthyr Tydfil working for Keir
Hardie, who was speaking for the fifty other nominees of the
Labour Party, and only appeared in Merthyr, well-nigh
voiceless, the day before the poll. She rejoiced with him in
the victory of twenty-nine Labour candidates; Labour was a
power to be reckoned with at last!

I was back again at College. Annie Kenney joined me at
Park Cottage with two pounds, advanced by Mrs Pankhurst,
'to rouse London'. We organized for the opening of Parliament, on 16 February, 1906, a procession of women and a
meeting in the Caxton Hall. Keir Hardie found a donor to
pay the cost. Alfieri, of the then new *Daily Mirror*, W. T.
Stead, and others, kept the movement in the news; already
the *Daily Mail* had christened us 'Suffragettes'.

On the day of the meeting, 400 poor women from East
London marched to the Caxton Hall. Already it was
thronged; Suffragists, nobodies, somebodies, were there to

see those extraordinary Suffragettes. Emmeline Pankhurst stood before them, appealing, compelling, wearing the dignity of a mother who has known great sorrow; her habitual elegance of dress and manner told with them as women. With scarcely a gesture, phrases of simple eloquence sprang to her lips, her eye flashed lightnings. Her wonderful voice, poignant and mournful, and shot with passion, rose with a new thrill. Deeply she stirred them; many silently pledged their faith to her for life. News came that the King's Speech was read, that it promised to democratize the men's franchise by abolishing plural voting; but to women offered nothing. She swept them out, and on with her to the Commons. The rain was pouring in torrents; that was the least of it; they were following her into the militant movement, and knew not whither the step might lead. For the first time in memory the great doors of the Strangers' Entrance to Parliament were closed during the session of the House. The Commons police were on guard to prevent the admittance of any woman. The militant and her following stood at the door defiant; Parliament buzzed with interest. At last the Speaker agreed to permit relays of twelve women within the Lobby. Hour after hour, in the rain, they waited their turn to interview legislators who promised nothing! The experience stoked the spark of militant impatience she had lit.

Within the citadel, Keir Hardie, replying to the King's Speech, as leader of the new Labour Party, demanded the removal of the 'scandal and disgrace' of treating women no better than the criminal and insane. Had the Party been ready to second him vigorously in that demand, there might have been a different history to write, for the Liberals were then keenly susceptible to the competition of the rising Labour movement. In this, as in much else, however, his colleagues failed to support him. They had fought the election on a programme of immediate demands, for which their constituents expected them to fight. Votes for Women had scarcely figured in that programme. It is true the Trade Union Congress had been pledged to Adult Suffrage for both sexes since its formation, and specifically to Votes for Women since 1884, but the Suffrage had not been made a vital question. Just before Parliament assembled, a resolution to support Votes for Women on the existing terms was brought before the delegate conference of the Labour Party. It was attacked by opponents demanding Adult Suffrage only, and was carried only by 446,000 votes to 429,000, a narrow margin indeed to arm Keir Hardie in a stubborn fight.

There was many an acrid and painful discussion in his rooms in the old Elizabethan house at 14 Nevill's Court, off Fleet Street, wherein he sat, dark-browed and silent, and Mrs Pankhurst wept and stormed. He was doing all he knew for the cause she loved, but it was not in him to argue or protest. She believed that to force through Votes for Women would buttress his power and that of the Labour movement. She was convinced he could do it if he were determined, and had the strong personal desire that he should do it out of his friendship for her. This strain made the contest more sharply poignant. She was torn between her affection for Hardie and the Socialist movement, her passionate zeal for the women's cause, and the growing influence of Christabel, who desired to cut the WSPU entirely clear of the Labour Movement; already she believed Votes for Women would be given by the Tories, because, to 'dish' the Liberals, they had given Household Suffrage to men in 1867.

The Labour Party decided that any places for Bills drawn by its members should be put at the disposal of the Party, to be allocated by majority vote. Keir Hardie nevertheless promised us that if he should draw a place himself, it would go to our Bill, whatever the majority might have to say. He was unsuccessful, but five places were drawn by other members of the Party. All foresaw that four of them must go to the repeal of the Taff Vale decision, the right of the unemployed to work, the feeding of destitute school children, and Old Age Pensions, for these were measures foremost in the Party programme. One place remained in doubt. Mrs Pankhurst demanded it should be given to Votes for Women, but the Party decided for a checkweighing Bill to protect the earnings of workmen. She could not forgive the blow. That the Labour Party won triumphant success in this first session only embittered her disappointment.

Despite all jars, when controversy could be thrust aside, Mrs Pankhurst was never so happy as in the hours spent with Keir Hardie during his very brief spells of relaxation, walking in St James's Park or on the Embankment, taking tea of his own making at Nevill's Court. Unswerving in friendship, he raised £300 to give the WSPU a start in London. Infinitely more important, he introduced her to one whom his discerning eye selected as the ideal honorary treasurer for the WSPU: Emmeline Pethick-Lawrence, a devoted social worker. She and her husband, Frederick Pethick-Lawrence, threw themselves unreservedly into the Suffragette movement; she ardent, eloquent and magnetic, he a great organizer, with tremendous drive and resource. They brought to the Union money and a considerable social circle, and developed the spectacular side of the propaganda, advertising the cause by kites, boats, poster, umbrella and horseback parades.

Speakers and organizers were engaged. The heckling of Cabinet Ministers increased, great meetings held in all the principal towns. Campbell-Bannerman was asked to receive a deputation. On his refusal, Suffragettes called at his official residence, 10 Downing Street. Denied admittance, they seated themselves on his doorstep, and were removed to Cannon Row Police Station. He sent to their cells a promise to receive a deputation shortly, and directed their release. Though the militants were accused of ruining the cause, it was leaping forward throughout the country as never before. Even in Parliament 200 Members formed themselves into a Women's Suffrage Committee and petitioned the Prime Minister to hear them. He consented to receive them with a joint deputation of all women's societies on 19 May.

Keir Hardie had won a place for a Parliamentary Resolution for Votes for Women, which assumed importance as a means of revealing the opinion of the new Parliament to Campbell-Bannerman, before his reply to the deputation.

Mrs Pankhurst anticipated the Resolution would be talked out like last year's Bill. She came up to London resolved that the insult should not pass without a resounding protest. Behind the heavy brass grille which screened its opponents from the House, the 'Ladies' Gallery' of the Commons was filled with her militants. She awaited impatiently an official statement. It was given by Herbert Gladstone; the Cabinet, being divided on the question, would leave the House free to vote as it chose. This failure to give hope of Government action, and hilarious sallies on the subject of woman and her disabilities, evoked angry retorts from the gallery. The Speaker gave orders for the police to clear it if anything more were heard. Samuel Evans, who had talked out Bamford Slack's Bill, rose to do the same again, turning occasionally to scan the clock with a sardonic smile. Keir Hardie, watch in hand, waited the moment to move the closure. The women in the gallery craned forward, waiting the signal of Mrs Pankhurst. Suddenly Irene Miller, daughter of a pioneer Suffragist, saw the police entering the gallery; fearing our demonstration would be prevented, she shouted, as they do in Parliament: 'Divide! divide!' We all joined in, flags were thrust through the grille. The police jumped over the benches to throw us out. The House was in a turmoil. Blown and dishevelled, we descended to the Lobby. A few women, Members' wives and a Suffragist or two, avoided us scornfully. Members crowded round to scold us, declaring we had destroyed all chance of a favourable reply from the Prime Minister. If Mrs Pankhurst, facing her opponents disdainfully, felt any qualms, she did not show them. Keir Hardie came forward to defend us, declaring the long ill-treatment of our cause, and the presence of the police in the gallery, sufficient explanation of our action, and overruling the intention of the non-militant Suffragists and their Parliamentary friends to exclude the WSPU from the deputation to Campbell-Bannerman.

When the representatives of 260,000 organized women, Suffragists, Co-operators, Temperance Workers, Conservatives, Liberals, Socialists, Trade Unionists, assembled in

Downing Street to plead for their vote, Emmeline Pankhurst uttered an unusual note of tragedy:

> We feel this question so keenly that we are prepared to sacrifice for it life itself, or what is perhaps even harder, the means by which we live!

There was the sharpness of actuality in her words; her business, now almost disregarded, was drifting to its end; her frequent absences from the registrarship were the subject of official rebuke; she might easily lose the position. Her daughters were not yet launched; her delicate son of fifteen was as yet by no means equipped to earn a living. Her old friend Noémie had written a harsh rebuke, telling her to leave politics alone and give her attention to placing her daughters in professions; but she could not settle down to that; she was driven by a desperate heart-hunger for the ideal. Still struggling, still unsatisfied, seeking a goal of beauty for her hard pilgrimage, she had seized on this quest of the vote as the fulfilment of her destiny, ready to die for it as the tigress for her young. At her note of passion, despite its dignity, carefully reared, conventional non-militants tightened their lips in disapproval; this surely was bad form!

Campbell-Bannerman expressed his personal belief in the justice of the cause, but excused himself from action: some of his Cabinet were opposed to it; he could 'only preach the virtue of patience'. 'Patience', replied Keir Hardie, 'can be carried to excess! With agreement between the leaders of the two historic Parties, it surely does not pass the wit of statesmen to find ways and means to enfranchise the women of England before this Parliament comes to a close.' Alas! the bald head of the Prime Minister shook gloomily in token of dissent.

Asquith, the Chancellor of the Exchequer, was named as the chief obstacle to Government action. He was to speak at Northampton. Mrs Pankhurst went before him to address a great meeting there. The President of the local Women's Liberal Federation assured her the disgraceful violence done to women in other towns would not occur in that enlightened city. She was accorded a front seat among the prominent Liberal ladies. Her plea that her question related to education secured her a momentary hearing, but she was violently ejected as soon as she mentioned the vote. The President of the Women's Liberal Federation and several of her colleagues resigned forthwith and joined the WSPU. A little later, when Asquith spoke in Aberdeen, Mrs Pankhurst was implored to hold off her stalwarts, on a pledge that he would answer the all-important questions quietly put to him by one woman: Mrs Black, the President of the local Women's Liberal Federation. When she rose, as had been agreed, she was hustled and howled down, whilst the Chairman, who was privy to the arrangement, declared her out of order. Mrs Pankhurst, rising to explain the situation, was violently ejected. Such scenes were typical.

For ringing Asquith's doorbell in London, and for heckling Cabinet Ministers in Manchester, more Suffragettes were imprisoned, amongst them Mrs Pankhurst's youngest daughter, Adela, who did not afterwards resume her position as an elementary school teacher, becoming a WSPU organizer. In June Christabel had graduated LLB, and left Manchester to become chief organizer of the WSPU. Mrs Pankhurst closed the dwindling Emerson's, and travelled from election to election. Her sister, Mary Clarke, whose marriage had proved unhappy, acted as deputy registrar, keeping the deserted home meagrely for the boy whose future was the subject of desultory and inconclusive debate.

In October, imposing headquarters were opened for the WSPU in Clement's Inn, Strand, where the Pethick-Lawrences had a flat. The Inn was at once a rallying-ground for women of all grades and classes, their pent desire for self-expression surging to this movement as a long needed outlet.

When Parliament reopened that autumn, Mrs Pankhurst again appeared with her militants. She communicated with the Prime Minister, through the Chief Liberal Whip, and received the plain answer that he held out no hope for Votes for Women at any time during the Parliament. Immediately there was a demonstration of protest in the Lobby of the House itself. Woman after woman sprang to a seat and attempted to make a speech. The police hurled themselves upon them; Mrs Pankhurst was thrown to the ground. Ten women were arrested, including her daughter Adela, Emmeline Pethick-Lawrence, and Annie Cobden-Sanderson, daughter of Richard Cobden, the great agitator against the Corn Laws. Next day they were ordered six weeks' imprisonment in the Second Division, on refusal to enter into recognizances not to offend again. I got a fortnight in the Third Division, for attempting a speech of protest on the steps of the Court. The country was thrilled. Parliament began to be concerned about the rigours of Suffragette imprisonment. Within a week we were transferred to what was termed the First Division, though it lacked the more important privileges given to men politicals. The slogan of the militant Suffragettes was always 'The Vote this year!' Even the patient, law-abiding Mrs Fawcett was impressed by the great stir; she addressed a circular letter to the Press, containing a frank admission: 'I feel the action of the prisoners has touched the imagination of the country in a manner quieter methods did not succeed in doing.'

The revolt of militant women made itself felt in the Parliamentary by-elections. The WSPU policy was simple: to urge the electors to vote against Government candidates until the Government agreed to grant the vote. When Cobden's daughter and her fellow prisoners were released, they rushed to a by-election at Huddersfield; huge audiences deserted the candidates to hear them. Though the Liberal poll was reduced, the Labour vote also fell; the Tory alone had gained. Labour organizers were dismayed; all the Suffragettes in the election were Labour women, Mrs Pankhurst still a member of the ILP Executive; yet they refused to advise the electors to vote Labour, stating that so long as votes were cast against the Government they cared not to whom they went! The resentment displayed itself at the next Labour Party Conference; a motion to support the Women's Enfranchisement Bill was overwhelmingly defeated by

605,000 votes to 268,000 in favour of accepting nothing short of Adult Suffrage. Keir Hardie, with poignant emotion, announced that if the resolution were intended to bind the action of the Labour Party in the House of Commons, he would consider very seriously whether to remain a member of it:

> The Party is largely my own child; I cannot part with it lightly or without pain. . . . If it is necessary for me to separate myself from my life's work, I do so in order to remove the stigma resting upon our wives, mothers and sisters of being accounted unfit for citizenship.

The Conference was shocked; many delegates would have reversed their votes if they could, but none of the leaders supported him. Ramsay MacDonald and Arthur Henderson were emphatic that after so decisive a vote the Party could no longer sponsor the Women's Enfranchisement Bill! Mrs Pankhurst was silent; she would not advise Keir Hardie to leave the Party, fearing he would be reduced to powerless isolation. She still hoped he would be able to induce the Party to push Votes for Women as a vital issue. Faced with his threat to resign, the Party Executive decided to leave its members free to choose between Adult Suffrage and Votes for Women on the existing terms. This meant the Party itself would take no action at all. Keir Hardie accepted the solution as the best he could get. He told me that but for his stand, the Party would have instructed its members to oppose the Women's Enfranchisement Bill. I sadly predicted to him that in the end the Suffragettes would be opposing the Labour Party as well as the Liberals. The WSPU appeared in great force at the ILP Conference, in Derby, that Easter. The resolution defeated at Belfast was brought up; Keir Hardie told the ILP it must choose whether or not it would retain 'some of its most valuable women members'. If he were a woman and this resolution were lost, he would be ashamed to belong to a Party which had turned its back on him. It was carried by a tremendous majority. An attempt to

censure the ILP members of the WSPU for publicly dis-
sociating themselves from support of Labour candidates was
swept aside. Mrs Pankhurst, with that great emotional appeal
which gave her command of popular audiences, averred that
till women were enfranchised she would never abandon the
independent election policy; rather she would reluctantly
surrender her ILP membership, though she pleaded she
had been 'loyal to Socialism on every other point'. A resolution congratulating the Suffragette prisoners* was opposed
by Ramsay MacDonald and by the defeated Labour candi-
date of Huddersfield, but Keir Hardie drove it through by
180 votes to 60.

It seemed for the next five years that of all the Suffragette
activities, the anti-Government election policy appealed
most to Mrs Pankhurst. She lauded it as the policy of Charles
Stewart Parnell, the great Irish leader; but Parnell's task was
easy – he had only to induce the men of his Party to follow his
bidding; she had to persuade men to vote against their Party
for women's sake. If any woman could appeal thus successfully, certainly it was she. Every newspaper in the country
declared that she turned large numbers of votes against the
Government.

For the opening of the Parliamentary Session of 1907, on
13 February, the WSPU advertised a 'Women's Parliament',
openly appealing for 'prison volunteers'. The Square was
thronged by spectators, the House guarded by an army of
police. It is indeed extraordinary to recall that literally
thousands of police on horse and foot were, time and again,
turned out to repel a few hundred women. The Caxton and
Essex Halls were both packed with the militants, who punc-
tuated fiery appeals to womanly valour from the platform by
cries of 'Rise up, women!' and answering shouts of 'Now!'
Then, hour after hour, repeatedly we sallied forth. Mounted
police, caricatured by the *Daily Chronicle* next day as 'London Cossacks', reared their horses over us. Foot police

---

*Twenty more women had been hustled into gaol for demonstrating in
and around Westminster before the close of 1906.

gripped us, rushed us along at arm's length, beating us with clenched fist between the shoulders, bumping us in the back with practised knees. At last fifty-four men and women had been taken to Cannon Row Police Station. The aged Mrs Despard, General French's sister, Christabel and I were among the prisoners. Our punishment ranged from ten shillings or seven days to thirty shillings or three weeks.

For the first time in the long history of the movement, the Member who drew first place in the ballot, a Liberal, W. H. Dickinson, gave his place for women. The Prime Minister had promised the Suffrage Society of his constituency: 'I will with much pleasure give my support to Mr Dickinson's Bill,' but when it came before the House, he decried it as applicable only to 'a small minority of well-to-do women'. Finally a Liberal, J. D. Rees, talked the measure out, the Speaker having refused to permit the closure. There was no protest from the Ladies' Gallery; it had been closed for the day! Rees was rewarded with a knighthood!

On 20 March, another 'Women's Parliament' met in the Caxton Hall and sent processions out to Parliament. Seventy-five women were arrested, one of them a portrait-painter of Rome, another an author of Norway.

The ceaseless contest with colleagues out of sympathy with his policy bore heavily on Keir Hardie. That April he suffered a sudden breakdown. He was removed from his solitary rooms to St Thomas's Home, but after some weeks there, left for his home in Cumnock still gravely ill. I feared he was dying and wrote so to my mother. She left Manchester immediately, arriving in time only to speak to him for an instant on the station platform. He was deeply moved that she had journeyed thus to greet him, and she to find him broken as an old man, unable to stand without support. Sadly, too, he had long departed this life when my mother was finally able to celebrate full women's suffrage just before her death.

Two
The Wicked Women

A Gang of Wild Girls

Moll Cutpurse

Lucrezia Borgia (1480–1519)

The World's Wickedest Woman?

The beautiful, golden-haired Italian noblewoman, Lucrezia Borgia, has frequently been labelled as 'The World's Wickedest Woman' for a life reputedly bound up with intrigue, sexual scandal, rumours of incest . . . and, of course, poisoning. Yet was the daughter of the power-mad Borgia family who was forced into not one but two marriages of convenience – one annulled on the grounds of impotence and the other by the murder of her husband by her brother, Cesare – really so black as she was painted? For this same woman was also said to be religious, charming and a noted patron of the arts. **Margaret Nicholas** uses the benefit of hindsight and new information to separate fact from fiction in the life of a truly extraordinary woman.

Lucrezia Borgia is, of course, the name on everyone's lips when you mention the subject of wicked women. She belonged to one of the most feared and hated families in history and the unspeakable crimes laid at her door include incest, not only with her brother, Cesare, but with her father, Pope Alexander VI.

The Borgias were certainly a terrible brood, but does Lucrezia herself deserve the reputation she has gained over the centuries?

Those who have written about her in modern times have come to the conclusion that she was used as a pawn by the brilliant, ruthless, Borgia men and sacrificed to their terrible ambition. It was under their influence and through their actions that she became 'the most execrated woman of her age'.

She lived in a world in which the concepts of decency and morality were very different from our own. The fact that her father, the libertine Rodrigo Borgia, could become head of the Catholic Church was evidence of that. But, says the historian Gregorovius, who is the most quoted authority on Lucrezia, 'she was neither better nor worse than the women of her time. She was thoughtless and filled with the joy of living'.

If she had not been the daughter of Alexander VI and the sister of Cesare Borgia she would have been unnoticed by the historians of her age, or at most would have been mentioned only as one of the many charming women who constituted the society of Rome. In the hands of her father and her brother, however, she became the tool and also the victim of their political machinations, against which she had not the strength to make any resistance.

Chroniclers of the day using scandal, innuendo and rumour, and the very real hatred felt for the Borgias, turned Lucrezia into a legendary monster and that is the picture that has endured.

Her family, Spanish in origin, had a meteoric rise from obscurity because within a relatively short span of time it produced a number of brilliant men, distinguished by their sensual beauty, force of intellect and ruthless ambition. One of these was Cardinal Rodrigo Borgia whose mistress, a Roman beauty called Vannozza, bore him several children including Lucrezia and the infamous Cesare.

Lucrezia was born on 18 April 1480. She was brought up in her mother's house on the Piazza Pizzo di Merlo, only a few steps away from the Cardinal's Palace. Rodrigo did not acknowledge the children as his own until he had been made Pope and was absolutely sure of his power.

Before she was eleven years old the first suitor had made a bid for Lucrezia's hand. Two months later another appeared and was favourably considered, but both were swept away as too insignificant when Rodrigo took the Triple Crown and desired a prestigious match for his lovely daughter.

He put her into the care of the two women who were closest to him, his cousin and confidante Adriana di Mila, who was married to an Orsini, and her daughter-in-law Giulia Farnese, an exquisite woman, said to be a poem in gold and ivory, who became Rodrigo's most famous mistress. These two tended the darling of the Borgia family like a hot-house orchid, keeping her apart in the splendour of the Palazzo of Santa Maria until she was prepared for her first marriage.

At thirteen Lucrezia was golden-haired and graceful, with a slender white neck and teeth like pearls; a delectable morsel to offer to the handsome Giovanni Sforza, Lord of Pesaro. They were married in a magnificent ceremony to which half of Rome was invited.

The marriage was not to last long. The Borgias saw to that. They soon realized they had underplayed their hand in marrying Lucrezia to Sforza when they could have used her to gain entrance to the powerful house of Aragon. They made up their minds to get rid of the unfortunate bride-groom.

Their method could not have been more humiliating. They announced to the world that Sforza had proved impotent and that his wife was still a virgin. The grievously insulted Lord of Pesaro called upon all the saints in the calendar to bear witness that he was a full man and had 'known his wife carnally on countless occasions'. Ripped from the arms of the child-wife he loved, he swore vengeance on the Borgias. But their power was too great. They forced him to sign a confession admitting his impotence and he fled Rome before anything worse could happen to him.

Although Lucrezia had not been averse to this first husband, she accepted the family decision without protest and retired to the convent of San Sisto on the Via Appia to enhance her virginal image in preparation for another marriage. When she left the convent the nuns were said to have been loath to see her go for she had turned the convent into a place of sophistication and fashionable pleasure.

Towards the end of February 1498 news spread through Rome that Lucrezia was pregnant. Her lover, it was said, was a Spanish gentleman at the Papal Court: Pedro Calderon, known generally as Perotto. A man of immense charm, he was certainly guilty of desiring her, if not actually seducing her. Cesare Borgia had Perotto thrown into prison and soon after his corpse was found in the river Tiber.

From this affair stemmed most of the stories of incest that hung like a foul miasma about the Borgias for ever after. Cesare, a dazzling man, handsome, hard and pitiless, certainly loved his sister with an intensity that seemed abnormal and could have been incestuous in motive although there is no evidence that her affection for him was of the same nature. Rumours began to spread that the child Lucrezia was said to be expecting was the result of incest. Sforza seized upon the gossip to get his own back and accused Lucrezia of sleeping not only with her brother but with her father, the Pope.

Whatever the truth – and Perotto was the most likely father – a child called Giovanni, who was later created Duke of Nepi, was born in Rome on March 1498. He grew up at Lucrezia's side but she always referred to him as her little brother. By others he was referred to enigmatically as 'The Roman Infante'. He remained a mystery.

The next match arranged for Lucrezia was, like the first, for political reasons. Alfonso, nephew of the King of Naples who created him Duke of Bisceglie for the alliance, was, however, of far more use to the Borgias than poor Sforza. Through him Cesare hoped to gain entrance by marriage to the house of Aragon.

All the omens were good. When Lucrezia first set eyes on the fair, incredibly good-looking Duke she was immediately won over. Although their marriage had been so coldly arranged, it was obviously going to be a love match. Cesare Borgia greeted him with signs of great friendship and when the wedding took place six days after his arrival in Rome, no expense was spared to make it an occasion of great splendour.

Alfonso promised to stay in Rome with Lucrezia for one year before carrying her off to his lands near the sea, and all seemed well until the blood-thirsty Cesare started his political intriguing once again. Before long he and the young bridegroom were at daggers drawn. Many in Rome saw the terrible signs of Cesare's jealousy and said prayers for the Duke of Bisceglie.

One evening Alfonso visited the Vatican. When he set out from there to make his way home to the Palace of Santa Maria, across the Piazza of St Peter's he was brutally attacked. His friends carried him home half dead with a split skull and terrible wounds to his body and legs. When Lucrezia saw him she nearly fainted. She nursed Alfonso back to health with great devotion but Cesare was determined to finish the job that had been so badly bungled.

One evening as Alfonso rested at home, a gang of ruffians broke into his room and one of them, a professional garrotter, killed him before he could cry for help. The affair marked a new phase in Cesare's career in ruthlessness and no one heeded his protests that the Duke of Bisceglie had threatened him.

Lucrezia was sent away from Rome to the Castle of Nepi where, for a time, she cried bitterly over the loss of her beautiful young husband. But she was a Borgia and in spite of her tenderness for the dead Alfonso, she dried her tears and waited to see what her father and brothers had in store for her next.

Recalled to the Vatican by her father, Lucrezia tried to amuse herself, in spite of being a widow. Lurid accounts were printed of the parties which Cesare gave to distract her. At one of these he was said to have strewn hot chestnuts over the floor of the Pope's apartment and forced naked courtesans to crawl along lighted candles to retrieve them. Other accounts of parties at which prizes were awarded in fertility contests and obscene theatricals were performed, reminded many people of earlier Roman orgies.

There is no record of Lucrezia ever taking part, however. Indeed about this time she began to be better known for her piety and gentleness.

She was about to be introduced to her third husband. The Borgias had chosen an alliance with the ancient and noble family of d'Este but negotiations had not gone as smoothly as they wished. Their prospective bridegroom, Alfonso d'Este, the Duke of Ferrara's son, balked at the prospect of taking to his bed a lady of such notoriety. He was also worried that he might suffer the same fate as her previous husband. His father, furious that his plans for the alliance were in jeopardy, warned his son that he would marry Lucrezia himself if necessary.

The two families argued and bargained and eventually the Pope settled a fabulous dowry on his daughter. Even so, it was only half of that demanded. Lucrezia was married for the third time in great splendour and at her wedding was seen to dance radiantly with the brother who had made her a widow.

She took leave of her father for the last time and set out with her new husband and a priceless trousseau including magnificent clothes, great works of art, jewellery and rare furniture to spend the rest of her days with the great Prince of Ferrara. He took her to the family's vast medieval castle at Vecchio where she continued to amaze him with her charm, grace and modesty.

For a time she continued to be a subject of gossip and speculation. Her name was linked with that of the poet, Pietro Bembo. Did she become his mistress or not? His poetry was widely believed to have been written in memory of the passionate hours he had spent in her arms. More dangerous was the friendship she cultivated with Ercole Strozzi, a fervent, elegant young poet who did not bother to hide his feelings for her.

There was a terrible scandal when Strozzi was found dead in the street, wrapped in a cloak, his body a mass of dagger wounds. Those who hated the very name of Borgia said she had organized the killing out of jealousy because the poet was about to take a wife. Others hinted that Strozzi knew too much and she had feared he might talk about the favours bestowed upon himself and Bembo by the Prince of Ferrara's wife.

Time passed, she became Duchess of Ferrara and poets and men of letters began to superimpose another image on Lucrezia, that of a supremely virtuous woman, flawless, perfect and angel of mercy. It was probably just as exaggerated as the one she had left behind in Rome.

All we do know for certain is that when she died in childbirth in June 1519 she was regarded with admiration and esteem by those who knew her. She was deeply mourned by the Duke of Ferrara who called her 'my dearest wife'.

Elisabeth Báthory (1561?–1614)

The Bloody Countess

Elisabeth Báthory, a Hungarian noblewoman sometimes referred to as Countess Nadasy, was undeniably
very wicked. Although beautiful and enjoying all the
trappings of belonging to a famous Transylvanian family, boredom with her life turned her first to sex with a
succession of lovers, then the practice of torture, and
finally an obsession with preventing herself from growing old by drinking or bathing in *human blood*. Assisted
by terrified accomplices, she slaughtered literally hundreds of innocent young serving girls for their lifeblood
– and for years was able to escape any kind of punishment because of her noble birth. **Peter Haining** re-
counts the gruesome history of Elisabeth Báthory, part
cannibal and part vampire . . .

At the beginning of the seventeenth century, sinister reports began to filter through the Carpathian mountains and across the lowlands of Hungary about the discovery of the bodies of dozens of young girls, all of whom appeared to have died in agony before their bodies had been callously dumped. But that in itself was not what most horrified the peasants who stumbled across the corpses in their woods and fields – it was the fact that each and every one had been drained of all its blood.

The area in which these grisly remains were found is, of course, famous today as the setting of Bram Stoker's classic novel *Dracula*, and such an outrage might easily be ascribed to his vampirism – if, that is, Count Dracula had been a real person and not a figment of his creator's imagination. In fact, the truth of this story is far more horrifying than any piece of fiction and exposed a human monster obsessed with a belief that blood was the elixir of youth and beauty. An obsession so strong that as many as 650 innocent young girls may have been slaughtered in the pursuit of these objectives.

The perpetrator of these gruesome crimes was no ordinary lunatic, however, but a famous society beauty and a member of one of the most aristocratic families in Europe, someone who would subsequently go down in history as 'a blood-thirsty and blood-sucking Godless woman caught in the act at Csejthe Castle,' to quote one report. Her name was Countess Elisabeth Báthory and according to at least one expert on the supernatural she has the dubious distinction of being 'probably the only reliably recorded instance of vampirism in the annals of Europe'.

The Countess, variously known as 'The Terrible Ogress' and 'The Tigress of Csejthe', developed her obsession with the blood of young virgins when still a young woman and pursued it with single-minded cruelty and gruesome ingenuity throughout the rest of her life. She slaughtered young girls without conscience and drained them so she could drink the blood, or alternatively use it to bathe in 'blood-baths', and thus preserve her looks. To some literary historians this vampire lady of the Carpathians was the real inspiration for Bram Stoker's novel.

The discovery of those pale and emaciated corpses in the year 1611 led to an official enquiry which soon tracked down the culprit to the residence of the Báthory family: the imposing Csejthe Castle situated in the Carpathian foothills. The scandal which resulted had such an impact on Hungarian society that a royal proclamation was handed down by King Matthias II that neither the Countess nor her crimes were ever to be mentioned in public. Indeed, it was to be almost 200 years before the full enormity of her crimes was to become generally known in Europe and elsewhere.

An Austrian scholar, Michael Wagener, was the first to assemble the facts about the life of the Bloody Countess in his book, *Beitrage zur philosophischen Anthropologie*, published in 1796. He was also the first to explain how her obsession had begun.

Elisabeth Báthory was thought to have been born in 1561 into a powerful, strongly Protestant, Hungarian family. Despite a strict upbringing, she quickly grew into a sexually adventurous girl with a streak of sadism in her character that developed rapidly once she had become a teenager. Perhaps already aware of her tendencies, Elisabeth's family arranged for her to be engaged at the tender age of eleven to the scion of another powerful family, Count Ferencz Nadasy. But this did nothing to inhibit her craving for peasant boys – and just before her fifteenth birthday she gave birth to a child, apparently fathered by one of these lads. A few months later, however, the infant was smuggled secretly out of the country and she was safely married to the Count at one of the biggest society weddings seen in the country for many years. Initially, says Michael Wagener, she tried to be a good wife to her new husband.

'Elisabeth was wont to dress well in order to please her husband and spent half the day over her toilet,' he states. 'Then on one occasion her chambermaid saw something wrong with her headdress, and as a recompense for observing it, received such a severe box on the ears that blood gushed from her nose and spurted on to her mistress's face. When the blood drops were washed off the Countess's face, her skin appeared much more beautiful: whiter and more transparent on the spots where the blood had been.

'Elisabeth therefore formed the resolution to bathe her face and her whole body in human blood so as to enhance her beauty. Two old women and a certain fellow called Ficzko assisted her in her undertaking. This monster used to kill her luckless victims, and one of the old women caught the blood in which Elisabeth would bathe at the hour of four in the morning. After the bath she appeared more beautiful than ever.'

In the years that followed, the Countess exercised her sexual and sadistic whims at every opportunity. She clearly enjoyed inflicting pain, and was merciless on any serving girl who displeased her. And to amuse herself during her husband's long absenses from the castle while furthering his distinguished career in the Hungarian army by successfully fighting the Turks, she conducted endless heterosexual and lesbian orgies at which perversions of all descriptions were not only permitted, but encouraged.

Nothing, it seemed, worried Elisabeth Báthory, or disturbed the cruel tenor of her life. Certainly not what she saw as her undisputed right as an aristocrat to do as she chose with peasant girls whom she probably did not even regard as human beings. Nor did such behaviour run contrary to her religious beliefs or her duty to her husband and family (she had four children to whom she was apparently devoted). Nothing, that is, except the fear of losing her beauty.

When Count Báthory died in 1604, worn out by the demands of his military campaigning, the first chill winds of ageing were beginning to blow around Elisabeth. Now aged forty-three, middle age was starting to appear in the form of tiny wrinkles around her mouth and eyes. Even her magnificent dresses and fabulous jewels could not hide every flaw. Yet still her appetite for sex and new pleasures was undiminished, and realising she could not do without the flattery and attention of men, she redoubled her efforts to preserve her looks and attract new suitors.

To satisfy her need for fresh blood with its supposed curative powers, the Countess demanded still greater numbers of pretty young girls to be brought to the castle, and her faithful procurers were sent ever further afield to recruit victims. Only those who had 'not yet tasted the pleasures of love' were to be recruited, she insisted. Quite why so many parents allowed their daughters to be taken away, when Elisabeth's fearsome reputation was already common gossip and disappearance followed disappearance, is one of the mysteries of this bloody saga. Fear of the Báthorys may well have been the spur, but the fact remains that at the peak of her obsession, the Countess was killing and draining the bodies of these girls at the rate of at least five a week.

'The unhappy girls who were lured to the castle under the promise that they were to be taken into service there were locked up in a cellar,' Michael Wagener states in his report. 'Elisabeth not infrequently tortured the victims herself; often she changed her clothes, which dripped with blood, and renewed her cruelties.'

The methods which the Countess used to drain the blood of her victims for her cosmetic needs were many and varied. One such method, reported in the later trial record, was to 'put a terrified naked girl in a narrow iron cage furnished with pointed nails turned inwards, hang it from the ceiling, and sit beneath it enjoying the rain of blood that came down.'

A still more gruesome method was a robot known as the Iron Maiden which had been designed to her specification by a German clock-maker and installed in the castle cellars.

'Shaped like a naked girl and covered with blonde hair and wearing red teeth torn from the mouth of some servant, the automaton also had red nipples and pubic hair,' says a contemporary report. 'It had eyes that opened and closed like an attractive doll and, when set in motion, would clutch anyone that came near it in a tight embrace and then transfix them with a series of sharp points that came out of the metal breasts. Other concealed spikes also pierced the victim's genitals. The blood of the girls ran down into a channel so that it could be collected, warmed over a fire, and then used for the Countess's bath.'

In her obsession to preserve her youth, Elisabeth would also drink blood from the wounds and burn blisters of girls who were tortured and dying. To satisfy her perverted nature she sometimes even forced her victims to eat the flesh of their predecessors.

According to the Reverend Janos Ponikenusz, the Lutheran pastor of Csejthe, who was one of those who took part in the downfall of the Countess: 'We have heard at Csejthe from the very mouths of girls who survived the torture that some of their fellow victims were forced to eat their own flesh roasted on the fire. The flesh of other girls was chopped up fine like mushrooms, cooked and flavoured, and given to young lads who did not know what they were eating.'

Occasionally Elisabeth herself tasted flesh. Dorottya Szentes, one of her accomplices, who also later gave evidence against her mistress, said:

'When she was not feeling well and did not have the strength to beat anyone, she would draw one of the serving maids suddenly to herself and bite a chunk of flesh from her cheeks and sink her teeth into her breast and shoulders. She would also stick needles into a girl's fingers and say, "If it hurts you, you famous whore, pull them out," but if the girl dared to draw the needles out, her ladyship ordered her to be beaten and her fingers slashed with razors.'

Despite all her endeavours and the ever increasing toll of the murdered girls, Elisabeth could do nothing to halt the process of ageing. She was seemingly on the point of despair when one of her accomplices, a woman named Erzsi Majorova who had apparently provided her with a number of useful potions, suggested that it was not the blood which was failing her, but the *type* she was using. The blood of peasant girls could not possibly have the properties she needed: only the 'blue blood' of those of noble birth had the power to regenerate her beauty.

'This was not quite so easy,' Reay Tannahill, a social historian who has made a study of cannibalism in her book *Flesh and Blood* (1975), states, 'but in the winter of 1609, with macabre humour, the Countess arranged to accept twenty-five daughters of the minor nobility whom she was prepared to instruct in the "social graces". It was the beginning of the end. Explaining away the deaths or disappearances of numerous well-born girls was very different from merely shrugging off the fate of peasants. And the Countess made another disastrous mistake. She had the bodies of four naked girls tossed over the ramparts one winter night when wolves were on the prowl, and the villagers found them before the wolves did.'

The murmurs of discontent from those living in the surrounding countryside now grew to a roar of anger. At last a few brave souls had the courage to stand up to the Countess and report what was going on to the authorities in Vienna. The sheer volume of unexplained deaths in the neighbourhood and the continuing gossip of terrible screams being heard from the cellars of the castle night after night gradually reached the ears of the King. Then Pastor Poni-kenusz smuggled to court a secret message in which he listed in detail the horrors he knew had been committed by Elisabeth and this finally prompted action.

On 3 December 1610, Count Gyorsy Thurzo, the governor of the province, who was also Elisabeth's cousin, set out with a party of soldiers, *gendarmes* and the village priest to raid the castle and arrest everybody in it. According to later reports, the men walked in to find themselves in the midst of an orgy of blood.

In the main hall, they found the Countess herself *in flagrante delicto* with two men. Nearby was the dead body of a girl drained of blood; another still alive whose body had been pierced with tiny holes; and a third evidently still being tortured. In the dungeons and cellars below they came across a number of other girls, some of whose bodies had already been pierced and – in the words of one of the rescuers – 'milked of their blood'. There were others still unharmed, 'plump, well-fed and like well-kept cattle in their stalls'. The dead bodies of fifty more were subsequently discovered in the most rudimentary graves.

The Countess herself arrogantly denied any knowledge of the deaths – and when her closest accomplices confessed their parts in the reign of bloodshed in the hope of saving their necks, she firmly laid the blame for any atrocities on them. As a member of the Hungarian nobility, she did not expect to be asked to account for any of her actions. Indeed, such were the laws of Hungary at that time that it would have taken an Act of Parliament to force her into any court of law.

As it was, the servants who had served her evil purpose were tried in the court of the nearby small market town of Bicse in January 1611 and all were ordered to be put to death. But Elisabeth did not escape retribution of a sort. King Matthias, being completely satisfied of her guilt though unable to exercise the death penalty, handed out the only appropriate sentence he could think of. She was to be walled up in Csejthe Castle for the rest of her life 'to repent her bestial ways'.

Subsequent reports state that the Countess was immured in a small room with the windows and door bricked over and only a hatch for food linking her to the outside world. For three and a half years Elisabeth Báthory lived almost literally the existence of the 'vampire lady' that history now calls her – locked in the icy tomb of her castle. She died there on 14 August 1614.

For years after her death, the Castle remained empty – four gibbets at each corner a constant reminder to everyone who passed of the horrors which had been perpetrated within. Then, one night in the eighteenth century, in a scene reminiscent of those which so regularly form the climax of horror movies, it was struck by lightning and burned to the ground. Although no trace remains today, the name of Elisabeth Báthory, the 'Bloody Countess' is still spoken of in whispers and with a shudder of disgust by those who live in the bleak Carpathian mountains . . .

Mary Frith (1584–1659)

Moll Cutpurse –
The First Highwaywoman

Mary Frith, who is better known to posterity as 'Moll
Cutpurse', stole a lead on all the famous highwaymen of
history by being the first person to take up pistols and
rob travellers on the roads of southern England. Born in
London, she was a tough, rebellious girl who graduated
easily into the city's underworld of crime and is described in one account as a 'bully, pick-purse, receiver,
forger and fortune teller [sic].' She also carried a sword
and often dressed like a man. Later Mary – aka 'Moll
Cutpurse' after her dexterity at picking pockets – became the head of a gang of thieves, and often flaunted
her popularity by parading around the capital. Such,
indeed, was her fame and eccentricity that she was
featured in a popular stage drama, wrote her autobiography and lived unscathed to the ripe old age of
seventy-five! Her larger-than-life story is recounted
by **Philippa Waring**.

In the early years of the seventeenth century a familiar sight on the streets of Holborn and Fleet Street was a flamboyant figure known as Moll Cutpurse, who dressed in men's clothing and invariably had a tobacco-pipe stuck rakishly in her mouth. As outlandish in her way as a modern punk, Moll turned many heads as she strode about the locality dressed in a pointed hat covering her dark, curly locks, a black cloak over a colourful doublet and hose, and with a sword hanging by her side. Tall of stature, with challenging blue eyes, she appealed as strongly, sexually, to women as to men, and rejoiced in the nickname public acclaim had given her, the 'Roaring Girl'.

Moll Cutpurse was also, the evidence suggests, the very first highwayman – not to mention 'The Mother of Highwaywomen', to quote the social historian Patrick Pringle. Though rumour and legend have done much to elaborate or alter many of the facts of this unique woman's life, research does lead to the conclusion that she highlighted her career of crime by appearing as a robber on the roads of London and was, at the very least, a contemporary of the first highwaymen if not their actual predecessor. Records also indicate that she claimed for herself the accolade of being the first female smoker!

Moll certainly possessed the capability to be a successful highwaywoman. She was a skilful horsewoman, knew the highways and byways of London and its suburbs intimately, and was a fine shot with a pistol. From childhood she had also developed a talent second to none at relieving the gentry of London of any valuables they might carry about their persons. Even when challenged by someone in authority it was said she spoke with the commanding tone of a general – although she was also perfectly capable of swearing like a trooper!

Small wonder, then, that a contemporary account says of her: 'There's a wench called Moll, mad Moll or Merry Moll – a creature so strange in quality a whole city takes note of her name and person!' (Interestingly, among those who 'took note of her' was a playwright named Shakespeare, who alluded to her in his play *Twelfth Night*, through Sir Toby Belch's reference to things being hid 'like Mistress Mall's picture'.)

Re-examining today the contemporary documents and accounts of the life of Moll Cutpurse produces a number of interesting facts which many of the later versions have avoided or glossed over – the writers probably being restrained from using the information by the moral attitudes of their times.

Some early sources, for instance, declare that Moll's neighbours believed she was a hermaphrodite – and even when the contrary was reported after her death, the belief nevertheless persisted in both story and ballad. In fact, she was bisexual, as happy to go to bed with women as men, and is quoted on this very subject by the Jacobean playwright Thomas Middleton, who with Thomas Dekker created a highly successful play, *The Roaring Girl* while the subject was still very much alive:

'I have no humour to marry,' Moll told the writer, 'for I love to lie a' both sides a'th'bed . . . I have the head of myself and am man enough for any woman.'

Her fondness for men's clothing should not, though, be seen as just an element of her sexual proclivities: disguise undoubtedly helped her in her criminal exploits, and by employing more than the simple face mask (which became the traditional sign of the highwayman), she used a full change into a dress to throw pursuers off her trail. It seems highly likely, too, that by impersonating a man, she ensured that many of her crimes were mistakenly ascribed to others, thereby making it impossible now, unfortunately, to estimate the number of robberies she actually committed.

Some authorities have stated that Moll was an ugly woman, dirty and mean-spirited, and more interested in masculine than feminine pursuits. This, however, hardly coincides with Middleton's description of her as a 'handsome and graceful woman', kind-hearted and generous in her dealings with other criminals; a woman who covered the walls of her house with looking-glasses and amused herself with lovers of both sexes – many of whom were seemingly unaware of her double life. This merely seems to me to confirm her mastery of disguise and deception!

Another claim, that she was really no more than a common pickpocket – hence her name – and only prospered through trading in the ill-gotten gains of other highway robbers – is also refuted by the first biographer of highwaymen, Captain Alexander Smith, who wrote in his now rare work, *A Complete History of the Most Notorious Highwayman* (1719), completed less than a hundred years after the event:

A long time had Moll Cutpurse robbed on the road, but at last robbing General Fairfax of 250 Jacobuses [gold coins struck during the reign of James I and variously worth between 50 and 125 pence] on Hounslow Heath, whom she shot through the arm in opposing her, a close pursuit was made after her by some Parliamentarian officers. Her horse failing her at Turnham Green they there apprehended her and carried her to Newgate, after which she was condemned; but she procured her pardon by giving her adversary £2,000. Now Moll being frightened by this disaster, she left off going on the highway any more and took a house within two doors of the Globe Tavern in Fleet Street where she turned fence, a buyer of stolen goods, by which occupation she got a great deal of money. Her reputation soon grew, the more so when tobacco became a great mode and she being mightily taken with the pastime of smoking, because of its singularity and that no woman ever smoked before her, though a great many of the sex since have followed her example.

Even in this terse account, it is not difficult to appreciate that Moll Cutpurse was obviously an extraordinary woman whose influence on the legend of the English highwayman is both important and enduring, and deserves further investigation. All the more so, I believe, in the light of another comment by a respected historian, Christopher Hibbert, who wrote in *Highwaymen* (1967), 'As a highwaywoman she seems, indeed, to have been more successful than any of her eighteenth-century male successors'.

The first interesting fact to be gleaned about Moll Cutpurse is that this was not her real name at all. She was born Mary Frith in the year 1584, the daughter of a shoemaker who carried out his trade in Aldersgate Street, in the Barbican district of London. According to a little booklet, *The Life and Death of Mrs. Mary Frith, Commonly Called Moll Cutpurse*, published in 1662 'for the Delight and Recreation of all Merry Disposed Persons', the child grew up as a 'very tomrig and rumpscuttle' – in other words, a tomboy. The anonymous work also reports that Mary was born with her fists tightly clenched, 'a sure sign of a wild and adventurous nature'.

Mary was an only child, and, despite her unruly disposition, was spoiled and indulged by her doting parents. She was given a good education and taught to ride, but soon found the pursuits of the opposite sex more interesting than her own and began falling into bad company. Before she had entered her teens she was frequenting bear-baitings and wrestling matches and proving more than a match for any young man who challenged her right to be in such places. 'She worsted many a pretty fellow in fair fight with a quarterstaff', according to the above account.

Mr Frith's original plan to put his rebellious daughter into domestic service was abandoned as her exploits about London grew wilder, and for a time he thought of agreeing to her demands to have 'a man's job' by apprenticing her to a saddler. Instead, though, he listened to the advice of his brother, a minister of the church, who maintained that the only cure for the troublesome girl would be to pack her off to America to work on a plantation! Mary was, in fact, actually put on board a merchant ship at Gravesend bound for New England, but somehow managed to jump overboard before the vessel sailed and swim to shore. From this moment, she was a free spirit determined to follow her own nature and inclinations.

Back in London, Mary naturally enough fell into a life of

crime to support herself, and, by the turn of the century, had become 'distinguished in the different characters of bully, prostitute, procuress, fortune-teller, thief, pickpocket, and receiver of stolen goods', to quote *The Life and Death*. Because of the generally accepted role of women at this time as servant or mother, Mary's deliberate decision to wear male clothing to enhance the impact of her height, as well as her robust language earned her her sobriquet, 'roaring', which was a less-than-flattering adjective for a woman of the era.

Quite when this 'lusty and sturdy wench', as Captain Alexander Smith called her, first took to robbing travellers on the highway is difficult to establish precisely; but certainly she had a reputation as a skilled thief and pick-pocket by the time she was fifteen, and was working in company with a gang who frequented the bear garden in Southwark. Her accomplices were not, it seems, altogether trustworthy, for male envy at her exploits soon led to whispers about her crimes reaching the authorities. A series of arrests followed which enraged Mary, now becoming widely known as 'Moll Cutpurse', and she decided that a solitary career in crime might carry fewer risks. Captain Smith has again recorded the relevant facts:

> But having been very often in Old Bridewell, the Compters and Newgate for her irregular practices, and burned in the hand four times, Moll left off this petty sort of theft and went on the highway, committing many great robberies, but all of them on the Roundheads or rebels that fomented the Civil War against Charles I.

Moll, with her skill as a rider, her ability to handle fire-arms, plus her mastery of disguise, was well-enough armed to confront and rob those foolish enough to travel the roads about London without protection. Early in her career, she found that the best pickings were to be had in the vicinity of Hounslow Heath, which was later to become such a popular spot with other highwaymen.

It was, though, to be some years before these audacious

robberies were ascribed to Moll, as all her victims swore they had been taken by a man. And, doubtless, even those who suspected the sex of the person behind the pistols were reluctant to say so for fear of ridicule at being robbed by a woman!

What undoubtedly cemented the fame of Moll Cutpurse was the play by Middleton and Dekker, *The Roaring Girl*, which was first performed in 1611 at the Fortune Theatre, and proved a huge success. The two dramatists had judged well the public interest in this larger-than-life figure in men's clothes who always seemed one step ahead of the law. Indeed, no member of the audience was left in any doubt that the 'heroine' was the self-same Moll who was currently reigning as the queen of the London underworld.

'She's the spirit of four great parishes', one character in the play declares, 'and a voice that will drown all the city. Methinks a brave captain might get all his soldiers upon her and never hold her.'

Another agrees with this verdict: ' 'Tis the maddest fantasticalest girl! I never knew so much flesh and so much nimbleness put together.'

What makes this play so valuable in any study of Moll Cutpurse's life is not just the fact that Middleton and Dekker were writing about a contemporary person, but that Dekker had, like Middleton, met the woman and caroused with her in the Fleet Street taverns which she haunted. The words which he puts in her mouth ring with the sound of authenticity.

'I know more laws', she declares at one point as she slips into the slang language, or cant, of the London underworld:

Of cheaters, lifters, nips, foists, puggards, curbers,
With all the devil's black-guard, than it's fit,
Should be discover'd to a noble wit.
I know they have their orders, offices,
Circuits, and circles, unto which they're bound,
To raise their own damnation in.

And, proud of her own reputation, Moll adds:

Condemn me? Troth, and you should, sir,
I'd make you seek out one to hang in my place:
I'd give you the slip at the gallows and cozen the people!

Not everyone admired Moll Cutpurse, however, for there
were those who objected to the way she cocked a snook at the
law and affronted decent society by dressing in men's clothes.
Indeed, action was taken after she had ridden across London
from Charing Cross to Shoreditch in a particularly outlandish set of clothes, waving a banner and blowing a trumpet, to
win a twenty-pound bet. For this she was arrested. The 1662
pamphlet 'quotes' the lady herself on this incident:

Some promoting Apparitor, set on by an adversary of
mine, whom I could never punctually know, cited me to
appear in the Court of the Arches, where was an Accusation exhibited against me for wearing indecent and manly
apparel. I was advised by my Proctor to demur to the
Jurisdiction of the Court, as for a Crime, if such, not
cognizable there or elsewhere; but he did it to spin out
my Cause, and get my Money; for in the conclusion I
was sentenced there to stand and do Penance in a White
Sheet at Paul's Cross, during morning Sermon on a
Sunday.

Swallowing her anger at this deception, Moll performed
her sentence – though another report claims that the tears she
shed were those of a 'maudlin drunk, it being discovered she
had tipple'd of three quarts of sack (six pints) before she came
to her penance'. Within hours, however, bold as ever, she was
back on the streets of Holborn in full male regalia and ready
to continue her career of crime.

Records indicate that Moll's most famous act of highway
robbery was the attack on Oliver Cromwell's man, General
Fairfax, on Hounslow Heath, which ended disastrously when
her horse went lame at Turnham Green and she was cap-

tured. Yet she had the money to buy her freedom – any prisoner who had not committed treason or murder could secure their release for a minimum of £500, popular legend had it – and thereafter she settled for a quiet life in a house in Fleet Street, almost opposite Shoe Lane and Salisbury Court. Here she became far-famed as the best fence (receiver of stolen goods) in London: so well known, in fact, that those who lost property to the depredations of pick-pockets or highwaymen soon took to visiting Moll's establishment, for there was every chance of their valuables turning up there and being readily redeemable for a consideration. As Charles G. Harper has explained in his important work, *Half-Hours With The Highwaymen* (1908):

> In those halcyon days of the receivers of stolen property, before the evil career of Jonathan Wild had caused an Act of Parliament to be passed, dealing with them on the same footing as the actual thieves, much was done in the way of ransom and ready brokerage, and, so long as it was done with discretion, with advantage to all concerned. The owners got their own again, with the expenditure of a comparatively trifling sum, the gang carried on their operations with a large degree of security, and the wily Moll made an excellent income. She was witty and original, and – such was the spirit of the age – she became rather the fashion among the riotous young blades of town, who were then 'seeing life'. The highwaymen knew her well, and resorted to her house when they had taken watches and jewellery they could not themselves, without the gravest risk, endeavour to sell. They trusted her, and the public, coming to redeem the articles, did the same; and indeed, as intermediary between losers and finders, she was honesty itself: absolutely beyond suspicion.

An interesting rumour that developed about Moll at this time – which she did nothing to dispel – suggested that her success at being able to recover stolen property was due to the fact that she owned a pair of magic glasses which enabled

her to 'see' where the missing valuables were and institute
their immediate recovery with the aid of her associates!

Captain Alexander Smith has also explained how Moll
pursued her sexual inclinations. He writes:

> In order to get money she would stick out to bawd for
> either men or women, insomuch that her house became
> a double temple for Priapus and Venus, frequented by
> votaries of both sorts; who, being generous to her
> labour, their desires were favourably accommodated
> with expedition, while she lingered with others, delaying
> their impatience by laying before them the difficult but
> certain attainment of their wishes. This served as a spur
> to the dullness of their purses, for the lady Pecunia and
> she kept the same pace; but still in the end she did the
> feat.

It seems likely that Moll provided refuge for a number of
highwaymen when the authorities were close on their trail.
As an ardent Royalist, she had little time for Cromwell's men
and during the years of the Commonwealth she happily
encouraged those who wished to persecute or rob the hated
oppressors.

Indeed, it is true to say that Moll Cutpurse's dearest wish
was to live long enough to see the restoration of the monarchy, and although her last years were spent in the comfort
provided by her trade in stolen property, she finally died of
the unromantic disease of dropsy at the fine old age of
seventy-five on 26 July 1659 – just one year before the return
of Charles II. She was buried in St Bride's churchyard,
appropriately in one of the suits of men's clothing that she
had worn during her life. Somewhat surprisingly, though,
considering all the money she had made as a highwaywoman
and fence, Moll left just £100 – of which twenty pounds, she
declared in her will, was to be kept for her friends and
associates to drink the health of the king when he was once
again on the throne.

With the passing of the 'Roaring Girl', highway robbery

may have lost its 'mother', but the 'sons' she left behind were already cutting a swath of robbery – around the outskirts of London and across parts of the English countryside – that history would never forget.

Mary Read (1682–1720)
& Anne Bonney (?–c.1720)

The Unique Pirate Duo

Mary Read and Anne Bonney were two headstrong, adventurous young women who infiltrated the all-male world of pirates around the turn of the eighteenth century and left an indelible mark on the history of buccaneering. Anne, the illegitimate daughter of an Irish lawyer, hoped to turn her marriage to a penniless seaman into a fortune from trading with privateers, but instead became the mistress of the infamous pirate, Captain 'Calico Jack' Rackham. Not long afterwards the two were joined by Mary Read, the daughter of a sea captain, who had been a 'powder monkey' on a warship before turning privateer. Almost immediately the two women became great friends and there have been suggestions that they might have been lovers as well. Their extraordinary union in crime is recounted here by **Stephanie Brush**.

As closely as historians can determine, the story started in an English port town in the 1680s when a comely, 'young and airy' sea wife gave birth to a robust baby girl. The mother's joy was marred by the somewhat glaring fact that her husband had been away at sea for more than two years. But she displayed a kind of ghoulish resourcefulness in dealing with the problem. Her legitimate baby son had recently died, and rather than report the death to kin, she dressed young Mary in the boy's clothes and hoped that no one would notice the deception.

At around the same time, an attorney of Cork, Ireland, was busy fathering a bastard daughter by his faithful serving maid (his wife had left him years before, for reasons not unrelated to this very event). With his legal practice to consider, the father dressed his daughter in boy's clothes and circulated the story that young Anne was the 'son' of friends and would someday be apprenticed to him to learn the legal business.

Perhaps it was only coincidence: young girls of the seventeenth century with a past of forcible transvestism could very possibly have survived the 'strain' and gone on to become wives or mothers or countesses or nuns. These two didn't. These two became pirates.

Savage pirates of the bounding main were Anne Bonney and Mary Read . . . and in that day, if you were a seafarer, you thought twice before setting sail with anything more valuable than library paste in the hold of your ship. Pirates meant business. They cut off your hands and feet. Sometimes they cut off your ears and nose, if they didn't like you. Or, they cut off your lips and broiled them in front of your eyes. And if they were of a merciful disposition, they then shot you in the head before leaving you for the flies. Pirates raped and they plundered, and their loyalty wasn't worth a brass farthing. They had scurvy, cholera, dysentery, rats, lice, maggots, and positively wretched manners. But Mary Read and Anne Bonney were the only two pirates history knows anything about who had breasts.

Puzzled historians have speculated that they were follow-

ing some obscure internal 'Robin Hood' code of ethics in
their strange choice of career. This is not untrue. They stole
from the rich, and they were their own favourite charity. It
was also said that they joined ship in order to be with
seafaring lovers, and this is also true. Both women were
devoutly heterosexual, and, in fact, had no disposition whatever for remaining chaste. In the end, however, their motivations were no more complex than this: they were partial to
blood.

In actuality, Mary Read's childhood was not in the least
unhappy. She never missed the trappings of little-girlhood.
Military life fascinated her. At an undetermined but tender
age, she left home and joined on as a 'footboy' on a warship,
then graduated to the rank of cadet in a land regiment. All
accounts profess that 'she behaved herself with a great deal of
bravery.' No human enemy ever got the better of her, but
biology did: during a period of exemplary service with the
English cavalry, Read's superiors began to notice that her
behavior was somewhat erratic, and it was feared that she was
going insane. In fact, she was not insane at all. She was in
love – with one of her messmates in the regiment. She finally
gathered the courage to inform the fellow to his face, hastily
proving the truth of her gender; and fortune, for a while,
smiled on both of them. They became engaged. The officers
of the regiment were entranced with the idea of 'two troopers
marrying each other' and 'made a great noise', pooling their
funds so that the two lovers could have a sound future – as
tavern keepers – together. Mary even took the plunge and
dressed in women's clothes for the ceremony.

We'll never know how domestic life would have suited her.
Her husband died soon after the marriage. Even more irk-
some to Mary was the fact that she could no longer follow her
chosen profession of soldier, because, for some unfathomable
reason, there weren't any wars going on. Luckily for Mary, in
those days the option of buccaneering loomed tantalizingly in
front of any able-bodied young soul with a purse to fill and a
good hand at the cutlass. There were actually two kinds of
pirates: the ones who made a lot of money, and the ones who

made great, filthy, heaping gobs of it. The ones who made
heaping gobs – the privateers – worked for the English
government. It was their job to patrol the seas: to see who
was copping the most plunder in the New World, and to
generally make life hell for the Spanish – which usually
amounted to the same thing. Sometime between 1700 and
1720, Mary signed on with the crew of Captain John 'Calico
Jack' Rackham, who had a very tidy little privateering racket
going. She'd finally found her niche. And it was aboard
Rackham's ship that Read was to meet her great friend and
co-buccaneer, Anne Bonney.

By the time Bonney was twelve years old, her fits of
passion were already somewhat legendary. 'Someone' handy
with a knife had dispensed with a servant girl after the girl
and Anne had quarrelled; Anne's alibi remained suspiciously
thin. It is fact that when a local youth tried to force her
maidenhood, she pounded his head into a bloody mess. Her
shiftless temperament took her to the Carolinas and the West
Indies. She married, left her husband, who 'wasn't worth a
groat anyway', and bounced about the West Indies for a time
'seeking her fortune', dressed as a man all the while. Well,
almost all. She bore a child in Cuba. The father of the child
was the very same Calico Jack Rackham. Having little interest in maternity, Bonney reassumed her masculine guise and
ran away with him to sea.

By the time Mary Read signed on with Calico Jack's crew,
Anne Bonney was already a hardened seafarer, with a hopeless passion for men. Bonney took one look at the strapping
new crew member and made a pass at 'him'. It was all right,
Bonney assured Read, because, what luck – Bonney was a
woman!

'A woman, eh?' said Read, because boy, did *she* have a
surprise for Bonney.

The two became fast friends, after quickly briefing poor
jealous Calico Jack, who had threatened to cut Bonney's new
companion's throat.

It seems incredible, but Calico Jack's crew never caught on
to the masquerade. In fact, they were a pack of lily-livers

when up against Read and Bonney's fighting style. Any kind of cowardice sent Mary Read into a towering rage. Whenever her ship was boarded, and the crew refused to come up on deck and fight, she'd fire her own pistols down into the hold to galvanize them into action. Fairly frequently, she'd kill one or two of them, but she thought it a small price to pay. Jack Rackham used to marvel that none amongst his crew 'were more resolute, or ready to board or undertake any thing that was hazardous', than Mary Read and Anne Bonney. If it ever happened – and apparently it often did – that either woman grew to fancy a crew member in *that* sort of way, she would come swooping down during skirmishes, sparing the object of her affection the dicey, messy task of having to save his own life. She would fight duels for him, if need be. In only one instance was Mary Read unable to control herself; she confided her gender to one such object of affection by (as he later confessed) 'carelessly shewing her breasts, which were very white'.

Read and Bonney were incontrovertibly good at being pirates, although we must reserve the judgment that they were *great* pirates. *Great* pirates, like great con artists and Mafiosi, don't get caught. Read and Bonney did. When piracy crack-downs finally came about in the 1720s, and Rackham's crew was captured and brought to trial, all defendants were requested to step forward and give reason why the sentence of death should not be passed upon them.

'My Lord,' said Read and Bonney, in what amounted to one of the most surprising sexual trump cards ever played, 'we plead our bellies'. And the court of the day was powerless, faced with the fact that two of the fiercest sea dogs ever captured and brought to justice were each four months pregnant. They had Calico Jack, bless his heart, to thank for that, but he was hanged anyway.

Charlotte Corday (1768–93)

The Angel of
the Assassination

Charlotte Corday was the daughter of an impoverished French aristocrat who became convinced she had a 'heroic destiny' to rid the nation of the revolutionary politician Jean-Paul Marat. A reserved but nonetheless ambitious woman, she came to regard Marat as a regicidal and murderous demagogue. Her mission to Paris, where she gained access to the politician and stabbed him while he was in his bath, has become one of the most dramatic and defining moments in history, subsequently earning Charlotte the epithet of 'The Angel of the Assassination'. **Margaret Goldsmith** examines the life and motivations of this complex woman with great candour.

Charlotte Corday – Marie Anne Charlotte de Corday d'Ar-
mont before she became plain Citizen Corday – was born on
27 July, 1768. She has often been idealized by biographers,
because many of them have not expected women to think
before they act, especially if they were young and very
beautiful. 'History', Carlyle writes of Charlotte Corday, 'will
look fixedly at this one fair Apparition of Charlotte Corday;
will note whither Charlotte moves, how the little Life burns
forth so radiant, then vanishes swallowed by the night.' And
Lamartine, who idealizes Charlotte Corday in his *History of
the Girondists*, defends her by saying that 'where there is
murder, history cannot approve; where there is heroism,
history dares not condemn.'

Charlotte, as these passages indicate, has frequently been
judged sentimentally rather than historically. Her tragic
death has made even some serious writers assume a Scar-
let-Pimpernel attitude towards the role she played in the
French Revolution. She, with other women of the past, has
been considered a great figure, because she gave everything
she had, including her own life, for the cause in which she so
fervently believed.

Her case shows how history has been more critical of men
than of women. The cause for which women died is often put
gallantly aside; the question is evaded whether their personal
and heroic sacrifices did not reflect a lack of brains; whether,
in fact, by acting emotionally and not rationally, they did not
harm their particular cause more than they helped it.

Men, on the other hand, have usually been considered
great only if they combined brains with character, determination, and far-sightedness, and if, apart from their fanaticism, they were rational human beings or original thinkers.
In history's judgment of men, courage has not been enough,
while young women like Charlotte Corday achieve lasting
fame by one outstanding act of bravery.

Charlotte herself left history no doubt about her beauty.
Her last request in prison before her death was that an artist
be sent to paint her portrait. She was a strong woman with a
beautiful complexion; her hair was brown and curly, and her

face a 'perfect oval'. She had clear greyish-blue eyes, long lashes, and well-shaped eyebrows. Her chin and nose were strong, but her full lips did not look like those of a fanatic. The most attractive thing about her seems to have been her voice, which left an unforgettable impression on every one who had known or heard her.

Her contemporaries report that, despite her beauty, she lacked self-assurance. She carried herself badly, and except in her great moments she held her head so low that her chin almost touched her chest. She appeared to be vaguely ashamed of something. She blushed at the slightest provocation, and her little vanities must have been a reaction to this extreme self-consciousness. When she went out among people, she dressed with the greatest care; perhaps she was seeking moral support from a well-groomed appearance. Before she set out for Paris on the journey from which she knew she would never return, she bought a pair of smart high-heeled shoes; and in prison she prepared for her execution by throwing away her ordinary hat and making a white Normandy cap, so that she should walk up to the guillotine as 'the woman from Normandy'. She gave everything she had, and with the utmost courage, to the demands of the moment as she understood them, but she never quite forgot the impression she would make on posterity.

By temperament she would never have grasped at great happiness, for she was essentially a woman who passionately desired above all to sacrifice herself, who longed to suffer so that the misery of others might be relieved. She was, in fact, the stuff of which willing martyrs have been made at any period of history. Martyrdom, Bernard Shaw once wrote in another connection, is 'the only way you can become famous without ability'.

Even had she longed for a gay, care-free existence, she would have found little happiness in her short life. In her early childhood Charlotte never knew a permanent home. She was a poor relation, frequently moved from one environment to another. Perhaps this is one reason why her mental processes remained jerky and confused to the end.

Her father was an impecunious landowner in Saint-Satur-
in-des-Ligneries in Normandy. He was one of those vaguely
liberal aristocrats of the pre-Revolutionary era, who read the
Encyclopædists, and went so far as to publish a pamphlet
against the rights of primogeniture, but who remained a
staunch Royalist at heart. Monsieur de Corday had a passion
for helping the poor. He gave so much money and human
kindness to the villagers living on his small estate Le Ronceray that little was left of either for his own children. He was
extremely proud of his wife's family – she was a direct
descendant of Corneille's younger sister – but this did not
prevent him from carrying on continuous lawsuits with his
wife's brothers. His legal activities no doubt gave him the
feeling that he was doing something to provide for his
growing family.

Finally, Monsieur Corday's children, whose mother seems
to have been rather a shadowy figure, were sent to the homes
of wealthier relatives. This happened before Charlotte was
six years old. She might have developed more naturally,
become less exalted and excitable, if she had stayed longer
in the peaceful country atmosphere at Le Ronceray. Until
her death, however, it never occurred to her that perhaps her
father should have been a more efficient provider, that
perhaps he had not been quite fair to his children. On the
contrary, even as a very small child she shared his passion for
indiscriminate giving. Though she saw her father relatively
little as she grew older, and when, years later, she lived with
him again for a short time, she disagreed with him politically,
she always felt the utmost respect for him. He represented
male authority, and though Charlotte achieved such fame in
the French Revolution, she was never a real revolutionary,
and much less a rebel. 'Forgive me, my dear papa,' she wrote
to her father before her death, 'for having disposed of my life
without your permission'.

From the country life at Le Ronceray Charlotte was moved
abruptly into an intellectual atmosphere. Her uncle, the
Abbé de Corday, who was the priest in the village of Vicques,
in Falaise, offered to take one of his brother's children into

his home. The priest taught Charlotte how to read from a cherished old volume of Corneille, so that she should learn her letters and respect for her family at the same time. She soon became a tremendous reader, and *Polyeucte* and *Le Cid* early gave her ideas of a somewhat pompous heroism.

She was growing pathetically serious and self-controlled beyond her years. Fits of spasmodic gaiety were followed by restrained severity. She had no companions of her own age; she never learned how to play, how to abandon herself to the joy of living. Her object in life, even at this youthful age, was to help others, to live with a purpose. Yet she never impresses one as a prig, but rather as a child who was forced into maturity. The years she spent with her uncle began to mould her into the woman, who later wrote with the utmost sincerity that her life had meant nothing to her whatsoever, 'except as a means of being useful'.

The secluded life at the vicarage caused her to regard others, who enjoyed themselves, with suspicion. The tales she heard of the pleasure-loving members of her own class would have made any serious child wonder to what this frenzy for enjoyment might lead. 'Our nation', she once wrote in her usual exalted style, 'is too light, too trifling; it needs retempering, regenerating; it needs to seek in mistakes of the past the traditions of the great and the true, the beautiful and the noble; to forget all frivolities which cause the corruption and degeneration of a people.'

In view of her uncle's firm though kindly influence, it is perhaps surprising that Charlotte's inborn fanaticism did not turn to religion, the most obvious outlet for her burning wish to contribute towards the salvation of the world. There were brief periods in her life when she wanted, passionately, to take the veil, but these moods soon passed. While she was still a child she refused to accept the doctrines of the Church unquestioningly, and the Abbé de Corday complained that she 'disputed everything inch by inch, and never gave in'.

She was soon to be moved into other religious surroundings. In 1782 her father left the country and took his family to Caen, where, so he felt, he could conduct his lawsuit against his brothers-in-law more efficiently. Existence in the town, however, was harsh; there were no grateful villagers to feed his self-regard. Apart from his financial struggle, Monsieur de Corday was made unhappy by the death of his wife and his eldest child during the first few months he spent at Caen. Charlotte, whom he had sent for as soon as he left Le Ronceray, and her elder sister Eleanore, a hunchback, kept house as best they could, and tried valiantly to keep the family together.

This time another relative, Madame de Louvagny, came to the rescue. She was a nun at the Abbaye-aux-Dames Convent at Caen, and she had heard of Monsieur de Corday's distress. This convent school, a modern establishment, was attended by the daughters of many of the French intellectual women of the eighteenth century. As a rule, boarders were not accepted, but Madame de Louvagny persuaded Madame de Belzunce, the Mother Superior, and her chief assistant, Madame de Pontecoulant, to give Charlotte and Eleanore a home. Charlotte did secretarial work for Madame de Belzunce and performed certain household duties. She made herself extremely useful. She was a poor relation no longer; at last she was independent, she was paying for her home and her education.

At the Abbaye-aux-Dames Charlotte was as happy as a young woman of her temperament could ever have been. She was liked and appreciated by every one at the convent. For the first time in her life she had friends, and she became deeply attached to Alexandrine de Forbin. She went regularly with the nuns to visit and help the poor of the town; she studied and read. She learned drawing and music, and, as one of her nineteenth-century biographers has expressed it, 'she became an accomplished artist both in crayons and embroidery'.

She was not always happy, however, for her adolescence brought with it attacks of morbid depression. She was often haunted by a tormenting fear of death. She was, in fact; at times so frightened of dying that speculations concerning her own future death developed into an unhealthy preoccupation.

For weeks at a time she would successfully repress these terrors. In other moods, her friends at the Abbaye-des-Dames noticed her 'dreamy melancholy', her introspection, and her curious detachment from the problems of everyday life. Her obvious instability was not, however, given much serious thought, for, as a rule, she appeared busy and contented, fully occupied with her work and reading and with new ideas.

Democracy was in the air, and politics were freely discussed at the convent. A new and better world, passionately desired by theoretical young humanitarians like Charlotte, seemed to be looming ahead and was already reflected in the literature of the age. Raynal's *Histoires*, which Voltaire once cruelly called 'rechauffé avec de la declamation', and which were published in Amsterdam and forbidden in France as early as 1779, made a profound impression on her. She once called Raynal her 'oracle', and his democratic doctrines moved her deeply.

She never realized that democracy could not come without a terrible social upheaval. She approached the problem emotionally; she longed for democracy without clearly considering the issues such a change would involve. 'I was a Republican before the Revolution,' she proudly declared at her trial, but this was true only in the sense that theoretically and sentimentally she believed in the Republic. Had she been at all conscious of the cost in human life involved in establishing the new regime, she would most certainly have been unwilling to pay the price.

She was developing a passionate sense of justice, or, rather, an acute sensitiveness to injustice. The poverty she had seen in the poorer districts of Caen and elsewhere roused her anger against the existing order. The misery of others was almost unbearable to her, and she hated cruelty as much as she was incensed by violence of any kind. She was the type of reformer who, by instinct, stands up for the underdog of the moment. The actual conflict involved in the struggle, or even a grudging realization that the cruel fighter may ultimately bring about a decrease of misery, did not touch her mind.

Stories which reached the Abbaye-aux-Dames of the luxuries indulged in by her contemporaries in Paris revolted her. She quite naturally sided with the poor, and she was reading Rousseau.

Her intense interest in the problems of the day never lessened her enthusiasm for the classics. She still worshipped the heroism of Antiquity, and she read Plutarch's *Lives* again and again. She longed to have lived in Sparta or in Rome. At the same time the convent was steeped in the Christian tradition of sacrifice, and in Charlotte's young and impressionable mind Christian sacrifice became confused with classic oratory and conspicuous acts of bravery.

When the Revolution broke out in 1789 Charlotte was still at the Abbaye-aux-Dames, and there she remained for some time, as convents were not suppressed by decree until the following year. Politics, among the ladies at the convent, changed from a subject of pleasant conversation to a somewhat grimmer reality. The families of many of the nuns, and the pupils, were involved in the upheaval. Occasionally an active participant in the Revolution came to call at the convent.

A nephew of Madame de Pontecoulant, Gustave Doulcet, who was later a member of the National Convention, stayed at the convent and answered Charlotte's eager questions by the hour. He was enthusiastic about the achievements of the Revolution, and Charlotte and her fellow-students were thrilled to learn that this gallant young man had willingly renounced his titles, sacrificing them to his democratic principles. Looking back at the stirring events in France at this period, it seems almost incredible that such a gesture can have been considered impressive.

When the news reached Caen that on the night from the fourth to the fifth of August the Legislative Assembly had abolished all feudal rights and privileges, Charlotte rejoiced. She was convinced that the new order had begun, for – and this should never be forgotten – her sheltered existence had given her no chance to learn about life. Though she belonged to the governing class herself, she sincerely believed that the

French aristocrats would willingly surrender the rights and privileges they had held for centuries without a fight.

Charlotte hated violence more than anything else in the world. It is only natural, therefore, that from the very beginning of the Revolution she supported those moderate Republicans, who later became known as the Girondists, and who came together in Madame Roland's famous salon. After the National Convention had been called in the autumn of 1792 the Girondists were bitterly attacked by the Jacobins for their non-terrorist policies.

When, at the Abbaye-aux-Dames, Charlotte first began to study the Girondists' pamphlets and ideas, they were still considered radical, for they were definitely Republican, whereas many of the other deputies had not yet given up their belief in a democratic type of Monarchy.

Charlotte's faith in the peaceful coming of the new order received a violent shock late in August 1789, when the Vicomte de Belzunce, a relative of the Abbess, who had insulted the symbols of the Republic, was killed in a street riot after it became known in Caen that the Nobility and the Clergy had joined the Third Estate. To celebrate this event, a wooden pyramid, painted to look like blue marble, had been erected in a Caen street, and on it were written the words: 'Vive le Roi! Vive Necker! Vive les trois orders!'

Beside himself with rage, young Belzunce had struck a shouting child among the enthusiastic onlookers, and as a result the mob literally tore him to bits.

It was a ghastly affair, and when Charlotte heard about it she was more shaken than she had ever been in her life before. She never quite overcame the shock this event gave her, and her horror was intensified by the inevitable realization that Belzunce's death was not really an event, but merely an unimportant incident in the Revolution as a whole. One of her conventional biographers must surely underestimate what the terrible end of a member of her immediate circle meant to her when he writes that 'she was distressed beyond measure'.

If she had been more far-sighted, more used to thinking in

terms of cause and effect, the violence of the Caen crowd
might have forced her to realize that her conception of a non-
violent revolution was fantastic and unreal.

The Abbaye-aux-Dames seemed less like a peaceful retreat
after this occurrence, and Charlotte was probably glad to
leave Caen when the convent was closed during the following
year. She and her sister went to stay with their father. The
household had already been broken up by the Revolution, an
atmosphere of fear prevailed in Monsieur de Corday's home,
and one of Charlotte's brothers had emigrated from France.

Monsieur de Corday was extremely nervous and less open-
minded than he had been. He was changing his mind even
about the rights of primogeniture. His liberalism had not
stood the test of a real upheaval. Charlotte, on the other hand,
was gradually forgetting, or repressing, the horror she had
felt at the death of Belzunce, and her optimistic belief in an
orderly establishment of a Republican regime was again
asserting itself. After all, she argued with her father, the
Legislative Assembly was functioning peacefully. The royal
family had been escorted by a crowd back to Versailles, and
Charlotte was firmly convinced that national unity had been
achieved, on the sixteenth of July 1790, by the *Fête de la
Federation* on the Champs de Mars.

Charlotte began to be annoyed with her father. Perhaps
she was not quite sure enough in her own mind to bear his
attacks on the Republic. She tried to revive his former liberal
views, but he remained unconvinced, and he was often angry
with her. Charlotte controlled herself, but at times the
friction with her father got on her nerves. She seriously
considered escaping from these conflicts by taking the veil.
Convents, however, no longer existed in France, and it is
doubtful whether any impulse would have been strong enough to cause her to leave the country and become an
emigrée.

In the end, therefore, she simply left home and returned
back to Caen. This was in June 1791. She went to stay with
an active old cousin of almost eighty, Madame de Bretteville.
As a child Charlotte had often stayed at Madame de Brette-

ville's estate at Verson, and the old lady had been consistently kind to her. Now she was living permanently at Caen, in the rue St Jean.

Some of Charlotte's biographers have described Madame de Bretteville's home as very 'gloomy'; they think it must have been depressing for a young woman as beautiful as Charlotte to live with her old cousin. Life in the rue St Jean does not, however, seem to have been as dreary as these writers believe, for, in so far as sociability was possible in such disturbing times, Madame de Bretteville continued to see her friends and to carry on her social life.

Charlotte had many admirers among the young men who came to Madame de Bretteville's home, but she was not interested in them. She was developing an unnatural aversion towards love and marriage. As the Revolution progressed, her emotional capacities were increasingly absorbed by her fervent preoccupation with politics. Perhaps she would have seen political issues more clearly if she had experienced a normal emotional outlet, but she was already becoming one of those fanatics whose attachments to human beings count for nothing as compared with their complete devotion to their cause. The cause came first, and she was already shrinking from human relationships which might involve her in responsibilities. When she went to Paris, knowing that she herself would die in a very short time, there was no one whom she regretted leaving, no one in whom she felt a need to confide.

Long before psycho-analysis was invented, students of human nature attributed her fanaticism partly to the repression of more human instincts. When Ponsard's *Charlotte Corday* was first produced at the Comédie Française in 1850, a dramatic critic, Theodore de Banville, startled some of his contemporaries with the following remarks in his criticism of the play:

'If Corneille's granddaughter had been a wife and a mother, the fair young blood that surged through her brain and heart and made her mad with fanaticism would have filled her breasts with milk to nourish beautiful children like

the child she kissed with tears in her eyes at the Palais Royal
. . . The angels who whispered into the ear of the heroine of
Vaucouleurs were the same as those who urged Charlotte
Corday to kill Marat; they were her youth, her life, and her
rebellious blood . . . The most outrageous part of the glory
and shame of these two girl martyrs was the virginity which
our barbarous laws make a duty.'

It is quite obvious that Charlotte herself never experienced any conscious conflict between her political interests
and her personal desires. She quite naturally chose as her
friends people who were concerned above all with politics.
She was very friendly with a young, self-educated man,
Augustin Leclère, who was Madame de Bretteville's steward and the manager of her affairs. Leclère was a keen
Republican, who shared Charlotte's aversion to violence. He
gave her the works of Voltaire, and buoyed up her hopes
that the Revolution would finally settle down into a peaceful
development.

By 1792, however, it had become obvious, even to optimistic provincials in Caen, that this was not to be. The news
of the King's flight and arrest at Varennes reached Caen
towards the end of June of that year. By the autumn the
growing restlessness of the town was apparent to every one.
The guillotine was first used in Caen in November, and, as
far as Charlotte was concerned, the Revolution was coming
very close to home.

On 5 November rioting broke out in front of the Church of
St Jean, near Madame de Bretteville's house. The curé, who
had refused to take the oath on the new Constitution and who
had been dismissed from office as a result, courageously
announced Mass for nine o'clock in the morning. Militant
Republicans expressed their disapproval of the priest by
throwing stones and attacking his supporters with their fists.

Rioting also broke out at Verson, near Madame de Bretteville's estate. In a letter to a woman friend, Charlotte has
left us an account of what happened in the village she knew so
well. Charlotte's letter is illuminating, for she describes only
the horrors of the uprising and not its causes. The Republic

itself is never mentioned, and the letter might have been written by a staunch Royalist.

'You ask me, dear heart, what has happened at Verson. Every conceivable abomination! About fifty people have been beaten and had their hair cut off, and women have been outraged. Apparently, it was only the women that they had a grudge against. Three died a few days later. The others are still ill, or at least most of them.

'On Easter Sunday the Verson people insulted one of the National Guard and even his cockade, which was the worst possible insult he could have been offered. Stormy deliberations! The administrative bodies were forced to give permission for people to leave Caen, and then the preparations for this lasted until half-past two. The people at Verson, who were informed in the morning, thought they were being fooled. Lastly, the curé had time to escape, leaving a funeral stranded in the middle of the street. You know that those who were there and were taken were the Abbé Adam and de La Ballue, Canon of the Sépulchre, the latter a stranger, and the former a young Abbé belonging to the parish. The women were the Abbé Adam's mother and the curé's sister; the major of the parish was also taken. They were only four days in prison.

'One of the peasants was asked by the municipality whether he was a patriot or not. "Alas, yes, gentlemen," he replied, "I am. Everybody knows that I was the first to put the property of the clergy up to auction, and you know very well, gentlemen, that honest men would have nothing to do with it." I don't suppose a witty man could have given a better answer than this poor fool, and even the judges, for all their solemnity, found it difficult to repress a smile.

'What more can I tell you in order to cut short this sorry chapter? The parish immediately veered round; it might have been a Club. They fêted the new converts, who would have set the curé free if he had come back.

You know the vile mob, it can change in a trice
And show hatred or love at a throw of the dice!

'That's enough about them! All the people you mention are in Paris. Today the rest of our good people leave for Rouen, and we shall be almost alone. What can one expect? Nobody is bound to do the impossible. I should have been altogether delighted to settle down in your district, especially as we are threatened with insurrection in the near future. But one can die only once, and my comfort in the midst of all these horrors is that I should be no loss to anybody unless my love for you means something to you. Perhaps you would be surprised if you could see how afraid I am; but if you were here you would share my fears, I am sure. I could tell you nice tales about the state of our town and the excitement everywhere!'

Charlotte was deeply distressed when she heard that, in August, the royal family had been imprisoned in the Temple. Her ambiguous attitude towards the King reflects her confusion of mind, her stubborn unwillingness to pay any real price for the Republic she claimed to support. At a farewell dinner party given by Madame de Bretteville for some friends who were leaving Caen – and it is interesting to realize that future refugees could have left the scene of the Revolution so conventionally – Charlotte refused to drink to the King's health. The guests, most of whom were Royalists, were deeply chagrined. By them Charlotte was considered a rebel. When they asked her why she would not toast Louis, who was 'so good and virtuous', she replied in her clear, beautiful voice: 'I believe him virtuous, but a weak King cannot be a good one; he cannot check the misfortunes of the people.'

This gesture shows how limited was her Republicanism. Danton once said of her. 'When she thought of Rome or Sparta, she was a Republican without reservations, when she thought of her own time, she could not help being critical.' She was later enraged when Marat, in reply to the Girondists' suggestion that an appeal be made to the people to save the King's life, wrote in his *Ami du Peuple*: 'I shall not believe in the Republic until the head of Louis XVI is no longer on his shoulders . . . There will be no security, no peace, until the tyrant's head has fallen.'

The news of the September massacres of the Royalists in the Paris prisons reached Caen with a communication from the Committee of Public Safety, in which the town was informed that 'a number of ferocious conspirators detained in prison have been put to death by the people'. Their executions were called 'an act of justice indispensable for terrorizing traitors into keeping within bounds'.

Charlotte's despair when she heard the details of the Paris massacres was so overwhelming that her mind seems to have suffered from the strain. She forgot about the new order; the Republic as such ceased to exist for her; she could think only of the horrors about which she had been told. It is a curious fact that despite her preoccupation with violence, she was never morbidly curious. She never witnessed an execution. On the contrary, when she herself was being driven in a cart to her own execution, and the guillotine on the Place de la Republique loomed ahead, she asked the driver to step aside so that she could see it: she had never seen a guillotine before. Perhaps her agony at the thought of these horrors was all the greater, as they lived entirely in her imagination and were stimulated by her abnormal fantasies of violence.

'The most horrible things that can possibly happen,' she wrote at this time to a friend, 'lie in a future inaugurated by such happenings. . . . All these men, who should give us liberty, have killed liberty.'

Charlotte was not strong enough, either mentally or morally, to face the ghastly realities of the Revolution. She refused to admit that at this stage bloodshed was unavoidable. The news of violent acts, which reached her daily, was unbearable to her, and she evaded inevitable mental conflicts by escaping into mystical conceptions; she made herself believe that the Republic could and would be maintained without further violence. She dreamed about a peace which would soon be restored in France, though as yet her ideas of how this could be done were vague and undefined.

The word 'peace' was beginning to obsess her. 'The Second Day of the Preparation of Peace', she heads the last long letter she wrote from prison, and the word occurs ten times in this letter. The last sentence she uttered at her trial was: 'The leader of Anarchy is now dead; you will have peace.'

She was gradually moving away from reality into an abnormal state of detachment. One of her great friends, Bougon-Langrais, who was executed a year after her own death, and who understood her well, wished that he, too, like 'dear Charlotte, could have lulled himself to sleep with a sweet and deceptive illusion into believing that soon order and peace would be restored in his country'.

Charlotte's troubled mind was groping to find some one individual whom she could hold responsible for the violence which had occurred. It was much easier to believe that peace would be restored, if she could persuade herself that, as a whole, her countrymen hated violence and that one diabolical being alone was causing the terrible bloodshed.

It is probable that Charlotte developed an *idée fixe* about Marat after 25 September when the Assembly attacked him for his terroristic measures. 'The people, obedient to my voice,' Marat had defended himself, 'saved the country by appointing themselves to the dictatorship to rid themselves of the traitors.'

Marat became Charlotte's symbol, the very essence of everything horrible. 'Striking at Marat,' she was asked at her trial, 'did you think you could remove all tyrants?' – 'Marat gone, the rest might fear,' she answered.

What she heard of his appearance stimulated her hatred, for already this was not too strong a phrase with which to describe her emotion for him. His physical ugliness made him more repulsive to her still: she was enraged when she thought of his short squat figure; of his head, so much too large for his body, his protruding nose, his jerky, awkward movements, his skin, terribly disfigured by the disease he had caught while hiding from his pursuers in the cellars of Paris.

Charlotte would never have acknowledged Marat's sincerity. She would have denied stubbornly that he had sacrificed everything for the principles in which he believed. She forgot, if she had ever known it, that he gave up a brilliant career as a physician and a scientist for his political convictions, that he went to prison for them, and that now he was dying from a disease contracted while he was defending them. If any one had told Charlotte that Jean Paul Marat was a tortured human being, as she was herself – except that his mind was keen – she would have been roused to passionate anger.

It is difficult to say at what point Charlotte began to complete her fantasy of the situation. She had found the solution: peace. She had found the means to attain this peace: the devil, who had terrorized France – Marat – must be removed. The person who killed him would be her country's saviour.

It is generally assumed that Charlotte vaguely thought of herself as this saviour after the so-called 'affair of 31 May' 1792, when a refractory priest of the parish of St Gilles was executed in Caen. By April of the following year, when the Convention attacked Marat, because he had encouraged a revolt against the Assembly, definite plans for saving France herself were maturing in her agitated mind.

A few weeks later, when Marat, through a deputation from the Commune, demanded the arrest of the Girondists, whom he considered active counter-revolutionaries, Charlotte became more resolute, but she must have experienced an agonizing conflict. Her every instinct was, after all, against violence, and yet she felt called upon to perform a murder as a sacred duty. Augustin Leclère later found a note among her papers. She had written: Will I do it? Will I not do it? – 'Le ferai-je? Ne le ferai-je pas?'

When, in June, a number of Girondists, who had fled from Paris, began to arrive in Caen, Charlotte's mind was made up. Though she utterly confused the issues at stake, and though her plan was a mad one, she carried out the details of it in a completely calm and logical manner.

She decided to murder Marat at a plenary session of the Convention. The crowds, so she believed, would then kill her at once or trample her to death. She would die an unknown heroine. She sincerely believed that an anonymous act of courage would serve her cause best, but in the end, when she actually went out to kill him, she carefully pinned her baptismal certificate and her 'Address to Frenchmen' to her clothing, so that every one would know who she was. This unconscious exhibitionism which reflects her longing to be acknowledged as a martyr is infinitely pathetic, for in her clear-sighted moments she wanted to sacrifice herself without receiving anything in return – even prestige.

The antagonistic attitude among her friends in Caen towards Marat stimulated Charlotte's intentions. When, in May, the Convention sent two messengers to the town to bring back the Girondist refugees, Caen did not obey these orders. Instead, the two messengers were kept as hostages.

Charlotte realized that she must find some pretext for going to Paris. Already she was extremely secretive about her plan. Her old friend, Mademoiselle de Forbin, who had emigrated to Switzerland, wanted some one to interview the Minister of the Interior for her and to arrange about her pension. As Mademoiselle de Forbin's family knew Barbaroux, a prominent Girondist then in Caen, Charlotte made this an excuse to go to him and to ask him for some letters of introduction to people in Paris.

Leclère, in whom she had confided as little as she had in any one else, escorted her to the *Intendance*, where she had an appointment with Barbaroux. He willingly agreed to give her a note to his colleague Deperret, who was still in Paris. Barbaroux asked Charlotte to come back in a few days and he would have the letter ready for her. Barbaroux's attitude in this case helps one to understand why men like Marat were enraged by the Girondists, who were willing to give public money in the form of pensions to counter-revolutionary Royalists living abroad.

On the next Sunday, it was the seventh of July, Charlotte dressed with great care and went to see the parade General Wimpffen had arranged in the hope of raising volunteers for a march on Paris. The demonstration was a failure, for only seventeen men stepped forward. Charlotte was deeply disappointed, but her manner was as calm and restrained as ever. She walked from the parade to Barbaroux's to fetch her letter of introduction. Then she went home, for Madame de Bretteville had asked some of the Girondists to spend the evening with her.

One of the guests spoke of Charlotte as 'the beautiful aristocrat, who had come in to see the Republicans'. For the first time Charlotte's composure was slightly shaken, and she answered somewhat sharply: 'You are judging me without knowing me, Citizen. One day you will know who I am.'

She was particularly casual the next day. She told Madame de Bretteville and her friends that she was going to Argentan, where her father was living. To him she wrote that she was going to England.

She went out to Verson to say good-bye to an old friend; she returned some books to Madame de Pontecoulant, who was still living in Caen. She bought the high-heeled shoes for her journey and mended her clothes; she reserved her place in the coach to Paris. No one could possibly have suspected that she was starting forth on her last adventure.

She left for Paris the next day. In the coach a stranger was unpleasantly attentive to her and, in the end, proposed to her. She appeared to be a young woman travelling purely for pleasure or, at most, on some trivial matter of business. She was apparently undisturbed by the thought that, a week from that very day, she would perhaps no longer be at liberty or even alive. During the night, this 'astonishing woman', as Madame Roland once called her, slept soundly and well. 'The murmured plaintive ditties' of her would-be admirer, as she herself admitted in a letter written shortly before her death, 'were extremely soporific', and 'she woke up only on reaching Paris'.

She had never been in Paris, but she was not at a loss. She did not seem like a provincial. She walked into the Hôtel de la Providence, in the rue des Vieux Augustins, as though she had stayed alone at hotels many times before. At the hotel, however, upsetting news awaited her, for the waiter told her that Marat was too ill to attend the Convention. She would not be able to kill him at a plenary session. Her plans would have to be changed.

The following day she went to Deperret's home to present her letter, but he was out. She returned, and he promised to go with her the next day to see the Minister. She then returned to the hotel, went to bed, and slept well.

The next morning Deperret took her to the Ministry, where she bought a knife with which to kill Marat, warned Deperret not to be seen with her too much, found out Marat's address, wrote to him asking for an interview, and went back to the hotel to write her exalted 'Address to Frenchmen'. She was quiet and unhurried; judging by her manner, none of these actions was more important to her than others. She would have given any one the impression that they were all in the day's routine.

Her 'Address', however, reflects her exaltation, her intense and abnormal excitement. 'Oh, France,' she wrote, 'your peace depends upon the maintenance of the Law. I shall not offend the Law by killing Marat, for he is condemned by the Universe; he is outside the Law . . . Oh, my country, your miseries break my heart. I have nothing to offer you but my life, and I thank heaven that I am free to dispose of it as I will . . .'

Marat was living in the rue des Cordelier where his devoted friend Simmone Evrard was taking care of him. As a physician he was fully aware that he had entered upon the last phase of his painful and incurable disease. He was a dying man, and Charlotte's sacrifice becomes all the more tragic, all the more meaningless, when one bears this fact in mind.

Marat was too ill to go to the Convention; he was free from pain only when, seated in a bathtub, he wrapped his body in wet towels. His energy, his will to save the Republic were, however, as dominating as ever. He still supervised the publication of his newspaper, *Le Journal de le République Française*, which had succeeded his *Ami du Peuple* after the proclamation of the Republic.

One day in July he received a letter in an unknown handwriting. 'Citizen, I have just arrived from Caen,' he read. 'Your love for your native place will doubtless make you desirous to learn about the events which have occurred in that district of the Republic. I shall call at your home in about an hour; have the goodness to receive me, and give me a short interview. I shall enable you to render France a great service.'

Marat, who was fighting the Girondists as bitterly as ever, must have been interested in any news from Caen, but despite this fact – perhaps he felt too ill – he obviously gave no orders that the signer of this letter was to be admitted to his house. For Charlotte was turned away when she called. She wrote once more and called again, but in vain. Finally, on 13 July, she was admitted.

At about half-past seven in the evening of that day Marat was seated in his bathtub. A board was laid across it, and on this he was writing. A young man named Pillet came in with samples of newsprint paper. Marat approved the paper, and asked the youth to open the window before leaving.

When Pillet left the house, so he later stated, he saw a handsome young woman arguing at the door with the concièrge. It was very hot, and the young woman was telling the concièrge that despite the heat she had come from Caen to see the 'Friend of the People'. Then Simmone Evrard joined the two women at the door and asked Charlotte to come in. Simmone took her up to Marat's room.

Charlotte was with Marat for about ten minutes. No one else was in the room, but she herself said at her trial that she had talked to him about the Girondists at Caen. He asked her for the names of the Girondist refugees who were then in that city. In the middle of their conversation Charlotte drew the knife she had bought from the folds of her dress and stabbed him. She was a strong woman who aimed well despite her casual manner. She had struck into his heart, and after one cry for help Marat died.

The room was full of people almost in an instant. We are told that Charlotte seemed shaken for a moment when she witnessed Simmone Evrard's grief, but Charlotte controlled her agitation almost at once. She was far more obviously distressed when, after she had been arrested and her hands tied behind her back, her clothing was searched for any documents which might incriminate possible accomplices. At her execution, too, she appeared to be disturbed only when the scarf was pulled off her neck and shoulders. Then her acute sense of modesty was outraged.

She was taken from Marat's house to the Abbaye prison. She spent the first day there mending the frock which had been torn when she was arrested. She also asked the warder of the prison for material to make the Normandy cap. She was equally busy the next day, writing letters. To Barbaroux she wrote:

'. . . It was through the lady who travelled with me that they found out I knew you and that I had spoken to Duperret. You know how resolute Duperret is; he told them the exact truth in answer to their questions. I confirmed his evidence by my own. There is nothing against him, but his resolution was regarded as a crime. I confess I was very much afraid they would find out I had spoken to him. I regretted having done so when it was too late, and I tried to make up for my mistake by making him promise to join you. But he was too obstinate to make any such promise. Knowing that he and everybody else were innocent, I determined to carry out my plan.

'Can you believe it, Fauchet is in prison for being my accomplice, Fauchet who did not even know of my existence! But they don't like having only an insignificant woman to offer to the shade of that great man! Pardon me, ye men, the word is an insult to your kind! He was a ravening monster, who would have devoured the whole of France through civil war. But now, *vive la paix!* Thank God, he was not a Frenchman born. Four of the members were present at my first examination. Chabot looked like a madman. Legendre insisted that he had seen me in the morning at his house. I never gave this man a thought. I do not think he is great enough to be the tyrant of this country, and I had no wish to punish so many people. All those who have never set eyes on me before said they had known me for a long time.

'I hear that Marat's last words have been printed. I don't know that he ever gave utterance to any; at all events I can tell you what were the last words he said to me. After writing down the names of all of you, and the names of the members of the Calvados Government who are at Evreux, he said, to console me, that in a few days he would have you all guillotined in Paris. These last words decided his fate. If the Department sets up his bust opposite St Fargeau's, it ought to have these words engraved in letters of gold.

'I shall not tell you any details about the great event. The newspapers will tell you all about that. I confess that what finally decided me was the courage with which our volunteers enlisted on the seventh of July. You remember how happy I was, and I promised myself that I would make Pétition regret the suspicions he harboured with regard to my feelings. "Would you be sorry if they did not go?" he asked me. In short, I came to the conclusion that it was foolish for so many brave men to die for the head of one man whom they might miss or who might drag down a number of worthy citizens with him. He did not deserve the honour. A woman's hand was enough. I confess that I made use of a treacherous trick to induce him to receive me; but the end justifies the means in such circumstances.

'When I left Caen, I counted upon sacrificing him on the summit of the Mountain; but he was no longer attending the Convention. I wish I had kept your letter; then they would have been convinced that I had no accomplices. But all that will be cleared up. We are such good Republicans in Paris that nobody can believe that a futile woman, who would never have been of any use however long she lived, could possibly sacrifice herself in cold blood to save her country. I was expecting to die at any moment, but brave men who are really above all praise saved me from the excusable fury of those whom I had made miserable. As I really acted in cold blood, the crying of some women upset me. But if one saves one's country one must not think of the price that has to be paid.

'May Peace be established as quickly as I hope it will. An

important step has been taken in that direction without which we should never have had it. I have been revelling in Peace for the last two days; my country's good is my own. The reward for every act of devotion is far greater than the pain one feels in deciding to perform it. I am afraid they may worry my father a little; he already has quite sufficient cause for distress in losing me. If any of my letters are found in his possession, most of them are portraits of you. If they contain any jokes at your expense, I beg you to overlook them. I gave way to the frivolity of my nature. In my last letter I led them to believe that I was terrified at the horrors of civil war, and was going to England. At that time my idea was to remain unknown, to kill Marat publicly and be killed myself at once, leaving the people of Paris to make a vain search to discover who I was.

'I beg you, Citizen, you and your colleagues, to take up the cudgels on behalf of my relatives and friends if they are molested. I say nothing to my dear aristocratic friends whose memory I keep in my heart. I have hated only one person in my life, and I have proved the strength of my hatred. But there are thousands whom I love more than I hated him. A lively imagination and a tender heart gave promise of a stormy life, and I beg those who may possibly regret me to remember this, and rejoice to see me enjoying my rest in the Elysian Fields with Brutus and the other heroes of old.

'Among moderns there are few true patriots who know how to die for their country; selfishness accounts for nearly everything. What a sorry people to found a Republic! But at least the foundations of Peace must be laid, and the Government will follow as best it can. At all events, the Mountain will certainly not rule France; you may take my word for that!

'I am treated with the utmost consideration in prison; the concièrges are the best and kindest of souls. I have been given some gendarmes to prevent me from being bored; that was all right during the day, but at night it is extremely disagreeable. I complained of the indecency, but the Committee did not think fit to pay any attention. I think it was Chabot's idea;

only a Capuchin could have thought of such a thing! I while away the time writing songs. I give Valady's couplet to anybody who wants it. I have assured the people of Paris that we are taking up arms only against anarchy, which is absolutely true.

'I have been transferred to the Conciergerie, and the gentlemen of the Grand Jury have promised to send you my letter; so I am continuing it. I have undergone a long examination; please get it if it is published. At the time of my arrest I had an Address on me which I had written to the Friends of Peace. I cannot send it to you. I shall ask for it to be published, though I expect it will be useless.

'I had an idea last night of presenting my portrait to the department of Calvados, but the Committee of Public Safety, to whom I addressed my request, have not answered, and now it is too late.

'It is astonishing that the people allowed me to be transferred from the Abbaye to the Conciergerie. It affords fresh proof of their attitude. Tell the good people of Caen this. They occasionally allow themselves the luxury of a little insurrection, which is not easy to keep in hand.

'Tomorrow at eight o'clock my trial begins. Probably by midday I shall have lived – to use a Latin expression. People must believe in the valour of the men of Calvados since even the women of the district are capable of determinations. I have no idea how my last moments will be spent, and it is the end that crowns the achievement. There is no need for me to feign indifference to my fate, for up to the present I have not felt the smallest fear of death. I never had any regard for life except as a means of being useful . . .

'I hope you will not cease to take an interest in Madame Forbin's business. This is her address if you find it necessary to write to her: Alexandrine Forbin, Mandresie, near Zürich, Switzerland. I beg you to tell her that I love her with all my heart.

'I am going to write a word to my father; I shall not say anything to our other friends. All I ask of them is to forget me quickly; their grief would disgrace my memory. Tell General

Wimpffen that I believe I have helped him to win more than one battle by paving the way to peace.

'Farewell, Citizen! I commend myself to the memory of the true Friends of Peace.

'The prisoners in the Conciergerie, far from insulting me like the people in the streets, looked as though they pitied me. Misfortune always arouses sympathy. This is my last reflection.

'Tuesday the sixteenth, at eight o'clock in the evening.

'CORDAY.'

That evening she also wrote to the Committee of Public Safety, and as a result Jean Jacques Hauer was sent to make a hurried portrait of her.

'As I still have a few hours to live' (she had written to the Committee), 'may I be allowed to hope, Citizens, that you will allow me to have my portrait painted? I should like to leave it as a memento to my friends. Moreover, just as the likeness of good citizens are cherished and held in honour, so curiosity may sometimes lead to a desire to know what great criminals looked like, since this would serve to perpetuate the horror felt for their crimes. If you deign to heed my request, I beg you to send me a miniature painter tomorrow. I take this opportunity of repeating the request that I may sleep alone. Assuring you of my deepest gratitude.

'CHARLOTTE CORDAY.'

On 16 July Charlotte was tried by the Revolutionary Tribunal. Two developments at the trial were extremely painful to her. In the first place, the Tribunal could not believe that she had killed Marat without powerful accomplices, that she alone, and with no confidant whatsoever, had carried out this murder. She, who had longed passionately to be the saviour of France, was accused of being merely the instrument of influential men.

Secondly, the judge, who was moved by her youth, urged her defending counsel to plead that she was mad. She vehemently rejected this suggestion. Had he succeeded, her deed, in her own eyes, would have been utterly futile. Nor would she have attained the height of exaltation towards which she was moving; she might have been pardoned and she would not have died, thus sacrificing herself for the cause of peace. Her whole life would have become meaningless to her. 'I killed a man in order to save thousands,' she said proudly at the trial.

Charlotte was executed in the late afternoon of the day of her trial, 17 July 1793. She was not quite twenty-five years old. It never occurred to her that her death might not bring peace to France – the fact that, historically speaking, the giving of her life meant nothing at all, never crossed her mind. And if she was afraid of dying, if, as the cart approached the guillotine, she felt regret for what she had done or at leaving life, she did not show her fear. Her self-control, her poise, her calm were perfect to the end. As Pierre Vergniaud, who had so strenuously opposed the institution of the Revolutionary Tribunal which had sentenced her to death, said of Charlotte and of Madame Roland: 'These women, if they cannot deliver us, can teach us how to die.'

Ethel Le Neve (1883–1967)

The Woman
Who Loved Crippen

Ethel Le Neve was the mistress of Dr Hawley Harvey
Crippen who has been described as 'certainly one of the
most dangerous criminals of this century'. Yet to many
people at the time, the timid-looking Dr Crippen
seemed more like a figure of pathos who had been
driven to distraction and then murder by his flamboyant, would-be actress wife. The curiosity of the case was
heightened when it was learned how Ethel Le Neve had
fled with him across the Atlantic on the *SS Montrose*
disguised as a boy; more so when the Doctor's last
request was that a photograph of her should be buried
with him after his execution. Le Neve herself was
released from custody after being found innocent of
any charges and at once disappeared from public view.
Thereafter, rumours abounded as to just *what* had
happened to this most enigmatic of women. It has taken
almost a century to solve the mystery which piles
surprise upon surprise, as **Alfred Draper** now explains.

Ethel Le Neve remains one of the most enigmatic women in the history of crime. She stayed in Britain throughout Crippen's long ordeal in the death cell. Yet her conduct was strange to say the least.

Sir Seymour Hicks, the actor manager, happened to be in Bow Street Police Station seeing a detective friend on the day Crippen's appeal was heard. 'Ethel Le Neve was in here a moment ago,' confided the detective. 'She came in to know if she could borrow the pair of trousers she wore when she was arrested on board ship – disguised as a boy.'

Ethel had explained that she had been offered a sum of money by a newspaper to be photographed in them. 'While I was discussing the matter with her the news came through that Crippen's appeal had failed and that he was to hang.

'The only Comment she made was "Oh." '

The photograph appeared in *Lloyd's Weekly News* three days before the execution. The same issue contained Crippen's farewell letter. 'In this farewell letter to the world, written as I face eternity, I say that Ethel Le Neve has loved me as few women love men, and that her innocence of any crime, save that of yielding to the dictates of her heart, is absolute. To her I pay this last tribute.

'It is of her that my last thoughts have been. My last prayer will be that God may protect her and keep her safe from harm and allow her to join me in eternity.

'I make this defence and this acknowledgement – that the love of Ethel Le Neve has been the best thing in my life – my only happiness – and that in return for that great gift I have been inspired with a great kindness towards my fellow beings and with a greater desire to do good . . .'

Nearly everything is known about the characters in the Crippen case . . . except Ethel.

Captain Kendall, the skipper of the *Montrose*, was commanding the *Empress of Ireland* when it sank on 29 May, 1914, with a loss of 1,062 lives at Father's Point, Quebec, the very spot where Crippen was arrested. Kendall was saved and lived to the ripe old age of ninety-one.

The *Montrose* foundered on the Goodwin Sands in December 1914.

The solicitor Newton who had made such a hash of the defence was sentenced to three years imprisonment in 1913 for fraud.

Bottomley, who tried to make money out of Crippen's plight, was jailed for seven years in 1922 for his infamous Victory Bond scheme.

How about Ethel – was she too a victim of the curse?

She, almost alone of the principals, appears to have escaped to lead a tranquil, if not completely happy, life up to the time of her death, aged eighty-four.

When last seen Ethel, in widow's weeds, was boarding the *Majestic* at Southampton en route to a new life in the New World. Then she seemed to vanish as far as press and public were concerned . . . though she was eagerly sought by reporters on both sides of the Atlantic.

In June 1932, a reporter claimed to have found her in Perth, Western Australia, 'looking out over the Indian Ocean, across which she fled many years ago to escape the public glare'.

But the real Ethel, her secret secure, was living at the time of that interview at No. 110 Parkview Road, Addiscombe, Croydon. Far from looking out over the waves of any Indian Ocean, Ethel looked out of windows on to a modest, tree-lined street where she could see her children playing.

After disembarking from the *Majestic* in New York on 30 November 1910, Ethel had hurried on to Toronto about which Crippen had spoken so glowingly. She got a job as a typist but it was not the paradise he had painted.

The Crippen case was still discussed in lurid terms by the girls with whom she worked and in tea shops where she took her meals. She lived in constant fear that she would be recognized although she had changed her hairstyle and made other efforts to alter her appearance.

She stuck it out until 1916 when she returned home to nurse her beloved younger sister Nina, who was dying. She was using the name Ethel Nelson and soon obtained a job as a typist at Hampton's furniture store in Trafalgar Square. There she met Stanley Smith, an accountant. They married and went to live in South Croydon, where they had a son and a daughter who grew up and married, and Ethel ultimately became a grandmother.

Then one night Stanley, who was said to have borne a strong resemblance to Crippen, died of a heart attack on his way home from work.

Ethel continued to lead a rather dull existence, broken only by visits from her grandchildren, and the occasional outing to the seaside with other old-age pensioners.

In 1954 she celebrated her seventy-first birthday, and soon after her real identity was at last discovered by the novelist Ursula Bloom. Miss Bloom wrote a fictionalized account of the Crippen case entitled *The Girl Who Loved Crippen*, which was serialized in a Sunday newspaper. When the first instalment appeared, Ethel's brother Sydney Neave – Neave was Ethel's family name – got in touch with her to complain about the way she had portrayed Ethel. 'Up to that point I wasn't even sure that Ethel was alive,' she said.

Neave was a night watchman at Baker Street Underground Station and Miss Bloom persuaded him to carry a letter to his sister.

Miss Bloom relates: 'I exchanged several letters with Ethel through the intermediary of her brother before Ethel, by then confident that I would not betray her true identity, agreed to see me.'

The encounter took place in June 1954. 'Ethel was much smaller than I anticipated,' recalls Miss Bloom, 'but at seventy-one she was still pretty, with grey hair gathered in a knot and intelligent grey eyes.'

Not surprisingly, Ethel turned out to be a human oyster, judging from the amount of information Miss Bloom was able to prise from her.

Perhaps it was that the habit of secrecy, of dissimulating even to her nearest and dearest, had become so engrained with Ethel that, even had she wanted to, she could not have unburdened herself to the other woman.

One thing was quickly established: neither her late husband nor her children knew that Ethel Smith was the once notorious Ethel Le Neve. Moreover the human oyster dropped no pearls but only inconsequential grit which Miss Bloom jotted down. 'She said she still loved Crippen.'

They obviously discussed the case for Miss Bloom recorded Ethel saying, 'We seldom used hyoscine, it was new and he never liked it.' Then she added. 'He did not die for any of these things. It was just that he loved me.'

'Her face was very white,' said Miss Bloom.

Finally, Miss Bloom noted, 'I looked at her. My eyes asked the question I could not put into words. 'He doesn't know,' she whispered. Neither did her son or daughter . . . In my notebook I wrote: I asked her if Crippen could have come back again would she marry him now?

'Her eyes almost pierced me. "Yes, I would," she said.'

And that was all. It was the sum total of information that Miss Bloom was able to extract at the interview and those that followed.

One result of Miss Bloom's enterprise was that until Ethel's death thirteen years later she was the novelist's exclusive: that is, only Miss Bloom and her editors knew about the house at No. 110 Parkview Road, Addiscombe.

Wolf Mankowitz and Monty Norman wrote the musical *Belle or the Ballad of Doctor Crippen* which opened at the Strand Theatre on 4 May 1961. But it died the death.

Wolf Mankowitz recalled: 'Miss Bloom reminded the public that Ethel Le Neve was still alive, and that she might be pained to find herself the heroine of a musical which poked fun at the Crippen tragedy. As a result there was a rush of sympathy for Ethel, and people stayed away from the theatre in droves.'

Miss Bloom had seen Ethel when plans for the musical were announced and she said: 'We have talked about it, she and I, sitting at tea in her room, with the cloth she embroidered herself and the cake she made with her own hands.

'No musical performance could coax her out of the quiet she has chosen. She asks only to stay as a shadow. For this poor woman does not forget . . . Ethel Le Neve has her own music about him, and it is the grand opera of very deep emotions.'

On Wednesday, 8 August 1967, the headlines were equally divided between the effectiveness of the United States' bombing of North Vietnam and the Biafran struggle for independence.

There was no mention of the death in Dulwich of a gaunt, grey-haired woman of eighty-four, whose name had once been in big headlines.

Widowed and living alone at the time of her death, Ethel had managed despite her failing eyesight to remain cheerful up to the end. She was always ready for a gossip over a cup of tea . . . except when the conversation touched upon her past.

Mystery of the Exotic Dancer

The life of Mati Hari was surrounded by such mystery that it has given her a special allure among the ranks of extraordinary women. Born Margaret Gertrude Zelle, the daughter of a wealthy clothing manufacturer in Holland, she originally had ambitions to become a teacher. Instead, she made an unhappy marriage, became a professional Oriental dancer called, initially, 'Lady MacLeod' (using her married name), and attracted a string of admirers and lovers with her erotic dances and scanty costumes. Her mystique increased still more when she changed her name to 'Mata Hari' and apparently became a spy for the German Secret Service just prior to the First World War. A short time later she claimed to be a double agent for the French! However, her arrest in 1917 and trial for espionage in Paris left even more questions unanswered, as **Ronald Seth**, himself an SOE agent in Germany during the Second World War, reveals in this account.

Without doubt the best-known spy in all the world is Mata Hari, The Eye of the Dawn.

At the height of her career she fostered the legend that she was a half-caste Javanese, who had been trained as a temple-dancer in Malabar.

It was a legend. Her parents were Dutch, and her maiden name was Margaret Gertrude Zelle. In 1895 she married an officer in the Dutch Colonial Army, called MacLeod, and went with him to Java. There a son and a daughter were born to them.

MacLeod was a brute, a sot, an adulterer. He beat her and heaped upon her every indignity. The son died in infancy, it has been suggested, of poison given him by a servant outraged by his father. It would seem probable that as a relief from the horror of her home life Margaret MacLeod studied the Javanese erotic books and spent a good deal of her time watching performances of the dancing girls, because when she later came to Paris in the role of temple-dancer, she performed well enough to deceive many Oriental experts.

In 1901 she returned with her daughter and husband to Holland. The following year MacLeod left her, taking the little girl with him. This seems to have stirred a latent power in the mother, because for the first time in her life she went on to the offensive, and obtained a court order for the return of the child and maintenance for both of them. She got back the child, but no money from MacLeod, and after three unhappy and difficult years, in 1905 she left her daughter with relatives, and disappeared – to reappear at the Musée Guimet in Paris, as Mata Hari, whose mother, a temple-dancer, had died in giving her birth, and who had been trained by the priests and dedicated to the god Siva in her mother's place. How she had come to Paris was not explained, and no one seemed curious.

She was an immediate success, because her dances, so she said, demanded complete nudity. The term for her meant complete nudity except for breast-plates, which she wore to conceal flabby, pendulous breasts. Her beauty was, in fact, concentrated, in her eyes and arms; her attraction in the eroticism of her olive-dark limbs.

Lovers came in their scores, and were drawn from such exalted families that she could afford to pick and choose. Her reputation spread to all the capitals of Europe, and she followed it to prove that she was all that rumour said she was. In Berlin, Rome, Vienna and Paris she gave her favours to Princes, Dukes, Ministers and Generals – in return for enormous fees.

When she made her first appearance at the Musée Guimet she was twenty-nine. When she faced the firing-squad at Vincennes she was forty. In the intervening decade she had established herself as the leading prostitute in Europe, and held a fatal fascination for men right to the moment that she slumped lifeless against the stake. As a spy she was not one-hundredth part so successful.

Berlin had always shown her the greatest hospitality, but if she spied for Germany, it was only because the Germans had been the first to ask her. The French have always maintained that her operational number was H 21, and that the Germans only used this initial for their pre-war agents. Yet for the first year of the war, Mata Hari kept herself well away from every scene of military activity.

The first notice we have of her, after 4 August 1914, comes in a telegram from the Italian Intelligence to the Paris authorities late in 1915:

While examining the passenger list of a Japanese vessel at Naples we have recognized the name of a theatrical celebrity from Marseilles, named Mata Hari, the famous Hindu dancer, who purports to reveal secret Hindu dances which demand complete nudity. She has, it seems, renounced her claim to Indian birth and become Berlinoise. She speaks German with a slight Eastern accent.

From the moment that that message reached Paris, Mata Hari was shadowed wherever she went, whether to Paris, London, Antwerp or Brussels.

But for another year no Allied counter-espionage service
could find any grounds for apprehending her. She performed
her dances as before; she dispensed her favours as before. But
she was never furtive; never displayed any fear.

Then, almost by chance, French counter-espionage discovered that she was sending her reports by the neutral
diplomats, upon whom she was now concentrating, and
who were exempted from censorship. Even so, the evidence
available would not have satisfied a court.

One of her former lovers had been a Russian, Captain
Maroff, who had been permanently blinded while fighting.
Maroff was now at Vittel, and Mata Hari applied for a permit
to go there to nurse him. Not believing her reasons for
wanting to go to the Vosges the French granted the permit
and she was more closely watched than ever before.

Again she disappointed French counter-espionage. It is
conceded now that of all the many men with whom she was
intimate the only man she ever loved was Maroff. Thwarted
and desperate the French decided that the only way they
could rid themselves of her was to deport her.

To their secret amazement, on being told of this decision
her nerve seemed to break. Vehemently she protested that
she had never spied for the Germans, but that if the French
wished to use her services, she knew many high-ranking
Germans and it would be very easy for her to obtain much
important information.

The French pretended to believe her and sent her first to
Brussels, to one of her former inamorati, General von Bissing, Governor-General of Belgium. Before she left they gave
her the names of six Belgian agents to whom she was to pass
von Bissing's secrets. But she had been in Brussels only a
short time when one of the six was arrested by the Germans
and executed.

The move in sending her to Brussels was not an exceptionally good one, because it was easy for her to pass, with
German help, to neutral Holland, whence she made for
neutral Spain, most surprisingly via England.

The behaviour of British Intelligence on her arrival is

equally surprising. She was taken to London where she was questioned by Sir Basil Thompson, chief of the CID at Scotland Yard, to whom she admitted being a spy, but in the service of France. In his book of reminiscences, *My Experiences at Scotland Yard*, Sir Basil states that he said to her: 'Madame, if you will accept the advice of one nearly twice your age, give up what you have been doing.'

With this sound advice she was permitted to continue her journey to Spain, where she made contact with the German Naval and Military Attachés, from whom she received her instructions. The Germans had realized by this time, however, that she was compromised so hopelessly that she was no longer of any use. She was also extremely expensive, and German Secret Service funds were running low.

She did not appear to have any idea of her danger, and went back to France fearlessly. The French knew she was coming, because the Germans, when they issued her instructions, had deliberately used a code which they knew the French had broken.

On arrival in Paris she stayed at the Hotel Plaza-Athenée in the Avenue Montaigne. The Germans had told her that the sum of 15,000 pesetas would be paid to her by a neutral legation. She had collected the cheque but not yet cashed it, when the French arrested her.

She was brought before a Court-Martial on 24 July, 1917. She was defended by the distinguished French barrister, Maître Clunet, who was one of the few who believed that she would be acquitted.

The President of the Court opened the proceedings by questioning her about a sum of 30,000 marks which she had received from von Jagow, chief of the Berlin police, on the outbreak of war.

'He was my lover,' she answered. 'Thirty thousand marks was the fee for my favours.'

That was the explanation she gave for all the large sums of money she had been receiving for years. The Court cited all the high-ranking Germans with whom she had been intimate – General von Bissing, the Duke of Brunswick, the German

Crown Prince, and Naval and Military Attachés engaged in espionage. She countered by calling as witnesses Jules Cambron, Permanent Secretary in the French Foreign Office, and a former Minister of War and others.

'I am not French,' she declared, 'so what is to prevent my having friends of any nationality I choose? If I wrote to high-ranking Germans it was only because they wrote to me and I returned their endearments, but nothing more. My letters that were sent in diplomatic bags were letters to my daughter in Holland.'

She became confused only when the Commissioner for the French Government, Lieutenant Mornet, began to question her about her offer to spy for France.

'I told the French authorities,' she retorted, 'many places in Morocco where German U-boats call to refuel. It was very useful information, I am told.'

'No doubt,' replied Mornet. 'But how could you know these things if you were not in contact with German Intelligence Chiefs?'

She launched a long explanation, which became more and more muddled as she went on, until she realized this herself and broke off.

'After all, I am not French. I have no duty towards this people.'

The trial, held *in camera*, lasted for two days. But she was condemned before it began.

Her lawyers fought desperately for her reprieve, but the President of the Republic refused to consider it. So did Queen Wilhelmina, who was pressed by her Prime Minister, M. van der Linden, one of Mata Hari's former lovers, to sign a petition to M. Poincaré.

Mata Hari was sentenced on 25 July, and the sentence was not carried out until 15 October. She comported herself with great calmness and courage to the last, refusing the bandage for her eyes, and faced the firing-squad with such composure that she drew the sincerest admiration from her executioners.

POSTSCRIPT

In January 1999 a new element of mystery was added to the story of Mata Hari when Britain's MI5 released a personal file on her that had been marked 'Secret' ever since the end of the First World War. In this it was disclosed that she had, in fact, been a marked woman and suspected of being a German spy from the moment she had first been interrogated by intelligence officers on her arrival at Folkestone in December 1915. There the exotic dancer had maintained she was on her way to France to give performances – although her new-found wealth, in the shape of elegant dresses and her expensive mode of travel, led MI5 to believe she must be in the pay of the Germans.

'Mata Hari is a *demi-mondaine* who during her sojourn in France made the acquaintance of many French and Belgian officers,' an MI5 official wrote at the time. 'She is suspected of having been in France on an important mission for the Germans.' Not surprisingly, this judgment led to her every movement being tracked. A report in December 1916 from an agent in Paris sealed her fate: 'I understand the French have ample proof of her activities on behalf of the enemy.' Mata Hari was, of course, subsequently arrested, tried and executed.

However, the MI5 file contains no actual evidence that she was ever a genuine secret agent capable of damaging national security or the operational effectiveness of the Allies. Indeed, the Germans had apparently written her off as 'a dud shell' and it was only gossip which claimed she was one of that country's most skilful women spies. More curiously still, a further document indicates that whatever Mata Hari may or may not have been, the service had a sneaking respect for her. 'She never made a full confession,' the file says, 'and never gave anyone away as her complice [sic]. She was a *femme forte* and she worked alone.'

Ulrike Meinhof (1934–76)

The Urban Terrorist

Ulrike Meinhof, the German extreme left-wing political activist who became known as 'The Most Dangerous Woman in Europe', came from a traditional
bourgeois family background. While a university student, she involved herself in the anti-nuclear movement
and also edited a communist journal, *Konkret*. Gradually Ulrike became involved in more radical groups, and
in 1970 helped to free another notorious activist, Andreas Baader. Together they formed the Baadar-
Meinhoff terrorist gang and carried out a series of bank
robberies, bomb outrages and murders aimed at authority in general and large industrial complexes in particular. Their violent activities made headlines around
the world until Ulrike was arrested in June 1972 and
sentenced to eight years in prison. She did not live to
complete her imprisonment, however, committing suicide in her cell on 9 May 1976. The bizarre story of this
female bomber is told by **Margaret Nicholas**.

Early in the evening of 16 June 1972 a tense German police-man, acting on a tip-off, knocked at the door of a flat in the suburban village of Langenhagen, near Hanover airport.

The door was opened by a sullen-looking woman with straggling hair, who immediately realized her mistake. Suddenly police were swarming everywhere. She struggled hysterically, fought and shouted obscenities. But it was all over for Ulrike Meinhof.

After the biggest and most sustained search in German police history, the middle-class anarchist, who had come to be regarded as the most dangerous woman in Europe, was in their grasp. As she was led away they opened one of her suitcases, packed for a flight from Hanover airport. They were not really surprised to find it contained three 9mm pistols, two hand grenades, one submachine gun and a ten-pound bomb.

With university drop-out, Andreas Baader, as her partner, Ulrike had been waging war on the established order for nearly three years. The terrorist group they formed committed so many crimes, ranging from murder to forgery, that it needed 354 pages to list them when they came to trial. Baader and two other gang leaders were already in prison. But until that June evening when Ulrike Meinhof was captured, the authorities could not rest for she was undoubtedly the intellect, the driving force behind everything.

The story of how she changed from an idealistic student into a fanatical anarchist ready to tear down everybody and everything is full of violence and hatred. Yet in the middle of it she remains a sad figure.

Ulrike Meinhof was born into an intellectual, upper-middle-class family at Oldenburg, Lower Saxony, on 7 October 1934. Both her parents were art historians but her father died when she was only five, her mother when she was fourteen. During her formative years she was fostered by her mother's friend, Professor Renate Riemeck, an intellectual woman of strong radical views. It was said that Ulrike learned from her many of her socialist ideas and the importance of never accepting the edicts of authority without first questioning them.

The attractive, red-haired girl soon showed signs of academic brilliance. In 1957, when she was twenty-three, she went to Munster University to study sociology and philosophy. She campaigned against the atom bomb, the Americans in Vietnam and most of the burning issues that radical minded students were interested in.

One day she was introduced to a thin-faced, handsome man called Klaus Roehl. He ran a lively, left-wing magazine called *Konkret* and when he asked her to join its staff she agreed.

Before long Ulrike had acquired a reputation as a first-class radical journalist, writing columns of such brilliance that she began to be talked about in circles outside the university. She probed into the economy of Germany, dealt with social questions many people felt were being brushed under the carpet and wrote about the misery that existed among those who had no part in Germany's so-called Economic Miracle.

Klaus Roehl made her his editor and his wife.

The magazine was successful enough in its own way, but not a bestseller. When Roehl hit on the idea of adding sex to the political content, it took off. They made a lot of money, lived in a fashionable house and drove round in a large white Mercedes.

Ulrike, now the mother of twin daughters, found herself the darling of radical chic society and became a familiar face on television. But the success and the gloss were superficial and inwardly Ulrike was burning with resentment. Her husband, she had discovered, was a womanizer. His affairs became too much for her and after seven years together, they were divorced.

She gave up her job with her marriage, moved to Berlin and put her daughters, Regine and Bettina, into an old-fashioned, strict-discipline boarding school. This left her free to mix with a group of well-off young people with extreme radical views, who believed the only way to change society was through violence. The idea took root. She was soon publicly defending arson, violent protest and the crimes of urban guerillas. But before she acted politically she had to get rid of some personal bitterness. She started a campaign against her husband and his magazine which culminated in a night of fury in which she and her friends vandalized the home in which she had once taken such a pride.

Through the grapevine she heard a lot about a young agitator and arsonist called Andreas Baader who was serving a prison sentence for his part in burning down a Frankfurt department store. One day she met Baader's 'revolutionary bride', a tall, blonde girl called Gudrun Ensslin, a pastor's daughter, who had studied philosophy. Gudrun told her his friends were determined to get him out and they wanted her to help. On certain days he was allowed to work outside the prison in a Berlin library, and it was decided to 'spring him' from there. On 14 May 1970 Ulrike led the raid with a gang of armed terrorists, leaving the librarian severely wounded and several prison guards with bullet holes. The violence had started.

After Andreas and Ulrike had had time to sum each other up, they agreed to form the Baader-Meinhof gang with a hard core of about fellow anarchists. Apart from themselves the leading members would be Baader's girl friend, Gudrun, and Jan Carl Raspe, who became Ulrike's lover.

Andreas Baader was officially the leader of the group. He was a dark, brooding, handsome man, attractive to women, who based his image on the young Marlon Brando. He was also indolent, spoiled and aggressive. Ulrike Meinhof supplied the drive and the brains in their partnership.

The four of them managed to flee the country after the raid and turned up in the Middle East to train with the Palestine National Liberation Front. But the Germans and Arabs did not get on too well, each accusing the other of being cold and arrogant. The two women were considered domineering and a damned nuisance and before long the PLO decided that their trainees were rebels without a true cause and asked them to leave.

Ulrike remained passionately pro-Palestinian. On her return to Germany she made the shocking decision to send her two small daughters to a refugee camp in Jordan to be trained along with Palestinian children to become *kamikaze* fighters against Israel. Fortunately for them, her plans went wrong. Karl Roehl had been scouring Germany for his children and had even engaged private detectives. He was tipped off just in time and they were snatched from a hideout in Palermo. They hated him at first because their mother's indoctrination had been very thorough. But for all his faults he was a good and devoted father and won back their affection.

The gang grew to be about 150 strong all told. Most of its members were from quite prosperous backgrounds, the only two working class recruits being garage hands, useful for dealing with stolen cars.

They were armed to the teeth with small fire arms, sub-machine guns, hand grenades and bombs and set out on a series of bank raids and robberies to raise funds to buy more. There was one particularly terrible assault on a branch of the Bavarian Mortgage and Exchange Bank in the small provincial town of Kaiserslautern, thirty-five miles west of Heidelberg, in which a police officer was murdered with callous deliberation.

Taking part in the raid was a new recruit, a long haired blonde called Ingeborg Barz. The girl was so horrified by the bloodshed that she made up her mind to go home. She telephoned her parents in Berlin. It was the last they ever heard of her. According to Gerhart Muller, who turned state witness, she was summoned to a meeting with Ulrike Meinhof then driven to a remote spot near some gravel pits where she was executed.

Violence piled upon violence while the ordinary man in the street watched with horror. During two years of urban terror five people were shot or blown to bits, there were fifty-four attempted murders, countless vicious assaults and a series of bombings directed against the American Army in Germany. Ulrike had developed a complete disregard for human life and categorized some people, including policemen, as 'pigs'. Her aspirations were supposed to be humane; to do something about the injustices she saw in human society. In fact she seemed to be using terrorism to work out of her system a load of hatred and bitterness.

The police put all their manpower into an attempt to crack the terrorist hold on West Germany and their chance came one day early in 1972 in a quiet Frankfurt Street. They had received an anonymous tip that a garage there was stuffed with ammunition. They drove up in two lorries loaded with sandbags and began to build a wall – but because they were dressed in overalls they looked more like corporation gardeners delivering bags of peat. After a time a smart lilac-coloured Porsche drew up. Three young men in leather jackets climbed out. Two of them went into the garage, the third, waiting outside on the pavement, was grabbed by the police. They found they had got Carl Raspe the arch terrorist who was also Ulrike's lover. After a long, tense seige, first a gang member called Holger Meins was brought out. Then, after a brief exchange of fire the police dragged out a dark young man writhing with pain from a bullet in the thigh. It was Andreas Baader.

Not long after Gudrun Ensslin was captured in a Hamburg dress shop when a shop assistant discovered a gun in her jacket and phoned the police. Ulrike began to feel very much alone. As the months went by she found that even her friends from the trendy left felt she was too dangerous to be associated with.

Then came the night in June when she decided to head for Hanover airport. She knew a left-wing teacher who had a flat nearby and turned up on his doorstep with several suitcases. He was in a terrible dilemma. He now held a respected position as Federal President of the Teachers' Union. The last thing he wanted was Ulrike Meinhof as house guest. He went to seek the advice of some friends and they urged him to phone the police at once. He made the phone call and stayed clear of the flat . . .

The rest of Ulrike's life was to be spent in prison or in the courtroom where she yelled and shouted abuse at her judges. The trial of the Baader-Meinhof gang was considered so potentially explosive that a fortified courtroom and special cells were built at the top security prison at Stammheim in Stuttgart. There was great fear that reprisals and counter measures would be launched by terrorists still outside.

Though members of the gang were kept apart she became aware as the trial went on of the enmity of the others, especially in the case of Gudrun Ensslin. Solitary, apart from her typewriter and her books, she began to brood. Eventually the pressure must have become too great. On the morning of 9 May 1976 she was found hanging in her cell.

Her followers refused to believe that she had committed suicide and for a time insisted she had been murdered by the authorities. Four thousand people marched in the cortège at her funeral in Berlin, many of them masked to avoid identification. The police felt they were watching over a time bomb and later they had to deal with revenge terrorist attacks.

But of Ulrike Meinhof a priest who knew her said afterwards, 'I think she finally decided she had come to the end of the wrong road . . .'

Phoolan Devi (1960–)

Law of the Bandit Queen

Phoolan Devi is today one of the best-known women in India: famous across the whole continent as 'The Bandit Queen'. For years, this petite, attractive young woman, whose name means 'Goddess of Flowers', defied the might of the authorities until she voluntarily surrendered to government forces in 1984. Her life on the run as a bandit, or dacoit, her shoot-outs with the police and alleged responsibility in the killing of over twenty people, made news far beyond the boundaries of India and has since inspired several books and a film, *Kahani Phoolan ki (Phoolan: The Bandit Queen)*, to which she has strongly objected because she feels it glamorizes the harsh realities of her life. But in a nation obsessed with social hierarchy, she has also been hailed as a champion of low-caste women and of women's rights in general. 'Phoolan Devi for Prime Minister' has been regularly scrawled on walls since her parole from prison in 1995 after serving eleven years. This is 'The Bandit Queen's' own version of her remarkable life as written shortly after her surrender in 1984.

My story is not the story of the film, *Kahani Phoolan ki,*
where I am shown as a romantic person dancing around in
the ravines of the Chambal. My story is one of poverty,
hunger and injustice, which finally led me to flee to the
ravines.

As far as I can recollect, my harassment began when I was
very young when my uncle, Bihari, made life impossible for
us in our village Guruakapurwa in Jalaun district, UP. My
father was a very simple, hardworking man who tilled his
own plot of land and we existed on whatever we could make
from the land. But my uncle, who was a very influential man,
would not have it that way. With the help of the other
powerful people in the village he usurped our land and took
all our crops. The result was that while my uncle lived
prosperously in a comfortable house, we lived in a hovel.
My uncle did not stop at this. He continued to harass us even
after that and, in fact, was instrumental in scuttling the
marriage of my elder sister, Rukmini, even though it had
been settled. When the *barat* reached our doors, he humiliated them and sent them back. Imagine the condition of my
sister who was sitting in the *mandap* ready to get married and
the humiliation that our family had to face in the village after
that. I don't know what my uncle had against us, but try as he
might he could not finally stop Rukmini from getting married.

After this incident, my mother was determined to get me
married as soon as possible and at the age of eleven I was
married to a man in Maheshpur who was about twenty years
older than me. Unfortunately for me, my marriage did not
help in making my life any happier. My husband was a
difficult person and used to treat me very badly. From dawn
to dusk I was made to work very hard. Finally, I could not
take the strain any longer, I fell ill and decided to return to
my parents, only to find that my uncle had in no way stopped
terrorizing my family.

Shortly after my return to the village I got my first taste of
it when my uncle decided to chase us out of the village. He
gathered some of his influential friends in the village and got

my mother beaten up. We were helpless: my father was old and weak, my brother only six years old at that time and the rest of us were women. We just took the humiliation quietly, not daring to protest. We didn't have money and the poor have no right to protest; even if they did, no one would listen to them. The *adhyaksh* of the village, Krishna, also beat me up and my hands and my back were swollen for days. Unhappy in Guruakapurwa and with mounting pressure from my family I went to live with my in-laws on a few occasions, but inevitably returned home ill after a few days. On the fourth occasion, I remember very well, my cousin Maiyadin went with me and told my in-laws (as I learnt later) that I had TB. My in-laws were naturally very upset and one of them took me home to my parents. By this time, I knew the ways of the world. In our malla community, women can be married twice and my mother, instead of sending me to my *sasural* (in-laws) decided on getting me married again. I protested against this and I requested her not to do so. In fact I assured her that I would earn my own living in the village. While the villagers agreed with my mother that I should get married again, my cousin Maiyadin said that he would see to it that I did not get married against my wishes. If the others had any objection to my staying in my parents' house, he would give me shelter in his home. That, I think, resolved the problem and I went to stay with Maiyadin. Once, while I was staying with him, I went to visit my in-laws, only to find that my husband had remarried and there was no place for me in their home. This was made abundantly clear to me by my in-laws during the short period that I was there, by constantly harassing me. I decided to go back to my village again.

By now Maiyadin was in no mood to let me stay in his house. Neither could I go back to my parents. So what could I do? In desperation, I went and sat down on the bank of the Yamuna, near our village. In the evening, my mother met me there and what she told me surprised me: 'Since you are unwanted in your husband's house and your parents' house, why don't you commit suicide by jumping into the well? It is better to die than live in such humiliating conditions.' With tears in her eyes my mother at last took me home.

Back at home, I could no longer tolerate my uncle's harassment and I used to protest quite openly. Often, I would even shout at my uncle. (It was perhaps for this reason that my uncle wanted me out of his way.) Besides my uncle, various other people in the village used to humiliate us. For instance, the loafers in the village used to tease me and very often humiliated me. I remember once the village *sarpanch*, Brijbihari's son teased me and I kicked him a number of times. In revenge, the *sarpanch's* son had me beaten with a shoe by the *mahipal's* son. I was so upset after the incident that I did not want to stay in my parents' house. I went to live with my cousin who is my aunt's daughter. Though I was not comfortable there, the days passed in comparative peace except on the few occasions when I spoke out against my uncle: the harassment would start again.

After a few days I went to visit Rukmini and I spent a fortnight with her. During my stay at her house I heard that a dacoity (a robbery by an armed gang) had been committed at Maiyadin's house and I was astonished to learn that Maiyadin in his report to the police had blamed me for the dacoity. He did not make a complaint against my father, perhaps because he was very old. Neither did he try to implicate my brother because he was a mere child.

I was arrested and taken to the Kalpi police station. The inspector there, Ganga Singh Sangar, beat me up and forced me into unspeakable indignities. He then put me in jail. I was in Uri jail for about twenty days and I remember I constantly cried over what had befallen me.

My cousin, in the meanwhile, announced in the village during a *panchayat* session that if anyone tried to bail me out, he would also be implicated in the dacoity. Thakur Phool Singh Mangrol of Narihar village was passing through our village on his way from the market. He stopped when he saw the *panchayat* session going on and found out why it was being held. When he heard about Maiyadin's declaration, he told my mother to go to the Uri police station and wait for him. He would bail me out, he said. And he did exactly that, after three days.

Within a short while of returning home, Maiyadin started his tricks again. He started meeting the village elders so that I would not be able to protest against the injustices of my uncle. At about the same time. I came to learn that Maiyadin had organized two dacoits, Babu Singh Gujar and Vikram Malla, to kill me. This was told to me by a boy from Khartala, who used to call me 'mausi' (aunt). The boy, a spy for the dacoits, told me: 'Mausi, please run away from home because the baghis (rebels) are coming to get you. They want to humiliate you. The outlaws are saying that you have come out of jail with the bail given by a thakur and were asking why you couldn't find anyone from your own caste (malla) to do that for you.' I told him: 'At least someone bailed me out. No one from the community came to help me.'

Although I tried to put up a brave façade I was frightened by the news that the boy gave me. I decided to go to Kalpi police station and ask for protection. When I lodged my complaint, the officer-in-charge of the police station told me: 'Phoolan, why are you lodging a complaint? The dacoits are mallas and so are you. If they abduct you, they will only keep you for a month or a month and a half. Then they will let you go. You can come home after that.' I told him: 'Sahab, by the time I return my honour will be gone. Probably they will kill me . . . How can I go with them?' The police officer seemed to take pity on me and said: 'Go home, the police will try to protect you . . .'

I reached home and waited for the police to turn up but there was no sign of them. If they had come to protect me, my story would have been different. It was a full moon in Shravan (July – August). The rivers, Jaundhar and Yamuna, were both in spate and everyone had gone to bed after dinner. It was probably midnight when we heard the first knock amidst the rain and thunder. None of us opened the door and then after a louder thump the door suddenly gave way and three men entered.

One of them, looking at me, shouted: 'Come, Vikram is calling you.' 'Why is Vikram calling me?' I asked. There was no reply to my question. One of them only said: 'Vikram is calling you. He is standing outside.' With that they also gave me a warning: 'If you try to run away we will kill you.' Picking up courage, I told them I would go with them.

When they turned to go, I ran and hid in a corner. When they discovered that I was not following them, they caught hold of my brother, Shiv Narayan, and dragged him outside. I could not bear to see my brother being taken away by the dacoits and so I came out of hiding and told them that they could take me anywhere, do anything to me, but they must spare my brother. Hearing my words, the dacoits shouted, 'We've found her, we've found her.' With that one of them caught hold of my hand and dragged me outside where I saw around thirty-five people.

A boat was tied on the banks of the Yamuna and the dacoits forced me into it. The people in the boat kept on telling me: 'Phoolan, do not worry. We are inspectors and policemen from Sikandra police station. We are taking you to identify Vikram so that we can kill him.' But when our boat reached Narihar village, the people in the boat cheered lustily: '*Babu Gujar, Singh ki jai! Vikram Singh ki jai!*' One of them shouted threateningly: 'If there is anyone who can bail Phoolan out, let him come forward. We would like to have a look at him.' It was only then that I realized that these people were not policemen but dacoits from the Babu Gujar-Vikram Malla gang.

Then Babu Gujar came up to me and asked, 'Phoolan, will you stay with me?' To this I replied, 'I do not understand what you are trying to say.' Babu Gujar then asked again, 'Will you stay with me or with Vikram? He has brought you here.' He then threatened me with dire consequences if I opened my mouth. But I would not keep quiet. I asked them: 'What have I done that you have kidnapped me? Neither have I spied on anyone, nor have I hurt anyone. Why have you brought me here?' Babu Gujar questioned me again,

'Did you do the dacoity in your uncle's house?' I was astounded. 'How could I?' I asked. This was greeted by jeers from the dacoits around us.

Babu Gujar then wanted to know who my associates were. I could not reply and burst out crying. Soon I heard a tussle going on about me. They were discussing whether one person would keep me as a mistress or whether I should be shared among every one. Up rose Barah Lal Kuka and he told them, 'Boys, do not harass her now. In one or two days, we shall have decided among ourselves who will keep her.' The dacoits would not agree to that and one of them said that I could be claimed for a price. The price rose from Rs one lakh to Rs ten lakh. But Babu Gujar, who was watching the proceedings, shouted out, 'I do not care if there is a price on her or not but all I can say is that she stays with me.' A minor tussle started between the dacoits with everyone claiming me as his own. Each one said to the other, 'If you touch Phoolan in front of me, you will die.' So, for the moment I seemed to be safe. But soon, Vikram told Babu Gujar, 'Have patience, once we reach Etawah district we will fix this up. Till then, if you want, you can keep her.' That very day, in the evening, Vikram shot Babu Gujar. Soon afterwards, Vikram took me to a village. There he asked me, 'Phoolan, are you willing to stay with me now? Already three people have been killed because of you. Will you keep on acting stubborn or come with me?'

I told him, 'Don't beat me or kill me. I will stay with anyone who treats me with respect.' Then a meeting was held to decide who would keep me. A unanimous decision was taken: since Vikram was the gang leader, I would become his mistress. Vikram's gang used to commit a number of dacoities and kidnappings and I was taken along with them. I remember the first dacoity after I was taken into Vikram's gang. It was at Kiratpur Devkali where the gang-members kept on shouting, 'Remember, this is not a local gang. This is Phoolan's gang!' The police arrived a few minutes later and we had a small battle with them. Even in front of the police, the gang members kept on shouting 'We belong to Phoolan's gang.' In spite of this, I was never given any weapon. It was only when my name became quite notorious, after nine months, that Vikram gave a .12 bore gun.

In our rounds, we went to my village and Maiyadin welcomed all of us. In fact, we stayed in his house. I was surprised to see that he gave each member of the gang a tip of Rs 500. When he came to me, he asked: 'Sister, I hope everything is all right now.' 'I am fine and my situation could not be any worse,' I replied. He had no answer to that. I was so angry that I even refused to eat in his house. It was ultimately Vikram who persuaded me to be more cordial towards my cousin.

Now that I was a member of Vikram's gang I decided to take revenge on all those who had humiliated me. So we went to Dharampur where Mansukh lived. He was the person who had teased me when I was in jail. I remember clearly that he used to taunt me, jeer at me and also make obscene remarks about me. Such was my anger that I told Vikram that unless he killed Mansukh I would leave him and join another gang. It was only then that Vikram killed Mansukh. After Mansukh's death Baladin, another dacoit, joined Vikram's gang. He even congratulated Vikram for killing Mansukh. The irony was that Baladin was Mansukh's brother.

From Etawah we travelled to the banks of Betwah, where in an encounter with some other dacoits Vikram was injured. We learnt later that the persons who had him shot were none other than Lala Ram and Shri Ram, who got Mahavir to do the job for them. Fortunately, Vikram was not fatally wounded though he was shot between the hips and his chest. As soon as Vikram was injured, I took him to Jhansi for treatment but there was no one willing to touch him. We then searched a number of places for a friendly doctor who would treat him: we went to Divyapur, a suburb of Etawah, and then on to Kanpur and from there to Deoria. When Vikram could not be cured even in Deoria we went to Nepal, where a doctor known to us put Vikram on his feet again. We then returned to the ravines, with Vikram vowing that he would take his revenge on Mahavir. What we did not realize was that Vikram would be attacked again and that this time he would not be so lucky.

Within about three weeks of returning from Nepal Lala Ram and Shri Ram again attacked Vikram – they had by now learnt that we were aware that they were behind the attack on Vikram – and shot him dead. It happened like this: Vikram and I were spending the night at Baijamau village and it was close to midnight when we were suddenly woken up by the sound of firing. I awoke instantly and told Vikram that we should flee, thinking that it was the police. Vikram got up, but before he could move he slumped forward as a bullet hit him. I rushed around the room looking for some weapon to protect ourselves. To my dismay I found that there was none around – somebody had taken the trouble of removing them. It was then that I heard Lala Ram and Shri Ram's voices, laughing and threatening me now that I was helpless. It was at this time that the other members of the gang fled in fright and taking the opportunity the Ram brothers came forward and shot at me thrice. Fortunately for me all three shots missed. Then Lala Ram decided to spare my life – at least for the moment – and instead decided to take me with him.

And so we set out on a boat to Simra and when we reached it was about ten in the morning. There we met Pandit Shiv Swaroop who on seeing my condition took pity on me and decided to take me back to my village. But Shri Ram would not hear of it; he lied to the *pundit* saying that the police had killed Vikram and that he would take me back to my village. Panditji, sensing that I was terrified, took us to his house where his wife looked after me. Then I told her exactly what had transpired and hearing this, she started weeping. Then both the *pundit* and his wife begged the Ram brothers to allow me to stay with them, but once again they insisted that they would take me back to my village. But what they planned to do was to take me to Churkhi Thana and kill me there. In the meanwhile, they decided to stay with the *pundit* for a few days.

While we were staying there I got friendly with some of the minions of Lala Ram and Shri Ram. In fact, after a few days they assured me that as long as they were there I should consider myself to be safe. What in fact they were planning to do was to kill the two Ram brothers, but I pretended as though I did not understand and told them that the only thing I wanted was to be free. Unfortunately, Shri Ram discovered the plot and thinking that I was instrumental in planning it decided to kill me without any delay. Once again Panditji came to my rescue and begged for my life and he assured both Shri Ram and Lala Ram that he would look after me. On that condition I was released along with some of the other people who had volunteered to protect me from them.

After they had gone we decided to go to my village. On the way we encountered some policemen who started abusing us and followed it up by shooting at us. We fled in fear and spent the night at Padh, a village on the way to Guruakapurwa.

It was while we were staying here that a message came from Balwan Gareriya, the well-known dacoit, saying that if anyone as much as touched me he would wipe out the village. The message was clear: Balwan wanted me to join his gang and that is precisely what I did. After about a month we met Baba Mustaquim and his gang and I decided that since Mustaquim's gang was bigger I would join it, especially since I was interested in taking my revenge on the Ram brothers for having killed Vikram and for having humiliated me.

But Mustaquim had other ideas. Though he had told me that he would make me the leader of the gang, what he, in fact, wanted to do was to keep me with him as his mistress. But I made it clear to him that I did not want that and this annoyed him. The only person who supported me was Man Singh who was then a member of Mustaquim's gang. However, after two months Man Singh and I broke away from the gang and formed our own gang.

After we had formed our gang we used to stay mostly in the jungles of Hamirpur, Jhansi and Banda and we did commit some dacoities and kidnappings so that we could survive. From here we shifted our scene of operations to the jungles of

Kalpi and there we encountered some trouble with other dacoits – namely the gangs of Ram Avtar and Raghunath, both of whom were *mallas* and they did not like the idea of my forming a gang with Man Singh, who is a *yadav*. So angry were they with me that they decided to kill me. They had, in fact gone to my house looking for me and beat up my parents when they could not help them to locate my whereabouts. Then Man Singh suggested that we flee from Kalpi as there were only four of us in the gang at that time. And so we left Kalpi and made our way to Hamirpur.

It was around this time that Ram Avtar's gang and Vikram's brother, Rampal, together carried out the Behmai massacre and after the carnage they raised slogans in my name so that the people of the village thought that I was responsible for it. Perhaps one reason for this was the fact that they wanted to get the police after us – and since we were ill-equipped, they were sure that we could not escape from their clutches.

When we reached Hamirpur we confirmed the fact that we had been framed for the Behmai massacre; I fell sad and wondered why God was placing so many difficulties in my path. Man Singh explained that difficult days would have to be endured. But I wondered how, considering that we neither had men nor arms and we were desperate to take revenge on Ram Avtar's gang. From there we went to Jalaun to find out the facts about the carnage and reached Gillauli village of Kalpi *thana*. In Gillauli the police surrounded us dangerously. With every passing day their cordon tightened and we stayed surrounded for three days. In between, in a few skirmishes with the police, five of my companions were killed. On the third day when even more police reinforcements arrived, we hid in a tunnel which we dug under a house. But we knew that we could not last long this way, with the police surrounding the entire village. So Man Singh and I changed our clothes – while he wore a *kurta* I wore a *salwar-kameez* – and easily slipped through the police cordon.

After this, the two of us roamed around without weapons and stayed in the jungles of Jhansi, Hamirpur, Chhatarpur and Panna. We did not commit any dacoities during this time. In just a couple of places we looted some people . . . to stay alive. We told the locals that they could loot in our name on condition that they gave us a share.

A year later we met Maniram and Alakh and slowly the gang grew. By this time some gang members of Balwan Gareiya, who had been killed in a police encounter, also joined our gang. It was then that the proposal for our surrender came. One day *havaldar* Parshuram, who was known to us, suddenly brought a man to us. We had him searched and discovered a camera, a tape-recorder and a pistol on him. I told Parshuram that he looked like an officer. He replied, 'Yes, sister, I am Rajendra Chaturvedi, the SP of Bhind.'

Mr Chaturvedi told me that a number of dacoits were surrendering and it would be better for us if we too surrendered. The government, he said, was trying to help the dacoits and would agree to our terms. I said that I was not willing to surrender because I had some problems: I wanted my father's land returned to him and I wanted to kill my enemies. Mr Chaturvedi left without saying anything but returned after three days, saying that the government would ensure that my father got his land back. But even then I did not agree to the surrender. I wanted my family to be safe from any attack after my surrender and I said this to Mr Chaturvedi. Once again he left to return a few days later – this time with the information that my family had been brought over to Gwalior and that there was no need for any apprehension.

After this, I did not see any reason why I should not surrender. God probably wants it, I thought. I discussed it with Man Singh and he agreed with me. Then came the formalities of laying down our conditions and a few days later we surrendered. I hoped that society would treat us with justice and realize the hardship which I had undergone.

I have no problems in jail now. But here too groups have been formed. In the jungle everyone was happy eating onions and *chapatis*. But here everyone seems to be demanding more. There are some complaints against the government that it has not fulfilled any of our demands whereas all the demands of Malkhan Singh, who is also in jail with us, are being met. For instance, Malkhan Singh has been given a large sum of money to build a temple but we have not got a single paise to do so. Again, as far as I know Malkhan Singh was given two and a half to three *bighas* of land while we have not got even an inch.

I will have no complaints if the government does not fulfil anyone's demands; but if it discriminates, then I feel unhappy and problems begin between us and the authorities. We have given up everything and we are suffering in jail so that we can return to society once again. But even then we have made mistakes. Perhaps, it would have been much better if I had committed suicide in the very beginning itself. But I did not do this. Nor did I give in to the tyranny of my uncle, cousins and others. Circumstances made me a dacoit and forced me into misdeeds. Will society ever realize the agony and the humiliation that I have suffered? Perhaps some people will understand my plight. I live in this hope.

Three

The Femmes Fatales

A Parade of Courtesans and Actresses

Nell Gwynne

Nell Gwynne (1650–87)

The Irresistible Sweet Nell

Nell Gwynne was the beautiful orange-seller turned actress who became the most enduring mistress of Charles II and certainly the best-known *femme fatale* of the Restoration period. Indeed, her legend has never dimmed. Nell first came to public attention at the tender age of fifteen, appearing at the Theatre Royal in Drury Lane, London, but it was her wit and vivacity off stage that also captured the imagination of some of the most distinguished men of her time, including the artist Sir Peter Lely who later painted her topless for the King's private collection of pictures. The beguiling Nell retained Charles's affection up to her death, and her influence was considerably more far-ranging than most people suspected. The remarkable story of 'Sweet Nell', an archetypal figure among courtesans, is told here by **Andrew Ewart**.

King Charles II of Merrie England had a barren queen, kept scores of mistresses and acknowledged fourteen illegitimate children. But the names of Marguerite de Carteret, Lucy Walter, Catherine Pegge, Barbara Villiers, Louise de la Valliere and Louise de Perroncour de Querouaille – to mention but a few – have vanished in the mists of the centuries. One of his favourites, however, has become a legend although she was reared in a brothel, earned a living as a pothouse wench, orange-seller, actress and whore before she graduated to the royal bed. Who has not heard of Nell Gwynne?

Not only has her reputation endured for 300 years, but each century seems to have adapted her story according to the mood of the age. In her own time she was the subject of hundreds of anecdotes (most of them smutty), lampoons, plays, memoirs and histories. Our Victorian forefathers, however, would not leave bad alone. To them she became 'sweet Nell of Old Drury', the classic example of the slum child who rose from poverty to palace – and died repenting her sins.

All the evidence available to us suggests that Nell was proud of being a royal whore – and didn't care who knew it. When her great rival for the King's bed, Louise de Querouaille, was created Duchess of Portsmouth, Nell wore 'an exceeding rich suit of clothes' to confront her. The new duchess said patronizingly: 'Nelly, you are grown rich, I believe, by your dress; why, woman, you are fine enough to be a queen.' 'You are entirely right, madam,' replied Nell, 'and I am whore enough to be a duchess.' And she once told her two sons by Charles that they were 'princes by their father for their elevation, but they had a whore to their mother for their humiliation'.

Today any mention of Nell Gwynne is still reasonably certain to produce a chuckle, a grin, or a knowing wink – but no malice. How is it that 'pretty, witty Nell' has ascended such a pinnacle of affection when more illustrious courtesans of the past are forgotten? According to one of her twentieth-century biographers, Arthur Irwin Dasent:

English men, and women too, have always entertained a peculiar liking for Mistress Nell, whilst rightly withholding their sympathy from such kittle cattle as Barbara Villiers and Louise de Querouaille, her two principal rivals in the King's affections. They, though of better birth and exposed to fewer temptations, are remembered, if at all, as having been two of the most rapacious and unscrupulous harpies who ever disgraced an English court.

On the other hand, Nell's invariable kindness to the poor and needy – the class from which she sprang – after she had been raised from grinding poverty to comparative affluence, has been the mainspring of the remarkable interest which has centred round her name.

Successive generations have extended to her an indulgence seldom conceded to the fair and frail in any age or in any country . . . There is abundant evidence that she had a generous and a tender heart, frequently exerting her influence with the King (to whom she was not only sincerely attached but consistently faithful) for good and worthy objects . . .

According to her horoscope, which is still preserved in the Bodleian Library, Oxford, Ellen Gwynne was born at six a.m. on Saturday, 2 February 1650. Her birthplace is in some doubt – London, Hereford and Oxford all claim the privilege – but it was probably in or near Covent Garden, at a small house in a squalid alley called the Coal Yard, Drury Lane. Little is known of her father but her mother was a thoroughly disreputable character who kept a bawdy-house in the Covent Garden district until Nell rescued her and set her up in a respectable Chelsea residence. Old Madam Gwynne was an enormously fat woman who smoked and drank to excess and in her youth had been 'skilled in acts of gallantry'. Nell is quoted as saying that she was brought up 'in a bawdy-house to fill strong waters for the guests'. In July 1679, after a hearty debauch, Madam Gwynne fell into a stream and was drowned.

In mid-seventeenth-century London it was a feat for a

slum child to survive, 'and by the time she was thirteen Nell had a lifetime of experience behind her – serving ale and brandy, selling herring and fruit in the streets, outwitting pickpockets and fending off seducers. Shortly after the Restoration of King Charles, two theatrical companies were formed – the Duke's Company and the King's Company – which established theatres in Lincoln's Inn Fields. The King's Company prospered and set up a larger theatre off Drury Lane. It was here that the thirteen-year-old Nell plied her celebrated trade of selling small oranges to the gentlemen who paid half-a-crown to sit on the backless benches of the pit. If she needed further education in the arts of badinage and profanity, Nell got it in the pit of the King's Theatre, working six days a week and augmenting her small earnings by obliging the gentlemen later. But she was determined to get out of the pit and on to the stage, so she learned to read (but not to write) and took lessons in dancing, singing and elocution. There was a desperate shortage of actresses and Nell soon got her chance – no doubt by way of the casting couch. Soon she became one of the most acclaimed comedy stars of her day.

Although the stage was a considerable step up from the pit, in those days acting was a disreputable occupation for ladies and most of the better-endowed ones were quick to leave if a suitably wealthy keeper offered himself. Nell's keepers had one thing in common – the Christian name: first the actor Charles Hart, a tall, handsome fellow; next Charles, Lord Buckhurst; and finally Charles II (whom she once remarked was her Charles III). Dasent gives this account of her first meeting with the Merry Monarch:

> Nell's personal appearance at this time – she was now seventeen – must have been extremely attractive. She was of middle height, exquisitely formed, with the smallest foot and the neatest ankle in all the town. Her hair was bronze-red, sun-kissed with streaks of gold, her luxuriant tresses falling in silken waves over shapely, snow-white shoulders. Her eyes were of the darkest imaginable shade of sapphire

blue, her mouth a perfect Cupid's bow, revealing when she smiled two rows of small but evenly matched pearly teeth. She had a complexion like the wild rose, a skin of satin and a well-shaped, if, as some say, a tip-tilted nose.

But perhaps the greatest beauty of her face, and it is one that is seldom or never found in those of plebeian birth, was that her eyebrows and eyelashes were dark, in striking contrast to her warm red hair.

He describes how young Villiers (the Duke of Buckingham) escorted Nell to a play in the rival theatre, the Duke's, one afternoon and found King Charles in the next box, incognito. Charles, to Villiers' embarrassment, struck up conversation with Nell, then invited both to supper where he saw to it that his brother, the Duke of York, was present to occupy Villiers' attention while he monopolized Nell. Dasent goes on:

They made a merry party of four at a neighbouring tavern, where Charles, who could make himself well-nigh irresistible to women once his desires were aroused, paid such marked attention to Nell throughout the evening that the quick-witted girl could not fail to perceive the inner meaning of his gallantry.

When the tavern-keeper, unaware of the rank and quality of his guests, presented his bill to the King as the senior member of the party, Charles fumbled in his pockets only to find that he had not enough money with him to discharge it. The Duke of York being found to be equally impecunious, Villiers had to pay the reckoning, not only for himself and his inamorata but for all four.

Nell, amused beyond measure at the comicality of the situation, burst into fits of laughter and, mimicking to perfection the King's tone and usual mode of expression, exclaimed: 'Odds fish! But this is the poorest company that ever I was in before at a tavern.'

Instead of being angry with her for laughing at him, Charles was so captivated by her high spirits that he promptly imagined himself to be head over heels in love. No doubt he had thought much the same dozens of times before, but so rapidly did this new-born passion develop that, before the party broke up, he declared his royal will and pleasure to be that Nell should retire from the stage at the earliest possible moment, and place herself under his protection.

Samuel Pepys the diarist – himself a great but unsuccessful admirer of Nell – notes for 11 January, 1668, that 'the King did send several times for Nelly, and she was with him . . .'

In Restoration England, freed at last from the shackles of Puritan repression, King Charles and his Court went on a gigantic debauch, with whoring and gaming the favourite pastimes. The men about town followed the pattern set from above and lechery was widespread among the monied classes. It was the done thing to keep a mistress and the husband who resented his wife's extra-marital activities was regarded as a spoilsport. There were many who regarded the two major disasters which overwhelmed London during 1665–7 – the Plague and the Great Fire – as a judgment of God on the wicked city. The theatres were shut down and the Court retreated to Oxford.

It was not until May 1670 that the fruits of her royal liaison became apparent – and she named her first-born Charles. The King, moved by her pleading, set her up in a small house at the east end of Pall Mall – one of the poorest dwellings in the neighbourhood. She had not yet achieved the decent status of mistress but was still his whore. She tried desperately to get her son acknowledged and badgered the King for dignities and pensions, but Charles did nothing. Nell changed the situation dramatically by doing something no royal favourite had dreamed of doing – she went back to the stage. The King's Company made her doubly welcome at Old Drury – now they could cash in on her notoriety as mother of a royal bastard. The sly topical allusions were too much for Charles – he started negotiations for the leasehold of a house on the better side of Pall Mall, the house Nell was to live in for the rest of her life. She had now arrived as a mistress. She gave sittings ('naked, leaning on a bed with her child') to the fashionable portrait painter, Sir Peter Lely – and the King made many visits to his studio. In 1671 her second son was born and she named him James, after Charles's brother (later James II).

Nell tried all she knew to win honours for her sons and herself, but when it came to court intrigue she was a hearty amateur compared to her chief rivals for the King's favours, Barbara Villiers and Louise de Querouaille, both of whom had wheedled the rank of duchess out of the weak and easy-going Charles. But in December 1676 a warrant was passed for 'a grant to Charles Beauclerc, the King's natural son (by Nell) and to the heirs male of his body, of the dignities of Baron of Heddington, Co. Oxford, and Earl of Burford in the same county, with remainder to his brother, James Beau-clerc, and the heirs male of his body'. And the King granted both children the right to wear the royal arms crossed with a bar sinister. At last, after six years of scheming, pleading and wheedling, her first-born was a peer of the realm and Nell could claim to be the equal of the court ladies. She had another great ambition, though – to be Countess Somebody-or-Other in her own right. Poor Nell died without achieving that status, but on 5 January 1684 her son was exalted to the title of the first Duke of St Albans with all rights and privileges vested in that rank. Her second son, James, died after an accident in France at the age of eight.

This preferment of her elder son dramatically changed the attitude of the Court towards her. No longer was she shrugged off as a rough-tongued comedienne, but she was accepted by all her aristocratic neighbours at the better end of Pall Mall and St James's. True, some of the King's diehard Ministers were reluctant to acknowledge her new status (as the mother of a royal duke) and a few haughty ladies were outraged at the appearance in their midst of an ex-actress and orange girl. The Dowager Duchess of Richmond told the King that 'she could not abide to converse with Nell and the rest of that gang'. Charles sharply informed her that those he 'lay with were fit company for the greatest woman in the land'. And the wife of the Keeper of Whitehall Palace dared to call Nell 'whore' to her face. She got the swift reply that if anyone else had called her so she would not have objected, but it afflicted her to be called so by one who had been 'an old notorious whore even before whoring was in fashion'.

There is, too, a famous story of her footman whom she found one day bleeding and dishevelled. She asked him to explain his sorry condition. He told her: 'I have been fighting, madam, with an impudent rascal who called your ladyship a whore.' 'Blockhead!' said Nell. 'At this rate you must fight every day of your life. Why, all the world knows it!' 'Do they so?' cried the footman. 'Well, they shan't call me a whore's footman for all that.'

When it became known that she was giving a birthday party for the King, Lady Shrewsbury hinted that she would welcome an invitation. 'No, no,' said Nell. 'One whore at a time is enough for His Majesty.' From time to time she had to beat off many such contenders for the royal bed. One of these was another actress, Moll Davis, and it is said that she and Nell at one time used to take it in turns to accommodate the lusty Charles. Nell decided to eliminate the other so she invited Moll to supper before visiting the King and put a powerful purgative in her food – with predictable consequences.

There can be no shadow of doubt that her natural wit and rumbustiousness captivated Charles II, who loved her in his own vicarious fashion as can be demonstrated from the remarkable fact that she retained her hold on his capricious affections for seventeen years despite the comings and goings of a succession of high-born ladies, the intrigues of courtiers and politicians against her, and the libellous pamphleteering of poets and playwrights who could not resist the target of a low-born whore with a drunken mother. King Charles was mulling over a plan to reward her long and faithful service to the Crown by making her the Countess of Greenwich and granting her heart's desire. But the years of wenching and hard drinking caught up with him. John Evelyn, the aristocratic diarist of that day, writes of Sunday night, 1 February, when he witnessed 'the inexpressible luxury and profaneness' of the Court at Whitehall with King Charles 'sitting and toying with his concubines, Portsmouth (Louise), Cleveland (Barbara), etcetera' (Nell – whose name Evelyn could rarely bring himself to write). When the party broke up Nell kissed her royal lover and was driven across the park to her house in Pall Mall blissfully unaware that she would never see him alive again.

The next morning the King had a fit as he was dressing and for four days he lay in extreme agony while the physicians tried all they knew to relieve him. His mistresses were kept in an ante-chamber while the Queen, his close friends and some of his natural children knelt by the bedside. He spoke tenderly to all and murmured to his brother, the Duke of York, that he was sorry to be so long a-dying. He commended his children to his brother's care and then added in a phrase which has come down the centuries: 'Let not poor Nelly starve.' He died on 6 February in the twenty-sixth year of his reign and fifty-fourth of his life. A few hours later his brother was proclaimed King James II.

No one is accorded less sympathy than a dead king's mistress, and Nell, who had just turned thirty-five, found a pack of creditors howling at her doors. She had enjoyed a pension of £5,000 a year from Charles but that ceased with his death and the unlimited credit she had been allowed with the King as collateral was now wiped out. James II, although by no means a generous man, was an honourable one, but he was surrounded by priests and she could not make an appeal to him in person. She managed to smuggle messages to him through the Keeper of the Privy Purse and received an assurance that the new King had her in mind and would take care of her business in due time. But he had plenty to occupy his mind, including a Spring session of Parliament, so Nell would obviously have to wait though her creditors would not. She mortgaged what she could, borrowed what she could, and raised some £6,000 on her jewels and plate, but was still some £700 short of satisfying all the Shylocks. In May she sent King James a note which began: 'Had I suffered for my God as I have done for your brother and you,

I should not have needed either of your kindness or justice to me.' This produced the desired effect and the King sent her a considerable sum of money with 'kind expressions and assurances for the future'.

Nell was delighted and replied: 'This world is not capable of giving me a greater joy and happiness than your Majesty's favour . . . All you do for me shall be yours, it being my resolution never to have any interest but yours, and as long as I live to serve you, and when I die, to die praying for you.' But she could not refrain from mentioning the dead Charles . . . 'He told me before he died,' she said, 'that the world should see by what he did for me that he had love and value for me . . . He was my friend and allowed me to tell him all my griefs, and did like a friend advise me and told me who was my friend and who was not.' In September she had another pleasant surprise from King James. He paid off the £700-odd that Nell still owed the tradesmen and in addition gave her a Treasury note for £1,300 to be drawn at once, and in December two cash payments of £500 out of the Secret Service funds. And he settled on her a pension of £1,500 a year from 1 January 1686.

She did not enjoy it for long for early in March 1687 she was stricken with apoplexy which paralysed one side of her body. Like her lover, Charles II, she suffered from what was euphemistically called 'the gallant disease' which she had contracted from one of her early lovers and which was now reaching its final stages, causing hardening of the arteries and high blood pressure. Clergymen surrounded her urging repentance, confession and piety. Nell was only vaguely aware that she had sinned. She had been a whore in an age when whoring was a recognized trade. She had loved pleasure but had given much, too, both as entertainer and lover. She was, however, prevailed upon to repent and make a will in which she remembered everybody and gave small bequests to the poor of St Martin's Church and added a request to her son, the Duke of St Albans, that he 'lay out twenty pounds a year for the releasing of poor debtors out of prison every Christmas Day'. Also she bequeathed £50 for the use of the Roman Catholic poor of the parish – to show charity to those who differed from her in religion.

Nell clung on tenaciously to life through the summer and autumn of 1687, but, on 14 November, she died and was buried three days later in the chancel of St Martin's with all the pomp befitting the mother of a royal duke. And Dr Tenison, rector of St Martin's, preached his funeral sermon on the text: 'Joy shall be in Heaven over one sinner that repenteth, more than over ninety and nine just persons who need no repentance.'

And so Nell Gwynne was given over to legend. One of her recent biographers, John Harold Wilson, sums her up thus:

Friendly and kind, witty and giddy, honest and loyal. Nell was above all ambitious and hard-working. By nature humorous, pleasure-loving and frankly carnal, she chose prostitution as an honourable and lucrative profession in an age when the successful courtesan was socially approved. Brought up in the rough schools of bawdy-house and Restoration theatre, she quickly grew skilled in the art of pleasing, and with honest realism she employed her skill to get far more out of life than her birth and breeding warranted. Although she never attained her ambition to be a countess, she kept the affections of King Charles II for seventeen years against formidable competition, founded a line of noble descendants entitled to wear the bar-sinister on their shields and left a son rich in dignities and property. She earned every bit of her success.

Madame de Pompadour (1721-64)

The Power behind the Throne

Madame de Pompadour, the name by which Jeanne Antoinette Poisson is best remembered, was the daughter of a French financial speculator who had to flee the country after a scandal. Nevertheless, she rebuilt her life and ultimately, as the mistress of Louis XV, became one of the most powerful figures in the nation. An intelligent and enchanting woman, she caught the eye and the affections of the King in 1744 and was shortly afterwards created Marquise de Pompadour. Once established at Court, she proved adept at frustrating the machinations of those who wanted to remove her as the monarch's favourite courtesan. For years she also played an active part in the artistic and cultural life of France, and is credited with the famous remark to Louis XV, '*Après nous le déluge!*' The story of this witty and highly influential courtesan is told by **Nancy Mitford**.

The King's mistress was a traditionally unpopular figure in France. She was also a convenient scapegoat. The French could thus love their monarch, while laying his more unpopular actions at her door. (Marie Antoinette, who doubled the role of wife and titular mistress, suffered in her turn from this long established attitude.)

After the Peace of Aix la Chapelle, in 1748, Madame de Pompadour became more unpopular every day. The public was displeased by the treaty and indeed, considering the splendid victories of French arms during the past years, it did seem rather unprofitable. The only advantage it brought to France was a not very exalted establishment for Madame Infante whose husband received the duchy of Parma. 'As stupid as the Peace,' said the Parisians, and blamed Madame de Pompadour.

Only those who have known what we call now a bad press can realize what a perpetual source of irritation it is, nearly always, to its victim. Nowadays the victim can at least answer back, with a dignified letter to *The Times*, or a less dignified libel suit, or he can hire a publicity agent. But the bad press of the eighteenth century was impossible to combat, taking, as it did, the form of horrid little poems and epigrams passed from mouth to mouth, posters, pamphlets and leaflets, all anonymous. Hundreds of these were directed at Madame de Pompadour, they were called the Poissonades; dull and dirty, they are untranslatable, since they nearly all depend on a play of words round her maiden name. Most of them originated at Court, with courtiers too stupid to realize that in thus attacking the monarch they were casting opprobrium on their own way of life. M. Berryer, the chief of police, a devoted friend of Madame de Pompadour, was crossing the state rooms at Versailles one day when he was rudely stopped by a group of courtiers who asked him how it was he could not run to earth the authors of the libels. 'You ought to know Paris better,' they said. He gave them a sharp look and said he knew Paris like the palm of his hand, but was not so much at home at Versailles. The Parisians lapped up the Poissonades, added to them and eagerly distributed them; the King was not spared and the two names were bandied about with evil intent. Nothing they could do was right. If they entertained they were wasting money, if they did not it was her fault because she wanted to prevent him from meeting other women. When they built the house at Bellevue, they were abused by half the public for spending too much, and by the other half for building such a wretched little house, smaller than that of a *fermier général*.

Each taxpayer felt that her houses, furniture and works of art were paid for out of his own pocket, and to make matters worse, her taste was for small things of an impermanent nature. Instead of great monuments like those of Louis XIV, the King's money was being frittered away on such toys as little wooden pavilions in the forest, built and furnished with amazing elegance, surrounded with large groves of exotic trees, and aviaries of tropical birds, visited once or twice and then taken down again so that the next year it was impossible to see where they had been. Croÿ describes a visit to Trianon with the King, who showed him the hot-houses, the rare plants, the hens (which he specially liked), the charming pavilion, the flower and the vegetable gardens; all arranged so prettily. Croÿ is full of admiration, but deplores the fact that Madame de Pompadour should have given the King 'an unfortunate taste for expensive little things which cannot last'. This view was shared by the public. Madame de Pompadour excelled at an art which the majority of human beings thoroughly despise because it is unprofitable and ephemeral: the art of living.

When the Marquise first arrived at Versailles she had four implacable enemies there, the Duc de Richelieu, the brothers d'Argenson (the Marquis and the Comte), and the Comte de Maurepas. The last three were ministers, of *bourgeois* antecedents, sons of ministers in the government of Louis XIV. The Marquis d'Argenson, already out of favour, was sent away in 1747, more through the influence of Madame Infante than that of Madame de Pompadour. He was not disgraced, since he was allowed to resign, but he left the Court and would never have been heard of again had he not kept a diary. Unfortunately for Madame de Pompadour, since it is largely devoted to envenoming her memory, this diary is far the wittiest and best written of the memoirs of her contemporaries. However, d'Argenson overdoes it and the reader ends by hardly believing a word he says. He is one of those diarists who are fond of prophesying and whose prophecies never seem to come true. The King is getting tired of her, she has completely lost her looks: old, yellow, faded and withered, her teeth have gone black, her neck is all scales, her bosom a terrible sight, she is spitting blood; the King cannot bear to go near her, she disgusts him, he will send her away and go to live with his family. Everything she touches turns to ruin, and so on. At the same time the other diarists, who, after all, lived at Versailles and saw her every day, entirely contradict him; they record that never has she been prettier, gayer, or the King more in love, and everything she does is delicious and delightful.

D'Argenson, scribbling furiously away in the country, was no menace to Madame de Pompadour in her lifetime, but the other two politicians were. Maurepas was the first to show his claws. He was a minister of thirty-one years' standing, at this time Minister of the Marine, and he had enormous influence with the King, who had, of course, known him from a child. He was a most entertaining, lively fellow, who roared with laughter, especially at his own jokes; except for the Duc de Richelieu, he amused the King more than anybody. Writing in his journal the best account we have of Madame de Pompadour's presentation at Court, he adds: 'She is excessively common, a *bourgeoise* out of her proper place, who will displace everybody if she is not soon herself displaced.'

It was his aim to see that this should happen, as quickly as possible. But, so far from her being displaced, he found her daily becoming more powerful. She was nearly always present when he saw the King; she would not hesitate to burst in, when they were working together, with some such request as the cancellation of a *lettre de cachet* issued by Maurepas.

Should he venture an objection, the King always took her side: 'Do what Madame suggests, please.' None of the mistresses had liked Maurepas but none had dared to treat him in such a way. 'M. de Maurepas,' she said, on one occasion, 'you are turning the King yellow. Good day to you, M. de Maurepas.' The King said nothing, and Maurepas was obliged to gather up his papers and go.

His revenge was to heap ridicule on her, to imitate her *bourgeois* ways as soon as her back was turned, and to invent Poissonades. He was an accomplished rhymester; all the most spiteful and beastly of these were attributed to his pen. Madame de Pompadour was determined to get rid of him, but Maurepas, quite well aware of this, was not at all alarmed; he thought himself indispensable to the King. This was a misapprehension under which each of Louis XV's ministers suffered in turn; it is very curious to see how little they seem to have understood the circumstances of their predecessors' exits. The King was too shy, he hated any form of embarrassment too much, ever to hint that somebody was displeasing him. He would let matters go on until, having had enough, he would strike with a dreadful swiftness; a letter of dismissal and banishment, couched in freezing terms, would be delivered to the unsuspecting offender.

In 1749, more and more hateful verses were being whispered round the Court until finally Madame de Pompadour, sitting down to supper, found, in her napkin, the famous quatrain:

> *Par vos façons nobles et franches,*
> *Iris, vous enchantez nos cœurs;*
> *Sur nos pas vous semez des fleurs*
> *Mais ce ne sont que des fleurs blanches.*

The disgusting implication of this rhyme, that Madame de Pompadour suffered from *fluor albus*, whether true or not, was perfectly clear to all who read it and the Marquise, usually rather philosophical about such things, was thoroughly upset. Dr Quesnay went to the King and said the whole affair was preying on her mind and making her ill; indeed she now had a miscarriage, followed by one of her attacks of fever. She told the King that she was thoroughly frightened, Maurepas would murder her, she said, as, some thought, he had murdered Madame de Châteauroux. But the King still hesitated to dismiss him. He was fond of Maurepas, old friend of all his life; he enjoyed working with him, and thought him good at his work. Above all, he loved his jokes. Madame de Pompadour made a temporary alliance with Richelieu over this affair; *Son Excellence* hated the minister even more than he hated the mistress and for the same jealous reasons.

Together they composed a memorandum, which they gave to the King, accusing M. de Maurepas of allowing the Navy to become dangerously weak. They had not entirely invented this; as early as 1745 the Duc de Luynes says that many people considered Maurepas responsible for the fall of Louisburg,* whose garrison he was supposed to have kept short of ammunition. He was also accused of an act of gross negligence – it was said that three ships of the Compagnie des Indes were captured by the English, because Maurepas had omitted to tell them the route which could safely have been taken.

Of course he answered this memorandum with the plausibility of an old hand at the political game; nothing had been his fault. The money, he added – with a dig at Madame de Pompadour – which should have been used for building ships, seemed to have gone into other channels. One morning, the Marquise ordered her sedan chair and, accompanied by Madame d'Estrades, she went to call on him. 'Nobody shall say that I send for the King's ministers.' Then, very sharply, 'When will you find out who it is that writes these poems?' 'As soon as I do find out, Madame, I shall of course inform His Majesty.' 'You are not very respectful, Monsieur, to the King's mistresses.' 'On the contrary, Madame, I have always respected them whoever they may be.'

*In Nova Scotia. Louisburg was razed to the ground by the English.

The Court was naturally buzzing with the news of this unaccustomed morning call, and that evening, at a party, somebody said to Maurepas that he seemed to have had an interesting visitor. 'Yes,' he replied carelessly, for all to hear, 'the Marquise. It won't do her any good, I'm not lucky to the mistresses. I seem to remember that Madame de Mailly came to see me two days before her sister took her place, and of course everybody knows that I poisoned Madame de Châteauroux. I bring them all bad luck.' These rash words were immediately reported to the private apartments; Maurepas had gone too far. Next morning at the King's *lever* he was in wonderful form, never had he talked more brilliantly and never had the King laughed so much at his sallies. He announced that he was going to Paris that afternoon for a wedding.

'Enjoy yourself,' said the King, as they parted. He himself was going to Madame de Pompadour's little house at La Celle, near St Cloud, with a few friends, including Richelieu. The next morning at eight o'clock *Son Excellence* was seen leaving for Paris, in such tremendous spirits that the onlookers wondered if some misfortune had not befallen M. de Maurepas. Also at eight o'clock the Comte d'Argenson, who had received a note from La Celle in the middle of the night, went to wake up Maurepas, sound asleep after his wedding party. One look at d'Argenson's face told the Minister what had happened. The wretched man, who lived but for society, politics and the life at Court, rubbed his eyes and read the following note:

M. le Comte de Maurepas, having promised to tell you myself when I have no further use for your services, I request you herewith to resign your ministry. As your estate at Pontchartrain* is too near, I request you to retire to Bourges during this week, without having seen anybody but close relations. Send your resignation to M. de Saint Florentin. Louis.

*A few miles from Versailles.

Smiling, imperturbable as ever, Maurepas got up, dressed and went his way. He knew his master well enough to know that this was final. Ministers who lost their jobs at that Court were always exiled, since the King did not care to see their gloomy, reproachful faces, with an implied, 'I told you so', when things went wrong. Nobody had ever been recalled. Maurepas, luckier than most, did return to Versailles; some twenty-five years later Louis XVI made him Prime Minister and was not well advised in doing so.

The Duc de Nivernais, Madame de Pompadour's *petit époux,* was married to Maurepas' sister, and a few months later (1749) he wrote from Rome to the Marquise:

. . . May I be allowed to describe his condition, without society, with nothing to occupy him, in a country which is literally a desert, where the air is unhealthy most of the year and where the roads are impassable from November to May . . . You know quite well how delicate Madame de Maurepas is; not a single day that she doesn't suffer either from colic of the stomach or from sharp pains in the head, where she very likely has a growth such as killed her father. Should she get a fever, she would certainly be dead before a doctor could arrive from Paris. She and her husband have this prospect ever before them; it goes to my heart to think of it; surely I can touch yours, and that of the King, always so good and understanding. All we ask, and it seems not unreasonable, is that His Majesty should allow him to live on his estate at Pontchartrain, to be understood that Paris would be out of bounds – his punishment would still be terrible enough . . . [Followed by two more pages on these lines.]

The Marquise merely replied that this letter did not surprise her at all; it was what she would have expected from such a nice person. In fact the King had been more thoughtful and merciful than he might have been in this matter. He had chosen Bourges because Maurepas' greatest friend and close relation, the Cardinal de la Rochefoucauld, was Archbishop there, and the Maurepas went to live with him. Four years later they were allowed to return to Pontchartrain, both in perfect health.

In September, 1749, the King decided to inspect his fleet at Havre and to take Madame de Pompadour with him. His popularity among the Normans was still as great as it had been at the time of Fontenoy and they do not seem to have been at all put out by the presence of a mistress instead of a wife; a double line of people waited to cheer them the whole way between Rouen and Havre. The only slight set-back was when the Bishop of Rouen, the Queen's Chaplain, indicated, by a respectful silence, that he would prefer not to have Madame de Pompadour under his roof for the night. They were obliged to make other arrangements. The account of this journey shows what enormous physical endurance Louis XV expected of his friends. The party left Crécy in the morning, Mesdames de Pompadour, du Roure, de Brancas and d'Estrades in a berlin, the King and the Duc d'Ayen *tête-à-tête* in a smaller carriage. They took riding horses and some hounds with them and hunted most of the way. That evening they arrived at the Château de Navarre, where the Duc de Bouillon gave a big party. All next day the King hunted in the forest; after supper they got back into their coaches and travelled through the night, arriving at Rouen at eight in the morning. They did not stop, but went straight on, through cheering crowds, to Havre, where they arrived at six p.m.

After an enthusiastic reception, the governor took them up a tower to look at the sea, which most of the party had never seen in their lives. A bitter wind soon drove them back to the Hôtel de Ville, where supper for twenty-eight was prepared. Next morning the King got up early to go to church while Madame de Pompadour received presents and compliments from the municipality, exactly as if she had herself been royal. All that day there were ceremonies, lasting well into the night, when 200 ships were illuminated in the harbour.

Next morning the party left for Versailles, only stopping once on the way.

Except with the Normans this journey was very unpopular; it was supposed to have cost a fortune and the King was blamed for taking his mistress with him so openly.

From now on Louis XV shut himself up in his houses and hardly ever left them again, never even going to Paris unless absolutely obliged to. He felt himself criticized unjustly, and misunderstood, and a serious riot which broke out in Paris confirmed him in this feeling. There were various causes for discontent. The Peace of Aix la Chapelle, which had been signed the year before, 1748, had brought no relief from taxation. Corn was scarce and prices were high. The immediate reason for the uprising, however, was the disappearance of a little boy. Waifs and strays, together with prostitutes and other undesirables, were rounded up from time to time by the police and shipped off to colonize Canada; the story went round that the police received so much a head, and Parisian parents lived in terror that their children would be picked up by mistake, or even kidnapped. The small boy of certain respectable citizens disappeared mysteriously; the frantic mother roused her neighbours; finally a whole quarter of the town rose in fury. Howling against Madame de Pompadour, the mob pursued Berryer, who was, justly, considered as her creature, to his house, threatening to kill him and burn it down. With great presence of mind he threw them a policeman, who was torn to pieces while Berryer opened all his doors and windows. The rioters, suspecting a trap, beat a hasty retreat.

Of course, neither Berryer nor his masters believed a word of the kidnapping story, and they were all outraged by the accusation. The King refused to drive through Paris when next he went to Compiègne – 'Can't see why I should go to Paris to be called Herod' – a new road was made for him across the plain of St Denis; it is still known as the *Chemin de la Révolte*. He suffered when his people behaved, as it seemed to him, so unreasonably. He felt that he and they were united by a religious link; he loved them, he lived for them, and like a father with naughty children he was vexed. But he was as far from understanding the root of the trouble as he was from knowing how it could be cured.

He had been brought up to consider that France was his property in the same way as an estate was the property of its owner. Taine, writing in 1875, says that the King would have thought it as surprising and unfair to be put on a civil list, as a modern millionaire if the State took away part of his income. A huge proportion of the national revenue was spent on the royal household. This had been regarded as a natural order of things by his subjects while taxes were low, but France had been at war for seven years, taxes were high, those who paid them thought they were not collected fairly and there was a great deal of murmuring. Unfortunately, like so many of the rulers of France, Louis XV did not understand money at all. When he was younger he came back from Paris one day so horrified by the poverty and famine he had seen there, that he immediately dismissed eighty gardeners. Then it was pointed out to him that these men and their families would die of starvation, so he took them back again. He had the irritating impression that he could never do right.

As for Madame de Pompadour, who loved Paris so much, she almost gave up going there. When she did so, it was at the risk of an embarrassing incident. If she went to the Opéra she would be greeted with ironical cheers, too loud, and lasting too long, to sound quite real; if she went to the convent to see her little girl, her carriage would be covered with mud; and on one occasion when she went to dine with M. de Gontaut, such terrifying crowds gathered that he was obliged to hurry her off by the back door. But none of this in any way affected her rise to power: after the exile of Maurepas and the journey to Havre she was regarded at Court as paramount. Only God or another woman, it was felt, could now bring a term to her ascendancy; no man could hope to do so.

Her enemies bided their time and bided it in vain, for it never came. Henceforward the King, though very faithful to his old friends, made no new ones except through the Marquise; favours and advancement could only be obtained through her. The courtiers assumed a new attitude towards her as she did towards them. Her staircase was thronged with people who wanted her to do something for them; she received them kindly and patiently and always tried to help them if she possibly could.

Marmontel describes calling on her, at her *toilette*, with Duclos and the Abbé de Bernis. 'Bonjour, Duclos, bonjour, Abbé,' with an affectionate tap on his cheek, and then, in a lower, more serious tone of voice, 'Bonjour, Marmontel.' He was, at the time, a penniless, unknown, unsuccessful young writer; he took her a manuscript which she promised to read. When he returned for it she got up on seeing him, and leaving the crowd of courtiers standing there, she led him into another room. They talked for a few minutes and she gave him the manuscript covered with pencilled comments. Back among the courtiers, Marmontel saw that the effect of all this on them had been prodigious. Everybody pressed forward to shake his hand, and one nobleman, whom he scarcely knew, said: 'Surely you're not going to cut your old friends?'

As in the Queen's bedroom there was no chair for her visitors, who were therefore obliged to stand, whatever their rank, even if they were Princes of the Blood. In the whole history of France no other commoner had ever dared to behave thus, and yet there only seem to have been two protests: the Prince de Conti dumped down on her bed one morning, saying 'That's a good mattress,' and the Marquis de Souvré perched on the arm of her chair while talking to her. 'I didn't see anywhere else to sit.' But these daring actions were not repeated, and the Marquise got her way in this as in most other things. She began to study Court usage of the previous reign and modelled herself on Madame de Montespan, sitting in the former mistress's box at the theatre and in her place in the chapel. It was noticed that she spoke of 'we', meaning herself and the King.

'We shall not see you for several weeks,' she said to the Ambassadors on the eve of a voyage. 'For I suppose you will hardly come all the way to Compiègne to find us.' Guests at her country houses were obliged to provide themselves with uniforms as at the King's little houses. Her retinue of fifty-eight servants included two gentlemen, decorated with the order of St Louis, and ladies of quality. She built the Hôtel des Réservoirs, in Versailles, to house them and as an overflow for her collections; it was almost an annex to the palace and joined to it by a covered passage. All these signs of power came gradually; gradually the courtiers understood that there were now two Queens of France within the walls of Versailles, and that it was not the wife of the King who reigned.

Lady Emma Hamilton (c.1765–1815)

The Beguiling Lady Hamilton

Lady Emma Hamilton, born Emily Lyon, the daughter of a humble Cheshire blacksmith, was undoubtedly one of the great beauties of her age. She was admired by the rich and famous throughout Europe and ultimately became the mistress of the great English seaman, Admiral Horatio Nelson. Alternately a servant, artist's model, prostitute and courtesan, Emma moved into high society as the mistress and then wife of Sir William Hamilton. But it was a meeting with Nelson in 1793 that proved her moment of destiny and soon after the Admiral's successful Battle of the Nile, they became lovers under the very nose of the unfortunate Sir William. As mistress to one of the nation's greatest heroes, her fame was assured – but after his death at the Battle of Trafalgar, Emma's love of money and high living brought her legend to a sad end, as **George Ryley Scott** describes in the following account.

If ever there has lived a modern Aphrodite it was Emma
Hamilton *née* Lyon. She captivated the epicurean Greville,
she pushed the doddering Sir William into marriage, she had
the peacocky Nelson running at her heels like a Pomeranian
dog, she had Romney worshipping her to such an extent as to
say, 'I think her superior to all womankind.'

The information respecting the astute Emma's birth and
early career is extremely scanty; quite as scanty, for instance,
as that concerning Nell Gwynne. The only person who could
have set down the truth was Emma herself and this she had
not the slightest intention of doing: her youthful escapades
she intended to remain buried; any references she made to
them were palpably untrue and gorgeously decorated.

Her father was one Henry Lyon, a blacksmith plying his
trade in the village of Great Neston, Cheshire: he survived
the infant Emma's birth by some two years. There is a tale to
the effect that Emma was not Henry Lyon's child at all; that
Mrs Lyon herself was not averse to extramarital adventure
and that the future Lady Hamilton could, if the truth were
told, claim to have in her veins blood as blue as ever any that
coursed through her husband's. No evidence of the truth of
the tale has ever been presented and the probability is that
Emma herself caused it to be circulated, just as she did her
utmost to circulate the myth that she received in childhood
an excellent education.

All that is actually known is that this Mrs Lyon had a
female child somewhere about 1763–5, baptized as Emily
Lyon on 12 May 1765. The mother, an ignorant bumpkin,
took the infant and herself to her native village of Hawarden
in Flintshire, and there in poverty the two of them lived until
Emma, as she was called, was old enough to go into service.

How many affairs, to give them no harsher name, Emma
Lyon figured in during those early days we shall never know,
but at sixteen we find her installed as the mistress of Captain
John Willet Payne. The birth of a daughter ended this
liaison. Her next affair was of longer duration – it lasted
almost a year – and was with no less a personage than Sir
Henry Featherstonhaugh: Emma was rising in value. An-

other pregnancy sent her once again to the streets. And on the streets she remained for some time with adventures the nature of which one can only guess until Dr Graham, an unscrupulous charlatan, hired her as the star turn at his notorious 'Temple of Health'. In addition to being the doctor's mistress Emma was trained to pose as 'Hebe Vestina', Goddess of Health. Ostensibly the exhibition was in the interests of hygiene, in reality it was merely a vulgar spectacular erotic show. But the seductive Emma was to turn her experience to good account in later years when, as Lady Hamilton, to the applause of the cream of Naples society, she repeated the poses she had learned under the tuition of the scoundrelly doctor.

What exactly led to the break with Dr Graham I can find no record of, but she next appears as artist's model for the sensual Romney; from which dubious position she stepped into the more elegant one of mistress to the Honourable Charles Greville.

Of women Greville was something of a connoisseur. He looked upon a woman much as he looked upon a picture, a piece of furniture or an ornamental trifle. Of love, in its real sense, he knew nothing. His was the sensualist's epicurean attitude. Well might he have said with Timon, 'Upon the day when I quit life the memory of three thousand women will not satisfy me.' There was, however, an obstacle to too free indulgence: the Honourable Charles's means were limited. However, he took Emma to his house in Edgware Row, where as his mistress she reigned in something approaching regal style; her mother acting as a sort of decorative housekeeper and in the process swallowing any qualms she pretended to feel at her daughter's doubtful position. For five years this arrangement continued, during which period three children were born. Of their destiny history is silent for Greville would acknowledge none of them, and Emma as Lady Hamilton chose to forget that she had ever had an accouchement.

Five years was a long time for the fickle Charles to keep a

mistress. The gilt was tarnishing and the admiration of his uncle, Sir William Hamilton, while on a visit to England, gave Greville an opportunity to get rid of Emma and at the same time do a remarkably good stroke of business for himself. As usual the nephew was heavily in debt, and what really took place was a sale of Emma to Sir William, the price agreed upon being the paying of Greville's debts. The deal was one calling for some niceness. There are indications that Emma Lyon was as sincerely attached to Charles Greville as it was possible for her to be attached to any mortal being. She was luxuriating in surroundings such as she was loath to leave; she naturally preferred the embraces of a comparatively young man to those of one verging on senility. From the first, Greville, who had aesthetic objections to his mistress betraying the manners of a charwoman, had given some attention to her education, and ostensibly in furtherance of this he sent her on a visit to Naples. Once installed in Sir William's establishment she was quickly acquainted with the fact that Charles Greville had finished with her: the choice of becoming mistress of Sir William Hamilton or clearing out was put in polite words. Not being a fool she accepted the proposition.

At this time Sir William Hamilton was fifty-seven. he was a man of unimpeachable heredity and character, possessed of great wealth, and holding a most important diplomatic post: representative of the British Government at the court of Naples. His first wife, a Miss Barlow, had died some five years before this. His hobbies were studying volcanoes and collecting antiques.

The court of Maria Carolina, Queen of Naples, was of its day perhaps the most licentious in all Europe. It was the rendezvous for the aristocratic debauchees of a continent. Nelson's description of it as a gathering 'of fiddlers and poets, whores and scoundrels', was no exaggerated one. Sir William Hamilton, as British Ambassador at Naples, was a frequenter of the court and it was to such an environment, that, in her twenty-third year, was brought Emma Hart, as she was now known, ex-prostitute. It took Emma five years to induce Sir William to make her his wife, but on 6 September 1791, while visiting England, the wedding took place and Emma, as Lady Hamilton, returned to Naples with her sixty-one-year-old husband. Emma was now publicly received at the Queen's court, became intimate with Maria; so intimate indeed as to participate in her plots.

There have been fierce and protracted disputes as to whether Lady Hamilton did give to the British Government the help to which she so persistently laid claim. While her apologists have admitted her claims to the hilt, her opponents have airily waved them aside as barefaced fiction designed to impose on the generosity of a nation. The truth probably lies between the two. Undoubtedly Lady Hamilton was in a position to obtain information of value to the British Government, and a woman of such duplicity and unscrupulousness would hesitate never a second in exhausting every artifice in this direction if it were to her own private advantage to do it. The fact that there were in existence no records of any truck which the Government had with Lady Hamilton says nothing. There would be no such records. True enough, the statements in the book published by Lady Hamilton after Nelson's death, written to her order by a literary hack, were miles from the actual facts. But Nelson, who of all persons should be in a position to know, admitted both his own and the Government's indebtedness to Emma's efforts. On 21 October 1805, before engaging in the battle which was to cost him his life, he made a bequest. It read:

Whereas the eminent services of Emma Hamilton, widow of the Right Honourable Sir William Hamilton, have been of the very greatest service to our King and country, to my knowledge, without her receiving any reward from either our King or country:

First, that she obtained the King of Spain's letter, in 1796, to his brother the King of Naples, acquainting him of his inclination to declare war against England; from which letter the ministry sent out orders to the then Sir John Jervis, to strike a stroke, if opportunity afforded, against either the arsenals of Spain, or her fleets: that neither of these was done is not the fault of Lady Hamilton; the opportunity might have been offered.

Secondly, the British fleet under my command could never have returned the second time to Egypt, had not Lady Hamilton's influence with the Queen of Naples caused letters to be wrote to the governor of Syracuse, that he was to encourage the fleet being supplied with everything, should they put into any port in Sicily. We put into Syracuse, and received every supply; went to Egypt, and destroyed the French fleet.

Could I have rewarded these services, I would not now call upon my country. But as that has not been in my power, I leave Emma Hamilton, therefore, a legacy to my King and country; that they will give her an ample provision to maintain her rank in life.

I also leave to the beneficence of my country my adopted daughter, Horatia Nelson Thompson; and I desire she will use, in future, the name of Nelson only.

These are the only favours I ask of my King and country, at this moment, when I am going to fight their battle.

May God bless my King and country, and all those I hold dear! My relations it is needless to mention; they will, of course, be amply provided for.

That this request was totally ignored is nothing to the credit of the nation. If a particle of Lady Hamilton's claims were true, and if one half of Nelson's claims on her behalf were true, she was at any rate undoubtedly deserving of the same treatment as was accorded Nelson's sanctimonious brother who got an annuity of £5,000, the which he had done nothing whatever to earn. George IV, then Prince of Wales, dissolute rake that he was, had a better sense of justice than the virtuous guardians of the nation's purse. He wrote: 'I hope that there is still in this country sufficient honour, virtue, and gratitude to prompt us to ratify and to carry into effect the last dying request of our Nelson.'

*　　*　　*

Like most popular heroes Nelson has been overrated. When living he was something to worship as a god; wherever he moved in society his opinions were listened to with awe. Whatever Nelson's genius as a naval commander, he needed his mother at his side when he first encountered Emma Hamilton. It was while visiting Naples in 1793 that the fateful meeting occurred: it was five years later, after the victory at the Nile, that Nelson became the slave of the woman who was fascinating European society.

To Emma Hamilton a man was merely another satellite. To see a male celebrity of passable looks and reasonable age was to see another to add to her already huge list of conquests. At her finger tips were all the wiles of the seducer, the Egyptian courtesan, the modern gold-digger. Nelson was almost too easy. The man was bursting with a colossal vanity, an insatiable appetite for praise. He had all of a Lord Mayor's, a lion tamer's, a Lodge Master's taste for prancing about on every possible occasion decorated with medals and ribbons: there are strong grounds for supposing that his inordinate love of show was the cause of his death at the hands of a marksman spotting just such decorated officers. In short, Nelson was a vulgar showman, greedy for every kind of honour, insatiable in his drinking up of every form of slobbering praise. With dazzling fame, he was tired of the plain and somewhat withered Lady Nelson: the young, beautiful, fascinating, gorgeously upholstered Lady Hamilton was just such a woman as he could proudly display: she appealed to the gaudy, circus-horse glitter that above all things Nelson loved. And there is no doubt whatever that the commander was hopelessly in love with Emma: he was infatuated if ever man was. By the closing months of 1800, when Sir William Hamilton and his wife, accompanied by Nelson, returned to England, he was Emma's slave.

The next phase in the drama is the most remarkable of all. It is marked by a degree of blindness on the part of Sir William well-nigh incredible. When Nelson returned with the Hamiltons to England all London knew that Lady

Hamilton was Nelson's mistress: in fact pretty nearly everybody knew it with the exception of Sir William himself.
Nelson was almost insane in his passion: he could not keep
away from his charmer. He made no efforts to conceal his
affair even from his own wife; he engaged with her in vulgar
quarrels in the presence of his mistress. In the end Nelson
and Emma concocted a precious scheme by which Sir William was induced to believe that Nelson's home life was
unendurable. The hospitality of the Hamilton house was
offered to Nelson and it was immediately accepted.

How the secret of the birth of Emma's child was kept from
Sir William remains to this day an impenetrable mystery.
The accouchement took place at 23, Piccadilly, on 31 January
1801. Emma's robustness enabled her to be about again in
less than a fortnight; the child in the meantime was smuggled
to the house of Mrs Gibson in Marylebone, and the whole
Hamilton household, heavily bribed by Nelson and his lover,
kept their tongues securely behind their teeth. Even with all
this one can only account for the success of the scheme by the
supposition that Sir William was in his dotage. Attempts
have repeatedly been made to throw doubt on the responsibility of Nelson for the child, but apart from the extreme
unlikelihood of the tottering seventy-year-old husband being
capable of fecundation, Nelson and Lady Hamilton, at any
rate, seem to have had no doubt as to the parentage. Mrs
Gibson's daughter averred that Nelson was a frequent visitor
to her mother's house when he 'played for hours with the
infant on the floor, calling her his own child'. Even more
conclusive is a letter written by Nelson to Lady Hamilton,
dated 1 March 1801, in which he says:

Now, my own dear wife – for such you are in my eyes,
and in the face of heaven – I will give full scope to my
feelings, for I dare say Oliver will faithfully deliver this
letter. You know, my dearest Emma, that there is nothing in this world that I would not do for us to live
together, and to have my own dear little child with us. I
never did love anyone else. I never had a dear pledge of

love till you gave me one; and you, thank my God, never gave one to anybody else.

Oliver was Nelson's confidential servant.

At this time Nelson and Lady Hamilton were corresponding with each other under the pseudonym of Thompson, and at Marylebone the child was baptized as Horatia Nelson Thompson. But an event was soon to take place which rendered these subterfuges unnecessary. It was no less than the death of Sir William on 6 April 1803. Turned out of the Piccadilly house by her former lover, Charles Greville, now Sir William Hamilton's heir, Lady Hamilton rented a house in Clarges Street where she spent such time as she was away from Nelson's home at Merton. For now the two, with their ostensibly adopted daughter Horatia, lived together openly.

The possession of a captivating, beautiful, seductive mistress is not all honey, as Nelson was soon to find out. Every time duty called him away he was the prey to the fiercest jealousy. While Sir William was alive there was a certain degree of peace of mind for the absent lover; with Emma free to do exactly as she pleased there was none. Naturally enough Nelson, in the throes of passionate love, looking upon his mistress as the most beautiful creature on God's earth, imagined every man putting greedy eyes on his treasure. He hated the thought of her becoming acquainted with any presentable man; he was maddened at the idea of the sensual Prince of Wales, a pursuer of every pretty maiden in London town, setting covetous eyes on her majestic beauty.

On her part Emma did nothing to assuage his fears. At her London house she gathered the gayest of society; Merton was the scene of the most voluptuous orgies. She visited the fashionable watering places and flirted industriously. She reported to Nelson, mainly with the idea of keeping him up to scratch, alluring offers of marriage which were wholly fictitious. Money she spent like water. The annuity of £800 left her by Sir William was a mere bagatelle. Week by week her monetary calls on Nelson increased. The man remonstrated with her, pleaded: all to no purpose. Probably he came to Merton time after time in a fit of temper, but she met him with honeyed words, with profuse sugary flattery, with the caresses and love-wiles of which she was such a mistress; and Nelson, the hero of the sea, the conqueror of fleets, became a bit of putty in her capable hands. Of Emma's real character Nelson never seems to have had an inkling. He fondly believed that he was the hero of her first real love affair; that Sir William Hamilton was the only other sharer of her bed. To his dying day had he never any knowledge of the four children she had borne before the birth of his beloved Horatia; of her adventures with Captain Payne, with Dr Graham, with Sir Henry Featherstonhaugh, with Charles Greville.

Thus, insanely jealous, but believing in the divinity of his love affair, Nelson reached that day in October that was to be his crowning glory and his day of death. Love for his Emma was on his dying lips.

On 21 October 1805, had she but known it the star of Lady Hamilton began to fade. Nelson's relatives and friends who had sycophantly worshipped at his mistress's shrine now deserted her. A consummate actress, she made frantic efforts to keep in the limelight. The scene at the opera when the 'Death of Nelson' was sung, and in full sight of the audience, Lady Hamilton fainted, grew stale after half a dozen repetitions.

The woman was not without money. Indeed had she lived reasonably, the £800 a year from Sir William, the £500 per annum left her by Nelson, and the interest on the £4,000 settled on Horatia, would have sufficed for her every need. But Lady Hamilton and extravagant living were indelibly welded. She gambled, she dressed, she had parties, she surrounded herself with a batch of loose women and looser men. For some time that aged roué, the Duke of Queensberry, kept her at Richmond. But her beauty was going. She was fat and not a little coarse. Her debts mounted until in 1813 she was arrested and actually went to prison for the best part of a year until some gallant provided the means for her release. Finally she fled to France, and at Calais she lived the remainder of her days, ending her career on 15 January 1815, practically penniless.

Catherine Walters (1839–1900)

'Skittles':
The Darling of London

Catherine Walters, the ravishing strawberry blonde courtesan who had London at her feet during the later half of the nineteenth century, was familiarly known as 'Skittles', from her reply to an insult from a group of drunken soldiers that, 'If you don't hold your bloody row, I'll knock you down like a row of skittles!' Her notoriety won her admirers among the nobility and literary men as well as promoting many accusations about the way she flaunted herself in public places. In 1862, for example, a letter to *The Times* complained that 'Skittles', appearance in Hyde Park, 'attracted as much attention as the international exhibition at the nearby Science Museum'. Her life was one long round of extravagant behaviour, intrigue and daring, with writers of all kinds vying with one another to immortalize her exploits. **Donald MacAndrew** here explains the furore which surrounded 'The Last Victorian Courtesan,' today commemorated by a blue plaque on her former home in Mayfair overlooking Hyde Park.

'As late as the 1860s and the 1870s,' wrote one who remembered them, 'there existed a sort of English *demi-monde* – Skittles and many women of the same kind being openly spoken about much as are the great Parisian cocottes of today.' That was written in 1913. Two world upheavals since 1913 have swallowed up even the last remaining great Parisian cocottes, so that to us, in our *terre à terre* universe, the species seems remote as medieval enchantresses. Yet well within living memory we find a luxurious *demi-monde* considered an ornament indispensable to civilization. What Balzac said in 1838 was true nearly forty years later. 'There can be no great age without its magnificent Aspasian figure. See how perfectly the Dubarry fits the eighteenth century and Ninon de I'Enclos the seventeenth . . . these women are the poetry of their age. Lais and Rhodope *are* Greece and Egypt.' And so on. In other words, the courtesan, afloat on its surface, epitomizes the age that drew her up from its obscurities: take her out of her surroundings and she vanishes, like the bubble that forms on a river. Any portrait of her, therefore, a mere sketch or a miniature portrait, must also in some sort be a microcosm of an age.

Nevertheless, the last great English courtesan – Catherine Walters, who was known as Skittles – seems at a glance to give Balzac the lie. Can this slangy hoyden, one wonders, really be an emblem of 1860? 1860, the age of high moral seriousness and social improvement? Or have we always been ridiculously wrong about our great-grandfathers and our grandfathers – wrong about what they liked and what they were like? In her youth, her contemporaries tell us, Skittles was horsey, hard-swearing, broad-talking and extravagant, with a strong propensity to show off in male society and an even stronger one to be rude to her own sex: traits every one of them, surely, quite distinctively un-mid-Victorian. Yet the future Duke of Devonshire set her up in a house in Mayfair and Mr Gladstone went to tea with her. Wilfrid Scawen Blunt made her the subject of his finest sonnet-sequence, and at least two kings to be – the Prince of Wales and the Crown Prince of Germany – were for years her devoted admirers. In addition, there are people alive today who smile indulgently over their recollections of her in her old age. Evidently, then, she possessed qualities on which her generation put a premium. A second generation, too, for she was the acknowledged 'queen of her profession' for at least twenty-five years. Indeed, seeing that no fewer than three yellowback 'biographies' of her, which first appeared in the mid 1860s were still being reissued nearly half a century later, one might say that the Skittles legend appealed to the imaginations of at least three generations. Faced with the evidence of a renown so prolonged and so indisputable, are we to discredit our great-grandfathers or to contradict Balzac?

The explanation is that the 1860s were first and last contradictory: no age in social history presents such melodramatic contrasts as the age that made Skittles possible. It looked forward to our own time in such benefits as its metropolitan policemen, its photographs, and its trains, but remembered the eighteenth century, and earlier periods, in the barbarity of many of its popular amusements and punishments. It was an age in which a stern sense of duty, religious and charitable, was counterbalanced by the rowdiest, the most spendthrift, dissipation: extremes which, for a rich man, were often personified by a wife and a mistress. He desired to see all the god-fearing, slum-visiting virtues concentrated in one lady and all the rowdiness in the other. Everybody knows the quiet tints of the Victorian wife, pious, noble, pure, highly progenitive. Reverse all these and you have the Victorian mistress. The age liked a mistress to be tough. It liked her to smoke and swear. It liked her to keep open house to her protector and his men friends every Sunday afternoon.

Undoubtedly the time was not out of joint for rich and unfaithful husbands. To isolate the courtesans completely from their wives the men of the 'upper ten thousand' had built a large new suburb to house them, and long before 1860 the whole area of St John's Wood was dotted with tiny dolls-house villas – embowered in shrubs, girt in by high walls, and many with a covered way leading from the gate to the stuccoed portico. Then a special drive had been marked off in Hyde Park for the courtesans to parade their equipages in, opera boxes were reserved for the display of their diamonds, and there was even a special hunt allotted them – the Queen's Staghounds in Buckinghamshire. So long as they knew their unmentionable place and kept in it, the age allowed them many amenities. The necessity for a *demimonde* was tacitly recognized by men of the upper and ruling class.

Skittles was the head and front of what the age called its 'submerged half': that to which all its rough and noisy features had been banished lest they contaminated the upper air. Thus far – and it is a good way – it will be seen that Skittles was a typical mid-Victorian. What, though, are her titles to be a symbol of the whole period? The answer is that she was a creature, like the age itself, of charming, if unsubtle, contradictions. These can best be pointed by what her contemporaries tell us of her appearance and her manners. She had, one chronicler tells us, 'the face of an innocent child', yet she could 'swear like a cabman'. Mid-Victorians found the contrast piquant. Another chronicler describes her as having 'one of the sweetest faces I ever saw . . . a face like a Magdalen with such an innocent mouth, and tender, timid eye,' but adds 'her language, should one tread on her dress, is a *caution*'. Wilfrid Blunt described her appearance thus:

> Her brow was pale, but it was lit with light,
> And mirth flashed out of it, it seemed in rays
> A childish face, but wise with woman's wit
> And something too pathetic in its gaze.

He also tells us how

> She went on talking like a running stream
> Without more reason, or more pause, or stay
> Than to gather breath and so pursue her whim
> Just where it led her, tender, sad, or gay.

So there was, it will be seen, a unity in, as well as a discrepancy between, her appearance and her manners. Both had been formed, apparently, expressly to charm men in the most simple-minded and sentimental epoch in history.

Catherine Walters was born in a Liverpool tenement, of Liverpool-Irish parents, the daughter of a customs officer who later became a captain in the merchant navy. When, again later, her father kept an inn in Cheshire, Kitty, as a mere child, used to follow the Cheshire hounds. At the end of the day she waited on the grooms and the huntsmen in the inn parlour. Perhaps Captain Walters, who seems to have been as happy-go-lucky as Captain Costigan, took pride in the fact that his daughter's 'beauty and boldness soon attracted a host of admirers'. At all events when he died, three years later, everything was sold to pay his debts, and Kitty and her baby sister (their mother had died in childbirth) returned to Liverpool to live with their maternal grandmother. The next stage in her career is related in a street ballad of the early 1860s:

> In Liverpool in days gone by,
> For ha'pence and her wittles,
> A little girl, by no means shy,
> Was settin' up the skittles.

Thus, through being employed in the skittle-alley of a Merseyside pothouse, Catherine Walters gained her lifelong nickname. She was then sixteen.

At seventeen she was in London, but a thick fog conceals her early activities there; it commonly does when a great courtesan is still in the lower grades of her profession. One pictures her dancing and supping in the many 'flash cribs' of the Haymarket, the centre in those days of London's night life.

The wide thoroughfare, we are told, 'blazed from midnight till dawn' with gaslight streaming from the plate-glass windows, and illuminated crescents, of a hundred Turkish divans, Cosmopolitan divans, Circassian divans, oyster bars and French restaurants. Dense crowds gathered outside the doors of the more fashionable night houses – the Piccadilly Saloon, the Argyle and Kate Hamilton's – to watch the broughams draw up and the heavy Dundreary 'swells' step languidly out to assist the ladies in their slow, and crinoline-encumbered, descent. Kate Hamilton's, the goal of every prostitute and night-reveller in London, was a huge subterranean temple extending from Oxendon Street to Leicester Square. It was in the famous plush and gilt saloon of this establishment that Skittles met, two years later, a well-known livery stableman and jobmaster, who was looking for a smart girl to show off his horses and drive his pony traps. Within a month of this encounter she became one of the most celebrated 'pretty horsebreakers' on the town.

Driving dashing little phaetons and riding high-priced hacks, she was to be seen everywhere: in Hyde Park, in the Cremorne Gardens, at meets of the Queen's Staghounds, at Ascot. She dined at Scott's and she danced at Mott's. She smiled at one from every West-End photographer's window. Even feminine fashion came under her influence. She invented the pork pie hat and revived the old-fashioned chimney pot for riding wear. Ladies adopted these styles never dreaming who had set them.

It was when riding one of her employer's hacks in the Row that she saw Spencer Compton, Marquis of Hartington (later eighth Duke of Devonshire). She had met him years before when she was hunting with the Cheshire; naturally the innkeeper's daughter remembered the son of the local bigwig, the heir, people said, to the seventh largest ducal property in the kingdom. Whether he, heavy, slow-witted, supercilious young man that he was, recollected the child of eleven is very doubtful. Skittles, however, was determined to make him take notice of her. Her horse collided with his and threw her on the turf just in front of him. As he helped her to remount Hartington could not but notice that she seemed to be on friendly terms with every man in the crowd that quickly formed about them. A month later he installed her in a house in Park Street, Mayfair.

Skittles was now a well-off woman with her own horses, carriages, and servants. More, she was now the everywhere-acknowledged 'Queen of her profession'. Sporting peers, foreign diplomats, even visiting royalty attended her Sunday afternoon baccarat parties. Not the least frequent of her visitors was the young Prince of Wales.

It was characteristic of Skittles that, instead of a roomy villa in Elm Tree Road, St John's Wood, such as realized the ambition of most of her professional rivals, she should consider a house in Mayfair, however cramped and uncomfortable, only proper to her queenly state. Similarly, when she rode to hounds she no longer now patronized the Queen's or the Surrey. She must needs follow the Fitzwilliam and the Quorn, crack subscription packs in High Leicestershire.

Before telling the best-known of all the Skittles stories – that of her expulsion from the Quorn Hunt – it is necessary to mention what even her admirers agreed to be her one completely unamiable trait: her wearisomeness, her boring stupidity, on the subject of other women. The man's woman, we know, has seldom much use for her own sex. But with Skittles the antipathy went a long way further than that. Her fundamental hatred of other women was almost pathological. She could not sit in the same room as another woman without at once talking at her. She could not hear another woman mentioned in conversation without starting a tirade against the whole sex. For virtuous women she cared nothing; it was her rivals who infuriated her. Her cruellest gibes, however, were reserved for those of her rivals who had become virtuous women.

Unfortunately it happened that the Master of the Quorn, the Earl of Stamford and Warrington, had married such a one. Mid-Victorian society refused to know Lady Stamford on the grounds that she, a game-keeper's daughter who had also been a show rider at Astleys and the Cremorne Gardens, could not have avoided, in the circumstances, being an

immoral woman. That she was naturally well-bred, shy and
retiring, and a good angel to the poor on her husband's estate,
mattered nothing. The half-dozen or so lady members of the
hunt (hunting had only lately become respectable for women)
united in cutting her dead in the field, while enjoying to the
full the magnificent sport that her husband provided. Seeing
this and believing that her own prestige and masculine
backing made her invincible, Skittles amused herself by
annoying the Master's wife on every possible occasion.
She ranged up beside her, she cannoned against her, she
twitted her about her former profession. She behaved so
outrageously that at last Lord Stamford was obliged to bid
her go away. He would call the hunt off, he said, if Skittles
ever showed her face with the Quorn again.

The next time the Quorn met Skittles appeared mounted
on a gaudy chestnut and wearing her own version of the hunt
uniform, which included a man's pink swallowtail coat and a
top hat. She approached Lady Stamford and began talking
loudly about exhibition riders at Cremorne. It was too much.
Lord Stamford sent word through his huntsman that he
would carry out his threat immediately if she did not clear
out. Skittles refused. When, however, she heard Lord Stamford telling his huntsman that the day's sport was cancelled,
and when, too, her particular friends urged her not to be a
spoil-sport, she at last sulkily obeyed. She turned her horse's
head homewards. But she had not gone far before a fox
scampered across her path, followed by the hounds in full
cry. Skittles could not resist. She leapt the hedge and joined
the hunt, which was going racing-pace over some of the finest
grass country in Leicestershire. The huntsman at once called
a check, and, after some further word-pelting, Skittles finally
departed. As she rode away, however, she bawled over her
shoulder, 'Tell Lady Stamford *she's* not the Queen of our
profession – I am.' Then having had the last word, she
trotted home in high feather.

Skittles gained both publicity and masculine sympathy
through her rudeness to Lady Stamford. Though banned
forever from the Quorn, she soon became a cynosure in other

aristocratic hunts, and could show off when out with these, and in Rotten Row, with impunity. Once, for instance, she larked her horse over the railings in Hyde Park for a bet of £100. Another time she left the skirt of her habit in a Leicestershire hedge and a sporting parson was obliged to retrieve it for her. Most remarkable of all is the story of her, when riding about between races at the Grand National Hunt Steeplechase at Market Harborough, suddenly clearing the eighteen feet wide water-jump in which three of the competitors had already had a bath, and which many others had refused. In 1861 Landseer exhibited an equestrian portrait of Skittles at Burlington House. For respectability's sake it was given out to be a portrait of Miss Gilbert, an entirely presentable tamer of lady's horses and equitation instructress. Unhappily the portrait bore not the faintest resemblance to Miss Gilbert but was a really speaking likeness of Skittles. For this reason 'The Pretty Horsebreaker' was the most popular picture of the year, though some people feared that Sir Edwin, late president of the Royal Academy, and friend of Queen Victoria, had forgotten himself.

Besides being 'the greatest horsewoman of the age' Skittles was an expert whip. Her miniature phaeton, and pair of tiny, perfectly-matched chestnut ponies – Viennese high steppers – was the gift of a Russian Prince, and universally voted the prettiest turn-out in Hyde Park. Crowds thronged the sidewalks every afternoon to watch her handling the ribbons. 'The dandy guardsmen, the perfumed loungers and the naughty old men in purple wigs and patent leather boots,' would, a contemporary tells us, 'lean over the park rails for hours in the hope of seeing her pass by driving her almost priceless ponies with a parasol whip'. When she appeared, hers was the passage of a sovereign through an avenue of doffed hats.

Eighteen-sixty-two was to see the World Exhibition at South Kensington. All sorts of foreign princes and potentates were expected, and Skittles, anticipating a bumper year, had the interior of her house 'entirely remodelled and decorated by a fashionable artist'. She had the drawing-room panelled, upholstered and curtained in a 'vivid cerise-coloured silk', while the woodwork was so sticky with gilding that it 'might have been suffering from a virulent attack of burnished jaundice'. The bedroom made extravagant use of saxe-blue coloured silk, while the dining-room had crimson repp with large clusters of gilt cupids. Even '*le cabinet*' had 'its seat padded in swansdown'.

That year she received as much publicity as even she could wish. Following the scandal of Derby Day, when Lord Hartington never left her side from morn till eve, was the 'Anonyma and her Ponies' letter in *The Times*, which complained that provincials making for the Exhibition found the roads across Hyde Park blocked by pedestrians, all waiting to glimpse 'Anonyma' (that is, Skittles) 'and her stepping ponies' take their morning drive down the Ladies Mile. Shortly after this, her sudden disappearance from the public scene, and Hartington's nearly simultaneous departure for America led, not unnaturally perhaps, to the rumour that the pair had eloped. Lastly, in November, *The Times* announced that the house in Park Street was to let: its furniture would be on view for a week before the auction sale. This was sensational news, and until the end of the year the papers complained about the 'prurient curiosity' of the 'mobs of fashionable women, mothers and daughters', who came to inspect the premises.

For all that, it was quite untrue that Skittles had bolted with Hartington. It is more likely, indeed, that Hartington's leaving the country just then, when his Parliamentary career still hung in the balance and when, too, he was vowed to the cause of the starving Lancashire cotton-spinners at home, was a flight from the universal coupling of his name with hers. Could it be that stories of his liaison had filtered into Buckingham Palace? Queen Victoria was very fond of Hartington, whom she hoped one day to see Prime Minister, and moreover she approved of him as a steadying influence on the young Prince of Wales. (He was likely enough responsible for introducing the Prince to Skittles). At any rate, Hartington had taken a trip to America to join his brother and to observe at close range the Civil War.

Skittles was drinking the waters at Ems when she learned that her protector had escaped, and she decided at once that the only thing to do would be to pursue him. There was one difficulty – who should escort her to New York? The honour fell upon an impressionable youth named Aubrey de Vere Beauclerk, who was staying at Ems. He, it seemed, would be glad to quit his newly wed wife and journey with Skittles anywhere. The publicity that he would get, the envy, would more than atone for any consequences.

Skittles dreamed of becoming a marchioness who would one day be a duchess: so intoxicating was the vision that it blinded her to realities. Hartington, apprised by the bell-boy that a lady awaited him in the vestibule, probably imagined that it was the American hostess who had given a reception for him the night before. Anyway, he strode majestically down the hotel staircase, never dreaming what he would find at the bottom of it. Nor when Skittles actually confronted him did he understand, just at first, what it was all about. He was a man of the slowest reactions. When his wrath did break out, however, it was so appalling that even she retreated, bewildered and stunned. She had failed to take the measure of Hartington's worldly wisdom. Because he had so often played at letting her do as she pleased with him, she had come to think that she really could. But behind all his apparent obtuseness and his lack of imagination lay an inborn, an absolutely straightforward and unquestioning, knowledge of men and women. Knowing the value of his titles and his wealth he took it for granted that women in all walks of life, wherever he met them, would quite naturally set their caps at him. Sudden glimpses of this may once or twice have startled Skittles in the past, but her mulishness, her innate cock-sureness, forbade her profiting by the lesson. Well, it had been forced upon her now. She realized with a sickening certainty that she could never have been Duchess of Devonshire. She also realized the impossibility of her returning to London for years. Her object in sailing to New York was known to all her rivals.

Accordingly she went to Paris – the florid, parvenu Paris of the Second Empire. Here fortune was once again indulgent, and she became the mistress of Napoleon III's finance minister, Achille Fould. Thanks to him, she rose immediately to the first rank of Second Empire courtesans: to the level of Cora Pearl, Giulia Barucci, Anna Deslions: women who owned estates in the country, besides houses in Paris, and who lived at the rate of ten thousand francs a day.

But though her prestige was equal to any of theirs, Skittles avoided the big gambling parties and masked balls that were given by her Parisian rivals. Seeing their outrageous manners, and their toilettes and equipages, either blinding yellow or flaming magenta, a spirit of English good form made her the sudden foe of all loudness. It was the beginning of a complete change in her habit, if not of her morals. 'Everything,' says a memoirist about her equipage, 'was so quiet. The harness and livery of her servants and she herself dressed always in dark colours, so that no one unless he knew her would have suspected that she was of the *demi-monde*.'

While in Paris she kept open house every evening to the young *attachés* of the British Embassy, and it was at one of these gatherings that she first met Wilfrid Scawen Blunt, then a slim, fair, remarkably handsome youth of twenty-two. The future poet and Oriental traveller who was destined to play such a disturbing part in Anglo-Indian, Arabian and Irish politics had been brought up by the Jesuits and had but lately himself renounced the idea of joining the priesthood. He now longed to savour life, but was fearful how to set about it. At this particular party, he tells us, he sat aloof and shy, listening to what he scornfully called the 'fool's talk' of his hostess, and his cheeks flamed when once or twice her eyes rested upon him. He 'wondered,' he says, 'that she did not wear men's patience out with her fool's talk,' but just the same when, after the party had broken up, he strolled about the midnight boulevards alone, unable to face the solitude of his room, he found that he could not expel either the vision of 'that gay face' or 'the torrent of her words' from his mind. He wandered into a fair-ground and, while gazing at, without seeing, some freaks in a booth, he felt someone in the crowd touch his arm. He turned swiftly round. Skittles had followed him through the night and was peering inquiringly up at him.

The ensuing liaison lasted twenty days. Since for Skittles the conquest of this beautiful proud boy, whose inexperience and virginity she had from the first divined, was merely the indulgence of a whim, it soon ended. She had set out to subdue Blunt, not to enslave him: and like all who openly delight in the pursuit of their quarry, she lost interest when the quarry surrendered. Her curiosity satisfied, she kindly, but resolutely, cut short her holiday and returned to business: returned to Fould and to the elderly *high-lifeurs* of the Jockey Club.

Blunt wrote of:

> The treasures of fair folly infinite
> Learned as a lesson from those childish eyes.

The lesson would no doubt have benefited that over-serious young man had not Skittles's vehemence of living and loving become an overmastering obsession with him. Now that all was over, the only balm he could pour into his bruised vanity and sensitiveness was to dramatize his loss. He began to see himself as one pining for a beautiful and cruel woman who had trampled upon him and spurned him. Alas! the downright and essentially unromantic Skittles had no aptitude for spurning. She was far too good-natured to be a destroying angel. She approved of the many poems that he wrote (and later published) about his passion for her, but she was bored by the passion itself. Most of her former lovers had since become her devoted friends. Why could not she and Blunt be lifelong friends?

Skittles spent the next few years rambling through Europe's capitals and pleasure resorts: Rome, St Petersburg,

Baden: with annual stays in Leicestershire for the hunting season. But as she approached thirty she began to tire a little of her solitary pride and independence. Not that she wanted a husband. Fate had denied her her duke, and the idea of marriage with a commoner held no allurements. Instead, since her distaste for other women did not extend to her own family, she adopted her sister as a permanent travelling companion. No doubt she dominated Mary-Ann and bullied her at times, but she was always generous to her, always protective. Mary-Ann was ten years younger than she, and much prettier; Skittles took a family pride in these virtues. Later she became warmly attached to Mary-Ann's daughter.

Though for some half-dozen years London had lost sight of Skittles, she was never to lose her hold on the imagination of Londoners. The three yellowback 'biographies' of her, published in her absence, kept her name alive in mess-rooms, in the clubs of St James's and also among errand boys. The first two, *Skittles, the Biography of a Fascinating Woman* and *Anonyma or Fair but Frail, with details of West-End Life, Manners and 'Captivating' People* were published simultaneously in January, 1864. *Skittles* was re-issued four times that year and *Anonyma* six times.

In addition, though such pseudo-pornography was, of course, unobtainable in Mudie's Select Library, many provincial subscribers became acquainted with Skittles through novels which presently began to circulate. She was, for example, widely recognized as the model for the Zu Zu, the hunting *demi-mondaine* in Ouida's *Under Two Flags* (1864), and for Lucy Glitters in Surtees's *Mr. Facey Romford's Hounds* (1865). Charles Reade admitted that a character in his *A Terrible Temptation* (1871) derived from her. Indeed, when in 1872 Skittles returned to London, she was talked of by thousands who had never heard of her in the days of her Hyde Park glory.

The year 1870, which saw the end of the Second Empire and the crinoline, public hangings, three-volume novels, and tiny

states in both Italy and Germany, is a turning-point in the
social as well as the political life of the nineteenth century.
Everything changed. Monte Carlo succeeded Baden as a
popular gambling resort; society was invaded by a horde
of Greek and Jewish capitalists; the heavy Dundreary 'swell'
became the slim and debonair 'masher'; the night-houses of
the Haymarket were replaced by the palm-decorated restaurants of Soho. Women, no longer mouse-like and retiring,
according to Victorian tradition, stepped forth as priestesses,
tall and classically featured, such as Lord Leighton was then
painting. The Prince of Wales, now social arbiter, was, like
Napoleon III before him, surrounded by lovely women.
Court Society, and indeed London life generally, had become a fretwork copy of the Second Empire – without,
however, the Second Empire's most distinctive and ornate
embellishment – its *demi-monde*.

The London *demi-monde* as a separate and mysterious
planet was, in this new, and virtually Edwardian epoch,
undergoing an eclipse. The recently developed 'fast set'
and the Gaiety chorus were stealing its lustre. Portraits of
stage and society beauties now filled every photographer's
window, and the *on dit* columns of the gossip Press recorded
their activities. Only in Paris, where the *haut-monde* remained exclusive, was the *demi-monde* still much in evidence.

But Skittles, thanks to the continued friendship of the
Prince of Wales, blazed as brightly as ever in the London
'hemisphere'. She had become a sort of institution, or public
monument, half-canonized by respectability. In 1873 she
rented houses in South Street, Mayfair, in Tunbridge Wells,
and in Paris, besides an apartment in Brown's Hotel, where
she and Mary-Ann principally resided. In 1878 she had three
houses in Mayfair simultaneously. In these she would entertain, besides European royalty, the Shah, British and
foreign diplomats, artists, sportsmen, Rothschilds. Even
Mr Gladstone, that other indefatigable talker, 'came along
to take tea with her' one Sunday afternoon.

One day she would play at being political hostess, the next
she was Art's enlightened patroness: the very avocations of

Society ladies in 1880. For the rest, her carriages were as ever a match for any in Hyde Park – unless it were Lily Langtry's. In Rotten Row she would appear mounted on 'a glorious chestnut', accompanied by her niece, a tiny girl on a Shetland pony.

In one respect Skittles in middle age was even more fortunate than Skittles in her youth. Most people, in early middle age, however they have spent their youth, wish that they had lived it differently. Skittles, for a brief while, seems to have regretted that she had always been too proud and spoilt to fall in love. As usual, however, fortune, like a kindly djinn, was ready to supply her wants. It was not only that an extravagantly handsome youth of half her age had fallen deeply in love with her, but that she too, this time at forty, fell quite comfortably, but, as the event was to prove, enduringly, in love with him. The Honourable Gerald Saumarez, while still an Eton schoolboy, had been introduced to the ageing painted courtesan at Tunbridge Wells, and now as a young man in London, he saw her every day. The attachment lost none of its force during the forty-one years that remained to Skittles of life, and to the end of his life – and he lived to be eighty – Saumarez used to declare that she was the only woman he could ever have married. The couple, apparently so ill-assorted, were, in fact, ideally matched. Both were irresponsible and gay, both loved a good laugh and both were tremendous talkers.

During the early nineteen hundreds, Skittles was a familiar figure in Hyde Park in a bath chair. Walking beside it one might see Lord Kitchener paying her elaborate compliments, or the tiny wizened Marquis of Clanricarde, that multi-millionaire who dressed like a tramp. When she visited Wilfrid Blunt on his Sussex farm he received her wearing Arab robes and a burnous. He kept a stud of Arab horses, and some of these were paraded before Skittles in his paddock. 'Though deaf and partially blind,' Blunt wrote in his Diary, 'Skittles is still unconquered in talk.'

Throughout the 1914–18 war Skittles's sole annual income was the £2,000 that had been settled on her by Lord Hartington. The South Street house was now mostly under dust sheets, and she lived almost exclusively in her bedroom attended by one old servant. Mary-Ann was in France. Apart from her doctor and a Catholic priest – she had been born a Roman Catholic – Skittles saw hardly anybody except the devoted Gerald Saumarez. He, when he was in London, called, as usual, every day.

He was there on that blazing August afternoon in 1920 when she was suddenly carried into the house in a fit, having had a stroke while taking her daily airing in the bath-chair. He was there two days later when she died. He saw to it that her wish that she should be buried in the graveyard of the Franciscan Monastery at Crawley, Sussex, was carried out. In her will she left the bulk of her property to Gerald Saumarez.

Skittles, being a symptom of her period, as well as a summary of it, could not possibly happen today. Doubtless there still are women who batten famously on the weaknesses of rich men, but they are not acknowledged courtesans, nor do they inhabit a strange, mysterious planet, whose ways sober-living persons can only guess at. 'Skittles,' says one memoirist, 'was the last of the great courtesans of the sixties.' 'We shall not,' says another, 'look on her like again.'

Sarah Bernhardt (1844–1923)

The Star Called
'The Bernhardt'

Sarah Bernhardt, whose real name was Henriette Rosine Bernard, was the illegitimate child of French and Dutch parents who became one of the greatest stars of the theatre. She was also one of the most eccentric, with a notorious love life and extraordinary versatility. Sarah first appeared at the Comédie Française, worked for a time as a burlesque singer, and then became an international star in what proved her greatest role, Marguerite, in *La Dame aux camélias*. Later she settled in London, made repeated tours of America and Australia, and in 1893 was honoured when the Théâtre de la Renaissance in Paris was renamed Théâtre Sarah Bernhardt. Although the final years of Sarah Bernhardt's life were dogged by unhappiness and ill-health, her compulsion to act was all-consuming. Even when she was in her seventies and one of her legs became infected and had to be amputated, she still appeared with a wooden leg. Some highlights from her life are described in this memoir by her granddaughter, **Lysiana Bernhardt**.

'The Bernhardt' was the name given Sarah by the Americans in the course of her United States tours in 1880, 1886, 1891, 1896, 1900, 1905, 1910, 1913 and 1916. They used the expression 'the Bernhardt' as they would say 'the Academy' or 'the Theatre'. In 1917 I accompanied my grandmother to the United States: the Americans still called her 'the Bernhardt'. She was then seventy-two.

When, on 8 November 1880, she made her first appearance in New York in *Adrienne Lecouvreur*, by Scribe and Legouvé, Booth's Theatre was completely sold out. The New York ticket agencies were more than grateful to Jarrett for having brought to New York this extraordinary, thin, eccentric person who received journalists lying flat on the floor in her hotel, and who bought dogs, materials and furs as other women bought powder, cosmetics or jewellery.

Yet the public as a whole hesitated to express its admiration for this foreigner who arrived preceded by a fanfare of trumpets. During the first act, certain people in the stalls thought each actress who appeared on the stage was Sarah Bernhardt. 'There she is! There's the Bernhardt,' they whispered.

Then someone in the third row of the stalls, annoyed by all this talking, leaned over to someone in the second row and said in a loud voice:

'Sh! Sarah Bernhardt does not come on in the first act.'

The third, sixth and eighth rows and even some of the circle heard the remark. Someone who misunderstood it got up and made for the exit. Another followed suit, and then a score of the audience, all asking for their money back because 'the Bernhardt' was not playing. An announcement had to be made from the stage to the effect that Sarah Bernhardt appeared in the other acts. Order was re-established and the curtain fell on desultory and perfunctory applause.

After five minutes of interval the public grew impatient and started stamping, clapping and whistling. For two months it had, by means of paragraphs and headlines in the Press, been promised a curiosity: and it was not going to brook any further delay. At last Sarah made her entry in the second act. The audience was silent, not knowing what to think. Sarah Bernhardt! But this woman was not even very pretty. Indeed, they had never seen anything like her. That slim outline, that proud, fascinating face, those eyes. And then Sarah began to speak. Her voice rippled out like a bubbling spring and held the audience spellbound with its music. Her nervousness could mar neither its purity nor its modulations. A murmur, swift as an electric current, ran through the audience and bound them together in their common surprise. They had not yet reached the stage of admiring her; they were still uncertain. They had heard so much of this transatlantic marvel! And here was merely a woman, more feminine than anything they could imagine or hope for.

Sarah Bernhardt herself admitted that she had more than once won over lukewarm audiences by her intense femininity. She could appear either lascivious, or quivering with fear, or in despair. Tears, real tears, were always near her eyes. She could make her voice metallic with terror or tender with love. Her expression could be either commanding, cunning or distraught with passion. Hands that shook with emotion, arms outstretched in token of surrender or of sacrifice. The bearing of a queen, of a coquette, of a mistress, of a mother, of a murderess; or floating over the earth like a fairy princess. She could interpret any feminine role, from the humblest to the highest, from the most malignant to the most virtuous. And that evening in New York, when Adrienne Lecouvreur, mistress of the handsome Maurice of Saxony, rebelled against the Duchesse de Bouillon, the hearts of the audience beat more rapidly. The spectators did not understand all the dialogue, but the inflexions of Sarah Bernhardt's voice, her gestures and her expression made them vibrate in sympathy with Adrienne's love and enthusiasm.

After *Adrienne Lecouvreur* Sarah gave *La Dame aux camélias*, with the handsome actor Angelo in the role of Armand Duval. While attending the final rehearsals of this play at Booth's Theatre, Sarah recalled that 19 July 1870 was the

day on which the younger Dumas, after escaping from the
boisterous attentions of her puma and her dogs, had left his
manuscript with her while the soldiers in the street were
rejoining their regiments.

La Dame aux camélias, Phèdre, L'Aiglon! Those were the
mainstays of Sarah Bernhardt's dramatic and lyrical career.
At the Théâtre de la Renaissance, and later at the Théâtre
Sarah-Bernhardt, when a new piece did not come up to
expectations, one of those three plays was quickly substituted
for it, and either Marguerite, or Theseus' incestuous spouse,
or the Duc de Reichstadt saved the situation, filled the box-
office and made up the deficit.

On the first occasion on which she played the part of
Marguerite Gautier in New York, Sarah, who never allowed
herself to hark back into the past, could not help doing so for
a moment. When, in the third act, Marguerite writes to her
lover to tell him that he must renounce her, Sarah, excited by
the hundreds of people who followed her movements and
hung upon her words, imagined herself back in the little
room in Brussels in which she had written that letter to her
Prince. Would he be pleased to hear of her success in the
New World? Would he even hear of it? She had sworn never
to see him again, but not to stop loving him. In her innermost
heart she carried a wound whose presence no one, save
Madame Guérard, ever suspected. She laughed, worked
and, in spite of this other memory, loved; no power on earth,
no man, could prevent Sarah Bernhardt from enjoying the
hour and the moment, or from listening to the ariettas, the
songs and the hymns which life orchestrated for her. Sarah
lived quite happily with her wound. She wore it against her
side like a dagger, but, if she did not take care, the steel could
still hurt her.

For a fleeting moment, Sarah, her face bathed in tears,
showed her despair to the audience. There, in the prosce-
nium, sat a fair young man who looked like her son Maurice;
in the same way that Maurice himself looked like the Memory. But the evocation only lasted for a second.

Already Marguerite Gautier, proud in her act of renunciation, had sealed her letter and fled into the night. And the house rocked with applause.

Jarrett could be courteous enough if he tried. His star's dressing-room, sumptuously furnished and filled with flowers, was adorned with dwarf palm trees and other green plants, not to mention, of course, Sarah's personal possessions, make-up bottles, cushions and fur rugs, all carefully arranged by the deft hands of Félicie and the loving ones of Madame Guérard.

'I am taking you with me as piece of my native land,' Sarah had told Madame Guérard before leaving France.

After the first performance of *La Dame aux camélias*, 'the Bernhardt', while removing her make-up, discussed finance with Jarrett. The receipts had surpassed their expectations and Sarah had been making plans: to pay her debts in France, to send some money to her son, to repay her mother.

'I'll be back in five minutes, madame. Don't forget that we are having supper with Abbey, the impresario, and a few New York notables.'

'Yes,' replied Sarah.

A tacit understanding existed between Jarrett and Sarah Bernhardt. Jarrett insisted on a minimum of co-operation from Sarah to maintain good relations with the battalions of reporters, and Sarah received their questions, their impertinences and their official dinners with unvarying good humour. 'The fierce gentleman', as Sarah dubbed him, knew quite well, as gentle Mother Saint-Sophie had known in former days, the exact words to use to calm the actress's nerves, or to cope with her revolts, which were sometimes justified. But that evening Jarrett's patience was tried pretty highly. This is what happened.

Several American women, who had been to Sarah's dressing-room to congratulate her, returned to the front entrance of Booth's Theatre. When the people loitering there saw these elegant women, with their escorts in dress clothes, they thought that Sarah Bernhardt was going to make use of the front entrance and hastened to warn the crowd collected

round the stage door. When asked about it, the amused
visitors declared that, on the contrary, she would be leaving
by the other door, where her carriage awaited her. So the
crowd all returned to the stage door, collecting other people
with them as they went. Several hundred people were soon
stamping their feet in the cold, hoping to see the young
woman and to accompany her back to her hotel.

The door opened on the brilliantly lit porch, and, warmly
muffled in a beaver cloak, with hair covered with a silk lace
scarf, Sarah appeared on Jarrett's arm; applause immediately
broke out and cheers went up in the chilly air while police,
holding hands, tried in vain to press the crowd back. Then
Sarah's coachman, in trying to bring up his horses, knocked
down a woman. Sarah screamed, but the woman quickly rose
and ran up to her, saying, 'Please sign my autograph book!'

This was a most unfortunate inspiration. As though by
magic, pieces of paper began issuing from pockets and
handbags: men thrust forward their cuffs or pointed to their
shirt-fronts or even their collars. Sarah signed and went on
signing. Elbowing her way roughly forward, a woman admirer approached the actress. She had fanatical eyes and full
red lips. Sarah, still signing, turned towards her.

'And what about me?' asked the girl in a hoarse voice. 'I
want your signature too.' And she held out her programme.

'Have you a pencil?' asked Sarah.

But the excited woman took a penknife from her pocket,
pulled down her glove, cut her wrist and, tearing a feather
from her hat, dipped it in the blood. All this occurred in less
time than it takes to write down.

'Oh!' cried Sarah, revolted.

'What does it matter? It is only blood,' replied her admirer,
passionately.

'The girl's crazy!' exclaimed Jarrett, shocked.

Jeanne burst out laughing and quickly hid behind the
group formed by her sister, Angelo, Piron and Jarrett.
The more the crowd grew, the angrier the impresario became. Important people were waiting supper for them and
there they were, hemmed in by these shoving men and

hysterical women. It was perfectly ludicrous. The 'fierce gentleman' called up a policeman and spoke to him in a low voice and then, turning quickly on his heel, he led Sarah back into the theatre.

'Aren't we going to supper, after all?' she asked, delighted that her admirers had succeeded in ruffling the usually phlegmatic impresario.

'We're waiting here for police reinforcements,' replied Jarrett, crossly.

'I've an idea. Let's put my cloak and scarf on Jeanne and then leave by the front.'

Jeanne, delighted by the idea, put on the beaver cloak and placed the lace scarf on her pretty fair hair and then, taking Angelo's arm, walked boldly out of the stage door. There she shook hands and signed autographs, delighted at the idea of impersonating her sister and playing a trick on everyone.

'Idiots!' she said to Angelo, who was protecting her as best he could. 'They can't see the difference between the sun and the moon.'

A few days later the Mayor of Chicago begged Sarah Bernhardt to be kind enough to entertain the convicts in the Joliet prison. Sarah refused. The Press would certainly find in it a new pretext for poking fun at her. Her rôle was to be a great artist, not a curiosity like Smith's whale. Although no prejudice could ever prevent Sarah from transforming a wish into a reality, she had learned to avoid grotesque exaggeration and idle scandal. No. She would not play to the convicts. Jarrett supported her in this decision.

Then the prison governor paid Sarah a personal visit. Quite amiably she pleaded previous engagements, fatigue and the refusal of her impresario. But the governor was persistent.

'I would have been so glad, madame, to give my men this splendid distraction from their troubles. An intelligent entertainment can do so much good to those prisoners who have some chance of becoming decent citizens again. And you would have met among us an old acquaintance, if you do not

mind me referring to him as such. Do you remember the one-
eyed man who saved you from the over-enthusiastic populace
on the morning of your arrival in Chicago? The unfortunate
man is shortly going to be hanged and he has asked me, as a
last favour, to try to get you to come and play for us.'

Sarah flushed. She often thought of the giant, the man who
had himself been recaptured because of her.

'Sir,' she said, 'I promise to have another talk with my
impresarios and to see what I can do; I may not act without
their authority; I am not free . . . either.'

The 'fierce gentleman' required a lot of persuasion, but,
as Jarrett was at the time in rather a difficult position as
regards the American theatre managers, he thought it more
diplomatic to meet the wishes of the officials of the great
American cities. So, when the Mayor of Chicago returned
to the charge in support of the prison governor's request,
Jarrett agreed, on condition that his star should be escorted
by plain-clothes detectives. The Company was to play an
act of *Hernani*.

When she arrived at Joliet prison, Sarah's heart suddenly
sank. Prison seemed to her to be an unnecessary mental
torment. The governor showed her all the smallest details
of his kingdom, all the latest humane or penal innovations; he
described the whole working of his institution to her.

Before the curtain rose, Sarah asked to be allowed to look
at her strange audience through the curtains.

In an enormous room, ranged on iron benches, sat between
600 and 800 convicts, clad in the usual American prison
dress, of alternate white and black hoops. At the back of the
room a wooden platform held other prisoners crowded together, either seated or standing. Round the room warders,
armed with rifles, formed a hedge, and lastly a little box,
fitted up actually on the stage, was reserved for the governor
and a few members of the prison personnel. Sarah gave an
involuntary shudder as she looked at these outlaws, murderers and thieves who were at the moment quietly awaiting
her appearance on the stage. 'The Bernhardt!' An actress
who was always being abused by the Press. 'The Bernhardt',

who had recently been saved by one of their number, a convict, a real criminal, a strangler.

When the curtain rose, the audience in its black and white uniform showed its appreciation by shouting and whistling, but the performance itself took place in complete silence. Not a sound, not a whisper interfered with the acting. The convicts did not let themselves go until the end, when the curtain fell for the eighth time on their applause and their cheers.

It was over.

The inmates of Joliet left the room in pairs. Some of them turned to take a last look at Sarah. What a contrast for them! They were returning to their reflections, to their companions in misfortune, their fetters, and their gloom. The vision must endure for those who wished to take it with them. Sarah remained on the stage until the last two convicts had disappeared.

'For twenty-five per cent of our number,' the governor subsequently explained, 'the performance you have been kind enough to give us will merely whet the basest appetites. For several hours, perhaps several days, the discipline of this minority will deteriorate; the instinct of vice will leap in among them like some horrible wild beast leaping out of the darkness into the revealing light of day. But for the other seventy-five per cent of my prisoners such a performance can do only good. It will bring them hope and light and will give them patience; it will bring happy memories back to them and remind them that their miseries will one day end. And now, with your permission, madame, Number 729 will read you the usual address of thanks.' And the governor added, 'We are hanging him the day after tomorrow and this is his last favour.'

The giant came forward, his chest filling out his hooped uniform and his single eye fixed on Sarah. He read a little speech of welcome in a halting voice, though it did not shake as much as Sarah's when she thanked him and shook him by the hand.

On the day on which 729 was hanged, Sarah was so upset

that she was quite prostrate and Jarrett suggested cancelling
the evening's performance. Sarah refused to allow this, but
for some nights afterwards the giant's face haunted her
dreams. She would wake with a start in her pretty bedroom
in Palmer House with the words ringing in her ears: 'You
whet the basest appetites. Twenty-five per cent will be only
more resentful.'

Sarah thought only of that minority. She decided that
never again would she play to convicts. And yet, in February
1913, thirty-two years later, she gave another performance at
the Saint-Quentin prison, before 2,000 prisoners.

The Bad Girl of Broadway

Mae West helped to bring sexuality out of its Victorian closet – not to mention providing the world with some of the most enduring *double entendres* of the twentieth century. Introduced to vaudeville shows by her mother when she was still a child, Mae made her debut as a dancer at just seven years of age. At fourteen, the direction of her career was set when she appeared as 'The Baby Vamp'. However, Mae's uninhibited language and provocative dresses mirrored a serious interest in all aspects of sexuality which was at last being discussed in the works of Freud, Jung, Adler and Havelock Ellis. Following the huge success of her 'autobiographical' play *Sex* in 1926, and the homosexual drama, *The Drag*, Mae moved to Hollywood and for a decade was one of the biggest money earners and highest livers in the film capital. Although pressure from censors forced her to make some of her later movies less outrageous, the legend was assured – thanks in no small measure to the famous one-liners such as, 'Too much of a good thing can be wonderful'. In this essay, originally entitled, 'SEX, More Sex, and the Cooler', Mae discusses her controversial opinions and how they made her a household name.

What kind of New York had I been preparing *Sex* for? Legs
Diamond, a gangster and blonde chaser, made bigger headlines being used as a public target than a great many Broadway shows. It was a wild, raucous period in American drama,
and we all tried to give the theatre patrons the feel and taste of
the times. Hecht and MacArthur had written the great fairy
tale of American newspapermen, a shoddy drunken lot at
times, in *The Front Page*. Plays like *Chicago, Broadway, The
Racket* and others showed that crime was a national sport like
basketball, and impregnating in rumble seats of Packards.

It was a time of night clubs, fancy speaks, and cabarets,
and I usually appeared on the town in my diamonds and with
my men, when publicity called for it. The Lido, Flamingo
and Silver Slipper were the finest places for meeting the best
and worst people.

We opened in New York at Daly's Theatre on Thursday,
26 April 1926. The show was a sensation to the opening night
audience. But the newspapers wouldn't print our ads in their
drama pages (or anywhere else in the paper). Not with that
word 'Sex'. An editor said: 'Up until now the word "sex" has
been taboo, except when used in such harmless phrases as
"the fair sex" or "the opposite sex". *The New York Times*
will *not* change now.'

I suggested that we keep the 'snipers', the men that go
around pasting up show posters, for the run of the show,
continuing to let them flood the town, all the five boroughs,
with one-sheets and three-sheets of the show. The boys
really went to work. Jim said, 'Any person who stopped
anywhere to look in a window would be lucky if he didn't get
a one-sheet of *Sex* pasted on his back.'

That winter New York taxis carried a sign reading: HEATED
– MAE WEST IN 'SEX' – *Daly's 63rd Street Theatre*.

Walter Winchell called attention to it and us in his column.
And I was a star in a legitimate theatre.

In the second week of the show, Chanin Theatre Corporation, owners of several theatres downtown, offered
Harry Cort fifty thousand dollars to let us out of our
contract with him and bring the show into one of its

theatres. Harry Cort refused the offer. 'I took a chance,' he said. 'I'll take more.'

Sex ran 375 performances. The show was such a hit that they were getting ten dollars for orchestra seats for the first six rows. At this time $2.80 was top price for dramatic shows.

A great many men entered my life. They first appeared as admirers of my play or acting, but stayed to be amused, or become serious. A chorus boy from one of the revues I had been in for the Shuberts brought two men backstage. One of them, an actor, was very good looking, with a deep, rich voice, and an unusual vital personality, so impressive that I wanted to know him much better. He was introduced as Mr Dupont.

When the men left my dressing room, the chorus boy came back. 'Dupont is out of his ever-loving mind about you, Mae. He is just utterly mad about you.' Then he rushed out like an elf.

The next day I got a lovely bouquet of flowers from Dupont. For a week I couldn't get this man out of my mind. I couldn't forget his voice; I couldn't forget his personality. I wanted to know him better. When I am attracted to a man, I am like an Amazon in battle; I hit out in all directions.

The following week I had a party at my apartment after the show. The chorus boy phoned, 'I am in the lobby with Dupont and sure would like to flit up and say hello.'

'Sure, come up.'

I got more than I wanted. I found out that Dupont had been married and divorced, and had a child. And he was also bisexual. I hadn't yet read Krafft-Ebbing or Freud. I had grown up in a world of odd men and women. Show business in its present form couldn't exist without them. Some of our greatest playwrights are homosexuals, and so are many of our actors, directors and producers.

But Dupont surprised me. There was nothing about him but a he-man charm. I wasn't too familiar with this phase of sex. The homosexuals I had met were usually boys from the chorus of some of the shows I'd been in. I looked upon them as amusing and having a great sense of humour. They were all crazy about me and my costumes. They were the first ones to imitate me in my presence. I suspected something wrong in Dupont; his being in the company of the types he was with when I met him. I began to study the problem. I read Freud, and Ulrich, who called them *Urnings*. I learned a lot about the yearnings of urnings.

I had no sexual desire for Dupont but I remained impressed with his personality. I asked myself: For what reason does this man interest me? Is it only interest as material for a play? Do I dare use it for dramatic purpose?

I was still playing in *Sex*. But I had to write this new play. Some force that was perverse, some strange thing, was compelling me to write it. I didn't understand.

There are many things in a person's life that, no matter how one tries, can never be fully explained. When I began to write my homosexual play, *The Drag*, I felt a strong compulsion to put down a realistic drama of the tragic waste of a way of life that was spreading into modern society at a time when any mention of it was met by ordinary people with a stare of shocked horror.

Oscar Wilde had gone to prison only a generation or so before for his effrontery of even hinting at his passions for other men. There had been discreet society scandals in Newport and other rich pleasure places here. But even the most daring, lurid editors of Sunday scandal sheets turned away from explaining or reporting any of it. There had been a homosexual upheaval at the court of the German Kaiser before World War I. And everyone who had been to England knew of the growth of the problem, resulting in the tainting of the English public schools, the Army and the theatre.

The American stage was soon no better. The entire Broadway theatre was filled with homosexuals in every creative field from costumes to playwriting. But when I first tried to set the truth down in a play I was almost alone. The only two plays that had tried were romantic, not realistic, and had been closed. A woman character got a bouquet of violets from another woman, in a French drama, *The Captive*, on Broadway, and the play was closed as 'an indecent display of

Lesbianism'. *The Green Bay Tree*, a romantic play delicately and artfully touching homosexual relationship, was no great success, for it never fully stated its theme directly.

My own desire to write a realistic play on such a daring subject was part of my stubborn character, which never resisted a challenge. And some mysterious, subconscious drive to see what kind of a drama I could make of it. I had no personal emotional relations to the ideas of the theme. I had worked with male homosexuals in the theatre, but I myself had almost no contact with women at all. I preferred male company at all times. I never had any private interest in a woman as a love object, and would have recoiled in horror at myself if I had. Yet here I was blithely writing a play that could only make trouble for me.

Was I a crusader? At the time I would have denied it. And perhaps I have never fully understood my motives when I wrote *Sex, The Drag*, and other plays that brought down the howl of the too pious.

I have explained many times that I freely chose the kind of life I led because I was convinced that a woman has as much right as a man to live the way she does if she does no actual harm to society. I saw no indecency or perversion in the normal private habits of men and women.

I now began to probe into society's secrets. I have always hated the two-faced, the smoother-over folk – the people who preach loudly one way of life, and then do something in private that they're against in public. In many ways homosexuality is a danger to the entire social system of western civilization. Certainly a nation should be made aware of its presence – without moral mottoes – and its effects on children recruited to it in their innocence. I had no objections to it as a cult of jaded inverts, or special groups of craftsmen, shrill and involved only with themselves. It was its secret anti-social aspects I wanted to bring into the sun.

As a private pressure group it could, and has, infected whole nations. The old Arab world rotted away from it. The civilization of Greece and Rome marched their really great ideas, philosophies and arts into being, but both were bisexual to a point where the family unit broke down, and the virility of its great and best breeding lines decayed under attacks from more virile and childbreeding savage tribal orders.

I was no daring pioneer in writing of this problem. But I do think no autobiography has yet carried details of its impact on contemporary life as simply and directly as I intend to do in this, my life story.

The Drag treated seriously the problems of a homosexual, and showed how his abnormal tendencies brought disaster to his family, his friends, and himself. It stated that an intelligent understanding of the problems of all homosexuals by society could avert such social tragedies.

The word 'drag', as used by homosexuals, means a big party or a ball, where they dress up as women for a kind of social romp. My play had a big scene that showed forty men, dressed as women, expressing themselves effeminately in song, dancing and dialogue. It was the oddest party ever produced on an American stage during a serious drama. I used comedy to make it exciting and interesting. Basically, the homosexual theme was given a clinical and serious treatment.

The play, directed by Edward Elsner, opened in Paterson, New Jersey. It created such excitement that the theatre was packed at every performance. Many of the audience came from New York, Boston, Philadelphia and other cities to see this play. They called long distance for reservations, and were paying as high as $50 for seats when they couldn't get reservations. It took an hour to empty the theatre after the final curtain. People just would not leave after the show was over, but would visit the actors.

When I was ready to take the show to Broadway, some New York officials came to Jim Timony and asked us not to bring the show into New York because it would 'upset the city'.

I gave in reluctantly and didn't bring the show into New York City. Too many odd important people in town were frightened at the idea of my play as a public exhibit. I had got back all my money for the production, and made about thirty thousand dollars from the two weeks the play ran in Paterson, New Jersey. I intend some day to put *The Drag* into novel form, and even hope to produce it again as a play and then a picture.

I had done what I had set out to do: write a realistic play on a modern social problem. I had not been permitted to bring it to Broadway, and I had presented no solution. For two weeks – one could see, and make up one's own mind.

I wondered if I should try radio when my play closed. I was never one to sneer at other mediums of entertainment and I had kept my eye on radio and motion pictures, knowing I'd be given a chance on them at some future turn of events. Radio has come up like a baby turning into a monster since its beginnings when it just announced ball scores and East Pittsburgh went on the air with its pioneering station KDKA.

Dempsey knocked out Carpentier for a radio public that still had crystal sets and earphones. In the middle thirties there were 563 radio stations on the air, and the public had spent that year forty-four million dollars for sets to hear, among other treats, Ibsen's *The Wild Duck*, starring Blanche Yurka; and still there were 20,000,000 golfers on nearly six thousand country club links.

Soon Paul Whiteman was getting $5,000 a radio show. Ben Bernie was replacing the first stars of the medium, The Happiness Boys, Billy Jones and Ernie Hare; and Amos and Andy emptied the movie theatres until after seven-thirty. I knew there was a place for me in radio if I waited for the right spot. I couldn't do what Will Rogers did on radio – burlesque President Calvin Coolidge so perfectly it fooled millions, even if Calvin was reported being 'not amused'.

When my time did come on radio I almost blew up the medium, but just then I was having trouble on the stage that took all my time, and landed me in jail.

As I saw the theatre, it didn't present answers, only questions – some of them in my case only whispered of before I beat my bells on the stage.

New York City was an unhealthy theatre that year. A place of very little courage or originality, it now fell before a windy attack of publicity-seeking blue-noses. *Sex* was in its forty-first week at Daly's when it was the victim of a puritan campaign instigated by John Sumner, the pompous Pope of the Society for the Suppression of Vice. My play had apparently wrecked no one's morals all those weeks, but suddenly it must have affected Mr. Sumner's.

The real trouble was that its success had stimulated a rash of plays with sex themes. Other authors and producers wanted to get in on the act, and they did. Most of their plays were repulsive; some filthy. Those few foul ones were the cause of the general clean-up.

While the playboy of fifty, Mayor James J. Walker, was on a vacation in Florida – perhaps conveniently, for he loved show business – the Acting Mayor Joseph V. 'Holy Joe' McKee cracked down on the sex plays, acting on the complaints and reports of John Sumner and his assistant guardians of public morals.

There was a list of plays allegedly objectionable, even such a fine one as *God of Vengeance* by Sholem Asch. Plays immediately affected by police action were *The Captive*, with Basil Rathbone and Helen Menken, *The Virgin Man*, and *Sex*. *The Captive* voluntarily withdrew from the stage. Rather than close, I chose to stand trial with my play.

I enjoyed the courtroom as just another stage – but not so amusing as Broadway. At the trial of *Sex*, the Assistant D.A., who was prosecuting me, could not find one line or one word in the play that was profane, lewd, lascivious or obscene. So he shifted gears and contended that 'Miss West's personality, looks, walk, mannerisms and gestures made the lines and situations suggestive.'

This contention was too hard to prove, beyond a reasonable doubt. In desperation, he pounced on an item of business in the second act 'where, to a sailors' jazz band playing "St Louis Blues", Miss West did a *danse du ventre*', frankly described as a belly dance (a dance now seen often enough, performed by loudly applauded native dancers from India and elsewhere).

'Can I do it in court?' I asked my lawyer.

He looked at the jury. 'I doubt it.'

Jim said, 'Let 'em pay if they want to see it.'

What I did on stage was nothing more than an exercise involving control of my abdominal muscles, which I had learned from my father when I was a child, along with other body-building exercises. Father may have had odd ideas on body building – but he never suspected his lessons would be called obscene. I performed the dance fully clothed, wearing a tight metallic evening gown. Of course I did it with feeling – I really enjoyed it.

The prosecutor questioned one of the arresting officers in detail about this dance. The officer blushed and testified.

'Miss West moved her navel up and down and from right to left.'

'Did you actually see her navel?' my lawyer asked him.

'No, but I saw something in her middle that moved from east to west.'

The courtroom roared.

Yet it was on this moron stutter alone that a conviction was secured.

Tammany Hall ran the town with its hands in the public pockets, and orders had come from certain pious heads to close several shows. New York City was at the time one of the most politically dirty cities in the world, as the Seabury Investigation was to show a few years later.

(Four years later when I played *Sex* on the road in Chicago, Detroit and other key cities, I had no trouble with anybody about the play.)

My manager, my producer and I were sentenced to jail for 'corrupting the morals of youth', and fined $500. I decided I could use those ten days as a well-earned vacation. In fact, when I was riding to the prison on Welfare Island I was thinking of the idea for my next play. And I did write some articles, one for *Liberty* Magazine, for which I received 1,000 dollars.

I objected to the underwear they gave me at the Island. It was rough on the body. 'I want to wear my silk underwear.'

'This ain't Saks Fifth Avenue,' said a toothless old hag.

The Warden, a distinguished looking gentleman with a fine military carriage and a resonant voice, blushed. 'Well, all right. Wear your own underwear.'

Welfare Island had landscaped grounds, and everything was freshly painted, clean and sanitary. What the conditions were in the men's building, I don't know, but I have no reason to assume they were not as good as in the women's quarters. The food was quite good. The prisoners got plenty of fresh air, situated as the island was in the East River.

I couldn't say the same about the Tombs prison, where I spent several hours before I was transported to Welfare Island. The Tombs was no rose. It was dirty and dismal. Everything that could not be painted grey was painted brown, and then permitted to damply peel. The confused, diseased, feeble-minded women were herded like animals, and though few ladies ever got there, the inmates were human beings, except for the prison rats and roaches. The very young and perhaps foolish, but certainly some innocent, were mixed with foul and decaying old biddies who knew every vice, and had invented a few of their own.

Humanity had parked its ideals outside, and the place was run by rewarded Civil Service ward heelers, relatives, and smalltime vote peddlers who were all busy feeding and stealing at the public's expense. They looked, in many cases, worse than the prisoners; their faces showed greed, stupidity and lust. It was very much everyone grabbing what he could for himself. The food was revolting and tasted as if it came from the garbage scows that the city sent to sea. Nothing fitted, nothing was new, and everything smelled of jail, bodies, bugs and the powerful odour of some disinfectant that did little but spoil the air. Fresh air – like hope – was kept out.

On Welfare Island I got into the cotton dress they gave me. I had a room for myself, and a view of river and bridges from large windows. There was a door, but it was not a cell with iron bars.

'You're a special guest, Miss West. The word has come down we give you our best.'

'Thanks.'

The second day I was there, the warden told me, 'All the women want to see you.'

'I'm not here to be on exhibition.' I was about to add, 'I don't want to see them,' when pity at their drab lives changed my mind. I said, 'All right.'

We went down long halls to another part of the prison. When I went into a large dormitory, all the women began applauding. 'Glad to see you!' 'Hello, Mae' I didn't care for the use of my first name, but I figured if I could make them a less miserable mob I was doing some good.

Looking at the raddled, torn and toothless faces, I shivered. It could happen to anyone.

After a few days, the warden said to me, 'I'm Mae West's secretary around here. Phone calls and mail seem all for you.' He asked if I'd do an article for *Liberty* Magazine.

'I'll write it if you'll give me someone to type it. I've never learned to use a typewriter and I have no desire to learn typing in here.'

'I'll see you get it typed up.'

I left Welfare Island after eight days, having got two days off my ten for 'good behaviour'. I talked to many of the girls and heard their pitiful stories. I tried to help some of them. But there were just too many sad cases.

Out of jail I looked around and thought of Hollywood and films. The motion picture industry had come out of its rented stores and was building film palaces, and vaudeville was in great danger. 'Vaudeville will go,' said *Variety*.

I read the reports of studio earnings and saw that vaudeville couldn't outgrow this new giant. In 1925 Paramount reported earnings of $21,000,000; Metro, $16,000,000; and First National, $11,000,000. Nice solid round figures that I liked. I gave some real thought to motion pictures and as to how they could use my style and personality.

But as yet I had no answer. The block-buster was *The Big Parade* with John Gilbert, and I didn't see myself in the trenches. Universal lost $2,500,000 on a version of *Uncle Tom's Cabin*. Cecil B. DeMille opened *The King of Kings* with a two dollar top, and I noticed there were 18,000 film theatres in the United States, and 47,000 in the world.

And vaudeville houses were closing. Hollywood had had a few bad moments when Fatty Arbuckle, one of the big box-office comedy stars, had to face a jury over the erotic death of a party girl. In the smell of burning opium pipes, William Desmond Taylor, a famous director, was found dead, and two stars, Mabel Normand and Mary Miles Minter were involved; the case was never 'officially' solved. Clara Bow was billed as 'The Hottest Jazz Baby in Films' and everybody began to say, 'Hot dog', 'That's the cat's meow', and 'The cat's pyjamas'. Not my type of dialogue.

The big stars were Gloria Swanson, Tom Mix, Marion Davies. I felt if films could only progress a little more to my style of entertainment I would go out to the coast; but the music and the sound of my voice would be missing.

By 1926, 97 per cent of the theatres were movie palaces; only twelve real vaudeville houses remained open. Two-a-day became 'continuous performances'. The Palace barred drum rolls and spotlights, and vaudeville acts now supported pictures. In a year or so the Palace put in films. Of the big stars only George M. Cohan and Al Jolson never played the Palace.

I decided to write another play. I had thought out my new play in prison: *The Wicked Age*. The idea had come to me the day I took the dismal ride to Welfare Island. When I got down to the actual writing of it, it was fairly easy. The play was to be an exposé of the bathing beauty contests of the 1920s – the Miss Americas, crooked contests and fixed winners. While I had little trouble writing *The Wicked Age*, and no difficulty financing its production, the show proved to be a hit and a headache.

The actor we signed for the leading male part had been in silent motion pictures, but didn't have much stage experience. When we opened out of town to break in the show, this actor did not project beyond the footlights. His personality, his delivery, his voice, did not get even to the first rows. He had a good enough speaking voice and charming personality in a room. But on stage, somehow, it just lay there.

Jim said, 'Maybe it is just due to nervousness. We'll wait for a few performances to see what happens.'

He did not do any better. I said, 'Only a fire under him will help.' Today with a microphone he could have been heard. But we didn't use microphones in the theatre at that time. The audience couldn't hear him and they started getting restless. In a legitimate show, once you lose an audience for a moment, the scene goes out the window and you can't get an audience back unless you blow up a few actors or fall into the orchestra pit.

Unfortunately this actor had a big male part, with many scenes; as a consequence, due to his lack of projection, each of his scenes went nowhere; certainly not to the audience, where they belonged, and where they were eagerly awaited out front. It was pathetic.

He had looked so good at rehearsals that we had given him a run-of-the-play contract. I said, 'We have the right play and the wrong actor with a run-of-the-play contract. Oh, great.'

Jim suggested, 'Maybe the mob could run him out of town for us.'

I said, 'I hope you're joking, Jim.'

'No, I'm not.'

I tried my best to keep the actor in the part. 'By the time we get to New York, he might be able to get over to the audience.'

But the managers of the theatre and of the show, with other people out front, were sure this Hollywood stick would not do. He also affected my performance. I had to repeat some of his lost lines so I would be sure the audience knew what he had said, and so that I would get my reaction on my own line that followed his.

It was a strain on my performance and on the other actors who had scenes with him. In desperation, I switched scenes and gave many of his to another actor in the show whom the audience liked very much.

'This,' he said, 'takes the importance away from me, the leading man.'

'Yes,' I admitted. 'But this at least doesn't spoil the show too much. It's impossible to open in New York and take a chance with you playing the scenes your way.'

'Nobody at Metro ever talked to me that way.'

Jim said, 'They don't talk in Hollywood. They point.'

'I shall take action.'

'Be better if you took a train back to California.'

'I have my contract.'

I stopped Jim before he told him *where* to bank it.

We had a big advance sale in New York, and the Hollywood actor complained to Actors' Equity that I had taken his part and given most of it to another actor because 'Miss West is having an affair with him and she is trying to make this favoured actor the leading man for that reason.'

This was mean, and, I am sorry to say, not true. Some of the actors in the show backed him; they were bit actors who were jealous of the man I gave the lines to. 'Actors,' John Barrymore once told me, 'are people, but not human.'

Actors' Equity stepped in opening day at Daly's in New York, and we had to give a performance for a committee from the actors' organization. We played the show for them both ways. With the complaining actor playing his original part, and then again the way it had been changed.

We went through an entire rehearsal of the show for the four members of the Equity committee. They sat in the front row and, being actors, were in sympathy with the Hollywood actor. Of course, sitting that close and in an empty house, they could hear him. In a packed house, which absorbs sound, they'd have realized that his voice didn't carry. They ruled, 'You will have to play the show in the original form, or this actor does not have to go on at all and you will have to pay him his salary for the run of the play.'

And curtain time on opening night four hours away I could open with a bad actor – there was no understudy for his part –

or close the show and pay all the actors two weeks' salary. We decided to go on with the sunkissed ham.

I was upset by these maddening conditions. It was hard for me to put the show back in the original version, as I had rewritten the scenes and learned them the new way.

'And now I am expected to go back and study the part the original way And I have to be in a pretty good mood to make people laugh. This is a comedy show.'

Jim said, 'Steady, Mae – two hours to opening.'

I was furious. I tried to offer a proposition to the actor. 'Play it my way for just a week, until we get another actor in the part, and we'll pay you your salary for the run of the play.'

He refused. We had to go through with it his way and he was no better in the part. However, the audience didn't pay much attention to him; they were much more interested in the play, and the laughs I was getting.

The show was going to be a hit, I knew. The critics' notices were great. One reviewer stated that there were 'enough laughs in the play for three shows'. But I had lost interest in the show. I was so irritated from fighting a bad actor that the fun was out of the show for me.

I said, 'I don't care what kind of a hit it is. I'm going to close it in two weeks. I am too tightly strung to go through with it, even if it is a screaming success. It's a strain on me to try to be funny.'

I ordered the show closed in two weeks.

'But, Mae—'

'Don't anyone say, "The show must go on." This one doesn't.'

I was very emotional in those years. If it had happened in later years, I would have engaged any other actor and let the unsatisfactory actor go, paying him the big salary he was getting and laughing it off. The truth was I had been living on my energy too long without a rest. I had depleted my nerve reserve and now it was catching up with me. Writing three plays in a row, producing them, and having to play in two of them, was suddenly too much. The inspiration was gone. I closed a comedy hit at the end of two weeks and ordered all the money from the advance sale returned to the public.

I wanted time to just think: Where was Mae West going – and just what did she want next? I got no answers – not satisfactory answers; not then. I became even more jumpy. It was Jim, in love with me, who said, 'Mae, this is no good.'

'What can I do?'

'It may sound funny, but I say, write another play.'

I certainly didn't want vaudeville again. It was nearly gone.

I felt I had gone on the legitimate stage at the right time. It was a strong theatre just then on Broadway, with such shows as *Kiki*, with Lenore Ulric, *Ladies of the Evening*, Jeanne Eagels in *Rain*. I tried to think of an amusing idea for a play.

I had noticed that at my plays there were more men in the audience than women. *Sex* had an audience 80 per cent men and 20 per cent women. At *The Wicked Age* I gained a bit: 70 per cent men, 30 per cent women in the audience. It disturbed me as to what I was doing, or wasn't doing, that kept women away. I played to parties of men, often twenty in a group. The only time I had women in any number was at matinees. They generally had to take balcony seats; the orchestra was always sold out in advance – to men.

In my new play, I would give a little thought to bringing in the women. I got to thinking I should do a period play of the Gay Nineties. I thought melodrama and nostalgia would please everyone. If I wrote a good play of the period and gave it modern pace, it would appeal to three generations: grandparents, the middle-aged, and the younger generation. Sex was perennial and would do no harm to the play.

I had always admired the fabulous fashions just before the turn of the century, when Lillian Russell and Lily Langtry were around. I had seen many photographs in the styles of the period and I thought them beautiful and alluring. It was style that really attracted me to the colourful background of the Nineties, and caused me to think of the idea that finally became *Diamond Lil*.

One night at my hotel, I stopped at the desk for mail, and the night porter said pleasantly, 'Miss West, your diamonds are the hotel's best advertising. They're really beautiful.'

I was wearing my small dinner set – a diamond brooch with a diamond chain, and a set of two and two-and-a-half inch diamond and platinum bracelets with a few emeralds set into them; a fine diamond wristwatch and a pure white perfect ten-carat diamond ring. I hadn't started out to collect diamonds, but somehow they piled up on me and in self-protection I became a gem expert.

I had received most of them as gifts from admirers and grateful male friends. I never asked for things, but felt it impolite to refuse a well-meant gift. One bracelet had been given to me by my friend and manager, Jim Timony. Another bracelet was from a judge, and the brooch I had accepted from a Wall Street admirer, who was in stocks and bonds and given to expressing himself in style.

The night manager of the hotel admired my diamonds again and said, 'My, my, they are something to look at.'

'I guess that's why I wear them.'

'What are you going to do next on the stage, Miss West?'

'I am thinking about doing a period play of the turn of the century.'

He started telling me his recollections of the Bowery in those years. 'I was a police captain down in that precinct when I was a young fellow. It's still wild and crazy and full of misfits and monsters.'

'You must have been some guy.'

'You wouldn't think it now.'

'I would. You look as if you have nothing to regret,' I said.

He began telling me about the Raines Law Hotels, which were saloons whose owners attached bedrooms to their taverns in order to be able to sell liquor on Sundays. According to the Raines Law, only a licensed hotel, having at least ten bedrooms, could do so. The Raines Law Hotels were really disorderly houses.

'You remind me of a sweetheart I had then, down on the Bowery. She had a lot of diamonds, just like you. And how the men did run after her!'

Suddenly I visualized the character who was to become a part of American folklore – Diamond Lil. But the name came later, when I remembered how my father playfully called my mother 'Champagne Til', because she didn't like hard liquor, but would sip champagne on occasion. This gave me the idea of a nickname for a title. I was going to call my play 'Diamond Til', but I finally decided on 'Diamond Lil'.

I went to my suite and thought about the desk clerk's talk and the old Bowery. It would be the best setting for my next play. I started at once getting the play down on paper.

A few items got into the newspapers (carefully planted) that I was going to do a play about the New York Bowery during the Nineties.

Jim got a call from a Jack Linder. 'I would like to produce a play with Mae West.'

Jim said, 'You're an ambitious fellow. What else have you got?'

'Let me come over and talk about it.'

At the first meeting with Jim, he said: 'You have Miss West's play about the Bowery. My brother, Mark Linder, has written a play about Chatham Square down there. What I really want is to produce my brother's play, and have Miss West star in it.'

Jim made the appointment for Mark Linder to read his play to me. The Linders were bright Broadway characters, and I saw no harm in hearing their play. It sounded like an old play that had been lying around for quite some time. It was tired in construction, banal in plotting, characterless.

'The play has nothing in it I like for myself,' I said.

Jim added, 'Miss West is finishing her own play. But it isn't quite ready for production.'

Jack Linder said, 'Maybe I can produce Miss West's show. I'd like to read it when it's ready. I've got plenty of backers' money and I want to become a legitimate producer on Broadway.'

'It's nice to feel ambitious,' I said.

Jim talked it over with me later. I said I wasn't too anxious to do business with them. 'This man's only been connected with smalltime projects. I don't think he would think along the lines we do.'

Jim saw more in the Linders than I did. When I had my play ready, Jim said, 'Linder's so anxious to become a big man I think he'll spend plenty of money on this production. And after all, his money is as good as anyone else's.'

An appointment was made for me to read my play to them. 'We're crazy about it,' Jack said. 'And there's a part in it for Mark here.'

Mark was an actor, besides being a playwright, and I saw nothing wrong in his playing in the show.

I was wary of the Linders, but they had the backers for putting on *Diamond Lil*.

When we were ready to sign contracts, Jack Linder said, 'We are going to do your play, not Mark's play. Maybe he could get some credit for suggesting the locale.'

Mark was grateful for the programme billing: 'Locale suggested by Mark Linder.'

I gave Mark Linder a part in the play. My original intuition proved correct, for these Linder brothers gave me a lot of headaches over this show. Years later I had to have a court prove to them once and for all how lucky they had been, and were entitled to no more and no less than I have stated here.

My sister Beverly was in the show, playing Sally, a young girl in the big city, whom Lil befriends.

We got a good director, Ira Hards, to stage the play, and we opened at Teller's Shubert in Brooklyn, during Holy Week, 1928, with a top-notch production, scenery, and costumes.

I spent a small fortune on my gowns for it; they were made by hand by skilled dressmakers who still remembered the styles of the period and could create the proper boning and fitting of the wasp-waisted, long-trained, heavy material dresses so that they would be authentic as well as handsome. I familiarized myself with every detail of the production so closely that once as I was lying in my golden swan bed waiting for the second act curtain to rise, I could tell that the lights in the strip above me had been mysteriously switched. By the last dress rehearsal everyone and everything in the entire production was letter perfect.

Holy Week is traditionally the worst week in show business. Jim thought not many people would be in the theatre the last week of Lent, so it didn't matter where the show opened. 'And opening in Brooklyn will save railroad fares for as big a company of actors as *Diamond Lil*.'

I was sure of the play and sure of myself. The only thing I wasn't sure of was would the younger generation like period costumes. We had all worked hard; the rehearsals had been long and involved. I was aware I had a fine play, and I tried to perfect it in every way.

We opened to a packed house to everyone's surprise, and that week broke the all-time box-office record of the theatre. The notices were colourful. On April 5, 1928, Robert Garland, the columnist and drama critic of the New York *Evening Telegram*, wrote:

When the justly celebrated Miss Mae West pulls a swift one . . . she opens a new play where Brooklyn's Monroe Street, Howard Avenue and Broadway come together, and you can't see the theatre's front door for the crowds that mill before it.

And mill they did last night between eight and eight-thirty. You'd have thought that a favourite bootlegger had come back from Atlanta or that some civic event of equal importance was about to happen . . .

The most casual investigation disclosed the fact that it was Miss West who was responsible for much of the turmoil. Miss West, author of that sterling home-and-fireside drama *Sex*, was staging her latest dialogic brain-child in Teller's Shubert Theatre, and half Manhattan was of a mind to get there.

Until yesterday I had not seen Miss West. That, of course, was my misfortune. But from now on, she's my favourite actress. From now on, I'm willing – anxious, even – to pay money to enjoy her. From now on, I intend to applaud her from the top lines of my column and the front rows of theatres in which she happens, by the grace of God and the laxity of the Police Department, to be playing.

She is, as a chap in a maroon sweater shouted, 'an actress and no fooling.' So regal is Miss West's manner, so assured is her artistry, so devastating are her charms in the eyes of all red-blooded men, so blonde, so beautiful and so buxom is she that she makes Miss Ethel Barrymore look like the late lamented Mr. Bert Savoy.

I'm here to tell you that *Diamond Lil* is a swell play . . . a grand 'Bowery folk play'. As for Miss West herself, in person, and a very moving picture, she's simply superb. It's worth swimming to Brooklyn to see her descend those dance hall stairs, to be present while she lolls in a golden bed reading the *Police Gazette*, murders her girl friend, wrecks the Salvation Army, and sings as much of 'Frankie and Johnnie' as the mean old law allows.

After the Brooklyn tryout, I didn't have to change a line or an actor. I had learned by now that I could say almost anything, do almost anything on a stage if I smiled and was properly ironic in delivering my dialogue.

We crossed the bridge to Manhattan and opened at the Royale Theatre. When the curtain rang down David Belasco, the old showman, came backstage and took me in his arms. He said, 'I couldn't have done better myself. It was excellent.'

The entire audience stood up and cheered the final curtain, and many of the New York critics came back to congratulate me on my success. I remember Walter Winchell, Percy Hammond and Heywood Broun. I was Diamond Lil off-stage as well as on. The champagne flowed and I knew the play was a hit. It got some odd comments. The New York *Daily Mirror* wrote:

Carl Van Vechten went to see *Diamond Lil* the other night at the Royale for the third or fourth time, bringing with him John Colton. After the second act, Mr. Colton sent a note back to Miss West.

'I've seen them all,' he wrote, 'from Bernhardt to Sada Yaceo (missed Rachel owing to delayed birth), but you surpass.'

I was enormously pleased – who wouldn't be 'But who,' I enquired, 'who is this Sada Yaceo?' Various erudite persons and horse players failed to solve the problem for me.

Percy Hammond, drama critic of the New York *Herald Tribune* put it this way: 'The Rewards of Virtue . . . Miss Mae West has become an institution in the Broadway drama . . . The Theatre Royale is crowded at each performance of Diamond Lil . . . Mae West, its star and author, is now more admired by her public than is Jane Cowl, Lynn Fontanne, Helen Hayes or Eva LeGallienne.'

'Mae is to the New York stage,' wrote Leonard Hall in the New York *Evening Telegram*, 'what a match is to a scuttle of gunpowder – what a hot fire is to a shivering wienerwurst. Just when the theatres wink out and the first nighters begin to deal timetables from the bottom of the deck, in flames Mae West in a sizzling drammer that sets Times Square to roaring.

'She is the prize tang-inserter of the American theatre. Probably no other stage in the world could produce such a phenomenon as this opulent girl whose acted works prove just because a lady is a little vulgar it is no sign that her heart isn't 22-carat gold.'

The more serious Stark Young, reviewing in *The New Republic*, said, 'Glamour Miss West undoubtedly has . . . She is alive on the stage as nobody is in life; she astonishes – shocks if you like – engages and puzzles you. In *Diamond Lil* all roads lead indeed to Rome. This Rome of all roads is Miss West . . . You may watch her performance and take it any way you like; the theatre, you perceive, is a place for your pleasure . . . Miss West is a part of the secret of Pan before the footlights.'

The puzzle of who was Sada was solved a few days later, in a note to the drama editor of the *Mirror*.

Dear Sir:

If John Colton meant Sada Yacco, the greatest Japanese tragedienne of her time, why didn't he say so? No wonder it wasn't recognized under Yaceo.

John Colton was the dramatist who wrote the smash hit play *Rain*, based on Somerset Maugham's story 'Sadie Thompson'. Also *The Shanghai Gesture*. He was an ironic cosmopolitan, mocking, witty and fun to have around.

Carl Van Vechten was a critically acclaimed avant-garde writer and novelist of the Twenties, who had written such bestsellers as *Peter Whiffle, Nigger Heaven and The Tattooed Countess*. I like best his intriguing book about cats entitled *The Tiger in the House*. Carl, buck-toothed, blond, chi-chi and bored, was the hunter of sinister sensations to be found in odd parts of New York.

Richard Watts, then drama critic of the New York Post, was the first to hail *Diamond Lil* as a 'modern classic'. Other critics followed suit.

In a sense I suppose it is. Certainly it is, as Bernard Sobel wrote, 'one of the few authentic stage pictures of tenderloin night life with its fashionable slumming parties, singing waiters, and "Frankie and Johnny" balladists.' It has warmth and humour, colour, variety and suspense. It is, in a word, 'theatre.' Anyone who wants to know how to write 'theatre' can 'Come up and see me sometime'.

With *Diamond Lil* I had it made. Through the years people have come to think of my characterization of Lil as my other self. Sometime, somewhere, I recall, someone quoted me as saying: 'Diamond Lil – I'm her and she's me and we're each other.' I hope I was not so ungrammatical, but however I said it, I spoke at least a partial truth. Lil in her various incarnations – play, novel,* motion picture – and I have been one.

From here on, Lil and I, in my various characterizations, climbed the ladder of success wrong by wrong.

---

*In 1932 I turned the story into prose narrative form. It was published by The Macaulay Co., and has sold over 95,000 copies.

I enjoyed my success with no false humility, and no coy hiding of my ego under a basket. I had worked very hard since a teenager. I was still young enough to think it would always be like this, and show-wise, and aware that it would be hard to follow. And that the public and my admirers would demand more and better things. Success is a two-bladed golden sword; it knights one and stabs one at the same time.

One thing it did: I was meeting a new type man – but not too different from what I was accustomed to. Hard as I worked, I would be lying to say I neglected all of my emotional side. I'm a girl who likes balance in everything and I now wanted to catch up on my love life.

Clara Bow (1905–65)

The 'It' Girl In Hollywood

In the late 1920s, the film star Clara Bow was described as 'the hottest Jazz Baby of the Jazz Age', and by Scott Fitzgerald as 'the quintessence of what the term "flapper" signifies'. She had escaped from an impoverished New York background after winning a movie magazine beauty contest which earned her a bit part in a film, and thereafter took Hollywood, literally, by storm. When she starred in *It* in 1927, Clara became a symbol of the new freedom of expression and behaviour for women: girls actually doing what their mothers had only dreamed about. She personified the 'new' girl who smoked, drank, wore revealing clothes and was sexually uninhibited. Overnight, she became a legend and in 1928 alone she received almost 34,000 fan letters, many addressed simply, 'The "It" Girl, Hollywood'. Over-work, mental instability and scandal about her private life brought her career to an end with the arrival of the talkies, but in popular mythology she lived on as 'flaming youth personified for an entire generation' to quote one of her obituary notices. This account of Clara Bow – 'the girl with the most desirable attribute of the decade' – and the cost of that fame is by **David Stenn**.

'She dislikes gossip and is unquestionably one of the most gossiped-about women in Hollywood,' wrote *Photoplay* of Clara. What the magazine did not mention was the town's tacit policy of excluding her from all social functions. Even twelve-year-old Budd Schulberg realized that 'there was one subject on which the staid old Hollywood establishment would agree: Clara Bow, no matter how great her popularity, was a low-life and a disgrace to the community.'

Her sin: In an industry trying to forget its outcast past and adopt affectations to suit its exalted present, Clara had remained herself, and as such was a constant reminder of her and, by implication, everyone else's lowly background. 'Her Brooklyn accent and dreadful manners would reproach [them] with their common origin, making her presence an insulting reminder of their uneasy position in "high society",' wrote Louise Brooks. When Brooks married director Edward Sutherland, she won instant access to the Pickfair-San Simeon set. Having idolized Clara since *Dancing Mothers*, Brooks planned to invite her to a dinner party, but when she mentioned it to her husband, 'Eddie recoiled in horror. "Oh, no, we can't have *her*," he said. "We don't know what she'd *do*. She's from *Brooklyn*, you know." ' So were several pillars of the Hollywood community, but they had renounced their humble beginnings. Clara had not, and her lack of pretension sealed her social fate. It is no coincidence that shortly after she and Tui Lorraine traveled to Yosemite National Park to visit Joan Crawford on location for *Rose Marie*, Crawford shunned Clara once she found future husband Douglas Fairbanks, Jr, and the social pinnacle of Pickfair within reach.

Clara's forthright sexuality alienated her from potential female sponsors within the Hollywood elite. 'Clara wasn't well liked amongst other women in the film colony,' says fellow outsider Lina Basquette. 'Her social presence was taboo, and it was rather silly, because God knows Mary Pickford and Marion Davies had plenty to hide. It's just that they hid it, and Clara didn't.' Unlike Pickford and Davies, Clara disregarded Hollywood's unwritten code of correct sexual conduct: a woman could do whatever with whomever, as long as she kept her door and mouth shut. Unique and sophisticated as it seemed, Hollywood actually possessed the same sexual double standard as any small American town: a man who pursued women was a 'stud'; a woman who pursued men, a 'slut'. Since a large majority of Hollywood actresses would have fallen into the latter category had they stayed in their hometowns, the emphasis on appearances was imperative, for all that separated Pickford and Davies from Clara was their self-made social position. 'The women in the film colony liked to put on the pure, virginal act,' says Lina Basquette, 'whereas Clara just called a spade a spade. She didn't care what anybody thought. She just went ahead and did what she wanted to do.' This brazen attitude outraged Hollywood socialites, who condemned Clara not for what she did not know, but because she did not care. Ignorance was forgivable. Rebellion was not.

As the rebel without a cause, Clara was often her own worst enemy. Though amusing, her social blunders were both blatant and avoidable: when director Frank Tuttle invited her to dine with his family at the elegant Beverly Hills Hotel, Clara arrived in a belted bathing suit. 'It was a shocker,' one of Tuttle's daughters remembers. It was also a violation of both the hotel's dress code and Hollywood's rule of formal dress for evening engagements, yet Clara couldn't fathom the fuss. Why should something *she* wore make someone *else* uncomfortable? And why did Mrs Tuttle get so mad just because she used their towels as makeup rags?

Clara even scandalized the scandalous, as Judge Ben Lindsey learned. The mild-mannered, middle-aged Lindsey had caused a furor with *The Companionate Marriage*, a book which advocated premarital sex as a crucial determinant of a couple's compatibility. If fewer women approached the altar as virgins, wrote Lindsey, fewer divorces would come before his bench in Denver. His theory lost Lindsey his judgeship, and when Colorado conservatives hounded him out of the state, he found refuge with empathetic Hollywood liberals like Ben and Ad Schulberg, who made the judge their house guest while a local bench was bought for him. The Schulbergs intended to present Lindsey to their equally enlightened friends, but he had other plans. As Budd Schulberg recalls, 'the apostle of unmarried sex in America wanted to interview one of its most celebrated practitioners'.

Judge Lindsey asked to meet Clara Bow.

With great reluctance, the Schulbergs invited her to their home. She arrived late and tipsy; ever genteel, they overlooked both details and introduced her to Lindsey. 'Hiya, Judge!' whooped Clara. 'Ben tells me ya believe people oughta have their fun without havin' t'get married. Ya naughty boy!' Giggling, she pulled Lindsey to her and planted a big, wet kiss upon his lips. Mrs Lindsey looked askance at her hostess. Ad Schulberg's expression indicated that she had expected as much.

Lindsey had planned to query 'the "It" Girl' about her views on sex and marriage. Clara had little interest in discussing either, demanding instead that the judge dance with her. Lindsey obliged, stumbling clumsily across the Schulberg living room as he tried to follow Clara's nimble feet. Meanwhile, and to everyone's mounting panic, Clara had begun a gambit of her own: 'beginning with the judge's top jacket button, she said, "Rich man . . . poor man . . . beggar man . . . thief . . .", her busy little fingers unbuttoning with each designation. By the time the childhood game had brought her to "Indian chief", Clara Bow was undoing the top button of Judge Lindsey's fly.' Clara was practicing what Judge Ben Lindsey preached; panic-stricken, he fled from her arms to his wife. The Lindseys left the Schulbergs' in a self-righteous huff.

Afterward Ben Schulberg reprimanded Clara, who sulked like a naughty child. 'Well gee whiz,' she pouted, 'if he believes in all that modern stuff like ya say he does, how come he's such an old stick-in-the-mud?'

Her point was lost upon her self-presumed social betters.

Shunned by socialites and forbidden to fraternize with Trajans, Clara found a friend and ally in Adela Rogers St Johns.

A novelist, journalist, and screenwriter (she wrote a draft of *Children of Divorce*) whose father, renowned criminal lawyer Earl Rogers, once defended Clarence Darrow on a charge of jury tampering, Adela was a tough, smart, and independent woman who believed her sex superior: 'This country got into trouble,' she once declared, 'when women came down to equality with men'. Though eleven years older and more worldly than Clara, the two women had plenty in common: both preferred the company of virile men (Adela married her latest lover, Stanford halfback Richard Hyland, that year, then divorced him when he called her 'half-witted'), and both were role models for other women. Adela had risen from a seven-dollar-a-week cub reporter for the Hearst syndicate to its 'World's Greatest Girl Reporter', covering major news events and interviewing movie stars with such revelatory results that she was called the 'Mother Confessor of Hollywood'. Aware that such pieces must paradoxically debunk yet perpetuate their subject's stardom, Adela could turn an ordinary life into extraordinary reading.

In the fall of 1927 Adela was assigned by *Photoplay* to profile Clara. She arrived at Paramount and was taken by a studio publicist to Clara's dressing room, located in the 'number one' spot on the lot (star prestige was measured by dressing room location; Clara's was on the corner closest to the executive offices). Clara was not there, which Adela later considered 'an omen. [She] is never, at least in my experience, where she is expected to be. Trying to locate her at any given time is a week's work, partly because she changes her mind with every new impulse and partly because she is always surrounded by thoroughly incompetent people whom she either happens to like or is sorry for.' Finally Clara was found with Tui Lorraine in a projection room watching the day's rushes, and Adela was introduced to 'a very young girl, with amazing red hair obviously but beautifully and effectively dyed, and the most restless, brilliant, and arresting black eyes I had ever encountered'.

Clara apologized for the mix-up and invited Adela to dinner at her home. Tui reminded Clara that it was the cook's night off and all that was left in the house was gin – 'and no lady ever drinks *gin*'. Clara tried calling her house to confirm this, but her phone number had been changed because too many people knew the old one and she could not remember the new one. She dialed several numbers which sounded right. All were wrong. Apologizing again, Clara invited Adela to dinner at the Ambassador Hotel the following night. Having extended the invitation, she immediately retracted it: 'Sorry, I forgot, I gotta date with a *gorgeous* man. 'Least, I *think* he's gorgeous. He'll prob'ly turn out t'be a dud.' Clara told Adela to drop by her house beforehand and wrote down her address. It was two blocks wrong.

The following evening Clara forgot to tell her maid a guest was coming, so Adela was denied admittance until Robert Bow appeared, allowed the journalist to enter, then disappeared without a word. Adela was left alone in the bizarrely decorated living room, 'unable to read because I couldn't find any books'.

Finally Clara and Tui arrived. Clara looked exhausted. 'She rehearsed a scene forty times with some sap leading man,' explained Tui. 'She runs errands for almost everybody over there.'

'Ya gotta be regular,' sighed Clara. 'Even more when you're up. I remember when I was scratchin' for a job. Pola Negri useta ride by me in her limousine like I was part of the roadbed. But I ain't gonna high-hat anybody. First, 'cuz I know how it feels. Second, 'cuz this is a funny game – you're here t'day and gone t'morrow. How 'bout a drink?' The three women had one highball each, which was all Clara allowed herself during shooting. Then Tui left. Clara was ready for her interview.

Adela was apprehensive. Her subject 'was slumped in the corner of the davenport. It seemed to me that she would give me nothing. She looked tired and almost stupid, in spite of the feverish glitter in her eyes.

'Then, as we started to talk, she came alive.'

The interview lasted until dawn. As Adela listened with

rapt astonishment, Clara spoke of her incredible past in vivid, unsparing detail. The tenements, the hunger, a life without hope or love. Frederick Gordon, and Johnny's deaths before her eyes. Her father's absences, her mother's 'spells'. The butcher knife. Sarah Bow's death, for which Clara still blamed herself. The Fame and Fortune Contest, coming to Hollywood, and then, five years later, becoming the biggest box-office draw in movie history. Men: Gilbert Roland, Gary Cooper, Victor Fleming. And despite her success and suitors, loneliness. Always loneliness.

Adela sat transfixed throughout. 'I do not know why she talked as she did,' she wrote later. 'Once started, she could not stop. It was as though a dam had broken and the words poured out without volition; as though she had not for years talked to anyone who might sympathize and understand.'

Adela called her all-night conversation with Clara 'the peak of my experiences. Before me rolled a mind entirely untrained, grappling in its own way with the problems of a sophisticated and civilized world. There is hammered into her soul a fear of life, and that is why she desires to live fast and furiously, why she must seek forgetfulness in mad gaiety.'

Beginning that night, Adela befriended the real Clara beneath her 'It' Girl veneer, and the truth behind the myth fascinated and frightened her. 'There seems to be no pattern, no purpose to her life,' she wrote at the time. 'She swings from one emotion to another, but she gains nothing, stores up nothing against the future. She lives entirely in the present, not even for today, but just for the moment. And you go on loving her, feeling sorry for her, and praying that she won't get into any real trouble.' Clara had acquired experience but not profited by it, and Adela feared that when she finally and inevitably did learn her lesson, it would be a devastating one. Given the disasters that would soon occur, her worries were justified.

Adela thought Clara's story too raw to retell in standard Mother Confessor style. Instead she convinced *Photoplay* to run it as a first-person narrative; the effect, Adela believed, would be most gripping coming directly from Clara, just as Adela had heard it herself. In an unprecedented decision, the magazine's editorial board agreed, and 'My Life Story, by Clara Bow as told to Adela Rogers St Johns' appeared in three consecutive issues. Though Clara's Brooklyn dialect and colorful vocabulary were cleaned up, the tale's grisly details were left alone. To her further credit, Adela did not concoct a happy Hollywood ending. From the first lines of its first installment, 'My Life Story' portrayed its subject unlike any prior magazine piece: 'I think wildly gay people are usually hiding from something in themselves,' wrote Adela for Clara. 'The best life has taught them is to snatch at every moment of fun and excitement, because they feel sure that fate is going to hit them over the head with a club at the first opportunity.' This was Clara's essential credo, and though she had neither the acumen nor ability to verbalize it, Adela did. The resulting life story, composed of Clara's facts and Adela's interpretation of them, remains gripping.

Ironically 'My Life Story' ensured Clara's social exile within the Hollywood community. Even those who reacted with sympathy recoiled at her candor, for in an era when poverty and mental illness were causes for embarrassment and shame, 'the "It" Girl' was associating herself with both. And in an industry which treated truth as a burden, not a virtue, Clara's unflinching honesty was considered yet another display of bad manners. While everyone else buried their pasts, she exhumed hers. While everyone else conformed, she rebelled. Now Hollywood rendered its hypocritical verdict: 'My Life Story' was touching, but was it truly *necessary*? What point was there in dredging up old, sordid memories?

Adela ignored such disapproval and appointed herself as Clara's protector. She arranged for her brother, Bogart Rogers, to take control of Clara's finances from Robert Bow, who had managed to squander much of Clara's $1,500-a-week salary on, among other investments, his cleaners and restaurant. She accompanied her to U.S.C. games, where Clara appeared in a bright red sportsuit, bright red slippers with high gold heels and buckles, bare legs, and a bright red beret perched jauntily over one ear.

Adela tried to reason with her new friend. All that red, she said, was positively *barbaric*. And a lady always wears *stockings* in public. And why come to a football game in *high heels?*

'Why not?' asked Clara innocently. 'I like 'em. They make me feel good.'

It was, suggested Adela, a question of *taste*.

Clara wasn't insulted, but she wasn't convinced, either. 'My taste suits me,' she replied. 'And I gotta live with myself more than anybody else does.'

Nonplussed by such reasoning, Adela said nothing.

Clara also became a frequent guest at Adela's ranch in Whittier, where she was re-presented to Hollywood society. Adela hoped her protégée would charm the assembled company and be granted a social reprieve, but Clara invariably turned opportunity into calamity. A typical blunder occurred at a gathering that included Colleen Moore, *It* scenarist Hope Loring, and guest-of-honor William Randolph Hearst. During dinner, Adela and Loring encouraged Clara to enroll in college courses, a daunting prospect for someone with a ninety-hour work week and seventh-grade education. Clara listened politely, 'agreed with us, admired our platitudes – and went right on being Clara Bow'. In this instance, being Clara Bow meant telling a dirty joke with graphic gestures and a punchline which, recalls Colleen Moore, had its narrator squatting to make her point. 'I was as shocked as everybody else,' Moore admits, 'but I had to laugh inside, she did such a first-rate job'. If others felt likewise, none were willing to say so in the presence of the prudish guest of honor. Clara's performance was received in silence.

Meanwhile the vigilant governess of Adela's two children, twelve-year-old Billy and ten-year-old Elaine, refused to allow her charges to sleep under the same roof as Clara. So vehement was the governess, and so intimidated was the normally formidable Adela, that the St Johns children were usually taken against their will to their grandmother's for the weekend. Both adored Clara: 'She was so warm and affec-

tionate, with soft skin; hugging her was like hugging a kitten,'
recalls Elaine. 'Of course, my governess disapproved of her
so heartily that I rarely got to see her.'

Clara knew it. 'I'm crazy t'see your kids,' she would tell
Adela as soon as she arrived. 'That little Billy is such a darb,
he reminds me of Johnny.' Adela knew about Johnny, so her
lame excuse that her son was spending the weekend with his
grandmother made her sick with guilt, especially when she
witnessed Clara's wounded reaction: 'her eyes met mine and
I winced. They began to smolder, her face hardened. "Oh
well," Clara said. "What'd I expect?" '

Although Clara preferred the company of the St Johns
children to Adela's adult guests, to Elaine's disappointment
she was invariably 'dragged down and made to watch the
tennis matches. She never played, just watched.' While Clara
watched the tennis matches, wives watched Clara. Adela
remembers one doubles game where she was partnered with
the wife of a handsome actor. During the match the actor and
Clara sat on a canvas swing beside the court, four feet apart
from one another, in full view of everyone. Yet when the
match ended, the wife stormed over to her husband and
smashed her racquet over his head. The couple departed
prematurely 'amid tears and recriminations'.

Clara couldn't understand it. 'Why do they always think I
want their husbands?' she would ask Adela wearily. 'Most of
'em are no bargains that I can see.' Aware of Clara's strict
code about married men, Adela nonetheless found herself
furious when her own husband, football hero Richard Hyland, scrambled eggs with Clara late one night. In the eyes of
other women or the presence of other men, Clara was guilty
until proven innocent, and although Adela remained a loyal
friend and ally, invitations to Whittier soon dwindled, then
disappeared. 'You'll fail as I did,' Hope Loring had warned
when Adela made Clara her Galatea. Adela later admitted as
much: 'I did fail as she had, as Elinor Glyn had. But I think
now it was because we were offering oyster forks to a
wounded creature who needed the true Bread of Life.'

Now Clara had neither. The most popular girl in America

was a Hollywood pariah whose presence was not even missed at the premieres of her movies (Clara would wait a month, then go incognito to a neighborhood theater). 'Mosta my friends're ones I knew before I paid income tax,' she told a fan magazine, 'and their names don't mean nothin' t'nobody.' To Hollywood society, this was precisely the point: Clara was without social prestige, and no degree of fame or adulation would secure it for her. Uninvited to private parties and unnerved by mobs which formed whenever she appeared in public, 'the "It" Girl' passed sleepless nights playing poker, Parcheesi, darts, or craps with her cook, maid, and chauffeur.

One premiere she missed would acquire historic significance. In December, 1927, as the Trojan season ended, Los Angeles audiences cheered a movie whose actions were accompanied by synchronized *speaking*. Despite frenzied public response to the onscreen songs of Al Jolson, *The Jazz Singer* was considered a novelty, not a threat to silent filmmaking.

There was no reason to believe otherwise, nor to suspect that in the wake of *The Jazz Singer*, a time bomb had been set, and that even for a career as phenomenal as Clara's, its clock was steadily ticking.

The Outrageous Tallulah

Tallulah Bankhead also broke away from her background when she won a beauty contest at the age of fifteen and headed straight for the New York stage. In her case, however, she was actually the daughter of William Brockman Bankhead of Huntsville, Alabama, the Speaker of the House of Representatives, who had her strictly and expensively educated. But after Tallulah made her début in *When Men Betray* at the Bijou Theatre in 1918, she began building an uninhibited and disreputable public persona which made her name a regular feature in the gossip columns of the world's press. Tallulah's gorgeous looks and unmistakable rich, harsh laugh were seen at their best in plays like *Little Foxes* (1939) and *The Skin of our Teeth* (1943), but it was her off-stage behaviour that qualified her as another of the genuine eccentrics of the twentieth century. She herself wrote the following account of her wild, wild ways complete with tales of drink, drugs and gambling in 1952.

Despite all you may have heard to the contrary, I have never had a ride in a police patrol wagon.

I have milked a mammoth, and I travel with adjustable window screens. I have been up in a balloon with Sir Nigel Playfair, and down in a submarine with Gary Cooper. I have scaled an elephant in a St Louis zoo, and christened an electric rabbit with a jeroboam of Lanson 1912. I have clerked behind a counter with Margot Asquith and sung duets with Margaret Truman. Charged with two double-daiquiris I have churned with the conviction that I can do the Indian rope trick.

My voice has been likened to the mating call of the caribou, and to the haunting note of a Strad. Apostates have hinted that I'm the ill-begotten daughter of Medusa and the Marquis de Sade. As against these slanders there are the hymns of my champions, equally inaccurate, that I'm a fusion of Annie Laurie, Bopeep, Florence Nightingale and whichever waif Lillian Gish played in *The Orphans of the Storm*. Somewhere in between these contrary verdicts lies the truth. With Montaigne 'I speak truth, not so much as I would, but as much as I dare; and I dare a little the more, as I grow older.'

I've had tea with Lloyd George, tiffin with Ramsay MacDonald, and I've aced Greta Garbo on Clifton Webb's court. Forced to vote for a Davis, I'll take Jefferson and give you Bette. To the consternation of the world of science my endorsement once glowed on the jacket of a book by Sir James Hapwood Jeans, the great astronomer. In it he was speculating on the age of stars – in the heavens rather than on the stage. To please the Maharanee of Cooch Behar I once togged myself out in a sari, and I won five pounds from Lord Birkenhead when he bet that Cleopatra was a brunette. Later I sued Birkenhead's daughter, Lady Eleanor Smith, for libel. She wrote in Lord Rothermere's London *Dispatch* that I was an Anglophobe. What's more, I collected.

I slept fitfully in Kimbolton, the haunted castle in which Henry VIII locked up Catherine of Aragon, and I suffer from chronic anaemia. (Just a minute while I take a look at the ticker! I want to get the last quotation on Billy Rose, common. Here it is. Nothing asked and nothing bid.) I've played Newcastle-on-Tyne and Terre Haute, Indiana, and when the London *News Chronicle* sought to rouse the parish with 'Do Brainy People Play Bridge?' I took the affirmative along with H.G. Wells and Rose Macaulay, with Bernard Shaw and John Galsworthy dissenting.

Under oath I'd like to refute the canard that I'm an old chum of Winston Churchill's – a fable that constantly bobs up in print. But he did come to see me five times when I was playing in *Fallen Angels*.

I have three phobias which, could I mute them, would make my life as slick as a sonnet, but as dull as ditch water: I hate to go to bed, I hate to get up, and I hate to be alone. My inability to cope with these prejudices leads to complications, excesses and heresies frowned upon in stuffier circles, circles I avoid as I would exposure to the black pox. My caprices, born of my fears, frequently find a vent in the romantic pursuits, enthusiasms and experiments at odds with the code affirmed by Elsie Dinsmore.

Though I say it who shouldn't, I was born an actress. I never had any formal instruction, never cased a drama school. Acting is an astonishingly easy profession. I've given no more thought to my best roles than I have to my worst. Asked about my technique, I grow evasive. I'm not aware I have any. I'm violating no confidences, least of all my own, when I say my performances have saved many a frowzy charade, prolonged their runs long beyond their deserts. I have a dark suspicion that only ersatz actors can explain the thing called technique. I could list a hundred right here, but there is little to be gained by starting a riot so early. I have enough feuds on my hands.

Acting is the laziest of the professions. A ballet dancer must limber up two or three hours a day, working or idle. The great musicians practise three or four hours a day, willy-nilly. Opera singers must go easy on cigarettes, learn half a dozen languages. The demands on an actress consist in learning the role, interpreting to the best of her ability the intent of the author as outlined by the director. When not on stage? She sits around chewing her nails, waiting for the telephone to ring. She toils not, neither does she spin. She may fume. She may even read. But she doesn't practise.

What would I do were platforms, microphones and screens denied me? That's easy. I'd go to the races, I'd sit up all night gambling in the most convenient casino, I'd enjoy an emotional jag while suffering with the New York Giants. I might glut myself with bridge could I find players agreeable to my wayward strategies. Cooking? Writing? These require powers of concentration and industry which I don't possess. The theatre has spoiled me for the more demanding arts.

You've heard, I'm sure, about Tallulah the toper! Tallulah the tosspot! Tallulah, the gal who gets tight as a tick! Let's face it, my dears, I have been tight as a tick! Fried as a mink! Stiff as a goat! But I'm no toper. No tosspot, I. In all my years in the theatre I've never missed a performance because of alcoholic wounds. I have never skidded into the footlights through confused vision. No curtain has been prematurely lowered on a play of mine that the litter-bearers might get an emergency workout. That's more than I can say of some of my contemporaries in the higher echelons. I shall not cite these contemporaries here. No use starting a pot-and-kettle controversy.

Before we pursue this delicate subject further it might be wise to define intoxication. If you wake up in bed with your hat on you, it's my guess you may have been addled on retirement. A friend of mine given to over-indulgence was horizontal for ten hours in his derby. It was three months before the ring on his brow faded. The hat theory doesn't cover me. I haven't worn one since Daddy's funeral. Joe E. Lewis, the night club cutup, heads another school of thought. It's Joe's conviction you're sober until, lying flat on the floor, you have to hang on to avoid falling.

Frankly, I have contributed a great deal to the carousing phase of my legend. When newspapermen question me on cosmic affairs and other irrelevancies, I ooze hospitality. Knowing their thirsts I'm quick on the bottle. Since I never drink alone, I would be remiss as a hostess did I not drink with them. Consecutive toasts lead to confusion. Most of my interviews reek of vermouth, bourbon and the smoky juice of barley. Whipped into frenzies through association with me and Manhattans simultaneously, my friends compose tales that echo the shore-leave sailors in *South Pacific*, James Barton in his 'Mad Dog' specialty, or one of Ernest Hemingway's heroes.

I do not wince at these gentle libels. They're the fruit of collusion. Because of my reputation for rowdiness and scorn of convention, my biographers feel they would be betraying their parishioners, false to their oath, did they paint me cuddled up before a grate fire, a cookie jar on the mantel, Louisa May Alcott's *Little Women* in my lap. And they would!

An actress who submits to interviews – one of the sweet uses of publicity – will get nowhere bellowing she's been misquoted. I've been misquoted often. I was all for sueing the newspaper *PM* and one of its feature writers, Robert Rice, son of Elmer Rice, the playwright, for hinting that my consumption was running well ahead of the output of the distilleries. In the end cooler heads prevailed. I'll have at him with my dirk do I ever get him in an alley.

I have been abstemious for long stretches but even deep in self-denial I am suspect. Once a rumour raced up and down Broadway that though I had forsaken intoxicants, I had found an astonishing substitute. By dissolving two aspirin tablets in a beaker of Coca-Cola and draining same down I was stimulated, said my foes, to the extent of four juleps. Had the charge been true I would rate with Pasteur and the discoverer of pencillin in the field of chemistry. Were such a concoction potent it would wipe out the saloons over night. Utter rubbish!

Let's not quibble! I'm the foe of moderation, the champion of excess. If I may lift a line from a die-hard whose identity is lost in the shuffle, 'I'd rather be strongly wrong than weakly right.' A congenital emotionalist, restive and wired for sound – I operate on either direct or alternating current – I frequently give the impression I'm awash when I haven't had so much as a snifter. On the edge of a crisis I shun the sauce. The climax behind me, I find drink stimulating. It's a worry-extinguisher that up to three in the morning makes for ease and confidence. At three-fifteen the issue may cloud up. I wouldn't think of tippling before an opening night. Once it is behind me and the decision beyond recall, I'm ready for such wassail as is available.

In any drinker's census you'll not find me in the two-cocktails-before-dinner file. After two cocktails I don't want any dinner, or any lunch. The so-called civilized drinkers who follow this tidy pattern are wrestling with desire and remorse at the same time. Food defeats the very thing for which you took the drink. It smothers the glow which the drink lets loose.

I like to drink best when I'm with challenging, exciting people. If I'm in the dumps liquor depresses me further. Circumstance rules my thirst. A thrilling knockout, a ninth-inning finish, a headline that stabs my spine – these can touch me off. I also find drinking pleasant, if not profitable, when I'm in love. It seems to give zest to my emotions, elevate the reading on my romantic thermometer. I'm not fascinated by the taste of liquor. A frozen daiquiri of a scorching afternoon is soothing. It makes living more tolerable. But, given any option, I'll bypass Martinis and Scotch highballs, stiff-arm those pink or purple concoctions, equal parts of bilge water, anisette and rum, with which hostesses sabotage a party. Asked to name my poison, out of loyalty to the South and my stomach I'll settle for bourbon. If the auspices are favourable, my host under no fiscal strain, I'll go for champagne, the most inspiring of all the juices. Racked with a hang-over I do my muttering over a Black Velvet, a union of champagne and stout. Don't be swindled into believing there's any cure for a hangover. I've tried them all: iced tomatoes, hot clam juice, brandy punches. Like the common cold it defies solution. Time alone can stay it. The hair of the dog? That way lies folly. It's as logical as trying to put out a fire with applications of kerosene.

When overheated I have a tendency to monopolize attention and conversation. I'm not content with boiling. I boil over! Havoc often ensues. I provoke some of my companions into controversy. Others grab their duffel and, to quote J. Caesar, put safety in flight. Edged, my conversation may be spiced with invectives and profanities, condoned in Hemingway, but not in Homer.

Drink reacts on its practitioners in conflicting ways. One brave can knock off a quart of Scotch and look and act as sober as Herbert Hoover. Another, after three Martinis, makes two-cushion caroms off the chaise-longue as he attempts to negotiate the bathroom. One gentleman of my acquaintance bolts upstairs to plough through Proust and James Joyce, after he's latched onto his fourth rum-and-coke. With the same handicap, another sobs his heart out when someone starts to monkey with 'Mother Macree' on the piano. As a rule of thumb, liquor sharpens and inflates our natural, if hidden, bent.

Of the mots coined to fit my deportment when on a rampage of good will, the most acid and accurate dropped from the lips of Dorothy Parker. Justly famed for her critiques, her poisonous impeachments of her sex, Dotty Parker is the mistress of the verbal grenade. Miss Parker, after seeing Katharine Hepburn in *The Lake*, wrote of her performance: 'She runs the gamut of emotions from A to B.' And it was Miss Parker, after swooning through two columns over the imagery and style of James Branch Cabell in *The Silver Stallion*, concluded by saying: 'To save my mother from the electric chair, I couldn't read three pages of it.'

A party-tosser of talent, Miss Parker touched off a shindig in tribute to Edie Smith, my secretary and confessor, shortly after my escape from Hollywood in the early thirties. To her hutch in the Algonquin she invited assorted wags, cynics and idlers, among them humorists Frank Sullivan and Corey Ford, screen director George Cukor.

Elated that my friend was to be saluted I made the mistake of taking a few nips before I got to the arena. There I added to my content. I distracted the guests with backbends, cartwheels and monologues. Enough of this shillyshallying! I was noisy, tight and obstreperous!

Miss Parker and Edie were in the kitchen setting up refills, when George Cukor, gentleman and diplomat, decided that in the interests of tranquillity I should go home. Through some ruse he tricked me to the street. Shortly after our departure Miss Parker came out of the kitchen, looked about, then said sweetly: 'Oh, has Whistler's mother gone?'

It's true that I once pinwheeled along Piccadilly, but it was three o'clock in the morning. The street was bare and silent. I was only answering a taunt of my companion – Prince Nicholas of Romania. You know those Romanian princes! Not all of them are on key.

When I came up from Washington to make my mark on Broadway, I had yet to take a drink other than a sip of eggnog at Christmas. I shuttled about quite a bit in my first two years in Manhattan. I lived for a time with Bijou Martin, a young actress. She was the daughter of Ricardo Martin, the opera star. Her mother was in Europe. I was broke. I welcomed the chance to share her apartment in West Fifty-seventh Street – a five-flight walk-up with two bedrooms, living-room and a bath. This shelter was an oddity in that all the doors opened into the corridor. The only way to get from one room to another was to prowl that hall.

One afternoon Biji came home with a bottle of port and suggested we sample it.

'Oh, Biji, I couldn't. I promised Daddy I wouldn't take a drink if he let me go on the stage.'

'This isn't a drink,' she said. 'It's only wine. In Europe children drink wine as we drink water.'

My resolve sagged. Eventually I'd get Daddy's permission. I must try everything once. 'All right! You're my friend and you'll take care of me. I'll see how it affects me,' I said.

We had no wine glasses so we used our toothbrush tumblers. Biji and I filled our mugs to the brim and tossed them off. I had no reaction. Disappointed, I said, 'Let's try another.' A third beaker, and the roof fell in. Both of us were so tight we couldn't walk. We had to crawl through the hall to our bedrooms on our hands and knees. I don't know which was greater, my horror or my surprise. I felt sick, and I *was* sick. The room was spinning like a top. In my agony I heard Biji moaning. I crawled back down the hall. Biji was trying to get into the bathtub. 'I want to take a shower,' she pleaded. I saw no flaw in this, though she was fully clothed. I put her hat on her head, she clambered into the vat, and I turned on the water. Then I crawled away to die.

We woke the next morning with devastating hangovers – me in bed, Biji on the bathroom floor. There was a note under the door from Biji's father: 'I came to take you and Tallulah to dinner tonight and missed you. You must have gone out.' Out indeed!

Numbed and nauseated, I was full of remorse. Serves me right for not minding Daddy, I thought. Thereafter, when offered a drink at parties, I'd say, 'No, thank you. I don't drink. Got any cocaine?' Thus did I start the myth that I was an addict. I talked so much, my manner was so animated, it was not hard to believe I was over-stimulated.

That was the sum of my drinking until I sailed for London two years later. Then I got a reprieve. Daddy came up from Washington to wish me Godspeed. General Coleman du Pont, who had served in the Senate with Granddaddy, gave us a dinner party in his suite at the old Waldorf Astoria. I felt important because the guests included General Pershing, Commissioner of Police Enright and my beloved Frank Crownishield. Dinner over, we were driven to the pier in General du Pont's car. On the gangplank Daddy gave me last-minute advice. 'Now, Sugar, I know you're going to be sea-sick (I used to get sick when he'd take me out fishing on Mobile Bay). When you do, take something simple: cold chicken, tomatoes and a glass of champagne. The champagne can't hurt you! It may help you.'

Thus with Daddy's benediction I started my champagne flight in London. Daddy's alarms about my drinking were born of his fear it might be hereditary.

★   ★   ★

In my first four years in New York I was constantly driven by the desire to appear daring and dashing. I used heavy make-up, slashed my mouth with crimson, touched up my brows. My talent my secret, I could cope with my betters and attract attention through heresies of deportment and conversation.

These ruses more than once defeated me. I hadn't been in New York long when Winthrop Ames announced a production of Maeterlinck's *The Betrothal*. The large cast called for six young girls of my age. When I presented my credentials to Guthrie McClintic, Mr. Ames' casting director, I was heavily made up – aping Pauline Frederick, Olga Petrova, Theda Bara and other screen sirens. Guthrie and Mr Ames decided I was far too mature for the gentle Belgian's play. I had my hair piled on top of my head, in the fashion of Elsie Ferguson, my momentary idol. I affected a slink and a world-weary air. The six girls elected for the play were all older than I was. They were brighter, too.

My 'have you any cocaine?' gambit turned up to haunt me. Repeating the line at a party, the host took me at my word. He led me into the bathroom, handed me a paper of glistening crystals. I was shaking in my boots but, after all my boasts, I couldn't back down. I hadn't the faintest notion how to take it, so I said: 'You take some first.' He took some on the end of a nail file and sniffed it up either nostril. My bluff called, in terror, I followed suit. I was sure I'd take off through the air like a rocket. To my surprise I experienced no sensation save that born of another achievement. For weeks I confused my friends by saying at every opportunity: 'My dear, cocaine is simply divine.' (I'll go into my excessive use of that debatable adjective, later, perhaps under the subhead, 'To err is human, to forgive divine.')

Months later when playing in Rachel Crothers' *Nice People* I went to a penthouse party. 'Like some cocaine?' said mine host. 'Of course,' I replied. This time the reaction was different. I didn't get exhilarated, instead had a woozy comfortable feeling. I wanted to sit quietly and smoke my cigarette – very un-Tallulah-like conduct. My escort took me home in the early morning to the apartment I shared with

Bijou Martin. I became violently ill in the taxicab. Happily there were few people in the streets at that hour, thus few witnesses to my shame. I was sick all the rest of the morning. The blood vessels in my eyelids turned purple. I couldn't keep a glass of water down.

With the knowledge that I couldn't make the matinée because of my up-chucking, I was desolated. Terrified, I phoned the theatre to say I had ptomaine poisoning from eating spoiled fish. Miss Crothers sent her doctor to me immediately. To my great relief he concurred in my verdict.

My deception confirmed, I resumed my retching, missed the night performance too. Here and now I swear on Equity's constitution and bylaws that those are the only two performances I've missed because of malfeasance. By way of atonement I've played when miserably ill. I've played when every move was agonizing.

Miss Crothers told me later she sent the doctor to me because she suspected my excuse. She felt I was masking some transgression. 'We know how young and excitable and spontaneous you are,' she explained. 'We thought perhaps you'd been out on a party and had been taunted into a drinking bout by unthinking people. I'm sorry we misjudged you.'

It was rash escapades like this that later led Mrs. Pat Campbell, that acid-tongued actress, to say: 'Talullah is always skating on thin ice. Everyone wants to be there when it breaks.' Now that I've introduced Mrs. Pat I may as well remind you she was the first woman to spit out 'bloody' on a London stage. When she loosed it in George Bernard Shaw's *Pygmalion*, she rocked the British Empire. 'Bloody' was taboo by the standards of costermonger or commoner.

Shortly I learned the reason for my illness following the penthouse party. I had been given heroin, not cocaine. Cocaine is supposed to exhilarate you, heroin to give you a feeling of ease and relaxation. I've never touched either since, except medicinally. In London, when I had one of my frequent attacks of the actor's nightmare, laryngitis, Sir Milson Rees, the King's doctor, sprayed my throat with a solution laced with cocaine. It stimulated my larynx, relieved strain on my vocal chords, reduced my chances of becoming mute during a performance. At a chemist, where I presented the prescription, I was given a bottle of pale little lozenges, labelled 'Cocaine and Menthol'. Obsessed with the desire to shock people, I whipped the vial out at every opportunity. I'd hold it out to my friends: 'Have some cocaine?' 'Tallulah, isn't it habit-forming?' 'Cocaine habit-forming? Of course not. I ought to know. I've been using it for years.'

Because of these blusters it is awkward for me to complain when charged with misconduct. Who started the rumour? Those winds I sowed are still whipping up clouds of dust.

Remember Prince Florizel of Bohemia in Robert Louis Stevenson's *New Arabian Nights*? The Prince, eager for adventure, was so rash as to enroll in The Suicide Club, was damn near bumped off for his pains. There must be a dash of Florizel in me. In London I visited a charming little house in Chelsea, with a top-floor room lined with tinfoil. A quite respectable friend asked me if I'd like to smoke some opium.

Acceptance was obligatory for a *femme fatale*. I was fascinated by the preliminaries, melting the pellets, tamping them into the bowl of the pipe. My imagination running riot, I felt like the daughter of Fu Manchu, Sax Rohmer's malign Chinese. The effects were pleasant and dreamy. The world seemed uncommonly rosy, but not for long.

Fortunately it was Saturday night. Two days before I had laid out fifteen pounds to talk with Daddy on Sunday afternoon by trans-Atlantic telephone. This, too, was an excitement. The only such call made up to that time had been a conversation between Washington and our Embassy in London.

On the way home to my service flat, my escort and I became actively ill. We were so sick that we flung ourselves on my bed and collapsed. There my maid found us in the morning, ashen and wretched. Panicky, I feared that in risking one thrill I had cancelled out another – that I would not be able to talk to Daddy. Between spasms I cursed my stupidity. I hoped against hope that through some miracle the call might be delayed. But there were as few miracles then as there are now. Punctually at three the bell tingled and Daddy's voice came through as if he were in the next room.

The conversation which ensued would have given Alexander Graham Bell a turn. It ran like this:

'Hello, Daddy, darling, how are you?'

'I'm fine. How are you?'

'I'm fine. How is Florence?'

'She's fine.'

'Well, how's Sister?'

'She's fine. I'll put her on.'

I told Sister I was fine, and she verified Daddy's report on her own health. Then it was Florence's turn – Florence was my stepmother – and, believe it or not, she was fine, too. After that we engaged in variations on the same theme, until three minutes and fifteen pounds had been ticked off. Then I collapsed again. Opium? Never again so much as a whiff!

Since I'm in my narcotic phase I might as well let you in on my reefer binge, if a handful of reefers spread over four weeks can be so classified. I was carrying on a lopsided duel with Cleopatra when I first tested marijuana on the cue of a friend who swore reefers were the next thing to ambrosia.

They may have been ambrosia to him, but my first one only brought on a fit of giggles and an overpowering hunger. Hunger is something I can't afford to create artificially, since I'm always either dieting or about to start. At the time I was deep in theosophy, and Madame Blavatsky's *Isis Unveiled* and *Secret Doctrine*. My giggles over, unreliable witnesses report I started to spout poetry of my own coinage. Very good it was, swore those perjurers. What with Cleopatra, back income taxes, a lost love and other considerations too gruesome to set down here, I was very depressed, not to say broke. The reefer consumed, I felt that I had the key to the universe. Never more need I fret and worry. The complexities of my life became crystal clear. For a few moments so vivid seemed my comprehension of the things that conventionally haunt me I felt kinship with God. In retrospect I

distrust my emotions. Perhaps it was the spell of Madame
Blavatsky. Perhaps I'd fused Poe and his laudanum with me
and my reefer. Thus exalted, shortly I repeated the experiment. It didn't come off. I was closer to the pawnbroker than
to God. That is the sum of my trifling. I was a noodlehead to
thus flirt with fire! Fortunately my skirmishes with forbidden fumes and philters never created in me any craving,
physical or mental, any desire to promote an experience to a
practice.

Tippling? That's something else again. I enjoy drinking
with friends, even though I know it occasionally leads me to
conduct not easy to condone. If, after four snorts, I'm
convinced I can do the Indian rope trick, the damage is
slight. You'll rarely find rope in a liquor closet. Indians? Yes!
When I go on the wagon my abstinence is not due to moral
scruples. The day that I find liquids jeopardizing my liveli-
hood or my health you'll find an arid Bankhead. I'm not a
compulsive drinker. I'll drink what and when I damn well
please.

My most notable attack of sobriety began the day the
British started to evacuate Dunkirk, while I was playing in
The Little Foxes in Chicago. That night in my bedroom I
dropped to my knees and prayed that through some miracle
the British might escape annihilation.

On the theory their deliverance might be effected through
the French artillery, I came into my living-room at the
Ambassador Hotel, nudged Room Service, and ordered up
three French 75s. This drink, served in a tall highball glass, is
a blend of champagne, gin, a spot of sugar, a squirt of lemon
juice, the whole topped off with a brandy float. Consumed in
quantity they can flatten a longshoreman. I drained all three,
then weaved to my feet and announced: 'As of now I'm on the
wagon! And I'm staying on the wagon until the British are
back in Dunkirk!'

This provoked the customary snickers. But I meant it.
Save when I contracted pneumonia making *Lifeboat* for
Alfred Hitchcock in 1943, I stuck to my vow. Then I took
whisky on the orders of the studio doctor. High as was my

resolve it couldn't match the potency of my legend. Playing in San Francisco, I was outraged to read I had been stoking up on mint juleps in the Omar Khayyam Restaurant. This was the invention of a columnist. He saw me dining with friends, saw them drinking, presumed that I must be. I blasted him to his editor, as a dastard and a poltroon, a disgrace to the name of Winchell. But I got no apology. Column writers, I have found, have delusions of omniscience. Never do you trap one in a retraction.

Why didn't the studio doctor recommend sulfa rather than bourbon? He did. More than once sulfa saved me, but I had evil reactions. Unwittingly I did violate my oath of abstinence. When low I found a dash of spirits of ammonia picked me up. The British were back in Dunkirk before I discovered aromatic spirits of ammonia have an alcoholic content of sixty-five per cent.

The flight from Dunkirk was not my only agonizing day in World War II. Another came in the spring of 1940, when Grover Whalen was wrestling with a World's Fair on the Flushing Meadows. To stimulate a becalmed box office the Fair management dedicated certain days to certain characters – in the hope the peasants would flock to the grounds to gaze upon this hero, that masquerader. I confess I glowed when 15 June 1940, was named 'Tallulah Bankhead Day'. I rejoiced in the ceremonials, wound up by reviewing the Boy Scouts. That evening I was to be guest of honour at a dinner at the French Pavilion.

Going up to the dining hall the girl elevator operator was in tears. Everyone seemed depressed. I had scarcely been seated when the head waiter approached me: '*Madame, j'ai peur . . .*' Then my heart broke. I had been honoured on the day Paris fell. The world wept.

That summer Daddy died. After the funeral my friend, Dola Cavendish, said: 'Tallulah, you need a drink. At a time like this you should not hold yourself to your vow. Circumstances alter all things.'

But this seemed the great challenge to my determination. 'I'm not going to break it, darling. Of all times, not now!'

Since I'm cataloguing my sins, I must embrace another defect I have long coddled to no profit: Gambling.

Aware the admission may win me the frown of Esters Kefauver and Senator Tobey, I'm fascinated by projects that enable me to get rid of money in a hurry. Sages have told me that gambling is a symbol of insecurity, as is drinking. In my case their theory leaks. My urge to gamble comes and goes like hot flashes. It's an outlet for excessive enthusiasm. Emotionally wrought up, I'll gamble on anything – ball games, fights, dice, *chemin de fer*, fan-tan or the sixth at Pimlico. Challenged by a cocky opponent I'll risk a few farthings to prove I can surpass him spitting at a crack, throwing playing cards into a derby.

With me gambling is a device to endorse my convictions. I'm not the cool calculating type. I never give a second thought to odds, past performances or form. A wishful thinker, I bet on the horse, the team, the fighter I'm rooting for. My bets are symbols of my devotion.

I became a fanatic horse-player in London because of my friendship for Steve Donoghue, greatest of all British jockeys. Didn't he win the Derby at Epsom three times in succession? Steve used to cue me on entering the paddock before a race. Did he think his nag was going to win, he'd hold his crop in his right hand. Convinced his mount was a beetle, in his left. My biggest killing was at Manchester. About to set off on a holiday in the South of France, after a season in *Her Cardboard Lover*, I won seven hundred pounds on a Donoghue tip, but not before I'd almost collapsed. I had backed this steed to win at 4 to 1, but he finished second. I was keening on the lawn when the winner was disqualified, my thoroughbred led into the winner's circle. Even then I didn't know the extent of my coup. It was five times as great as I thought. I didn't distinguish between pounds and dollars.

Two years earlier I had an unholy run of luck at *chemin de fer* at Deauville. I was down to my last fifty pounds when I went there with Sister and her husband, Morton Hoyt, for a weekend holiday. We stayed three weeks and on our departure I still had my fifty pounds, after picking up all the tabs. Our first night in the casino a crusty dowager nodded at me, then said to Sister, 'Wouldn't you know that that rich young American in those huge pearls would make a killing?' My pearls were paste, put out by Chanel. Hoyt? He's the one Sister bagged three different times. He was the brother of Elinor Wylie, the poet and novelist.

I get just as much fun out of playing two-bit limit with the stage hands as cashing in on a long shot, and get just as excited. When playing in *The Little Foxes* at the National Theatre in New York, I wasted a lot of sleep playing the match game with newspapermen at Bleeck's saloon around the corner. One night I reduced Stanley Walker, long-famed city editor of the *Herald Tribune*, to bankruptcy with my fey playing.

Since my bets are rooted in emotion, the New York Giants have cost me a pretty penny in the past ten years. They even addled my nest egg when they nosed out the Dodgers in '51. Electrified by their last-minute victory, I bet all my friends they'd pull the rug out from under the Yankees in the World Series – at even money when I could have got 11 to 5 at any cigar store.

Here's a rule I recommend. Never practise two vices at once. High as a kite of an early morning in Milwaukee, I invaded a gambling house with Donald Cook. Thanks to excessive optimism I lost all my cash at the roulette table within an hour. But the management was gracious and was only too glad to cash my cheque for a hundred dollars. I lost that, too. At the end of the month, I was reminded of my folly. The cheque so rashly cashed had been tilted to a thousand dollars. What's more, my bank had cashed it. And why not? It bore my signature.

The Natural-Born Exhibitionist

Madonna, the professional name of recording star and actress Madonna Louise Veronica Ciccone, is probably today's best-known *femme fatale*. Born in Detroit, she studied dance at the University of Michigan's School of Music, before setting out single-mindedly to develop a new image which mixed sex appeal with an exhibitionist's talent for the outrageous. Since her records 'Material Girl' and 'Like A Virgin' in the mid 1980s, Madonna has been at the forefront of a whole new generation of uninhibited female performers. She has taken effortlessly to appearing on TV, in films – including the award-winning *Desperately Seeking Susan* (1989) and the typically controversial *In Bed With Madonna* (1991) – and has also published a notorious book, *Sex* (1992), which was described as 'profoundly immoral' and has sold millions. Her popularity and regular assaults on current sensibilities will no doubt keep her name in the headlines far beyond the Millennium. This account by **Andrea Stuart** explains how Madonna combined the great showgirl tradition with the allure of the *femme fatale* to create a unique contemporary icon.

Madonna, the showgirl superstar of the MTV generation, has been accused of being simply a 'marketeer' but her gift for scrolling back through visual culture and utilizing its most popular and evocative images is hard to distinguish from the wider tendency of our times. Indeed her work is similar to that of many lauded contemporary artists. She 'samples' her material, taking a bit of this and putting it with a bit of that, creating effective collages. But Madonna is more than just a post-modern pastiche, a glorious grab-bag of images. Whatever her banditry with the showgirl's visual codes, she of all contemporary performers has maintained a curious spiritual fidelity to her mythology. She even got her big break dancing as a latter-day chorus-girl in a disco revue that Patrick Hernandez took over to Paris in the early 1980s. If the stage still offered a girl the opportunities it once did, no doubt she would have found her home there. However today's showgirl could only have emerged in the movies or as a pop star. Nowadays it is the music or film business, not the staid and overcontrolled world of the theatre, that provides the possibilities for mega-stardom and notoriety.

The oft-recounted tale of Madonna's arrival in New York, a young hopeful with single suitcase in hand, is worthy of any Busby Berkeley movie. Originally from Detroit, Madonna was born in 1958, the offspring of devoutly Catholic, second generation Italian immigrants. She moved to New York in July 1978, after a stint studying dance at the University of Michigan's School of Music. Once in New York, Madonna became one of the more visible birds of Manhattan's Bohemia, then dominated by graffiti artist Jean Michel Basquiat and Keith Haring. This milieu, with its strong gay and ethnic presence, shaped Madonna's creative life. In The Mudd Club, the Palladium and Danceteria, the heirs to Warhol's 1960s Factory – Debbie Harry, Mapplethorpe, music-man Nile Rogers and Warhol himself – partied amongst the sycophants eager to usurp them. Camp, streetwise and given to pastiche, the attitudes of this world, personified by media manipulators such as Jeff Koons, have had a consistent influence on Madonna's work.

Mae West spent her entire career turning the working-class sexual subcultures of her youth into performance and Madonna has done the same with this alternative 'downtown' New York culture. She anticipated and then translated underground trends like voguing, black dance music and sexual ambiguity into the mainstream at the opportune moment, and then reaped the commercial results. Just like West and Eva Tanguay before her, Madonna exploited an explosive contemporary cocktail of sex, race and transgression to consolidate a popular following. As Jelly Bean Benitz remarked, Madonna 'crossed over a lot of boundaries 'cos everyone in the rock clubs played her, the black clubs, the gay, the straight . . . and very few records have that appeal'.

Madonna showcased her talent in much the same ways as performers like Mistinguett and Josephine Baker. Her videos are celluloid performances. Like filmed music-hall sketches, they present her cleverly constructed pop tunes within a carefully plotted story line, jazzing them up with extravagant costumes and adventurous sets. Her live shows are a direct steal from the showgirl iconography of a bygone era. With the 1990 'Blonde Ambition' Tour, for instance, Madonna's goal was to create 'a combination of a Busby Berkeley musical, *Cabaret, A Clockwork Orange* and Frederick's of Hollywood'. The resulting meticulously staged extravaganza, which featured Madonna looking like a showgirl from the Crazy Horse in metallic Barbarella bustier and Dietrich style top-hat, was worthy of the mighty Ziegfeld himself.

From the beginning of her career Madonna has used traditional showgirl narratives and fused them with contemporary concerns in order to create a thoroughly modern image. The video for 'Material Girl' (1985), a turning point in her early career, was a tongue-in-cheek tribute to Monroe's showgirl in *Gentlemen Prefer Blondes*. Her dress for the video, a shocking pink, cut-to-the-thigh gown, was an exact replica of Bill Travilla's design for Monroe in 1953. But Madonna's video version was truer to the spirit of Anita Loos's original book than Monroe's happy-go-lucky 1950s musical, in which love triumphs over filthy lucre. Written in

1925, *Gentlemen Prefer Blondes* is a tale for our times. Its heroine, Lorelei Lee – a fusion of all the corrosive narratives that had surrounded the showgirl for generations – saw diamonds, not romance, as a worthy investment. In the video Madonna strutted around in Monroe's dress, a knowing and unrepentant man-magnet with a fondness for dripping diamonds, her platinum-plated philosophy recalling the Lorelei of old and providing the perfect image for the 'greed is good' 1980s.

The video for 'Material Girl' reflected Madonna's regard for Marilyn Monroe. 'I'd love to be a memorable figure in the history of entertainment in some sexual comic tragic way. I'd like to leave the impression that Marilyn Monroe did, to be able to arouse so many different feelings in people,' she declared. Perhaps the most important thing that Madonna borrowed from Monroe was her hair colour. Angela Carter describes blondeness as 'a state of ambivalent grace, to which anyone who wants it badly enough may aspire'. It is a comment with which Madonna would agree: 'Being blonde is definitely a different state of mind. I can't really put my finger on it but the artifice of being blonde has some incredible sort of sexual connotation. Men really respond to it. I love blonde hair but it really does something different to you.' Amazed at the international success of her book *Gentlemen Prefer Blondes*, Anita Loos asked a Chinese scholar, Dr Lin, how a country with no blondes could understand the concept. He replied, 'Blondeness is not resigned to pigmentation.'

All of the best blondes – West, Monroe, Harlow, Bardot, Deneuve, Madonna – were originally brunettes. There is something about the artifice of the 'voluntary blonde' that only adds to her allure. Perhaps it is because blondeness too is an act, and the non-blonde is dispassionate enough to perform it best. Monroe, who went blonde on the instruction of her agent in 1946 ('I have a call for a light blonde, honey or platinum'), created a version of blondeness that became inseparable from her persona. Her hair's translucence contributed to her vulnerability. For Angela Carter, blondeness is inseparable from masochism, 'their dazzling fair skins are of such a delicate texture that they look as if they will bruise at a touch, carrying the exciting stigmata of sexual violence for a long time, and that is why gentlemen prefer blondes'. These sorts of blondes are the ones 'who look most beautiful when they are crying'. But Madonna based her persona on early Monroe, when she made her name as the triumphant gold-digging showgirl Lorelei Lee, before revelations about her pain-filled personal history stained Monroe's myth with tragedy. From her full-figured and pouty-lipped image, Madonna created a Marilyn without tears and combined her with the overt sexuality and tough girl bravado of the blonde Mae West.

Later in her career, tired of the Monroe tag ('Marilyn Monroe was a victim and I'm not. That's why there's really no comparison'), Madonna created a new blonde role for herself. She remodelled her blondeness on another showgirl predecessor, Marlene Dietrich. She said, 'I wish I had slept with [Marlene Dietrich] she had a very masculine thing about her, but she maintained a sexual allure.' Dietrich's version of blondeness was summed up in her song, 'Those Charming, Alarming Blonde Women' in which she warns men of the deceptive dangers which lurk behind any romantic encounter with a blonde woman. Historically the *femme fatale* was a product of masculine anxieties about the emerging New Woman of the 1890s. Characterized as autonomous and sexually ambiguous, she devours and castrates the male, luring him down a path of destruction and death. Madonna had flirted with this image before in 'Open Your Heart' (1986) in which she paraded in a black corset, suspenders and high heels. By the early 1990s she was increasingly constructing her identity around the female destroyer in both looks and language. From the 'Blonde Ambition Tour' to *Sex* to the 'Girlie Tour', Madonna – with her slicked-back blonde hair, ruthlessly plucked eyebrows, and top-hat and tails – played with the imagery of bondage and S&M, pain and power.

From 'Material Girl' to the 'Girlie Tour' Madonna also

utilized another very important component of showgirl
mythology: the word 'girl'. In the early days of the century,
no tag had more charm. Flo Ziegfeld, the pioneer of the
American spectacular revue, did more than anyone to po-
pularise its showbusiness use. For 'The Glorifier of the
American Girl', the word was synonymous with female
allure. 'In one word, I would say it was promise; a promise
of romance and excitement – the things a man dreams about
when he thinks of the word "girl" – that haunting quality.'
The market value of the word 'girl', which simultaneously
evokes sexual innocence as well as frivolity and beauty, was
immensely important to Ziegfeld as he packaged sexual display for a mass market audience.

Today most women demand the right to be called women,
but the word girl still maintains its enchantment. It has been
reclaimed in much the same way as the description 'black',
turning what was once a restrictive put-down into a badge of
identity. By disregarding its anachronistic connotations (pas-
sivity, triviality and shallowness) women now enjoy the word
'girl' in a knowing, parodic and subversive way. It harks back
to a time before husbands and children, crow's-feet and
compromise; a time when a woman is unencumbered, blissfully unaware of her limitations, heady with her unexplored
potential. So when a contemporary female star like Madonna
uses the word, it evokes a certain complicity with other
women. It is no wonder that in 'Material Girl' Madonna
is still a girl – when she wants to be. The word is a *cri de coeur*
to a whole new generation of women who associate it with
feminism, lesbianism and other outlawed female identities.

Madonna did not only use the showgirl's terminology and
visual devices; she also wove around herself the same racial
and sexual mythologies. She deliberately revived the showgirl's links to the sexual underworld *à la* Mistinguett by
playing with the iconography of the prostitute. The meta-
phor of commercial sex was evident in songs like 'Material
Girl' and 'Open Your Heart', and also in the names she chose
to call her companies. With a large dose of irony – 'There is a
wink in everything I do' – she dubbed her music company

Boy-Toy, called her film company Siren, and christened her video company Slutco. 'Madonna has not only taken the stereotypes that have kept women trapped in their cultural roles and used them to her own advantage, but has also turned them upside-down and shrewdly capitalised on them,' crowed *Vanity Fair* in 1990.

Like many of her showgirl predecessors, Madonna exploited the *frisson* of racial difference. She generated an ersatz sense of 'racial otherness' from the earliest days of her career by fabricating a background in the predominantly black Motor City ghetto. 'I was definitely the minority in my neighbourhood. White people were scarce there.' The truth was altogether more prosaic; she spent most of her childhood in the fairly affluent, and largely white, suburb of Rochester in Michigan. On a trail that took her via Josephine Baker right back to the Hottentot Venus, she exploited the symbolic blackness that supposedly existed within every showgirl. 'If being black is synonymous with having soul, then yes, I feel I am,' she is quoted as saying. Like Mae West whose 'shimmy' and swagger were taken from the 1920s' black entertainment scene, Madonna deliberately affected black style to attract a wider audience. In 1983, when she released her début album *Lucky Star*, her face was not on the album cover. Many consumers had assumed she was black and she had her best exposure on black radio stations. Record executives weren't happy revealing she was white, apparently, because they felt it might alienate her embryonic audience.

Like Barbette and Dietrich before her, Madonna also titillated her audiences with touches of lesbianism and cross-dressing. In the video 'Express Yourself', she dressed in male drag and monocle, and grabbed her crotch. This performance coincided with her much publicized relationship with Sandra Bernhard. A showgirl herself, Bernhard's live one-woman shows, such as *Giving Till It Hurts*, are a manic mixture of sarcasm, strip-tease and song. As one reviewer remarked, they recall 'Broadway's forgotten era of all-singing, all-dancing entertainers'. The pair had become close when Madonna was in New York doing the Mamet play *Speed-the-Plow*, and Bernhard was doing her own off-Broadway show. Quite apart from their similarities as performers, they both enjoyed teasing audiences with their sexual ambiguity. Bernhard, in particular, was very open about her lesbian affairs. In comparison to earlier showgirls' Sapphic shenanigans, Madonna's behaviour with Sandra Bernhard was tame, but she reaped the publicity benefits none the less. She christened her all-girl gatherings the Snatch Batch (a reference perhaps to Dietrich's Sewing Circle) and appeared on David Letterman's show with Bernhard in matching outfits, joking about notorious lesbian haunts like The Cubby Hole. 'Sandra and I were just fucking with people. But then when I realized the reaction we had gotten, of course I couldn't leave that alone,' Madonna later remarked gleefully.

Having exploited the same tactics as previous showgirls, it was no wonder Madonna provoked the same incendiary response. The language used to assault her reflected the hysterical moralism of a bygone age. One tabloid screamed 'Man-Eater Madonna Used Sex to Climb to the Top!' whilst others called her an 'eye batting gold-digger' with a vampiric appetite for men, and 'a slut who strips and sings professionally'. Her unfortunate influence on young women was particularly stressed. Dubbed a 'corrupting Pied Piper' by one newspaper, Madonna outraged members of Planned Parenthood who felt that she 'encouraged the young into illicit sex and thoughtless procreation' when she decided she was 'keeping her baby' in the song 'Papa Don't Preach'. Scandal succeeded scandal, each gaining Madonna priceless publicity. The controversy about 'Like a Prayer', in which Madonna kissed the feet of a black Christ, was followed by the 'Blonde Ambition' Tour. It was so eventful that it almost put Josephine Baker's 1928 tour to shame. Captured in the film *In Bed with Madonna*, it depicted a performer consistently in conflict with the guardians of morality. In Toronto, the police threatened to close the show and arrest the cast for public indecency, if she insisted on simulating masturbation on-stage. Meanwhile the outraged Boston University president, John R. Silbert, declared she 'has no more right to set this example for our kids than Adolf Hitler did or than Saddam Hussein does'. On the Italian leg of the tour, the Catholic Church condemned her concerts as blasphemous, and demanded that those being held in Rome and Turin be banned. Madonna asked the clergy to come and judge for themselves. 'My show is not a conventional rock concert,' she declared loftily, 'but a theatrical presentation of my music, and like the theatre, it poses questions, provokes thought, and takes you on an emotional journey.'

Madonna had created a reputation almost as outrageous as her predecessor, Mae West. She attracted a cumulative cloud of disapproval and discomfiture which came to a head with her next big project. Seventy years after Mae West's play *Sex* had scandalised Broadway, Madonna produced a book of the same name. It was the biggest literary launch ever, with 750,000 copies of *Sex* on sale simultaneously in the United States, Japan, Britain, France and Germany. Embargoed from actually seeing the book until publication, journalists were despatched from all parts of the globe in search of an interview with Madonna herself. (The rare few who did get a look at the product were forced to sign a release form, preventing them from divulging its contents). In a veritable Madonnafest of music and interviews, BBC Radio One declared 14 October 1992 'Madonna Day'. As the big day dawned, missives from *Sex*'s official launch in New York made front-page news.

Madonna's *Sex* is not so much a book as a performance. Its packaging, all shimmery silver aluminium, reflects the retro-chic glamour of the showgirl and the high-tech perfection of a space capsule. Inside are 128 pages of words and pictures. Madonna is everywhere, on every available surface, in every conceivable sexual pose. S&M and rape scenarios intermingle with a lesbian *ménage à trois*; interracial sex features rapper Big Daddy Kane and model Naomi Campbell. Madonna, it seems, does not just go both ways, she goes *all* ways.

Like Mae West's play, Madonna's book was a grand-stand

star vehicle, masquerading as a sort of sex manual that claimed to be exposing us to dangerous territory, guiding us through unfamiliar sexual subcultures. Those unaware of the showgirl's legacy dismissed it as a sign of the depravity of contemporary culture. For those familiar with the showgirl's history, *Sex* – 'the dirtiest coffee table book ever published' – was a direct descendant of the 'girlie shows' of burlesque. Focused on the display of female sexuality – tacky, shiny and determined to shock – this fusion of porn and pop art was faithful to the spirit of the showgirl's mythological and aesthetic legacy.

Sex proved as great a watershed in Madonna's career as it had been in Mae West's. The book was deemed 'profoundly immoral', in 'execrable taste' and 'crassly commercial'. 'In a world where nothing is taboo the amoral slut is queen,' concluded the *Daily Telegraph*. '*Sex* is no more than the desperate confection of an aging scandal-addict who, with this book, merely confirms that she is exhausting her capacity to shock,' wrote Martin Amis. It was so explicit, some argued, that it had left her with no more frontiers to cross. What may have upset her audiences, though, was not the fact that Madonna had revealed too much but that she had revealed too little. '. . . you should have had a beaver shot of yourself', reproached Norman Mailer, 'Given the number of nude and semi-nude pictures of you in costume, I thought that was an evasion.' The journalist Andrew Neil, probing relentlessly as to whether the pictures reflected her personal experience, sought to expose not photographic revelations but 'admissions' about her private life.

Madonna has teased her audience with titillating prospects of self-revelation throughout her career. The film *In Bed with Madonna* (known in the USA as *Truth or Dare*) was marketed with the provocative slogan: 'The Ultimate Dare is to tell the Truth.' The publicity build-up to the film's release attracted headlines like 'Nothing is too private for Madonna to flaunt in public' and 'Madonna lets it all hang out: The shameless one stages a raunchy revealing self-portrait.' In response to endless speculation about just *how much* she would reveal, Madonna teased, 'While you can argue that I chose to show what I wanna show, I can also say that what I chose to show is very revealing.'

Many critics were disappointed. Despite scenes in which Madonna simulated fellatio with a bottle, frolicked with her dancers, and engaged in private conversations with her father, they felt that the film still didn't reveal enough of its star. But as Colette and Josephine demonstrated, the private life of the showgirl has always been as carefully staged as any other part of her existence. Those hoping for a slip, a chink, any vulnerability, waited in vain. After all, as one reviewer remarked, 'When a natural born exhibitionist exhibits herself, is it the 'real' Madonna, or are we watching an artful imitation of reality?' With *Sex*, many thought that Madonna would have no choice but to reveal herself. In a society such as ours, which believes that sexual secrets are the ultimate clue to personal identity, a book about sexual fantasies seemed certain to provide a key to the real self. But in the end it was all a tease. Madonna presented such a proliferation of sexual scenarios that readers had no sense which, if any, of these images reflected her real proclivities. She says as much on the first page: 'nothing in this book is true'. As Suzanne Moore wrote in the *Guardian*, 'What upsets us most though is not the nakedness of her body but the nakedness of her ambition. For all her antics, all she ever exposes are the mechanics of stardom in the late twentieth century.'

Madonna's frustrating elusiveness is in striking contrast to an icon like Marilyn Monroe. We love Marilyn because we think we know her. Her revelations provide us, we feel, with a genuine insight into her 'inner life'. We are touched that she allows us to invade her privacy, that she tells us her secrets. Unlike Madonna or Mae West, she does not appear to withhold anything from us. It does not occur to us that this particular strip-tease might be as calculated as any other showgirl's, or that Monroe's revelations are just part of her act. The parading of her pain simply reassures us that we really do possess and know her. Even Gloria Steinem is taken in. As she writes in *Marilyn*, 'Yet I also see the why of it, and the woman behind the mask that her self-consciousness creates.' But do her revelations really explain the magic of her on-screen presence, or the cunning and tenacity with which she pursued her rise to fame? That is not to say that her suffering is not genuine, just that it is not the answer. In the end, Monroe allows us to think that we have stepped behind the façade, only to show us another mask. Madonna offers no such consolation. As she declared in *Vanity Fair* in 1991, 'you will never know the real me. Ever.'

Four
The Military Girls

A Gallery of Women at Arms

Christian Cavanagh

Queen Boadicea (? – AD 61)

The Revenge of
the Warrior Queen

Boadicea, who was also known as Boudicca, is generally regarded as the first English military heroine: a woman of gentle upbringing who was forced to take up arms against what seemed like impossible odds. In AD 60, Boadicea gathered together the Iceni, a tribe inhabiting those parts of East Anglia now covered by Norfolk and Suffolk, to do battle with the occupying Roman forces after they had seized her lands and brutalized the people. Her victories at Colchester, London and St Albans were among the greatest setbacks ever suffered by the mighty legions of Rome and ensured her a place among the great military figures of history. The story of the Warrior Queen is told by **Jean Thorley**.

Among famous women, the dynamic and colourful character of *Boadicea* puts her on a par with Cleopatra, Elizabeth I and Florence Nightingale, although she was only in the limelight for a few short months. Yet during this time she gave the Roman legions the greatest shock which they encountered during their conquest and occupation of Britain, and was the first of many females in British history who have struggled and died in the cause of liberty.

When she was a teenager, the Iceni tribe of Norfolk were preparing to fight for their independence against the powerful tribe of the Catuvellauni who had advanced into what is now Essex and made Colchester their capital. But the Roman invasion of AD 43 released the pressure by the defeat of the Catuvellauni. It was the turn of the Iceni and their allies to suffer defeat at the hands of the Romans in 47–8, and a new ruler, *Prasutagus*, became a puppet king, allied to the Romans, whilst they spread their rule northwards into Lincolnshire. For a dozen years there was a peaceful penetration of Roman ways and influence in Norfolk. The tribal queen, *Boadicea*, would notice the increase of luxury, the foreign pottery, jewels, furnishings and clothing. Her richer subjects were encouraged to borrow from Roman capitalists – to get the new fashions 'on tick'. The dependent kingdom was prosperous.

Then in AD 60 *Prasutagus* died. He had hoped to save half his possessions for his two daughters by leaving the other half to the emperor, *Nero*, but the Romans made a 'take-over' without any previous bid. They helped themselves to the lot! The royal palace was looted, and no doubt *Boadicea* objected. She was given a thorough beating like a disobedient slave or a common thief. Her daughters were not only robbed but raped as well. Seething with indignation, she had no difficulty in rousing her cruelly oppressed subjects to strike for vengeance.

Most people picture her as young and beautiful, with long black hair. She was more middle aged, having two grown-up daughters, and her hair was certainly long, but, according to *Dio Cassius*, it was white. The rest of his description is more in line with our traditions: she was tall, majestic, severe-looking, her voice masculine [perhaps he means deep and powerful]. She wore a chain of gold, had a tunic of several colours, all in folds, with a sort of blouse ['vest'] of rough material.

Mounting on a throne made of turf, and bearing a lance in her hand, she harangued her followers: 'Better Liberty than Servitude! . . . We are despised and trampled underfoot by people who are only fit to usurp what belongs to others. If we get the victory we will put them to the sword. If they win we can take refuge in the marshes and mountains . . . They cannot, like us, bear hunger or thirst or cold or heat . . . We are better acquainted with the country . . . Let us march boldly against them and make them know that they are a parcel of hares and foxes that have the rashness to pretend to command dogs and wolves.'

She let a hare loose, which had been concealed, and drew a good omen from its course. *Boadicea* made scathing reference to *Nero*, saying he was in effect more like a woman, 'since he sings, plays on the harp and dresses himself like those of that sex'. She thought the Romans equally degenerate, 'bathing themselves in hot water, eating exquisitely, drinking deliciously, covering themselves with perfume and indulging in undignified behaviour with pet boys'. All this was rather the writer's indictment of the debauchery of the court than the eloquence of the Queen of the Iceni, though she may have heard of the Roman scandals. She represented a simpler, more primitive and nobler mode of life.

The Romans were supposed to have been warned by a series of omens foretelling the wrath to come. The statue of Victory at Colchester fell on its face. Women rushed about screaming and prophesying disaster. Strange noises and confused laughter were heard coming from the empty council chamber. The appearance of houses were seen in the Thames and in the Channel the water was stained as it were with blood, and figures of bodies were traced on the sand as the tide receded.

With a swarming multitude of perhaps 230,000, *Boadicea*'s

chariot led the attack on Colchester, which had a garrison of
but 200 men. There were no walls of defence and the town
soon fell, though the temple on its mound (where now stands
the castle) resisted for two days. The Britons took a ruthless
revenge for their wrongs, being especially severe on the
priests and servants of the temple. No quarter was given,
no captives taken. Hanging, fire and sword destroyed the
town and its inhabitants.

The nearest legion was at Lincoln and its commander,
Petilius Cerialis, hurried to meet the rebels, but was too late
to save them. *Boadicea* advanced to meet him and, heavily
outnumbered, his infantry were cut to pieces. Only the leader
and the cavalry escaped.

The rebellion had a flying start because the main Roman
army and the governor, *Suetonius Paulinus*, were far away on
the island of Anglesey, stamping out the main headquarters
of the Druids, a task achieved with great thoroughness and
success. *Suetonius* heard of the rising and with an advance
guard rushed to London. He soon realized that he had not
sufficient strength to save the city, which was a commercial
centre but not the capital in those days. With a host of
refugees he marched north to link up with his main forces.

Boadicea took advantage of his departure to sack London,
and then marched north to do the same at St Albans. As
Tacitus says: 'The barbarians glutted themselves with the
blood of the enemy.' Historians estimated that *Boadicea*'s
forces destroyed 70,000 men, women and children altogether. The carnage and the loss of three cities appeared
so much the more disgraceful as having been occasioned by a
woman.

But the Romans had a reputation for courage in adversity,
for making sure of winning the last battle in a campaign.
Suetonius met the rest of his army from North Wales and
collected together some smaller detachments. With 80,000
disciplined men he carefully chose his field of battle, like
Harold at Hastings, but with better results. He positioned
himself with forest to the rear, level ground for manoeuvring
in front and woods on either side to prevent the more

numerous opponents from outflanking him. The site has never been ascertained, but was somewhere north of St Albans, probably along Watling Street. The Romans as usual had the infantry in the centre, and the horsemen on the wings. Probably light-armed men came in between.

They must have viewed with some trepidation the approach of *Boadicea*'s savage horde, flushed with victory and the easy success of destroying three open towns. The chariots must have looked formidable with the knife blades like scythes sticking out from the wheels ready to maim anyone getting too close as the wheels whirled round. But, as *Tacitus* remarks, 'military skill was not the talent of the barbarians'; their tactics consisted of a wild charge. So confident were they that they stationed their wives in the waggons, to have a grandstand view of the battle. These waggons must have contained food and plunder and were drawn up behind the army. There were also a lot of cattle.

According to the tradition of historians of Roman times, *Dio Cassius* puts a fiery pre-battle speech into the mouths of each of the two leaders. He credited the British queen with the sentiments of fighting for liberty and revenge, and says she reminded her warriors of their success against *Cerialis*, and their overwhelming superiority in numbers. She told her forces 'On this spot we must either conquer or die.' *Suetonius* also harangued his men and maligned the enemy. He said 'In all engagements it is the valour of a few that turns the fortune of the day,' and finished with an exhortation 'Keep your ranks: discharge your javelins; rush forward to a close attack: bear down all with your bucklers, and hew a passage with your swords . . . Conquer, and victory gives you everything.' His words were received with enthusiastic acclamation and he gave the signal for a charge.

The centre advanced silently in wedge formation, and the light-armed men and cavalry rushed forwards. The legionaries threw their javelins. The Britons shot their darts. Roman archers fired at the chariots and wounded horses were thrown into confusion and charioteers were disabled. The wedge stood firm against the chariots, and the Britons were

driven back. Discipline and training prevailed against reckless valour. As the rebels fled how they must have cursed
those waggons which barred their flight! The light-armed
troops of the conquerors killed many among the baggage, and
in the woods. The cattle, women and camp followers were
alike slaughtered. Amongst those who escaped in the confusion were *Boadicea* and her daughters. Rather than face
capture the brave queen committed suicide. She is generally
supposed to have poisoned her daughters and then herself, in
which case she would have had the poison ready with her in
case of necessity. *Dio Cassius* says she perished from sickness.
Perhaps it was a deadly illness caused by poison. In any case,
she died as she had fought, bravely.

The commander of the legion in the West Country, stationed at Gloucester, had done nothing to help the defeat of
the rising and, stung with remorse, he fell on his sword and
perished likewise by self-slaughter. Of the rank and file the
rebels are said to have lost about 80,000 and the victors a
mere 400 killed and about the same number of wounded.

They proceeded to take a terrible revenge on the Iceni. With
re-inforcements of 2,000 infantry, eight auxiliary (allied)
cohorts and 1,000 horsemen they ravaged the homeland of
the rebels. The men had rallied to the cause of the Queen and
most of the customary crops had not been sown. Much that
was grown was burnt by the Romans. In addition to the loss
of life through battle, famine stalked the land. It was one of
the most awful times in the story of East Anglia.

Suetonius was as merciless as his opponents had been, but
there were those who realized that a ruined countryside
would not yield taxation. A special imperial envoy was
despatched from Rome to make enquiries, and soon afterwards, on the excuse of the loss of a few ships on the coast,
the governor was recalled, the punitive measures were
brought to an end, and slowly the province recovered.

It has been supposed that the draining of parts of the Fens,
with farming in the Downham Market-Wisbech area, was
accomplished by the employment of 'convict gangs' from the

territories of *Boadicea*. Perhaps they helped the Romans build the Carr Dyke which served the double purpose of fen drainage and barge transport from Lincoln to Peterborough. The farms prospered until the rise of the water level towards the end of the fourth century reduced the land to marsh again.

Another result of the rebellion was the erection of a tall watch tower at Thornham on the eastern side of the Wash. Signals of fire by night or smoke by day would be visible across the water in Lincolnshire and troops could be sent from the garrison at Lincoln. But they were never needed, for peaces reigned after the holocaust. Perhaps the fact that there were only two Roman towns in Norfolk (Caistor by Norwich and Caister by Yarmouth) is further evidence of the poverty which followed the ruthless suppression of *Boadicea*'s revolt. She had brought to her people brief triumph and lasting glory, but long retribution followed.

Countess Agnes Dunbar (c.1312–69)

'Black Agnes': The Scottish Amazon

Agnes Dunbar was the granddaughter of the Scottish King, Robert the Bruce, and demonstrated extraordinary courage when defending the besieged Castle of Dunbar from invading English forces in 1337. She had been left to hold the fort – one of the few still in Scots hands – while her husband, Count Patrick Dunbar, was away campaigning against other troops from the South. Agnes's defensive skills, combined with her bravado and the contempt she hurled onto the English soldiers from her position on the battlements, made her a heroine throughout the nation when the enemy finally withdrew after six fruitless months. The story of 'Black Agnes, The Scottish Amazon' – as she became known – is told here by **Harry Graham**.

Up to the beginning of the eighteenth century the domestic annals of Scotland strike one as being singularly squalid. Deeds of violence abound on every page. Human life is held to be of little value, and murder is a crime of such frequent occurrence as scarcely to call for comment or excite attention. The early Scottish chronicles comprise for the most part descriptions of the public torture of criminals, the commission of agrarian outrages, the forcible abduction of desirable heiresses, the sequestration of undesirable wives, and the worrying of witches. They are largely devoted to unedifying accounts of family feuds, of forays, of brawls between rival clans and rival factions. 'For a long series of centuries,' as Sir Walter Scott says, 'the hands of rapine were never folded in inactivity, nor the sword of violence returned to its scabbard.' And though he was referring particularly to the Border, the same words apply with equal truth to the rest of Scotland, and more especially to the Highlands.

The lust of blood was a vice common to both noble and peasant. It was not confined to the uncivilized or uneducated half of the population. In October of the year 1396, for instance, the King of Scotland and all his court assembled on the bank of the river Tay to witness a duel to the death between two bodies of Highlanders, each thirty in number. The combatants were armed with dirk and claymore, and so bloody was the fray that at the end only one man remained alive on the one side, and on the other only ten, all of whom were grievously wounded. Such an affair as this was probably the result of a clan feud, a form of hostility too often marked by a cruel and vindictive spirit expressing itself in deeds of the foulest treachery. Thus at the beginning of the seventeenth century we read of the Macleods driving the Macdonalds to the shelter of a cave in the Island of Eigg, and deliberately smoking them all to death. Again, in the raid of the Clanranald against the Mackenzies of Kintail, as late as 1603, a whole congregation of the latter was burnt alive in the Church of Gilchrist, while the Macdonald pipers marched round the building drowning the cries of the unfortunate victims with inap-

propriate music. In this same year, too, the Clan Gregor
decimated the Colquhouns of Luss in Glenfruin in the
Lowlands – Tobias Smollet, the novelist's ancestor, being
among the slain – in what was probably the last savage
battle fought between the clans.

In early days the passions of Celtic feudalism could not be
restrained from acts of bloodshed and devastation. They
found a satisfactory outlet in this ceaseless battling of clan
with clan. There was a perpetual feud between the Lindsays
and the Ogilvies, between the Grants and the Gordons,
between the Scotts and the Kers. The hatred of the Ma-
claurins of Balquhidder for the Lenies of Callander was only
one degree less violent than that of the Maxwells for the
Johnstones. The Macleans were for ever quarrelling with the
Campbells, the Campbells with the Macdonalds. The Macdonalds and the Macgregors combined against the Drummonds, and the Drummonds themselves were busy harrying
the Murrays.

In such squabbles as these, women – 'generally the witnesses of men's imbecility', as Dr Chalmers declares – took
an active share. They were, indeed, in many instances the
very cause and object of the strife. The system of 'hand-
fasting', which allowed two persons to contract a temporary
connubial alliance, terminable at the end of a year, was
another prolific source of bloodshed.

The dames of bygone days did not spend their whole time
at the distaff. They were not all the timid, retiring ladies of
whom we are accustomed to read in romantic fiction. Some,
indeed, like Lady Bridekirk, seem to have been almost too
bold and masculine. This good lady was long famous in the
Annandale border both at the bowl and in battle. She could
drink a Scots pint of brandy with ease, and 'when the men
grew obstreperous in their cups, could either put them out of
doors, or to bed, as she found most convenient'. Lady Brux
provides a good example of the implacable, vindictive spirit
common to the women of the sixteenth century. Her husband, Cameron of Brux, had agreed to meet one Muat of
Abergeldie, with whom he was at feud, each being attended

by twelve horse only. Muat treacherously took advantage of the literal meaning of the words, and provided each of his twelve horses with two riders. In the fight that ensued at Drumgaudrum, near the Don, Brux and his party were outnumbered and slain. His widow thereupon offered the hand of her daughter, now heiress of the Brux estates, to whomsoever should avenge her husband's death. A young gallant named Robert Forbes challenged Muat to single combat, and killed him. On presenting himself to Lady Brux, that bloodthirsty old lady clasped him to her bosom, declaring that the marriage should take place at once, while Muat's gore was yet reeking upon the bridegroom's knife.

Lady Johnstone is another instance of a similar type of Scottish Amazon. The Johnstones and the Maxwells were fighting outside the gates of Lockerby Castle, where Lady Johnstone anxiously awaited the result of the struggle. Becoming impatient to receive news of her husband's safety, she sallied forth to the scene of the fight, armed only with the keys of the fortress. Among the dead and wounded on the field of battle she found Lord Maxwell, chief of the rival clan, slowly bleeding to death. The old man begged for mercy, but in vain, Lady Johnstone's only reply being to raise her heavy bunch of keys and dash out his brains. Again, during a feud between the clans of Gordon and the MacIntosh, the chief of the latter, finding that he was getting distinctly the worst of the argument, decided to submit himself to the goodwill of Lord Huntly, chief of the Gordons. While the marquis was away from home, the MacIntosh took the opportunity of surrendering himself to the tender mercies of Lady Huntly. As a sign of complete submission, he laid his head on a butcher's block which chanced to be in the kitchen where the interview with this lady took place. His hopes that such a token of humiliation would melt her heart were not fulfilled, for the marchioness calmly gave an order to the cook, and the wretched MacIntosh was neatly decapitated on the spot.

When from time to time Scotsmen agreed to sink their private differences in order to unite against their own kings or a common Southern foe, women continued to play a prominent part in the proceedings. It was the murder of his wife by the English at Lanark that increased the fury of William Wallace, and made him vow never to rest until he had slain the man who was guilty of this deed. And an old historical legend long attributed the murder of the Regent Murray to Hamilton of Bothwellhaugh, who, sentenced to forfeit his property as a traitor to James VI, saw his wife turned out of the house in an almost naked condition – an outrage which drove her insane – and found a speedy means of avenging the tyrant's brutality.

The Scot, like Robert Browning, was 'ever a fighter'. He could always agree with that old Earl of Buchan who declared, in his letter to Pitt, that 'if the privileges of Scotland are endeavoured to be violated, I shall know how to make my porridge in my helmet, and stir it with my sword!' And his womankind naturally inherited much of that admirable patriotic spirit. It was not required of every one of them to emulate the achievements of that unknown Amazon who, in the disguise of a knight, accompanied Guy, Count of Namur, when he marched upon Edinburgh to fight the Earls of Moray and March on the Borough-muir, in the early part of the fourteenth century, and engaged with a Scottish esquire in single combat which proved fatal to both. But the women of that age were reared in an atmosphere of stress and turmoil; the familiar din of battle and the clash of arms to which their ears were ever accustomed helped to strengthen their characters, and rendered them fit mates for warrior chieftains.

Women were often to be seen upon the battlefields of those days. King Edward I of England used, it is said, to summon the ladies, as well as the earls and barons of his kingdom, to attend him in war. In the year 1291 he called upon the ladies of Cumberland and Westmorland to meet him at Noreham, a village near the Scottish border, provided with horses and accoutred with arms, 'the consequences of which summons', says a chronicler, 'it is believed Scotland will never forget'. And the list of ladies of Scotland who at that time swore allegiance to the English king, of which the original is preserved at the Tower of London, contains over a score of well-known Scottish names.

The women of that violent period of history were, indeed, imbued with the universal spirit of martial ardour which then pervaded Scotland, and have handed it down as an heirloom to their descendants.* Even as late as the middle of the eighteenth century, we find an example of a woman taking a personal part in actual warfare. During the Rebellion of '45, the MacIntosh of MacIntosh, laird and chief of the clan, remained loyal to the reigning sovereign, and held a commission in Lord Loudon's army. But his wife, Anne, a daughter of Farquharson of Invercauld, was one of the Pretender's most active partisans, even going so far as to raise a small body of troops to uphold his cause. 'Colonel Anne', as she was nicknamed, led this corps in person, and a story is told of the MacIntosh being captured by the insurgents and brought as a prisoner to his wife's headquarters. 'Your servant, captain,' said the fair lady, as the captive was led into her presence. 'Your servant, colonel,' was the laird's laconic reply. Charles Edward remarked at the time that the prisoner 'could not be in better security or more honourably treated', and subsequently favoured the gallant 'Colonel Anne' with a visit to Moy.

Many a zealous adherent did the Young Pretender find among the ranks of women. The Duke of Perth would never have espoused Prince Charles's cause so warmly but for

---

*Near the border, between the parishes of Maxton and Ancrum, there is a ridge of hill called Lilliard Edge. Here, in 1547, a battle was fought between English and Scots, wherein the latter obtained a victory, though inferior in number. The success was ascribed to a young woman named Lilliard, who fought with great courage on the Scottish side. Some remains of a tombstone erected upon her grave on the field of battle can still be seen, with this inscription:-

Fair maiden Lilliard lies under this stane,
Little was her stature, but great was her fame;
On the English lads she laid many thumps,
And when her legs were off, she fought upon her stumps.

his mother, the duchess, who proclaimed the Chevalier from the battlements of Castle Drummond and recruited a regiment on his behalf. She herself accompanied the Scottish army to England, and at Carlisle, when the expected reinforcements failed to put in an appearance, threatened to lead the troops in person against the enemy. She was finally taken prisoner at Culloden, a fate which she shared with another Scottish woman – the short-tempered but courageous Lady Ogilvy.

Since that day more than one Scotswoman has turned amateur recruiting sergeant. The regiment of Gordon Highlanders was raised by a woman, Jane, Duchess of Gordon. Another duchess, Elizabeth, Duchess-Countess of Sutherland, when a girl of twelve years old, raised a Sutherland regiment, at the time of the American Declaration of Independence, declaring that she was only sorry she could not herself command it. This brave child subsequently reviewed her troops, 1,000 strong, from the windows of her aunt's house in Edinburgh, and later, in 1793, when she had reached womanhood, exerted herself to raise another corps of 'Fencibles' which was eventually embodied in the famous '93rd' Regiment. In our own time the successful enlistment of a body of Scottish Horse, which did splendid work in South Africa during the war, was largely due to the exertions and influence of a woman.

Of such women as these it may truly be said that they inherited something of that spirit of courage and patriotism which more than four centuries ago inspired two successive Countesses of March in their celebrated defence of the castle of Dunbar.

The history of the castle is a romantic and interesting one. The antiquity of the fortress is unknown, but must be considerable, for we hear of its being burnt and levelled to the ground by Kenneth, King of Scotland, as long ago as the year AD 856. Two hundred years later, when the stronghold had been rebuilt and fortified by all the artificial means then known, it was given by another Scottish king, Malcolm Canmore, to Patrick, Earl of Northumberland, who fled thither from England after the Conquest.

Built on a cluster of high rocks, round which the sea beat fiercely at high water, Dunbar Castle was, by reason of its natural situation, practically impregnable. It came consequently to be regarded as the key to the eastern portion of Scotland, and played an important part in the martial history of that country. In 1296, during the wars of Bruce and Baliol, when Edward I occupied the throne of England, the governor of the fortress, Patrick, 8th Earl of Dunbar and March, seceded to the English side and fought in the army of King Edward. But his wife, Margery Comyn, who held the castle in the absence of her lord, regarded the English with feelings of deadly hatred, and entered into secret negotiations with the Scottish leaders to deliver her charge into their hands. Margery was forced to choose between disloyalty to her country and the betrayal of her husband, and readily chose the latter. The Scottish besiegers, assisted as they were by the chatelaine of the castle, found little difficulty in capturing it, and expelling the few defenders who still remained true to England. Hearing of the treacherous surrender of Dunbar, Edward I at once despatched the Earl of Surrey with a force of 10,000 foot and 1,000 horse to recover the fortress. But the Scottish garrison were not easily to be daunted into submission, and for some time succeeded in repelling the English attack. Margery Comyn and her Scottish men-at-arms meanwhile stood on the battlements and hurled insults at the Earl of Surrey's soldiers. 'Come on, ye long-tailed: hounds!' they shouted, 'and we will cut your tails for you!' In spite, however, of these suggestive taunts, the English force persevered in the siege, and was eventually rewarded by the capitulation of the fortress and the unconditional surrender of its garrison.

Patrick, 10th Earl of Dunbar and March, has been described by one historian as 'at that time the most outstanding man amongst the Scots', and by another as a noble who stood 'almost alone' in the position of a man 'whom no promises could entice, nor any dangers force to submit to the English'. Yet he seems to have had some difficulty in fixing his allegiance permanently to the cause of any particular monarch. His sympathies were at first entirely on the side of the English, and he allowed Edward II to take refuge at Dunbar after the battle of Bannockburn, and thence to escape to Berwick by sea. Later on, however, he tendered his allegiance to Robert Bruce, fought in command of the Scottish troops, and was appointed governor of Berwick Castle. But in 1333, after the battle of Halidon Hill, he surrendered once more to the English, and became a loyal subject of Edward III, a temporary allegiance which he renounced in the following year, when he was once more to be found fighting on the side of the Regent of Scotland.

In the earl's absence on the field of battle, the castle of Dunbar was left in the charge of his second countess. 'Black Agnes', so called from the darkness of her complexion, was a daughter of the famous Randolph, Earl of Moray, and the alleged grand-niece of Robert the Bruce, and in her capable hands the fortress was safe against the attacks of the most persistent foes. A powerful English force, under the command of Montagu, Earl of Salisbury, proceeded to besiege it, and for five long months sought in vain to accomplish its capture. A cordon of troops was drawn up round the fortress, closing in upon it from day to day, while two Genoese galleys were ordered to manœuvre in concert with the land force, and watch that side of the stronghold which overlooked the sea. But the problem of its capture was not so easy as Montagu had perhaps imagined. The defender of Dunbar – though only a young woman of twenty-five – was a foe worthy of his steel, resolute and fearless, if (as an early bard would have us believe) she was not altogether without pity.

The castle of Dunbar was boldly situated on two rocks which projected far into the ocean, and were connected by a natural reef of stone consisting of two archways, through one of which, serving as a porch to the water-gate, the Bass Rock might be seen in the dim distance. It was the Earl of Salisbury's intention to prevent any friendly force from coming to the rescue of the beleaguered garrison, and thus he hoped in time to reduce the defenders to starvation. He had to reckon, however, with the courage and determination of a peculiarly determined and courageous guardian of the fortress. 'Black Agnes' was a born leader of men, valiant and full of resource. 'She performed all the duties of a bold and vigilant commander,' says an enthusiastic old chronicler; 'animating the garrison by her exhortation, munificence, and example,' and extorted even the praise of her enemies by her warlike bearing. In the words of one of the English minstrels of the time:–

> She kept a stir in tower and trench,
> That brawling boisterous Scottish wench;
> Came I early, came I late,
> I found Agnes at the gate.

Day after day she exposed herself fearlessly upon the battlements, deriding (like her predecessor Margery Comyn) the futile onslaughts of the English invaders, and rousing them to the fever pitch of fury by the fierce and ceaseless witticisms in which she indulged at their expense. When the huge stones from the besiegers' catapults struck upon the castle walls, 'Black Agnes' would scornfully send one of her women to wipe off the dust with a white napkin – a particularly felicitous manner of displaying her indifference to their attacks.

Salisbury at last brought up a huge military engine called the 'Sow', which had been used with great success at other sieges, and which he now hastened to erect against the walls of this stubborn fortress. This machine resembled the Roman *testudo*, and consisted of a vast wooden shield, under cover of which the besieging force was intended to advance and undermine the foundations of the castle. The arrival of this contrivance inspired Black Agnes to burst into verse for probably the first and (let us hope) the last time. Stepping forward onto an overhanging parapet, she shouted out the following couplet – in which, claiming the licence of the true poet, she sacrificed the correct pronunciation of her adversary's name to the exigencies of rhyme–

> 'Beware, Montagow' (she cried),
> 'For farrow shall thy sow!'

As she uttered this masterpiece, 'Black Agnes' gave a
preconcerted signal, and the defenders paused in the admiration of their leader's poetic gifts sufficiently long to allow
them to drop an enormous rock on to the top of the 'Sow',
crushing it to pieces, and killing a number of the unfortunate
soldiers who were sheltering beneath it. As the bruised and
wounded Englishmen fled from the wreck of their machine,
'Black Agnes' added insult to injury by jeering loudly at
them, declaring that her metrical prophecy had been fulfilled, and that they reminded her of nothing in the world so
much as a new-born litter of pigs.

Finding that force was unavailing, the Earl of Salisbury
determined to try other means to secure the downfall of the
castle. He sent to England for the Earl of Moray, 'Black
Agnes's' brother, who was a prisoner there, and, displaying
him to the defenders of Dunbar, declared that he would kill
him before their eyes unless they surrendered immediately.
The countess was not to be moved by such a threat. She
retorted that the castle was not her property but that of her
husband, and that she could not, therefore, deliver it without
his authority, however much she might desire to do so. 'If
you slay my brother,' she added coldly, 'I shall be the heiress
of the earldom of Moray!' Salisbury was humane enough to
appreciate the truth of her argument, and refrained from
putting his prisoner to death. Moray was sent back to
England, and survived to fight at the battle of Durham,
where he was killed in 1346.

The scheme of terrorizing the defenders having failed
ignominiously, Salisbury now had recourse to guile. He
bribed the warden of one of the castle gates to admit a
portion of the English into the fortress at nightfall. This
the man readily consented to do, but wisely omitted to
inform the earl that he had every intention of betraying this
typically southron scheme to his Scottish mistress. When,
therefore, the scene was wrapped in darkness, a body of the

besiegers crept stealthily up to the gate and gave the signal which was to secure their admittance. The portcullis was silently raised and the English made their way quietly into the fortress. Suddenly the defenders, who had been watching events from a hiding-place on the battlements, gave a loud shout, the portcullis was once more dropped into position, and the invaders found themselves caught in a trap. The Earl of Salisbury happened to step back just as the gate was lowered and so managed to get away, the defenders having mistaken one of his men-at-arms, Copeland by name, for the commander, and let down the portcullis a moment too soon. As he made good his escape, 'Black Agnes' called after him, begging him earnestly to come back and sarcastically expressing her regret that his lordship could not stay to give her the pleasure of his company at supper. She had a strong sense of humour, a quality which Salisbury no doubt appreciated, as he was not himself wholly deficient in it. One morning when he was riding near the wall in company with a knight in full armour, a Scottish archer, named William Spens, shot an arrow from the battlements and stretched the knight dead at his feet. 'That is one of my lady's tiring-pins,' said the earl, with a smile, as he withdrew the arrow from the corpse of his companion. 'Black Agnes's love-shafts pierce to the heart!'

For five weary months the siege continued, until at length the garrison was reduced to extremities. The supply of food began to run short, and things looked bad for the gallant defenders of Dunbar. But the celebrated Sir Alexander Ramsay of Dalwolsey heard of the straits in which the castle was placed and made up his mind to attempt its relief. Ramsay had collected a small band of Scottish swashbucklers, and was lurking in the caves of Hawthornden, whence he issued now and then to harry or cut off detached parties of the English. Being a chivalrous man as well as a brave one, he lost no time in arranging plans for the relief of 'beauty in distress', as exemplified by the chatelaine of Dunbar. Secure within the caverns of Hawthornden, he concocted an elaborate scheme for turning the tables upon the hated English and rescuing the hard-pressed countess and her little band of men-at-arms.

Hawthornden was a perfect hiding-place for such a man as Sir Alexander Ramsay. It is famous in Scottish history as the refuge of many early patriots. It is still more famous perhaps as being the residence of the poet and historian, Drummond. Hither in the year 1618 Ben Jonson walked all the way from London on purpose to visit his Scottish friend, an occasion on which their greetings took the form of an impromptu couplet:

D. – 'Welcome, welcome, Royal Ben!'
J. – 'Thank ye, thank ye, Hawthornden!'

which has acquired (though it scarcely seems to have deserved) immortality. The house itself was the scene of many a memorable conflict in the past. On the gable of the old mansion was a tablet with the inscription: 'To the memory of Sir Lawrence Abernethy of Hawthornden, a brave and gallant soldier, who, at the head of a party, in 1338, conquered Lord Douglas five times in one day, yet was taken prisoner before sunset.' The caverns, known as 'Bruce's Bedchamber' and 'Bruce's Library', which were close to the house, have been considered by archæologists to date their origin to very early times, when they were perhaps the stronghold of the old Pictish kings. It was from these caves that Sir Alexander Ramsay and his forty resolute followers emerged to the rescue of 'Black Agnes'. Contriving by some means or other to get into communication with the defenders of the fortress, one dark and stormy night, at the head of his gallant little force, Ramsay eluded the vigilance of the Genoese galleys, approached the castle from the sea, and was gratefully admitted at the Water Gate by 'Black Agnes' herself.

Next morning, before the besiegers had time to realize the addition that had thus been made to the garrison, the latter sallied forth under Ramsay's command and inflicted a serious defeat upon the Earl of Salisbury's troops, on the same ground where, 300 years later, Cromwell defeated the Scottish Covenanters. The English now acknowledged themselves foiled by a woman's wit, determined to abandon the siege, and made a truce favourable to the defenders.

There are numerous other instances in Scottish history of women who have defended hearth and home at the point of the sword. In 1336 King Edward III made a successful expedition to relieve the beleaguered Countess of Athole and her garrison in the castle of Lochindorb. Sixty years later the castle of Fyvie in Aberdeenshire was held by Margaret Keith, wife of Sir James Lindsay and daughter of Sir William Keith, Great Marischal of Scotland, against the attacks of her nephew, Robert de Keith, who was the centre of a family quarrel. And in the Privy Council Records at the General Register House at Edinburgh there is an account of how 'Dame Isobel Hepburn, Lady Bass', and her son, George Lauder, defied their creditors from the safe shelter of an impregnable tower on the Bass Rock, where they long remained, bankrupt but undaunted, 'presuming to keep and maintain themselves, so as to elude justice and execution of the law'.

Of 'Black Agnes' we hear little more. Her husband changed his mind once again, in 1363, when he rebelled against King David. He was speedily suppressed, however, and five years later resigned his earldom. Some say that he and his countess had no children; others that their daughter Agnes became mistress to David Bruce and was perhaps the cause of that monarch's divorce of Margaret Logie. Patrick died about 1639 at the age of eighty-four, and his death was shortly followed by that of his wife.

The castle of Dunbar is now nothing but a ruin on the seashore. If the old stones could speak, what strange stories they would have to tell of 'far-off things and battles long ago'. A thousand romantic memories cling to the fallen battlements. It was at Dunbar that the luckless Mary sought refuge after Rizzio's death, and from the gates of this castle she set forth to the disastrous Carberry Hill where she surrendered. But there is nothing more stirring or remarkable in the annals of its history than that lengthy defence maintained by the gallant body of Scotsmen who owed their success and safety to the intrepid leadership of 'Black Agnes' of Dunbar.

Christian 'Kit' Cavanagh (1667–1739)

'Mother Ross': The Bold Dragoon

Christian Cavanagh was the daughter of a prosperous Dublin brewer and in 1693 disguised herself as a man to follow her first husband, Richard Welsh, into the army. Described as a rough diamond, strong and self-reliant, her exploits at arms against the French in Holland became legendary and it was not until she was wounded at the Battle of Ramillies that her sex was revealed. Following the death of Richard Welsh at the Battle of Malplaquet, Kit was to marry again, twice – once to a grenadier, Hugh Jones, and later to another soldier named Davies – before spending her last years running a public house in London where her fame attracted many customers. She died in 1739 after a period in Chelsea Hospital and was buried with full military honours. The following year, *The Life and Adventures of Mrs. Christian Davies, commonly called Mother Ross* was published, having allegedly been 'taken from her own mouth when a pensioner at Chelsea Hospital'. This more recent account of Kit Cavanagh's life makes use of that now very rare source and is written by **Charles Thompson**.

Among the women who posed as men and served as soldiers in the British Army in the early eighteenth century, none showed more courage and bravery than Christian Davies. The story of her career and adventures marks her as a woman of extraordinary determination and character, who faced the dangers of a soldier's life with the greatest equanimity.

She was born in Dublin in 1667, her father being a maltster and brewer in a good way of business in that city. Her parents gave her the best education possible at the time, and afterwards her lively and active disposition led her to help her mother with the work on a farm they rented. She loved country life and learned to follow the plough and thresh the corn; she could turn her hand to any work as well as the best of the men on the land.

She was a good rider and often rode astride a favourite grey mare, jumping the hedges and ditches across the countryside. When in some districts the Irish rallied to the cause of James II, her father sold the corn on the farm and joined the Army in support of the King. The battle of the Boyne, however, put an end to his hopes for the cause, and after their defeat, in company with a Frenchman, he made his way home. His companion, who was known as Captain Bodeaux, fled with him to his house and was afterwards placed in command of troops at the siege of Limerick, where, while defending the bridge with great gallantry, he was killed. When they came to remove his uniform and clothes it was discovered that the Captain was a woman, an incident which probably left an impression on Christian's mind.

When the war was over she went to live with an aunt with whom she remained for four years, and on her death she was left heiress to all her aunt's property, including a well-furnished house. Here Christian, now provided with means, carried on with farming and kept a number of horses, her overseer being a young man called Richard Welsh, who had been in her aunt's employ. She describes him as 'handsome in appearance with a manly face, an open temper, sober and active in business, and a man any woman might love'.

It is little wonder, therefore, that Christian developed a

strong affection for him. At first she thought it would be beneath her to think of marrying a man who was really her servant, but love overcame her resolutions, her pride vanished, and she awaited his declaration.

Although Richard adored Christian he was too bashful to broach the subject of love to his mistress and first sought the good offices and advice of a friend of hers. This friend told him that she was sure Christian wished to marry him and was only waiting to be asked. So Richard plucked up courage and acted on this advice; finding Christian at her house he offered her his heart.

'Believe me, my dear mistress,' he exclaimed, 'I have no views of interest. I love you for yourself and not for your money. I will never pretend to be other than a just steward should you consent to make me the happiest of men.'

Christian did not need much persuasion, and embracing him she replied that she had long been waiting for him to ask her, and consented. They were married within a week and settled down very happily in their new relationship. All went well with them for a few years, during which time Christian gave birth to two children.

One day Richard Welsh left the house in the morning to pay an account of fifty pounds which was owing – and did not return. As day after day went by Christian became prostrate with grief and anxiety. She could not account for his sudden disappearance, his desertion of herself and the children, yet she could not believe he had met with his death.

At length she learned that he had paid the money owing and had then left in company with an unknown man. A year went by and Christian heard nothing more. She threw herself actively into the work of her farm, which, with the care of her children, occupied all her time.

After a further twelve months Christian received a letter from her missing husband. In explanation of his absence he declared that he had become completely intoxicated after drinking with a stranger in a tavern, and he knew nothing until he found himself on board a ship carrying recruits. By the time he had recovered from the effects of the drink, the ship had reached Helvoet Sluys, where he was put on shore without a penny in his pockets. He had tried in vain to find a ship to take him back home, and the ensign in charge of the recruits advised him to enlist in some regiment. As he was without money he was compelled to do this, and much against his will he joined up with a regiment of foot.

When Christian read this letter she was at first completely overcome and could not understand why Richard had been so long in communicating with her. She decided to go and find him and bring him back.

At first she had no idea how this was to be done; then, probably recalling the incident of 'Captain Bodeaux' and how she had succeeded in disguising herself as a man, Christian did not see why *she* should not conceal her sex and join the army and go to Flanders. At length she made her plans and placed her children in the care of her mother and a nurse and her house and land with friends. She then cut her hair short and dressed herself in a suit of her husband's clothes; she took the precaution of quilting the waistcoat and bought a wig, a hat, some Holland shirts, and a silver-hilted sword. She managed to conceal fifty guineas in the waistband of her breeches so that she could carry it without suspicion, and having thus completed her preparations she set out on her quest.

Riding to the town she disposed of her horse and made her way to the sign of the Golden Last, where Ensign Herbert Lawrence kept his rendezvous for beating up recruits for the army in Flanders.

She offered him her services to fight against France and show her zeal for King William. The Ensign, after declaring that she looked 'a clever, brisk young fellow', gave her a guinea as enlisting money and a crown to drink the King's health. He ordered her to be enrolled as 'Christopher Welsh' in Captain Tichbourne's company of foot, in the regiment commanded by the Marquis de Pisare; the lieutenant in charge of the company being called Gardner. After staying a short time in Dublin, Christian was shipped with other recruits to Holland, where they were landed at Williamstadt and then marched to Gorkum. Next day they set out for Landen, where they were incorporated in various regiments.

Christian threw herself wholeheartedly into her training and soon became proficient in drill and military exercises; she was even commended by the officers for her smartness and aptitude. Her regiment was now ready to join the Grand Army, which was in expectation of a general battle as they were now within cannon-shot of the enemy.

Shortly after she reached Landen Christian was ordered on the night-guard posted at the bedroom door of the Elector of Hanover. While she was there on duty, she tells us, 'Mustapha, a Turk and valet to His Highness introduced to his master's room a fine, handsome, jolly lady, a black beauty dressed in rich silk and a bedgown tied with ribbons from her breast to her feet'. She goes on: 'I thought the lady went in with a great deal of alacrity. I believed many more of our sex would visit a sovereign prince with a particular satisfaction, especially if he was as agreeable in his person as the Elector, who then wore his own hair – the finest I ever saw.'

As the French Army drew nearer and the troops of the Allies engaged, Christian heard the shot rattle about her. It made her afraid at first, but she soon recovered her courage. She was ordered by Lord Cholmondeley to return to her regiment, and while she was trying to do so she received a wound in the leg from a musket-ball. Lord Cholmondeley, who saw her fall, ordered her to be carried off the field.

Christian was disabled for two months with the wound. By the time that she was fit for service again winter was approaching, and her regiment was ordered into quarters at Gertruydenberg.

The village was near the dykes, and while the regiment were there they began to give way. The English soldiers were ordered to assist the Dutch in repairing them, and the men were obliged to work night and day up to their waists in water. Christian, who, with Lieutenant Gardner, was busy in a trench, narrowly escaped drowning, for the tide rose rapidly, and they had to wade out hand in hand.

The following summer was spent in marches and counter-marches, watching the movements of the French. One day, when Christian's detachment was engaged in foraging, the French suddenly attacked the party. Thus surprised, Christian and sixty of her comrades were taken prisoners, and after being robbed of their belongings they were taken by tedious marches to St Germain-en-Laye.

On their arrival the Dutch and English soldiers were herded together, but on the following night, owing to the intervention of the English Queen, who was then at the Court of St Germain, they were separated and given clean straw every night to sleep on. They were allowed five farthings each daily for tobacco, a pound of bread, and a pint of wine. The Duke of Berwick came to visit them to see that they were not ill-treated, and he advised them to take service with the French. When he thus spoke to Christian, she replied: 'I have taken the oath to King William and I could not in honour break my engagement.'

After they had been imprisoned for some nine days a Mr Van Deden arrived to effect an exchange with some French prisoners, and Christian with her comrades was liberated.

'We went to the Palace,' she says, 'to return Her Majesty our grateful thanks. She consented to see us and told me I was 'a very pretty young fellow' and that it grieved her much that I had not had my liberty sooner.

'On rejoining the army we heard the news of the death of Queen Mary in England, and soon afterwards we drew off again into winter quarters at Gorkum.'

While there Christian had an adventure which is best told in her own words. She says: 'I began to indulge my natural gaiety of temper and lived very merrily. In my frolic I made my addresses to a burgher's daughter who was young and pretty. I squeezed her hand whenever I could get an opportunity and sighed when in her company, I looked foolishly and practised upon her all the ridiculous airs which I had often laughed at. The poor girl grew really fond of me.

'When I was with her she always regaled me in the best manner possible – nothing was too good for me. It was true she did not scruple to own she loved me, but she avowed she loved her virtue better than her life.

'If I had dishonourable designs on her I was not the man she loved,' continues Christian. 'She told me that in the course of this affair a sergeant of the regiment had also fallen to her charms, but finding I was preferred he resolved to make a desperate assault on her virtue. One day when I was under arms, the sergeant came bravely to her and tried to obtain by force what he could not gain by assiduity. She defended herself stoutly but in the struggle which ensued she lost her cap and most of her clothes were torn off her back. Attracted by her cries, friends came to her assistance and the sergeant beat a retreat.

'No sooner had she recovered from his assault than she came in search of me, to find me in my rank, standing at arms. She told me what had passed and begged me to revenge the insult on her. When I was dismissed by my officer I went in quest of my rival and demanded to know how he had dared attempt the honour of a woman who, for aught he knew, was my wife? I told him his conduct cast a reflection on the corps and required immediate satisfaction. He called me a proud insolent coxcomb.

' "I leave Billingsgate language to women," I replied. "If you have as much courage in the force of a man as you have in assaulting defenceless women, come with me at once to yonder windmill and I will soon convince you that General T——— had too good an opinion of you when he took his livery off your back to put on the King's and gave you a halberd.'

'I knew the fellow had been footman to General T——— and this reproach stung him to the quick. He replied that he would soon cool my courage and we went off together to the windmill where we both drew and engaged.

'The first thrust I made gave him a slanting wound in his right breast which well nigh finished the business. He returned this with a long gash in my right arm, but before he could recover his guard I gave him a thrust in the right

thigh about half a span from the "Pope's eye". The next
pass he aimed at my breast, but it hit my right arm, though
it was little more than a prick of a pin. He then grew weak
with loss of the blood which now flowed plentifully from
his wound.

'By this time some soldiers on duty had seen our first
attack, and a file of musketeers under the command of a
sergeant came up and took us prisoners, disarmed us both
and sent him to hospital. As my wounds were slight and I was
the aggressor and but a common soldier I was taken to
prison, for the sergeant was thought to be mortally wounded
and he did not recover for a long time.

'I sent my sweetheart an account of what had happened
and where I was confined. She acquainted her father with the
villainous attempt the sergeant had made upon her and let
him know it was her quarrel which I had taken up. The father
at once acted and made a proper representation of the affront
offered to a member of his family, with the result that in four
days' time I received a pardon from King William and an
order for my immediate release. My sword was returned, my
arrears paid, and I was given my discharge from the regiment.

'The moment I was released I went to thank my deliverer,
and she gratefully acknowledged the risking of my life in
revenging the insult done to her. In the end she made me a
proposal of marriage.

' "My dear," I said, "you offer me the greatest happiness
this world can afford me. Will you give me leave to ask your
father?"

' "My father!" she cried. "You cannot imagine that a rich
burgher will allow his daughter to marry a foot-soldier? For
though I think you merit everything, yet my father will not
view you with my eyes."

'This answer was what I expected, for it was because I
knew her father would refuse his consent that I had asked to
speak to him.

' "What then can be done?" I asked.

' "I will run the hazard of your fortune in case my father

proves irreconcilable after our marriage," she replied: I told her there were two obstacles to that proposal and declared I must gain a commission or purchase one in order to deserve her.

'Thus I got off from this *amour* without loss of credit and was discharged from my regiment.

'I was uncertain what to do, but loath to leave the army. So I sought Lieutenant Keith and rejoined in Lord John Hayes' regiment of dragoons.

'We were soon ordered to the siege of Namur which King William had invested. He opened the trenches before the city in two different places and it capitulated on 4 August, but the French bombarded Brussels to save the citadel. This made the Allies redouble their efforts at Namur.

'Never was more terrible fire seen, for no less than sixty large battering pieces and as many mortars played incessantly on the outworks. Marshal Boufflers, seeing no likelihood of saving the citadel, retreated when most of the fortifications of Namur were demolished.

'Nevertheless we lost 1,000 men in the assault on the new castle and while the King was preparing for a second attempt, Marshal Boufflers surrendered on terms, and the Allies took possession on the evening of 1 September.'

Christian continued in the same regiment of dragoons until the King reviewed the Army on the Plain of Breda, after which it was disbanded.

Her thoughts then turned to home. She knew not what might have happened in her absence, and to assure herself she set out for Dublin, which she reached in safety. She decided not to make herself known, so after ascertaining that her mother and children were well, she resolved to continue a soldier's life.

After all the vicissitudes and the adventures she had gone through Christian could not remain idle for long. On hearing that a new war was breaking out in Italy and that the Dutch were massing troops near Rosendaal, she again took ship for Holland. On arrival she sought out Lieutenant Keith, her previous commander, who was reforming her old corps, and she at once re-enlisted in the dragoons under Lord John Hayes.

The first action in which the regiment engaged was at Ninmeguen, where they were roughly handled by the French. After this they took part in the siege of Kaisersweert, during which Christian formed one of a party of horse and dragoons detached from the main army for reconnaissance, under the command of General Dompré. They fell in with a superior force of French cavalry and put them on the run, but Christian escaped unwounded and afterwards took part in the sieges of Stevens, Weert and Ruremond.

When the Army went into winter quarters Christian at length began to think of her husband, whom she had come to seek. She had made many enquiries in various places, but all had been in vain; she concluded he must have been killed and that she had lost him for ever.

In March 1703 the Duke of Marlborough landed in Holland and took command of the Army to open a new campaign. On 24 April they invested Bonn, which capitulated in four days. Then came disaster for Christian, for at Donawert she received a ball in her hip which lodged between the bones and deprived her of the use of her thigh and leg. She was carried to a hospital near Schellenberg and received attention from three of the best army surgeons, Wilson, Laurence and Sea. While there, the secret of her sex, which she had managed to conceal successfully for so long, was nearly discovered; but eventually she got her discharge with her secret still intact. On leaving the hospital, she was glad to receive her share of the plunder taken at Ulm and the cities in Bavaria, whither the Army had marched.

Christian was next engaged in the battle of Hochstet, and, although she was often in the thickest part of the fight, she escaped without a wound. Afterwards her troop was detached to guard the prisoners and march them to the plain of Breda. On the way, during a halt, while watching the women bewailing the loss of husbands and brothers who had fallen at Schellenberg and Hochstet, she noticed a woman talking to a man whose face seemed very familiar to her. She drew nearer to the palisade where her horse was tied and looking through saw the man turn to embrace the woman. She was struck with amazement when she recognized him as Richard Welsh, her missing husband. She was so surprised that she shook with emotion and for a moment was paralyzed. After she had seen him embrace the Dutch woman, she resolved not to make herself known to him yet. She joined a comrade, who asked her what was troubling her (for she was trembling from head to foot), and told him she had just encountered her brother, Richard Welsh, whom she had not seen for twelve years.

She pointed out the man, who was in the uniform of Orkney's regiment, to her comrade and told him to find out if his name was Richard Welsh, and to ask when he had last heard from his wife. He went at once and she saw him speak to the soldier and receive a reply, but he had hardly returned when the drums and trumpets sounded to resume the march to Breda.

On arriving there, after housing the prisoners, Christian went in search of the soldier who she believed to be her husband, and on enquiring at the main-guard, was told he was in an ale-house nearby. She entered it and passed through an outer room to the kitchen, where she saw the man drinking with the Dutch woman. Taking a good look at him she was now sure that he was indeed her husband.

Christian then asked the landlady to show her to a private room; she was no sooner there than she was convulsed with grief. She lay down and cried until her tears ceased; then she bathed her face and calling the landlady ordered some beer to be brought. When the woman had brought it, she asked her to go and tell the soldier of Orkney's regiment who was drinking in her kitchen to come and speak to her.

'I sat with my back to the light,' says Christian, 'so that he might not see my face. Presently he came in and I saluted him by name, adding that I had the advantage, for I found I knew him although I appeared to be a stranger to him. "Sir," I said, "you are not unknown to me. Pray when did you hear from your wife and children?"

' "Sir," he replied, "I have heard no news of them these twelve years though I have written no less than a dozen letters to her which I am apt to believe have miscarried."

' "There are many pretty girls here, no doubt, who served to compensate for her absence," I remarked.

' "Sir," he replied, "you take me for a villain and you lie."

'A sudden tremor seized me of which he who had his hand on his sword took notice, and looking in my face more intently he stepped forward crying: "Oh Heavens! Is this possible? Can I believe my eyes or is it a delusion. Do I really see my dear Christian?" He clasped me in his arms, kissed me in rapture and bedewed my cheeks with tears of joy.

'As soon as I could disengage myself, I told him of my search and all I had been through to find him and how I had left children and home to face the dangers of a soldier's life for his sake.

' "My dear Christian," he said, "do not embitter the joy of this meeting by cruel and undeserved reproaches. Had you received my letters you would have learnt of my misfortunes. It was not my fault. I gave you a true account."

Meanwhile the Dutch woman, who had been waiting in the kitchen below, came upstairs, knocked at the door, and asked why he had left her so long alone?

Stirred by jealousy, Christian called to her: 'Is this man your husband?'

'Yes,' the woman replied.

'Richard denied it, but she declared they had lived together as man and wife.'

He bade her leave them, and after she had gone Christian told her husband that she liked her life in the army so much that she was going to continue it. If he would pass as her brother and not claim her as his wife, and would promise not to reveal the secret of her sex, she would give him all that he wanted. To this arrangement he eventually agreed, and after giving him a piece of gold he took leave of her with a passionate embrace and they separated to their respective camps.

For a time they saw each other every day, like brothers, and their real relationship was kept secret.

The Dutch army, at this time not being strong enough to keep the field, was entrenched under the guns of Maestricht, while the French left their lines and invested Huy, and after taking it laid siege to Liège. The Duke of Marlborough had no sooner arrived at Maestricht than the French abandoned Liège, raised the siege, and withdrew. At the battle of Ramillies, Christian was again in the hottest part of the fight, and escaped unhurt until the French were defeated, when a shell (fired from a steeple on which before the battle they had placed mortars and cannon) burst close to her and she was struck by a fragment, which fractured her skull. She was carried to Meldret, a small town near Louvain, and taken to hospital, where it was found necessary to trepan her and it was ten weeks before she recovered. For some days she had been unconscious and during that time the surgeons who were attending her discovered her true sex. They at once informed Brigadier Preston, who was in charge of the British, that his 'pretty dragoon' (as Christian was usually called) was in fact *a woman*. He was loath to believe it, and on seeing Christian told her he had always looked upon her as 'the prettiest fellow and the best man he had'.

He sent for Richard Welsh and said: 'I am surprised at a piece of news these gentlemen tell me. They say your brother is in reality a woman!'

'Sir,' said Richard, 'since she is discovered I cannot deny it. She is my wife and I have had three children by her.'

Christian's story soon spread throughout the camp, and among others who heard of it and came to see her, was Lord John Hayes. He asked her no questions, but spoke to a comrade who had formerly shared her tent, and he declared that he never knew or even suspected she was other than a man.

Lord John then called Richard and asked him to explain the meaning of the disguise. He gave full and satisfactory answers and told him how he had first met Christian and married her, also how they came to be separated.

Lord John was greatly interested in the story and ordered that Christian should want for nothing and her pay should be continued. He sent her a parcel of shirts and sheets to make clothes and Brigadier Preston made her a present of a handsome silk gown, while all the officers of the regiment contributed something to pay for dresses. Lord John also spoke to her about her treatment of Richard and now that her sex had been discovered he told her there was no longer any reason for disguise.

'My Lord,' said Christian, 'the discovery of my sex has now removed the cause and I have no objection to living with him as is the duty of an honest wife.'

'Well,' said Lord Hayes, 'we will have a new marriage.'

'All the officers of the regiment were invited,' says Christian, 'and we were wedded and bedded with great solemnity. The sack-posset was eaten, the stocking thrown and every one on leaving kissed the bride and left a piece of gold.'

Although she had resumed her married life, Christian could not remain idle for long, so she offered to undertake the cooking for the regiment, returning to her husband's quarters every night. After that she turned subtler and was allowed to pitch her tent at the front, while the others were driven to the rear of the army.

Christian Davies records but little more of her army experiences, although we learn she served as a soldier on General Webb's expedition, when between Ostend and Ghent a convoy was attacked by the French. She followed her husband to Ghent, where she took a hand in some smuggling operations that were going on. Here she came in for more plunder and got 'a bay horse with silver-capped pistols and laced housings'. She also occupied herself in fishing up with a grappling-iron plate and copper which had been thrown down the wells.

One day, towards the close of Marlborough's campaign in the Low Countries, Christian was walking through a wood after an engagement when she came across a dog which led her to a wounded man. He proved to be her husband, who had been badly hurt. She attended to him and seeing he was in a serious condition went to get assistance. On returning, it was evident that he was too ill to be removed, and in a few minutes he died on the spot where she had found him.

All her hopes of future happiness were now shattered and she finally decided to give up army life and return home. She obtained a pass to England and eventually landed in Dublin.

Nothing is known of the fate of her children or of how she became so impoverished that she had to open a small beer and pie-house in Dublin. She received a pension of a shilling a day, which was afterwards reduced by the Lord Treasurer to fivepence. Later on she returned to London and first kept a pie-shop in Westminster and afterwards a public-house in Paddington. Her adventurous career as a soldier made her famous and brought many customers, including certain noble patrons who asked her to their houses – more for a joke than anything else – so that she could entertain the guests with her stories.

In the end she took asylum in Chelsea Hospital, where she lived out her last years in peace. She died there after reaching the great age of 108 years. She was interred according to her wish among the old pensioners with military honours, and three volleys were fired over her grave.

So ended the life and career of this remarkable woman whose determination and courage make her conspicuous among the others of her sex; a woman who played the part of a man and who fought with great bravery in the British army.

Hannah Snell (1723–92)

The Brave Marine
of Pondicherry

Hannah Snell was the granddaughter of a soldier who died at Malplaquet and in all probability knew Christian Cavanagh. Like her predecessor, Hannah disguised herself as a man in order to find a recalcitrant husband and enlisted with a regiment fighting the Stuart rebellion in Scotland. When she went to the aid of a young girl protecting herself from the advances of a lecherous sergeant, she received 500 lashes for her pains and afterwards deserted. She then went to sea as a marine and even after being badly wounded in action in Pondicherry, still managed to conceal her identity. However, in 1750 when Hannah returned to London, she revealed all in a sensationalized autobiography, *The Female Soldier*, and used the proceeds to open an inn called – appropriately – The Female Warrior, which proved every bit as popular as the establishment of 'Mother Ross'. This version of the life of Hannah Snell is told by **John Laffin**.

It is safe to say that Hannah Snell was born with soldiering in her blood and, as genealogists have discovered about many people, she had more in common with her grandparents than with her parents. Her grandfather, Captain Samuel Snell, began his military life as a cadet and fought in the wars of William III. He probably knew Kit Cavanagh. He so distinguished himself at the capture of Dunkirk and was so dangerously wounded that he was offered a place at Chelsea Hospital, plus a good pension. But he petitioned Marlborough to allow him to serve abroad again, and Marlborough, with a soft spot for any brave soldier, consented. Snell fought with the Welsh Fusiliers at Blenheim and was again dangerously wounded. He must have had an iron constitution to survive two such woundings, for survive he did, only to be mortally wounded on the field of Malplaquet. His career was a proud one. Not only had he fought in twenty-two engagements; he had also reached his rank by sheer merit in an age when promotion had to be bought in hard cash.

Perhaps his son saw nothing heroic in war, for he became a haberdasher of sorts in Worcester, where, on St George's Day, 1723, Hannah was born. She was one of nine children, all of whom, except one girl, became soldiers or sailors or were married into the services.

When her parents died in 1740, Hannah went to live with an elder sister in Wapping and, inexperienced and ardent, she fell for a young Dutch seaman, James Summs. Hannah took the romance very seriously and perhaps Summs did, too, initially, but seven months after marrying Hannah in 1743 he went to sea again. Nothing was heard from him but despite the more mature misgivings of her sister and brother-in-law Hannah was sublimely confident that James would return. She never doubted that he loved her and convinced herself that something was preventing him from returning – something like having been pressganged into the Army or Navy; such things were known to happen all too frequently. When her baby died at six months Hannah appropriated some of her brother-in-law's clothing, bound her breasts, and in 1745 set out to trace her husband. She was not so well equipped as Kit Cavanagh; she had practically no money, no ability to handle horses and men and no real experience of the world. She was armed indeed with nothing more than courage.

Feeling that her husband might be in Coventry, where troops were gathering to counter the Pretender's rising in the North, Hannah marched northwards and before long enlisted in Guise's regiment of foot. The corporal who enlisted her was a rogue, as so many recruiters were, but it is doubtful if Hannah was tricked into joining the colours. She was intelligent and sober and she probably realized that without money she needed to be a soldier to exist and to travel. Travel she did, for soon after joining she marched to Carlisle – twenty-two days on the road. Carlisle was a harsh town in 1745. The rebellion in Scotland had just been quelled and many survivors of Culloden were being tried and hanged. Hannah must have seen men led out to die amid the jeers of the populace and of the English soldiers.

Many troops in those days were bovine and dull, but Hannah so quickly learned to handle her arms and to drill that the company officers noticed her. She was making good soldierly progress until she became involved with Sergeant Davis, a crude lecher. Davis wanted to either seduce or rape a particular girl in Carlisle and practically ordered Hannah to help him achieve his ends. Hannah could perhaps have taken the easy way out and evaded the importunate sergeant's demands; instead, she went to the girl and warned her. Hearing about this, Sergeant Davis was furious, concocted a charge of neglect of duty against Hannah, and had her sentenced to 600 lashes.

This was a vicious but not uncommon sentence, and the lash was vigorously laid on. Hannah was tied to the barrack gate which would have hidden her breasts; this is perhaps the reason her sex was not discovered. Usually the victim, stripped to the waist, was triced to the halberds or pikes. Hannah could, of course, have escaped the flogging by proclaiming her sex, but she said nothing. Many soldiers broke down under the lash, but Hannah Snell bore 500 lashes without a whimper, though her flesh was torn and bleeding. It is tempting to consider that she so loved her husband that she could not bear the thought of being discharged from the army and having to start her search again. Perhaps it was her grandfather's spirit which saw her through the ordeal, before the Commanding Officer cancelled the final 100 lashes. All the officers, it seems, admired the fortitude she showed.

Nevertheless, when her lacerated back had mended a little Hannah deserted, emotionally because of the injustice she had suffered, practically because she had recognized as a recruit a neighbour from Wapping and feared exposure. She stole some civilian clothing and made for Portsmouth, her main adventure on the way being to thrash the landlord of a Winchester inn who thought the good-looking male guest, Hannah, was trying to have an affair with his wife.

Portsmouth was buzzing with martial activity and able-bodied men were being cajoled, tricked, tempted and forced into uniform. Hannah, now known as James Grey, joined Frazer's Regiment of Marines and was posted to Captain Graham's company. At this time Admiral Boscawen was preparing a fleet expedition for the East Indies and when it was known that many marines would be taken there was an instant wave of desertion. The East Indies was notoriously dangerous and unhealthy. Hannah Snell held her ground and was sent aboard the sloop *Swallow*, commander Captain Rosier. It has been said that probably she was the only marine on board who sailed cheerfully.

She was cheerful throughout the voyage, too, which was noteworthy considering the dreadful conditions of shipboard life with its interminable boredom, poor food, cramped conditions and rigid discipline. In the Bay of Biscay a hurricane hit the squadron and Hannah with the others worked at the pumps, and, of course, stood her turn at watch. How she managed to find privacy enough to carry out her natural functions only she could tell. She was so helpful about the ship that Lieutenant Wyegate asked her to become his mess sergeant. During a delay at Gibraltar she nursed

Wyegate through a desperate illness, but he was not fit enough to sail on with the squadron.

Boscawen's first objective was an attack on the island of Mauritius, but the enemy were too strong for him to make a frontal attack. A party, including Hannah Snell, was sent close inshore in longboats to determine the depth of the water and here she came under fire for the first time. She was commended for her self-control and calmness.

The next objective was an assault on the major French post of Pondicherry on the Indian coast south of Madras. Before Pondicherry could be taken the river fort of Areacopolong had to be reduced and here Hannah found herself one of 2,500 infantry committed to the action. In the first attack thirty-five officers and men were killed or wounded and the French in a counter-attack suffered severely. During the continual artillery fire that followed, a British shell exploded the main French ammunition dump, forcing the French to withdraw with the British at their heels. Again James Grey won the respect of officers and men for her steady courage. Example counted for a great deal in those days when every member of a small unit was visible to every other member. But Pondicherry with its 300 guns and perhaps 500 mortars well placed behind fortifications was a difficult nut to crack.

The British worked hard at preparing their attack while the French tried to disrupt these preparations. An enemy patrol caught some Marines moving stores on the beach, killed one and wounded their officer before Hannah Snell calmly shot dead one of the Frenchmen.

Gradually, the British moved closer to the inner defences. Under gunfire, Hannah, with a band of soldiers, forded a river at chest height to capture French reinforcements. The monsoon now began and the British, virtually without food, crouched in wet and muddy trenches. Realizing the danger of losing the initiative, Boscawen at the end of September 1748 ordered a combined naval and military attack, with the Marines advancing under their own guns' protection.

Hannah, not surprisingly, was in the first wave and managed to fire thirty-seven aimed shots before suffering multiple wounds – six in one leg, five in the other, and a musket ball in the groin. Taken to hospital, she did not mention this wound to the surgeons, realizing that her sex would be discovered under treatment. Her agony was intense.

A contemporary writer noted: 'This wound being so extremely painful, it drove her to the precipice of despair. She often thought of discovering herself . . . but the resolution was soon banished and she resolved to run all risks, even at the hazard of her life, rather than that her sex should be known . . . She communicated to a black woman who waited on her, and who could get at the surgeon's medicines . . . she intended to experiment on herself to extract the ball . . . yet she did not tell the black that she was a woman.'

After bribing the woman, Hannah probed the wound with her finger until she found the ball, then 'thrust in both her finger and thumb' and pulled it out. This was a very rough way of 'proceeding with one's own flesh, but of two evils, she thought, this was the least . . . After this operation was performed she applied some of the healing salves the black had brought her, by the help of which she made a perfect cure of the dangerous wound.'

Her other wounds also healed, perhaps despite what the surgeons did to them, and after three months Hannah left hospital, officially classified as being unfit for Marine duty, which would have been less arduous than the deck-hand's jobs assigned to her. Eventually, after a time aboard the *Tartan*, she was sent aboard the man-o'-war *Eltham*, bound for Bombay.

But she now made another enemy, the ship's chief officer, the dictatorial Lieutenant Allan. Wanting a little amusement and knowing that Hannah had a fine voice he rudely ordered her to sing for him. Hannah said she was unwell and when Allan swore at her pointed out that it was no part of a soldier's duty to sing. Her comrades enjoyed the bully's discomfiture, so vindictively Allan accused her of stealing one of his shirts and put her in irons. The more humanitarian captain was ashore so Hannah endured the degrading irons for five days, after which she was given twelve lashes on the bare back. It is said that this time she concealed her sex by tying a large handkerchief around her neck and spreading the ends over her breasts. Her shipmates detested the officer and even the petty officer ordered to inflict the whipping used much less violence than would have been expected of him. Hannah, to complete her sentence, spent four hours at the masthead. The officer's steward later found the missing shirt in his locker, further angering the men. It was no accident that when the ship docked in London a heavy weight fell from the rigging and crushed the officer's skull.

Throughout her travels Hannah had not failed to ask for news of James Summs. In Lisbon, on the way to England, she met a man who knew that Summs had stabbed a man to death in Genoa and had been executed by being thrown into the sea in a sack weighted with stones. It was rather an anticlimax and after all these years Hannah was not deeply distressed. But all reason for posing as a man had vanished, so when the *Eltham* arrived in London in 1750 she returned to her sister in Wapping and changed her male attire for woman's garments.

Somehow her story soon became known, probably through Hannah's proud sister. She became known as 'the heroic marine of Pondicherry' and the Duke of Cumberland, intrigued by her career, permitted her to wear men's clothes, a laced hat and cockade, sword and ruffles. He may actually have ordered her to don this attire, for a contemporary writer noted that Hannah was 'not to alter the military dress till further orders from the Duke'.

To earn a living she agreed to perform in a theatre act in a double roll – as Bill Bobstay and Firelock, popular terms for a sailor and soldier respectively. The producer thought that this would bring in customers interested in both army and navy. The critics applauded her as 'masterly and correct . . . in the manual and platoon exercises' and found her songs 'lively and diverting'. She even appeared at Sadler's Wells theatre, before she leased a Wapping tavern which she renamed 'The Widow in Masquerade, or the Female Warrior'. Added to the money she made from her tavern came a

Sovereign's grant of £30 a year for life. She married twice more but in 1789 developed symptoms of insanity and was taken to Bethlehem Hospital where she died in 1792. Having no noble patrons she did not win a military funeral, but many years later her portrait was hung in Chelsea Hospital. A son by her second marriage had a successful life in London commerce.

Hannah Snell–James Grey was outstanding for her patient acceptance of all her trials and sufferings. In this she was more of a woman than Kit Cavanagh. Where Hannah was almost passively courageous Kit was aggressively brave. It has been said that as she was habitually cheerful she could not have been particularly intelligent. I do not think that this necessarily follows, but it is true that Hannah had a simple purpose and lived life as she found it. She must also have kept her femininity because she did not become coarse in speech or manner.

Charlotte Walpole (1758–1836)

Mrs Pimpernel Atkyns

Charlotte Walpole was a beautiful Irish actress who delighted London theatregoers with her vivacity and then married into the British aristocracy. During the French Revolution, however, she revealed a quite different side to her nature and became a real-life 'Female Pimpernel' in the same mould as Baroness Orczy's great fictional creation, 'The Scarlet Pimpernel'. Driven to try and rescue the French queen Marie Antoinette and her son, the Dauphin, Charlotte risked death every day as she cleverly outwitted the French secret police, disguised herself as a man in soldier's and sailor's outfits to avoid capture, and arranged the most daring rescue plans. This love of excitement did not desert her when she returned to England, and she achieved still more notoriety as 'The Brazen Widow' during an election campaign in 1806. Her story is told by Norfolk historian **Howard Swales**.

Ketteringham Hall, between Wymondham and Norwich, is a handsome Tudor-style mansion rebuilt about the middle of the last century round a genuine Tudor core. It stands in a large park with two lakes and a stream. Fragments of the west window of Norwich Cathedral may be seen by the end of the lake near the house. They probably date from the time when the cathedral was being restored in the middle of the last century. More than 300 years earlier, before most of the present hall was built, the tragic Nine-Days Queen, Lady Jane Grey, spent her childhood at the old hall.

At the end of the eighteenth and beginning of the nineteenth century Ketteringham Hall was the home of a beautiful and romantic lady known in France as Milady Atkyns. She was a former star of Drury Lane theatre, and became an intimate friend of Marie Antoinette, for whom she risked her life during the French Revolution. Mrs Atkyns was a Scarlet Pimpernel of real life, not a mere character in a bestseller, but she attempted to save royalty, not just aristocrats, and though unsuccessful in such ambitious schemes, she risked her life and spent her husband's fortune in trying to save the queen and the dauphin of France.

She was Irish by birth, but was said to be a distant connection of the famous Norfolk family, the Walpoles. As Charlotte Walpole she entertained the public by her singing, dancing and acting on the stage at Smock Alley in Dublin, and she was recommended to the great dramatist, Sheridan, who was stage manager at Drury Lane. The immortal David Garrick had retired but kept an eye on things at the theatre, and Charlotte no doubt benefited from the advice of the maestro. After a few minor roles she made a hit in the early months of 1778, as Wilhelmina, a Dutch girl, singing and dancing (in clogs) in *The Waterman*. With her Irish brogue and her vivacity she repeated her success as Widow Brady in *The Irish Widow*. In the autumn she was the leading lady in *The Camp*. In the part of Nancy of the Dale she disguised herself as a recruit in order to be with her lover. Military uniform seemed to suit her.

Edward Atkyns, the rich young lord of Ketteringham

manor, was enjoying life in London, and became a regular patron of the plays in which Miss Walpole appeared. He was her most fervent admirer and they spent much time together. At the height of her success she gave up her stage career and they were married in June, 1779. After the honeymoon they settled down at Ketteringham. The ladies of the local county families were keen to meet the stage star, but they soon satisfied their curiosity, and then ceased to treat her as one of themselves. The birth of a son and heir in 1783 was celebrated by the tenantry and must have been some consolation to the former actress for the snobbish behaviour of the Norfolk aristocrats.

In 1785 Charlotte met an old friend of Drury Lane days, Mrs Robinson, 'the exquisite Perdita', who had been the mistress of the Prince of Wales, and had been abandoned by him. On a visit to Paris, Mary Robinson had attracted the attention of the romantic queen, Marie Antoinette, and had given her the locket which she herself had had from the prince. Mrs Atkyns' imagination was captured by what she heard about the glittering life at the French court, and she persuaded her husband to take a villa at Versailles. Charlotte was invited to meet the queen and soon became her intimate friend, spending most of her time at Marie Antoinette's special palace, 'Le Petit Trianon'. The queen was fond of amateur theatricals, and often took parts of servant maids and confidantes. Charlotte's experience at the leading London theatre probably gave a professional touch to the production of the plays at the private royal theatre, and she was honoured by being made a Queen's Pensioner.

The frivolity of Versailles was abruptly ended by the events of the Revolution, and in 1789 the royal family were forced to move to Paris by the action of a revolutionary mob. The Atkynses could not accompany them, but remained in France, living at Lille. The husband must have felt neglected for a considerable time, and his wife soon had an affaire with a handsome young officer, Louis, Chevalier de Frotté, who remained her devoted admirer for many years. Perhaps it was through some mood of retaliation that Edward Atkyns became the father of an illegitimate son, born in Lille in March, 1791.

By this time Louis de Frotté had been transferred with his regiment to Dieppe. At the time of the king and queen's flight to Varennes (which led to them being brought back as prisoners) the chevalier and his brother officers slipped over the border to join royalist supporters in the Netherlands. Later he was to be one of the chief leaders of the underground forces against the Revolution, the 'Chouans' of north-west France, till he was ambushed, captured and shot early in 1800.

Mr and Mrs Atkyns returned to Ketteringham, but Charlotte was soon in touch with French émigrés in London, especially Jean Jacques Peltier who had started the first French royalist paper in London. She induced him to find agents in Paris to try to rescue the king and queen from the Temple prison. At first he attempted to get in touch with two former servants of the king, who knew the two physicians attending him. But the two servants had prudently made themselves scarce. Then Peltier employed the services of a clever international spy, the Baron d'Auerweck, and paid his expenses. About the same time Mrs Atkyns chartered three patrol ships to hover near the French coast, dodge revolutionary vessels and pick up fugitives, agents and despatches from France.

The execution of Louis XVI was a blow to the hopes of the plotters. Marie Antoinette was removed to the Conciergerie and separated from her son, the dauphin. Mrs Atkyns was determined to see the widowed queen, and at great personal risk she slipped into France and got to Paris. Through her paid agents and by liberal bribes she actually managed two interviews with her royal friend. In the first, she was disguised in military uniform again, as in her acting days, but this time in the loose-fitting dress of a National Guardsman, and she was allowed to take the prisoner a bunch of flowers. But inside the bouquet was a note, which was certainly not allowed. When she entered the cell and saw the humble circumstances of the queen (her possessions were in cardboard boxes) and when she saw the white hair and the thin, pale face of the woman she idolized she was so overcome that she fainted and dropped the flowers. The note fell out! But she recovered in a flash, grabbed up the bouquet, snatched the note and put it in her mouth. Fortunately the gendarme on duty had seen nothing untoward, and she was hustled out, leaving the prisoner mystified.

Nothing daunted, Charlotte expended more money and got a pass for a private interview with the queen. She probably intended to persuade her to change clothes and escape, while her devoted admirer faced the consequences. The interview was held, and must have been an emotional one. Marie Antoinette refused any immediate chance of freedom for herself, and begged her old friend to try to rescue the dauphin instead.

Some time after the female 'pimpernel' had returned to England the queen she had sought to save went bravely to her death amid the execrations of the blood-thirsty mob. It was a sad, but not unexpected blow for her admirer at Kettering-ham. To add to the depression Mr Atkyns died of consumption in 1794. Charlotte kept in touch with agents in Paris and schemed and lavishly poured out money in attempts to organize the rescue of the dauphin from the Temple prison. The poor child was made to sing revolutionary songs. After a while the victim was confined in a room with the shutter fastened, no light but candles, and food passed through a grill. After six months of this solitary confinement he was unable to talk coherently. Some supposed that the prisoner was a deaf mute who had somehow been substituted for the dauphin, and that the real prince was concealed somewhere else in the building. Charlotte's agents had written of success though they attributed it to others, and General Paul Barras, who succeeded Robespierre as strong man of the Revolution, may have favoured a secret substitution in the expectation of personal benefit if the son of Louis XVI ever became king.

If any agents of Mrs Atkyns, or other schemers, did get the real dauphin out of his cell they did not succeed in conveying him to sympathizers abroad. The prisoner in the Temple

died on June 8th, 1795. Most of the royalists, even the
Chevalier de Frotté, swore allegiance to Louis XVI's brother, but Charlotte was convinced that the real dauphin was
still alive – somewhere in France. In September 1799 she
again crossed the Channel, this time probably disguised on
the voyage as a sailor in order to avoid being shot as a spy if
captured at sea. But she disembarked safely and made her
way to Paris once more. It was either as a secret agent of the
British government, or on a private attempt to locate the little
prince, that she spent the winter in the city. By March she
had roused the suspicions of the secret police, under their
notorious leader, Fouché. In the neighbourhood of her
lodgings questions were being asked about her movements,
so she resumed her male impersonation act, and as James
Bruce, citizen of the United States, she left her rooms and
managed to get on a coach travelling to the north. She was
sheltered in Anjou by friends she had known in Lille. She
tried to get an interview with Jean-Marie Hervagault, who
claimed to be the dauphin, but he had been arrested and
transferred to a fortress before she could see him.

She returned to Ketteringham after two and a half years in
France. Her father died in March 1803, and her only son,
Edward, barely reached his majority before dying from the
same complaint as his father, in November, 1804.

Charlotte won great notoriety as 'the brazen widow' in the
disputed election of 1806. The two Whig candidates, Thomas William Coke, the famous agriculturalist and 'Weath-
ercock' Windham, Pitt's war minister (till 1801) were
opposed by the Tory, Colonel Woodhouse. The Atkyns
carriage was painted with the Tory colours, yellow and
purple, her horses had harness of the same colours, she
and her friend Mrs Berney dressed in fancy costumes of
yellow and purple and were attended by coachman and
footman in livery of yellow and purple. The gay equipage
lent colour and excitement to the streets of Norwich as the
two ladies canvassed for the colonel. The riff-raff on the
opposition side did not greet them with silence or politeness,
and the Press referred to 'the brazen-faced widows'. The

climax came when, after a few days, opponents burlesqued
them with an old crock of a coach, drunken drivers, ber-
ibboned carthorses and two notorious strumpets decked out
in the election colours. The mock coach was attacked by
Tory supporters on Castle Hill and wrecked. After such
riotous scenes the two Whigs were duly elected. It was said
that the three candidates had spent £70,000 between them on
the election. That was not the end of the affair, for on a
petition of corrupt practice, the victors were unseated and a
new election had to be held. Mrs Atkyns did not make an
exhibition of herself this time.

In 1810 there were great celebrations at Ketteringham for
George III's Golden Jubilee and two young oak trees were
planted in the park.

Charlotte adopted as her heir, her godson, Edward Atkyns
Walpole. He was her father's nephew and his widowed
mother had recently remarried. The heir could not expect
a wealthy heritage as the estate had been mortgaged and the
money spent in the attempts to help the French royal family.

When Napoleon's rule came to an end and Louis XVI's
brother reigned as Louis XVIII (the dauphin being counted
as Louis XVII), she spent anxious years in France trying to
obtain repayment of all the money she had spent in her
efforts to save Marie Antoinette and her son. The new
monarch recognized her service to his family, but there
was a host of other loyalists clamouring for rewards and
recompense, and the French claimants got priority. Charlotte
did receive some small amount, but if the dauphin were to be
found alive, his uncle would lose his crown, and as long as she
persisted in believing it possible, Louis XVIII in his own
interest was against her. She refused to accept the story of the
death of the dauphin and the king refused to accept her claim
for expenses on behalf of the dauphin. When Charles X
succeeded his brother, the position was the same, and more
promises and delays were all she ever got in answer to her
further claims.

In 1817 there were two Pretenders claiming to be the
dauphin. The first, an American, Bruneau, paid the penalty

for his claim by being given five years' imprisonment, and she visited him in his cell. The second pretender, a Berlin watchmaker, had some intimate documents of Louis XVI. It was afterwards thought that the papers had been concealed in the king's chair in prison. The royal valet had obtained the chair and presented it to the Prince Regent, who had given it to the Duke of Cumberland. He took it to Berlin and it was sent for repair to an upholsterer, who discovered the documents and gave them to Nauendorff. On the strength of these papers he made his claim to the throne of France. Charlotte probably came to the conclusion that he was a fake, but she never gave up hope that the real prince would be found.

She had another grave disappointment in 1824 when her adopted son decided to go with his mother and stepfather to Australia. Mrs Atkyns made over the estate to her sister-in-law in return for an annuity, and was allowed to continue her residence at Ketteringham, but she returned to France when her mother died. She was in touch with yet another Pretender after the revolution of 1830. Eventually she died in 1836, and it was fitting that her end came in Paris, the city where so many important events in her life had occurred. By her will she desired that her body should be brought to Ketteringham for burial, but she was buried in the French capital, and her grave is unknown. Long, long afterwards, Frederic Barbey, an author, came across a bundle of letters labelled 'Milady Charlotte Atkyns' in a lawyer's office in France, and the fascinating story of the 'Scarlet Pimpernel' of real life was at last made known.

Sarah Emma Edmonds (1842–98)

Heroine of the American Civil War

Sarah Emma Edmonds claimed that the source of her inspiration to become the most famous woman soldier in the American Civil War was a 'penny-dreadful' novel, *Fanny Campbell*, or *The Female Pirate Captain*, in which – like her – the heroine escaped from the clutches of a cruel and dictatorial father. She was still only a teenager when she took on the disguise of a man – cutting her hair, changing her clothes and emerging as Franklin Thompson, Bible salesman. Starting in 1861, Sarah served for two years in the Second Michigan Infantry Regiment before leaving the army and once again assuming a female role. In 1867 she married her childhood sweetheart, Linus Seelye, raised a family, and wrote a best-selling biography about her life, *Nurse and Spy in the Union Army*. She died in Texas in 1898, but three years later her body was moved to a place of honour in the Washington Cemetery, Houston. **Julie Wheelwright** examines Sarah Edmonds' adventurous life and, in particular, a series of remarkable and very revealing letters between her and another soldier, Jerome Robbins . . .

The American Civil War's most famous female soldier, Emma Edmonds, claimed after her retirement from the army that her inspiration to take up arms came from a nascent understanding of her oppression as a woman. But along with her 'hatred of male tyranny' she remembered being struck forcefully by the imaginative power of a character in a favourite childhood book. Dreaming of escape from drudgery and her father's volatile temper, Emma turned to her heroine, a female pirate, for hope.

Fanny Campbell, female pirate captain, blue stocking and bold saviour of deserving men, graces the frontispiece of Lieutenant Murray's 1815 novel. The intrepid heroine stands defiantly on the wood-planked deck of her ship gazing out into some foreign sea. She grasps a black flag embossed with a skull and cross bones in her left hand and in her right she sports a menacing sabre that reaches to the floor in a graceful arch. The captain's hips are hidden beneath a short but modest skirt, a hint of short curls adorns her peacock-feather hat and frames the delicate features of her face. Her lips are touched with the faintest hint of a smile.

Murray succeeded in creating an appealing figure. So thought teenaged Emma Edmonds, who surreptitiously read the novel on a spring day when she should have been planting potatoes with her sister on the family farm in Prince William parish, New Brunswick in 1854. Emma's copy of *Fanny Campbell or the Female Pirate Captain* was a gift from her mother. It was the first novel Emma had ever read and she felt honoured that of her four sisters, she the youngest, had been the recipient of this kind gesture. Unlike Emma, her heroine Fanny's parents spared no expense in educating their daughter – hers was a life of writing poetry rather than planting potatoes. But Fanny was no effete intellectual. She was equally adept at rowing a boat, shooting a panther or riding the wildest horse in the state. She wrote thoughtful prose and her friends respected her talents as a scholar. 'Fanny Campbell was none of your modern belles, delicate and ready to faint at the first sight of a reptile,' wrote Murray, 'No, Fanny could . . . do almost any brave and useful act.'

Thirteen-year-old Emma was delighted with the novel and intoxicated by the simple ingenuity of Fanny's disguise; with just a blue sailor's jacket, breeches, a haircut shorn of her long, brown curls she stepped 'into the freedom and glorious independence of masculinity'. While Emma scorned Fanny's low ambition to masquerade merely to rescue her lover William Lowell, the heroine's ability to transcend her femininity seemed, to her, touched with genius. As the realization that Fanny's adventure lay open to her as well, Emma tossed her straw hat in the air and let a lusty cry of sheer delight ring out into the surrounding fields – salvation was hers. 'All the latent energy of my nature was aroused and each exploit of the heroine thrilled me to my fingertips . . . I was emancipated! and could never again be a *slave*.' As she crossed the fields home that evening she plotted that, one day, she would emulate Fanny's brilliant scheme. Like many of her fellow female warriors, a longing to escape was the central theme of her early life.

While still in her teens, Emma became a partner of Miss Henrietta Perrige in a Moncton millinery store, giving her some degree of independence from her tyrannical father. But her moment for escape came when he announced her impending engagement to a local farmer. She consented to the engagement but only 'in obedience to orders' and covertly planned her escape. *Fanny Campbell* was a novel of her youth but at the age of nineteen Emma self-consciously followed her heroine's plot and 'unceremoniously left for parts unknown' in male clothing.

She began a new life as Frank Thompson selling family bibles door-to-door for a publishing house in Hartford, Connecticut. During her transition from Emma to Frank she ventured out canvassing the good book only by night and sleeping in the woods by day until she became accustomed to her new identity. Frank began selling bibles 'in earnest' only when New Brunswick was a safe distance behind her. She settled in Flint, Michigan for a year where she lived in the home of Reverend Mr Joslin, a Methodist pastor. She sold her books in the surrounding area with great success and spent her free time taking her lady-friends on country rides in her stylish, horse-drawn buggy. Her friend Damon Stuart, who knew her first as Frank Thompson, described 'him' as, 'glib of tongue, thoroughly business-like, and had an open persuasive manner that was particularly attractive'.

She returned to visit her mother in New Brunswick after a year. She recounted in 1883 that her family had failed to recognize her when she ate supper with them, although when she stepped into the barn, the farm animals greeted her. 'My mother,' she said, 'looking up through a mist of tears asked my sister, "Fanny, don't you think this young man looks like your poor sister?" ' Emma then burst into tears and was forced to prove her identity before her mother would accept her miraculous transformation. But her visit was brief because she feared encountering her father and she left that afternoon.

Frank Thompson, 'after a strange catastrophe', lost all her worldly possessions except a bible which she sold for five dollars to see her through to Hartford, Connecticut. Frank then found work with a publishing company selling books in Nova Scotia. Her sales throughout the province were highly successful, clearing $900 in ten months. While on the road she stayed in good houses, ate well and 'came near marrying a pretty little girl who was bound I should not leave Nova Scotia without her'. During this period Frank Thompson was buoyed with confidence and recalled later: 'Oh how manly I felt; and what pride I took in proving (to my employers) that their confidence in me was not misplaced.' But Frank left 'his' sweetheart in Halifax for the lures of the West and returned to Michigan at the beginning of the American Civil War.

On 12 April 1861 Confederate forces fired upon Fort Sumter and President Abraham Lincoln swiftly called for 75,000 military recruits. Five days later Frank Thompson enlisted in a local militia unit that was accepting men for the second Michigan volunteers. While living in Flint, Frank had befriended William Morse, captain of the Flint Union Greys and enlisted in time to attend a mass meeting and to help choose its officers – Morse among them. The Greys' departure was marked by a parade of the 'boys' and an address from Morse. Each soldier was ceremoniously presented with a bible courtesy of the Methodist Episcopal church, the Flint ladies pinned a rosette inscribed, 'The Union and The Constitution' on each volunteer and Reverend Joslin pronounced the benediction.

The reasons for Emma Edmonds' decision to enlist remain obscured by her own writing on the subject. In her autobiography, *Nurse and Spy in the Union Army*, she recounted ironically that she was working for a foreign missionary society when war broke out. As a Canadian she could easily have returned home but instead turned to 'the Throne of Grace' for advice. Her prayers directed her to sign up as a field nurse for the Union army. In her autobiography, however, she carefully veils the fact that she was actually disguised as a man when she joined the Greys and she never acknowledges Frank's previous existence. Although religious moral conviction as the sole motive for enlisting wears slightly thin, her story is typical of many female soldiers.

Emma is vague about her childhood yearning for freedom that led to her initial metamorphosis into Frank. Quite possibly she thought her readers would be less sympathetic toward a woman whose decision to join up was stimulated more by a need to perpetuate her deception than to fight for the Unionist cause. The first edition of *Nurse and Spy*, published in 1865 while the war was still raging, has the quality of a polemic. Emma's adventures are seen through the lens of patriotic sacrifice rather than feminine liberation. Though the warrior heroine was well-known in balladry and in popular literature in Britain and the US during this period, none of these heroines openly declared Edmonds 'dormant antagonism' towards male tyranny. Even Emma Edmonds' earlier incarnation as Frank and her proto-feminist statements came to light years after her Civil War experience when she spoke from the perspective of wife and mother. But the published testimony of her enlistment, her motives and their later popular representations and misrepresentations shed much light on the warriors' experience.

What Emma Edmonds shares with her fellow female combatants is her sense that, like Fanny Campbell, she too could grasp 'the freedom and glorious independence of masculinity'. Like those women who went before and after, she sensed that donning trousers, a transformation as simple as changing a suit of clothes, would transport her to another, more privileged, world. Shorn of their long, flowing locks and no longer encumbered by stays, bodices, skirts and petticoats these women discovered new freedom of movement. They shed any concern for their appearance along with their feminine modesty. In shirts and breeches they strode forward, capable of expressing themselves in ways they had only dreamed about. As late as 1929 clothing still carried such significant value that this miraculous shift was convincingly made. No audience had difficulty believing that clothing, literally, made the man.

One of the most fascinating records of friendship is revealed in the correspondence of Emma Edmonds and another Civil War soldier, Jerome Robbins. Throughout the war Jerome Robbins of the Second Michigan Infantry Regiment kept a detailed diary of his army experiences. On 30 October 1861 Jerome, then assistant surgeon, refers to his friend Frank Thompson (Emma Edmonds) who also worked at the regimental hospital. The friendship blossomed over the following weeks as Jerome found Frank an entertaining conversationalist, 'a good noble-hearted fellow' and a keen intellectual companion. Together they attended prayer meetings, took long walks and on 7 November Jerome noted that he 'arose greatly refreshed after a sound sleep in a couch with my friend Frank'. Soon after Jerome's intimacy with Frank prompted him to write: 'The society of a friend so pleasant as Frank I hail with joy though foolish as it may seem a great mystery appears to be connected with him which it is impossible for me to fathom.' Despite his unease, which Jerome brushed off as 'false surmise', the friendship grew. The soldiers shared a deep religious conviction and their work kept them in close contact, occasionally filling in for each other or staying up to talk on night duty in the hospital.

Only two weeks later, after a 'long and interesting conversation' with Frank, Jerome returned to his quarters and wrote in his crabbed hand, 'my friend Frank is a female'. Jerome was distraught, not from any moral conviction that women had no place in the army, but from his sense of personal betrayal. A more than platonic love for 'his' stalwart companion may have prompted Frank to reveal 'his' true identity. When Jerome spoke about his intended bride, Anna Corey, Frank volunteered an explanation for 'his' decision to leave New Brunswick in male disguise and to join the army. Frank Thompson had enlisted in the Union Greys on 17 April 1861 and Jerome was probably the first person, after eight long months of subterfuge, to learn his friend's secret.

Contrary to all Emma Edmonds' published accounts about her life as Frank, Jerome Robbins states in his diary that she left her home town, Mandan, New Brunswick because of an ill-fated love affair with Thomas, a local merchant. 'My friend describes him as pleasing in manner and so won her heart as to cause the object of love to be nearly worshipped,' wrote Robbins. 'But a change came; her lover seemed cold, reserved and exacting, which was too much for the nature of my friend.' The lovers separated, Emma became seriously ill with scarlet fever and after several weeks languishing in bed, she recovered and abruptly left Canada. Emma possibly invented this story because she doubted that Jerome Robbins would believe anything else but it is equally plausible that her lover did exist. She would wisely have left the mysterious Thomas out of her published and self-censored autobiographies that fashioned her into a more conventionally acceptable war heroine. According to her own account Emma left home when her brutal father forced her into an engagement with an odious farmer and, inspired by the lively heroine of Lieutenant Murray's novel, *Fanny Campbell or the Female Pirate Captain*, she took on a new identity as Frank.

The story so far adds another dimension to Emma's own words that her alias allowed her to escape from an unhappy home life. There is no reason to doubt Jerome Robbins' record of this conversation since he carefully protected Emma's confession from accidental discovery. Jerome gummed together the pages for this entry and wrote across the top, 'please allow these leaves to be closed until author's permission is given for their opening'. Jerome kept his friend's secret throughout the remainder of his diary, never mentioned the conversation but always referred to Frank in the masculine pronoun. Though Jerome burned with resentment about Frank's deception he still regarded the friendship 'as one of the greatest events of my life'.

Despite this assurance, however, Jerome Robbins found a replacement for an increasingly surly Frank. On 6 December his moody companion watched as Jerome had 'another long conversation with Russell in which he expressed to me the deepest friendship that even a brother could not'. Two weeks later Jerome wrote of Frank: 'I am little fearful our natures are not as congenial as at first supposed by me yet I feel he is the same friend.' For the next few weeks the friendship appeared to deteriorate, Jerome noting that Frank, 'acts strangely', and was 'very much out of humour'. He suggested that Frank might be jealous of Jerome's fiancée and wrote, 'Perhaps a knowledge on her part that there is one Michigan home that I do regard with especial affection creates her disagreeable manner.'

At the end of December 1861 Frank left Camp Scott to nurse at an army camp in Alexandria. According to Jerome, Frank left because of constant teasing about 'his' feminine appearance from a cook and other men in the camp. But when they met again a year later in Alexandria, they resumed a warm friendship. They continued their evening walks, often discussing religion, nursed each other when sick, swapped magazines, stories and on 14 February Frank, Jerome and another soldier shared a 'pretty, warm berth' on a cabin floor. When Frank failed to pay a visit for a few days, Robbins wrote, 'I feel quite lonely without him.' One evening Frank came to visit when Jerome was out but left a note between two pages of Robbin's journal saying that 'he' had read it 'for spite'. Such was their intimacy that Jerome was amused rather than angry about his friend's disregard for privacy.

But on 16 April 1863 Frank deserted the army at Lebanon, Kentucky and soon after Lieutenant James Reid of the 79th New York Volunteers, followed. Throughout that spring Jerome made note of Frank's 'particular friend', Reid, who was 'a fine fellow and seems very fond of Frank'. Although Jerome knew his friend planned to leave, he felt cheated and deceived when it happened. 'He did not prepare me for his ingratitude,' wrote Robbins '. . . to repay kindness, interest and the warmest sympathy with deception [is] the petty attribute of a selfish heart.' Reading between the lines of Robbins' journal it is clear that he was smitten with jealousy and wrote on 4 April while nursing Frank through an illness: 'It is a sad reality to which we awaken when we learn that others are receiving the devotion of one from whom we only claim friendship's attention.'

This was not, however, the end of Jerome's friendship with Frank. During the last two years of the war they corresponded and in Emma's letters she reveals her affection for Robbins. A month after leaving the army she wrote from Washington, D C: 'Oh Jerome, *I do miss you so much*. There is no person living whose presence would be so agreeable to me this afternoon as yours.' Two years later Emma still addressed her friend wistfully. 'I daily realize that had I met you some years ago I might have been much happier now,' she wrote from a camp in Falmouth, Virginia. 'But providence ordered it otherwise and I must be content.' Reid told Emma that he and Jerome had discussed her which prompted her to ask Robbins: 'I want you to write me the import of [that conversation]. Will you please do so? [Reid] says he wants me to come and visit his wife who is very anxious to see me.'

There is very little evidence of Emma's relationship with Reid but if she was in love with him, it must have been an excruciating situation. Her relationship with Reid jeopar-

dized her position in the regiment and her friendship with
Jerome. Her affair with a married man appears quite contradictory to her Christian principles and was probably the
source of vicious rumours that she later took pains to quell in
her published life-history. In *Nurse and Spy* and other
autobiographical accounts Emma left the army because she
was seriously ill with malaria and only then because a request
for a leave of absence was denied. But in reality her relationship with Reid may have become uncomfortably public and
since Robbins says that Frank prepared him for 'his' eventual
departure it was probably not spontaneous.

Apparently Reid and Robbins were not the only men who
knew Emma's secret. William Boston also of the Second
Michigan regiment wrote in his diary on 22 April 1863: 'Our
brigade postmaster turns out to be a girl and has deserted
when his lover Inspector Read [sic] and [General O.M.] Poe
resigned.' Several years later Poe was willing to testify that
'her sex was not suspected by me or anyone else in the
regiment,' although he alludes to her fear of detection as
the reason for her desertion. Her comrades' extraordinary
loyalty in keeping her secret [in Poe's case to help her get a
pension] suggests her fellow-soldiers' acceptance of a woman
in the ranks. Emma was an exception but one who had
'proven' herself in battle and in the camp, working tirelessly
in the hospital. When Robbins discovered Emma's secret
there was no mention of turning her in or divulging her secret
to a commanding authority. Even Poe and Reid – both
officers – accepted her presence. It is only later, public
accounts of her story that wrestle with questions about a
woman's appropriate role on the battle field.

Jerome Robbins' documentation of his relationship with
Emma Edmonds reveals the complex inner workings of a
double identity. Jerome struggles to make sense of his conflicting feelings for Emma as a woman *and* as a comrade in
arms. He implies that Emma too yearns for more than a
platonic relationship and the opportunity for physical intimacy – the nights they shared a warm berth – presented
itself. Their mutual interest in religion may have provided a

space where their corporeal conflict was felt less keenly. It remains surprising to a contemporary audience that Robbins' reaction to Emma's confession is confusion about his friendship with her and anger at her deception while he is unconcerned with the gender issues that figure so large in public discussion of women in war.

Constance Markievicz (1868–1927)

On the Run with 'The Red Countess'

Countess Constance Markievicz, nee Connie Gore-Booth, was the Irish nationalist politician known as 'Madame' or 'The Red Countess'. A noted society beauty in her youth, she was initially involved in the cultural and national renaissance in Ireland, but then driven on by her convictions became an active participant in the 1913 Dublin Strike and 1916 Easter Rising. She commanded 120 Republican soldiers and became a familiar figure in her green Irish Citizens' Army uniform. When surrendering, Constance struck a symbolic pose by kissing her revolver before handing it over. She was condemned to death for her activities, but this was subsequently commuted to life imprisonment. After the 1917 amnesty, the Countess stood as an MP for a Dublin constituency, but refused to go to Westminster, preferring to be involved in the armed struggle. She was repeatedly imprisoned and went on hunger strikes – all events which established her as one of the heroines of Ireland. She is represented here by a series of letters written in 1919 to her sister, the poet Eva Gore-Booth, while 'on the run' from the British authorities. They speak more eloquently about the woman and her ideals than any short biography.

Undated.
'On the Run.'

Darling – I was so glad to hear from you. What on earth is the meaning of their latest move? It's such a funny selection. Old Kelly always describes himself as a 'Man of Peace', and it is an admirable description. Irwine is quite unknown to most people.

Was it not lucky that I was away? I hear that Mrs. C— asked to see the warrant and that the detective in charge said there was none. She then asked what I was charged with and they said they did not know. They had orders to arrest me and that was all. There were some police and a lorry-load of soldiers and they searched the house to her amusement. She made them look everywhere and waste a lot of time! If you see Cecil, you might try and find out with what awful crime I am charged this time! It's enough to make any one curious.

I've a sort of feeling that it may mean strained relations with America and nothing more. We have created a delightful situation in America for the enemy, thank God! G—'s return with his tail between his legs is rather significant. It was wonderful, when you come to think of it, how few were caught. Of course we are on the run most of the time, and no one who respects themselves lives much in their homes.

Wasn't it a shame to stop the Aonach? It was just a fair and nothing more: you hire a stall and sell. Shopkeepers and industries count on making a nice few pounds, and manufacturers hope to get Irish goods on the market through it. It was political to the extent that it is organised to help Irish industry and trade to hold their own against English, German, or any other foreign industry or agencies. It gets customers for the shops that are willing to put themselves out in their efforts to help their country's struggling industries. Of course this is treason, as the enemy wish all Irish men and women to emigrate or starve. M— attributed all the trouble in Ireland to the stoppage of emigration during the War.

I believe the English are trying to goad us into another rebellion, so as to murder a large number of intelligent and brave patriots. Everything that is done points that way, but I hope that the country is too well in hand for anything of the sort to occur. The people are wonderfully steadfast, under the most ridiculous persecution and provocation. No one knows at what moment they may be arrested on some vague charge, and any house may be raided at any moment. The police are employed entirely as an army of occupation, and I believe that there are several gangs of English thieves making themselves very busy. This does not of course get into the papers, but our own crowd are constantly held up and robbed, both in their houses and on the streets.

One of T—'s sisters married Sean M— the other day, and as they were going home one night last week from her people's house in Brunswick Street to Queen's Square, they saw two soldiers and a civilian hold up a man with revolvers. They ran! The robbers had white handkerchiefs over the lower part of their faces. Next day they found that quite a lot of people had been stopped and relieved of their watches, money and jewelry. This is an everyday occurrence just now, and invariably some of the assailants are soldiers. It is generally supposed that Barton the detective was shot by one of these gangs, as he was employed for years in hunting down the cross-channel thieves, but of course it's put down as a 'Sinn Fein Outrage'.

No one can see any sense in the motor-permit Order, except to cripple Irish trade. Motors have been very little used by us, except in Elections: we have not the money! Of course, S.F. traders can be hit that way and their businesses ruined. All this fuss may be to upset our organizations for the elections, and to prevent our people in the slums learning the intricacies of P.R., but I don't think that the enemy will gain much. The situation appeals to the imagination of the people, and they love the excitement. They are not afraid and they have a great sense of humour. It gives them endless joy when they outwit 'the Hun', and vast and pompous military raids result in the arrest of two harmless pacifists.

How is your health? I hope that you are none the worse for your exertions during my visit.

I am going to keep quiet for a bit and then dodge them and go about as usual, as there is much to be done.

                                        'Somewhere in Ireland.'
Beloved Old Darling, – I have succeeded in getting *Ossian* at last: it was evidently second-hand, as it was cut. P. S. O'Hegarty has been looking for it since before I was on the run. Awfully funny things are happening, and we manage to have many a good laugh. The enemy raided Mrs. F— and found only two women in the house. They tried to terrorize her into telling them where her husband was. In the middle of the altercation the lights went out. It was a penny-in-the-slot machine. The officer ordered her to put in a penny. She refused point-blank. 'Put it in yourself,' she said, and she watched them relighting the gas. They went away empty-handed, the officer saying that they would get him in spite of her.

                                             'On the Run.'
A thousand thanks for your letter and lovely gift, which actually got to me in time! I was delighted and overjoyed and surprised. It's wonderful to have a birthday 'on the run'. It's an awfully funny experience. Mrs C. will tell you some of it.

I spoke five times for various women in the elections and had some very narrow shaves. At one place I spoke for Joan, and they sent an army, just about an hour too late. At another, I wildly and blindly charged through a squad of armed police, sent there to arrest me, and the crowd swallowed me up and got me away. The children did the trick for me.

Of course I don't keep quiet, and the other night I followed some of the Army of Occupation round about the streets. They had a huge covered waggon, and they seized some fellows and put them inside and searched them. They charged the crowd with bayonets too, and children were knocked down and terrified and women too.

Shawn and some boys were held up by detectives last night when they were leaving the public library. One of them said he thought there was a detective watching the people reading, when two men stepped past them and poked revolvers at them through their pockets, in the American way, and said that they were talking of them, and demanded to know what they were saying. Of course they just humbugged, and the two men finally moved away.

'On the Run.'

You were an angel to send me such an interesting parcel. Thank you so much, and Esther too, for the book.

I sent a hamper between the two of you. I hope you got it alright. I had to get someone to choose the contents, as I was taking no risks before Christmas, as I did so want to have one at liberty. I told them to put in a turkey for Esther and other carnivorous friends!

It is awfully funny being 'on the run'! I don't know which I resemble most: the timid hare, the wily fox, or a fierce wild animal of the jungle!

I go about a lot, one way and another, and every house is open to me and everyone is ready to help.

I fly round town on my bike for exercise, and it is too funny seeing the expression on the policemen's faces as they see me whizz by! There are very few women on bikes in the winter, so a hunted beast on a bike is very remarkable.

Things are going ahead alright, so it does not much matter. People are subscribing to the Loan, in spite of, or perhaps because of, the fact that it has been made a jailable crime by the enemy.

I wonder how you are getting along and how you spent Christmas. I had *two* Christmas dinners at the two extremes of Dublin and had quite a cheery time, everyone congratulating me on not having been at home!

Poor Alderman K—! No one can understand why he was taken. He is a pacifist and he was never mixed up with anything violent. The housing of the poor and building up industries was his line. His nickname, given to him by himself, was 'the Man of Peace'. Some of them think that a 'plot' is being fabricated to prove that everyone who has been keeping rather quiet was engaged in secretly conspiring to shoot policemen! But I think that this is too absurd a lie, even for Ll— G—, M— and Co.! You can write to me at any friend's address or at Liberty Hall. I always keep in touch when I move around, and my letters get to me alright.

No date, no address.

Dearest Old Darling, – I was much relieved to read the list of things that S. wants! It does not look as if he were in any great straits to live! I had quite a happy laugh when I read the list of 'frivolities' that he wants. Evidently he can't be in serious want, or any real danger. Such a blessing! I doubt if one could get all he wants for £20! Of course he has no idea of prices. Do you think that anyone could be found to bring him sweets? Stockings, handkerchiefs and sweets and tobacco are the only things that would be practical to send. There is no use sending hats, gloves or shoes on chance. I can't get at any of his things at present, and I think it really would be folly to send him things like English novels just now. I fancy that the camera, handbag and footwear were all stolen. The clothes were all too small. He exchanged his cabin trunk for mine and it has vanished. Of course I will send him things in place of them in time, but just now seems rather a bad time. When I was on the Continent, English cameras were a great nuisance, for you could not get plates to fit and it would probably be better for him to get a French or German camera. Would not the person who takes clothes bring a business letter (open) just to tell him these things?

I am sorry, too, that there was no woman in the Albert Hall. I suppose that Mrs Skeff. could not get away. She is President of the Court of Conscience, Mrs Clark of the Children's Court, and Mrs Wyse Power Chairman of the Public Health Board, so the women have done well in the Corporation. It was very difficult to get women to stand for Municipal honours. It was part of our policy to run women. I could not get any woman to stand in either of the wards in S. Patrick's. I got Mrs Clark, who of course headed the poll, and Mrs M—, a stranger to them: but the Committee, mostly men, worked hard for her and it was given out that they had selected her because I was not qualified to stand myself, and more than all she is pleasant and has a good personality and the right kind of brains. But most of the people who got the votes got them because they were known personally to the voters, and men as well as women who were on our ticket did not get in, not being known.

Shawn is working hard to get into College, and Maeve herself is very busy. She seems quite fit and well and is looking lovely, though thin.

It is rather wearying when the English Man-Pack are in full cry after you, though I get quite a lot of fun out of it. Even the hunted hare must have a quiet laugh sometimes. You don't know what a joke it is sometimes to speak at meetings and get through with it in spite of their guns and tanks and soldiers and police. I had some very narrow shaves. The other night I knocked around with a raiding party and watched them insult the crowd. I was among the people and I went right up to the Store Street Police Barracks where the military and police lined up before going home. Night after night they wake people up and carry off someone, they don't seem to mind who. Some of the people they took lately did not belong to our crowd at all. When they could not find Mick S—, they took his old father, aged sixty, and his baby brothers!

Mrs C— had a very funny scene with them. They found a pair of socks in her old room and asked whose they were in a most insulting manner. Of course she gave it them hot! She wound up by saying that even Sinn Feiners occasionally put on clean stockings, when they still continued to believe that they were not her husband's. Of course I can't tell you how people escape and where they all are because of the Enemy's accursed spies who open our letters.

We all have very cheerful news from Dev. and we feel sure that we are at the end of the British tyranny over here.

Dorothy Lawrence (c.1890–1967)

The Sapper at the Front Line

Dorothy Lawrence came from a typical middle-class English family. But right from the days of her childhood, she was something of a rebel and bridled against the tradition that seemed to have her set on the road to marriage and child-rearing. For, above all else, Dorothy wanted to be a writer. The outbreak of the First World War seemed to her an ideal oportunity to further a career in journalism, so she simply disguised herself as a man and set off to write about life on the Western front. In 1915, 'Private Denis Smith' appeared in the midst of a British Expeditionary Force Tunnelling Company and initiated one of the most curious episodes of the entire war. **John Laffin** relates the story of Dorothy Lawrence and the promise she was forced to keep about her identity until the hostilities were over . . .

It might be thought that in a war which lasted from 1914 to the end of 1918, which involved so much fighting that more than 800,000 British soldiers were killed and which took place to a large extent only a few miles from England, a number of women might have found their way to the front disguised as soldiers. In fact, only one woman served as a soldier with the British army in France.

Among all the gallant nurses, ambulance drivers and others who were simply women in uniform doing jobs approved for women, this one woman soldier stands out as an oddity. And odder still is the little that is generally known about her.

Despite her almost obsessional desire to 'get to the front' it is difficult to find points of similarity between her and other women soldiers. She lived in an age when women were expected to know their place and to keep it, when warfare had become such a bloody business that parties of women no longer drove in coaches to vantage points to watch the thrills of a battle. (They had done this as late as the American Civil War.) And Miss Lawrence had to use a great deal of guile to get herself to the front.

Brought up in a middle-class family, Miss Lawrence first tried orthodox means of approaching battle. She managed to wangle introductions to editors and even to press proprietors, hoping to be employed as a war correspondent. But in the early days of the war there was no shortage of highly regarded and experienced correspondents, none of whom could get to the front themselves, because officialdom had decreed that all information would come through the Official Eyewitness. This was a measure as crude as it was stupid, despite the competence of the eyewitness himself, Lieutenant-Colonel Swinton.

Gone were the days when a Kit Cavanagh or an Emma Edmonds could simply don male clothing and be accepted into the Army. The medical inspection was now complete and every organ was examined, not so much to make sure that no woman got into the Forces as to ensure that no woman had got to the enlisting man. The Army was very conscious of what V.D. could do to an army. Lord Kitchener went so far as to warn his soldiers against having anything to do with women in France. Thus Dorothy Lawrence was forced to resort to stratagems never contemplated by earlier martially inclined women.

It was however fairly simple to get to Paris, even with a bicycle, which Miss Lawrence foresaw as an essential part of her equipment. In mid-1915, when she launched her operation, the French front line was a mere twenty miles from Paris, although earlier in the war it had been only fifteen miles distant, running through the town of Creil.

Miss Lawrence next cycled to Creil, which she made her base. She was not too conspicuous as some Frenchwomen had returned to it when the war moved a little way off and, indeed, there were some English nurses there. Being bilingual, she could fit into the background of either nationality. As a would-be reporter, she had many interesting conversations with the French soldiers who filled Creil. Some of their stories would have made fascinating reading, for these men had been in battle and were in the front line when not resting in rotation in the town. It was through her questioning that she realized that what she proposed to do would be difficult and that, if achieved, would be no picnic. But this only made her all the more determined.

Getting any further forward was virtually a physical impossibility. French police sealed off the forward area from the rear area, partly to prevent spies from getting too near the front, equally to stop troops from leaving without authorization. The French were very touchy and Dorothy, who was no fool, knew that it was not safe for her to stay in Creil. She could prove she was no spy, but she certainly could not escape bodily removal from the front.

Working on the well-tried theory that it is safer to seek authority before it seeks you, Miss Lawrence applied to the town hall for a pass to visit Senlis, which she estimated would be nearer the front. The theory worked once more and armed with her piece of paper Dorothy made for Senlis. But at Senlis she found the French very much more sensitive than in Creil. Gendarmes, military police and ordinary army patrols were everywhere, checking on anybody in the least suspicious. There had been a number of spy scares, a few genuine spies had been captured and authority was taking no chances. Officials told Dorothy Lawrence that the pass from Creil – which in any case they were reluctant to accept – entitled her to only two nights' stay. This forced her to act without proper preparation and when she cycled out of town towards the front she was arrested and escorted back to town. The French, in no mood for compromise, said that as she had broken the rules she must leave Senlis at once and return to Paris.

She made a show of riding away from the front, but when safely out of sight hid the bike in a shed and, taking rations, walked towards the front, hoping that the forest of Senlis would hide her approach. Englishwomen have long been renowned for what they can endure in adversity. In appallingly difficult times as widely separated as the Indian Mutiny and the Japanese invasion of Malaya they have survived by sheer courage and that unshakeable conviction of the Englishwoman abroad that she can outlast people of an 'inferior' race. But Miss Lawrence's venture into the forest of Senlis was self-determined and not an adversity decided by fate; perhaps this was one of the reasons she found the going very tough. The nights in the open were cold and damp, the days long, hot and tiring, and while a definite plan might have made the discomfort bearable Miss Lawrence soon realized that she must find some other way of reaching the front.

After forty-eight hours in the woods she returned to Paris where she set about planning her next move. By now she had accepted that to get into the war she must have a khaki disguise, something she might have realized sooner had she been more familiar with the stories of earlier women soldiers. However, unlike her predecessors, she could not obtain a uniform merely by enlisting, and was forced to cast around for help. Eventually, she met two private soldiers who had, as she said, 'the faces of clean-minded boys', and they agreed to supply her with what she wanted. Whether they were as clean minded as she supposed is another matter, for they said that when she first approached them, they took her for a prostitute. But, taking it all as a good joke, and apparently quite unaware of the risk they were running, they brought her every item of uniform she would need.

But once again there were difficulties not faced by earlier Amazons. A soldier already at the front would be expected to have had some training; at least he would be able to stand at attention when addressing a superior, to salute, to march, to know how to hold a rifle and so on. At training sessions in side-streets the two soldiers enjoyed themselves immensely teaching the girl how to get away with her deception.

There were still more difficulties. A modern soldier has a mass of documentation. The conspirators could do nothing about acquiring a paybook, but they did manufacture a leave pass of sorts, entitling 'Private Denis Smith' to be absent from his battalion, a Leicestershire formation, until some date late in August. Miss Lawrence now reported in person, as a woman, to the local town hall for a pass that would take her as close as possible to the front. She told the official who signed passes quite an elaborate story. First, she would take a train to Amiens, in the Somme region, then she would cycle to Bethune, further north, where she wished to visit a friend, and finally she would make for Calais *en route* to England. The official gained the impression that the Englishwoman planned to use her bicycle to avoid cluttering trains proceeding further northwards and this helped to make him more amenable to granting the pass.

At this point an unexpected hitch occurred, Miss Lawrence could not get a haircut. She could not ask a Parisian, or indeed any French barber, for a British army type basin-cut for fear that their imaginative suspicions would be aroused, and apparently her two assistants were either no longer available or could not be trusted to do a neat enough job. In the end she found a most unlikely helper – a Scottish military policeman! He not only gave her a competent haircut, but helped her aboard the train to Amiens. If he knew

what her brown paper parcels contained the knowledge
apparently did not bother him. But in Amiens, one of the
key towns of the Allied defensive system, the sight of a
strange woman did bother a gendarme and he was so difficult
and suspicious that Dorothy left town before anything
further happened.

She took the road north-east towards Albert. Even then
Albert was a famous town in British military history. In 1915
it was a key point in the British front line, though an
uncomfortable one, for German eyes observed it and German
guns opened up frequently. The road between Amiens and
Albert, therefore, was a major routeway and for much of the
distance was packed with military traffic of all kinds. At this
time, too, small parties of refugees were still trickling westwards out of danger. Dorothy Lawrence saw all this activity
with some dismay; she was so uninformed about the state of
the front – a tribute to security, perhaps – that she had
expected to find it serenely empty. Instead, she came upon
several French-manned posts whose duty it was to check
passes and credentials.

What the many soldiers on the road thought of the woman
on the bicycle heading *towards* the front, and what the
French guards thought when they examined her pass we
shall never know. They were reluctant to let her proceed, but
the French are peculiarly impressed with an official document and they allowed her to go on. If it seemed strange that
she was heading via Albert for Bethune and Calais they
shrugged and made no objection. Eventually she reached
the last French post, though she did not immediately appreciate that it was the last, and with even more reluctance
the Frenchmen passed her forward. She was, of course,
travelling now in her own name as an Englishwoman and
it is extremely likely that as this was the British front the
French sentries were much more tolerant than had she been
approaching the French front.

The traffic had so thinned out by now that Dorothy made
the last part of her journey in company with a lone soldier on
a horse. When they parted company she entered the ruined

town alone. It must have been an eerie and frightening moment, for Miss Lawrence realized as she saw the lonely wreckage that she was very close to the fighting. She had got through.

Then came sheer shock. 'Halt!' a Scottish voice said and she saw a bayonet levelled at her. Astonished to find a woman at the other end of the weapon, the soldier called his mates and several of them escorted her to the nearest officer.

Miss Lawrence saw at once that it was hopeless expecting to be able to make a deal with these private soldiers, and the officers who interviewed her, while courteous, were also unhelpful. Albert was an impossible place for a woman, they said. As it was nearly night it was also impossible for them to put her out, but in the morning she must go. After a shock – and being challenged by the sentry *was* a shock – a person is apt to make damaging admissions and Miss Lawrence was indiscreet enough to tell the officers that she was a reporter looking for stories. This not only appeared to give the lie to her pass – which the officers had examined – but obliged them to be all the more dutiful in reporting the presence of an Englishwoman at Albert. But for some reason they took no such action. Chivalry? A feeling that having come so far she deserved not to be penalized? Laxity? But when they provided breakfast for her the following morning they gave her no hope of further generosity. She must leave – westwards.

Disappointed, her ambitions obstructed at the last hurdle, Miss Lawrence cycled away, though not before a rough, woman-hungry soldier had attempted to molest her. It was not even possible for her to don her disguise, for all the soldiers she saw around her were kilted Scots. During the incident with the amorous soldier she met a smaller, conventionally uniformed soldier, one 189467 Sapper Tommy Dunn, from Lancashire, serving in a Tunnelling Company of the Royal Engineers. He was friendly and interested, and Dorothy Lawrence found him as pliable as her two earlier helpers. He was prepared to help her get into the trenches and was in a position to do it. Up to this point Dorothy Lawrence had not had any luck as such, but meeting and gaining the co-operation of an engineer of all soldiers was luck. Engineers and signallers were frequently detailed in small groups to carry out unattached duties; their badge and the duties that went with it gave them a freedom of movement denied mere infantry, cavalry or artillery. An engineer or a signaller could also legitimately be found at any part of the front, whereas it might be difficult for, say, a soldier of the Grenadier Guards to explain why he was the only member of his unit in an area defended by the Sussex Regiment. Similarly, it would be difficult for a man to claim he was a member of the regiment for a particular part of the line, for he could be asked which company and which platoon and the game would soon be up if he were an impostor. But nobody could point the finger of accusation at an engineer.

The sapper took Miss Lawrence back towards Albert and found a cellar in a wrecked house, where she changed into uniform. Presumably, it was at this point she bandaged her well-shaped breasts. Dunn meanwhile went off to scout for her, returning to suggest that she should lie low for the rest of the day. Despite her 'training' and the improbability of her being spotted he did not wholly believe that her disguise was good enough. He wanted her to stay in the ruins until he himself was a member of a party detailed for trench work, when he would be able to help her more actively.

Alone in the ruins that night Miss Lawrence was, in fact, under fire. Many shells burst around the area and fragments were continually falling into her immediate vicinity. Even spent rifle bullets thudded into the masonry. When she ventured to look out she could easily see the flashes of guns and of explosions, and signal flares bursting over the battle-field. As night edged into dawn she saw British troops moving forward and back. The ruins were uncomfortable in more ways than one, for they were crawling with lice. At one time a French civilian came into the place to use it as a latrine. As the girl was undressed and washing the moment was potentially disastrous, but she was able to cover her embarrassment and the man brought her some coffee. She lived in the rubble for a few days, before Sapper Dunn found himself detailed for forward trench duty at night. He collected Miss Lawrence, drew her into the party and pushed her in front of him as a sergeant gave the order for the mixed working party of engineers and infantrymen to move off. After a short distance in the open they entered a communications trench. The smell of war was here – the compound of sweat, fresh earth, cordite. The sounds were there too; the swearing and muttering of men jostling both ways in the trench, the *thunk* of tools in earth, the small noises of equipment. Dorothy Lawrence's senses took in everything; it was like a moment of destiny. In fact, destiny lasted about twelve nights.

Sticking close to Sapper Dunn, Dorothy Lawrence made herself busy with pick and shovel, as the men strengthened the trenches, dug new ones and did some mining. Nobody showed any interest in Miss Lawrence, which is not too surprising for men on a job of this kind at night have no energy or concentration to spare for small talk. They barely glance at their neighbours. But the woman found the going tough; for one thing she had little to eat, only whatever Sapper Dunn could contrive to bring her and sometimes that was very little. The cold ruins and the damp trenches brought on aches and pains. Probably because she was worried about how she could continue to stand the strain unless she could get more food and some bedclothing, Miss Lawrence now tried to expand her luck. She told Sapper Dunn she wanted to meet the engineer sergeant, so that she could ask his help. Would the sapper act as go-between, explain the situation to the sergeant and bring him to the hide-out? The imagination balks at the sergeant's immediate reaction on being told a woman had been working for him, but he agreed to meet her.

It takes a lot to startle a British sergeant and this one was matter-of-fact when he was introduced to the stranger in army uniform. Now that she was not attempting to pose as a man Miss Lawrence's femininity was obvious. He listened carefully to the woman's plea as she stressed that he would be doing nothing to be ashamed of in helping her, for she was a loyal Briton doing her bit for King and country. After a time the sergeant took his leave, making no promises but somehow leaving Miss Lawrence with the impression that he would help her. She was disillusioned and furious when he returned a few hours later to arrest her.

It is difficult to say if Sapper Dunn or Miss Lawrence was the more naive in expecting any NCO to cover up her presence in the line, but by her own account she felt that this particular one had betrayed her. The sergeant took her to the nearest regimental headquarters, where a lieutenant-colonel received her and reported her presence to Division, which in due course sent an Intelligence officer to escort the intruder to the rear. On the way to see General Rawlinson he suggested that a good way to keep out of this sort of unwomanly behaviour would be to marry.

In some ways the most extraordinary part of the whole incident now began. Kit Cavanagh and the others would have been astonished and amused at the fuss which now enveloped Dorothy Lawrence. The trouble was that nobody could accept the simple truth – that a curious woman wanted to see what war was like. Division felt the potato was too hot to hold and passed it on to Third Army H.Q. Senior Intelligence officers, the Judge Advocate's Department, the Provost Marshal, all were drawn into the developing web. At one time a board of three generals interviewed her. Being men, all these self-important soldiers had convinced themselves that this woman was the hub of some sinister espionage network. They could not believe that a woman would otherwise go to such lengths and endure so much knowing she could only land in so much more trouble. One officer did point out sagely that no woman, other than a really desperate or dedicated spy, would go to the lengths of having her hair cut off.

In the end investigation showed quite clearly that Miss Lawrence's story was as true as it was simple, much to the disappointment of those eager officers who felt they had caught a master spy. Still, the Army salved its pride by keeping her in a convent at St. Omer until any secrets she may have acquired no longer mattered. With so much happening towards the end of 1915 this was a matter of only a few months and, as Dorothy was a heroine of sorts, young officers came to talk with her through the convent grille and to offer her books. Finally, on the orders of the Commander-in-Chief himself, Sir John French, she was released. The Provost Marshal warned her to stay away from the front and said that the results of disobedience would be too unpleasant to contemplate. She was provided with an escort all the way to London, and thus ended the military career of Dorothy Lawrence.

Miss Lawrence has been much maligned for making a nuisance of herself, for causing needless difficulties, and for having 'the reprehensible motive of sheer curiosity', among other things. I am unable to see what is reprehensible about sheer curiosity and feel that she can only be accused of one major fault – that she led men much simpler-minded than herself into doing things which could have had them severely punished. There is no record that they were punished, but the possibility appeared not to bother her. Much later she said that her purpose in embarking on the adventure was to show that an enemy agent, even a woman one, could pierce the security screen. But this does an injustice to her own adventurous spirit. Although Miss Lawrence was no heroine in the physical sense that Hannah Snell and Deborah Sampson were, she had no opportunity to be. Without decrying her personal courage, perhaps it was just as well for her that she did not have to go over the top. But she did endure enough enemy action during her brief stay at the front to establish a certain amount of courage. Men – and women – are usually judged by what they succeed in doing, not by what they would like to do. It was Dorothy Lawrence's misfortune that she did not save the day, the guns or the colonel's life. Had she done something as spectacular as this she would have been acclaimed a heroine. I doubt if she ever forgave the Army for not allowing her to become one.

Josephine Baker (1906–75)

The Secret Life of 'Nefertiti'

Josephine Baker, the brilliant American revue dancer whom Picasso once called 'the modern Nefertiti', secretly worked for the French Resistance during the Second World War and afterwards was awarded several honours by the grateful nation, including the Croix de Guerre and Légion d'Honneur. Born in St Louis, Josphine had always wanted to dance and after making her début at the Cotton Club in Harlem became an international star when she crossed the Atlantic and appeared in many spectacularly successful revues at the Folies Bergères and the Casino de Paris. Her dancing was celebrated as 'très sauvage', but underneath the glamour and spontaneity beat the heart of a patriot, as **E. H. Cookridge** reveals for the first time in this essay.

The inimitable Josephine Baker enhanced her reputation and retained her integrity by becoming involved in espionage. This she was able to do because she helped a cause in which she believed. She agreed to perform these duties out of her own passionate free will.

The story of Josephine Baker, the entertainer of world repute, is well known. The story of Josephine Baker the secret agent is, in accordance with her own wishes, hardly known at all. It has never been told before to the English-reading public. I have the account of her war-time activities from Captain Jacques Abtey, who recruited her. She was very modest about these achievements, and her attitude was revealed when she was offered money for her efforts on behalf of the Allies. She refused any reward.

'It is France which made me what I am,' she declared. 'We coloured people could live in France happily, there was no colour bar or racial prejudice. I have become the darling of Paris, and to Paris and France I owe eternal gratitude. They gave me their heart, and I gave them mine. Today I am ready to give my life for France . . .'

The story of Josephine Baker, intelligence agent, starts one evening in September 1939, soon after the outbreak of the war. Captain Jacques Abtey, who had just left his post as adjutant of the garrison of Nantes to rejoin the counter-espionage section of the military intelligence in Paris, was sipping an apéritif in a boulevard café. He was hailed by an old friend, Daniel Marouani, the well-known impresario who looked after Josephine's theatrical interests.

Marouani told Abtey that Josephine was anxious to do some war work. Within a few minutes the two men agreed that she would make an excellent secret agent. Josephine already had some experience in this field. As one of the *correspondants honorables* – the honorary correspondents of M. Gianviti, head of counter-espionage at the Paris Prefecture – she had furnished some discreet information concerning an Italian diplomat. Abtey reported his conversation with Marouani to his chiefs, Colonel Schlesser and Commandant Palloile of the 'German Section', which was then domiciled at 2, Avenue de Tourville, and known as the 'Tourville Bureau'. Josephine was accepted into the organisation before she even knew herself that she was an agent. Abtey was ordered to be 'attached' to her.

Thus Josephine and Jacques embarked on an Odyssey which led them from France to Spain, Portugal, Morocco, Algeria, Tunisia, Libya, Egypt, Iraq, Syria, Lebanon and back to liberated Paris. For a time during these war years she worked with British intelligence in the Middle East.

Her exploits, as one would expect, had their lighter moments. She rarely assumed anything but her own famous name and personality. Neither did she discard some of her charming foibles. At one time she insisted that at least part of her private zoo should be despatched across Nazi-occupied France to North Africa. Anyone who has come under her spell, either as a personal friend or a member of her world-wide audience, knows that Josephine is that supreme rarity, a woman endowed with all the most desirable qualities of her sex but also with high intelligence and a rich sense of humour. She could always afford to mock herself, poke fun at her audiences and even at her Nazi pursuers. Jacques Abtey gradually turned her into a fully-fledged intelligence worker who learned to employ all the techniques of a trained operative.

Abtey was ordered to collect Josephine from her sumptuous château in the Dordogne. The cabaret star, who had amassed a fortune from her appearances on stage and screen, lived at the Château des Mirandes near Castlenau-Fayrac, a turreted fifteenth-century manor which she had modernised luxuriously. Abtey gave a memorable picture of his first visit. The star had a household of nine, all of whom were later to play a courageous part in the Resistance. There was her secretary, Emmanuel Bayonne, born in Mexico and a former French naval officer, and Joseph Boné, her pilot. Josephine was a keen flier herself. She owned a private aircraft and held one of the first *brevets de pilot* issued to a woman in France. In addition there was Malaure, a blacksmith and odd-job man; Dartain, the gardener; Madame Larenne, the house-

keeper; François, the valet; Paulette, the lady's maid; and
Père and Mère Jacob, a Belgian refugee couple who presided
over the kitchen. Other lively inhabitants of the castle were
Bonzo, the Great Dane; Glou-Glou, a black howling monkey, 'full of malice'; Mica, a fierce baboon; Gigusse, a heavily
mustachioed saki, and Bigout and Point d'Interrogation, two
white mice who usually nestled in Josephine's dress. It took
some persuasion before Josephine agreed to leave her zoo in
the castle. She wanted to take them all on her journeys.

For the first few weeks Josephine worked in Paris, mixing
with Belgian and French refugees, among whom were a
number of German spies planted by the Nazi espionage
service. Then came the fall of France and Abtey was ordered
to go to London to receive his instructions from the Free
French and British intelligence. He travelled with a forged
passport under the name of Jacques Hebert. In the meantime
Josephine had received permission from the German military
authorities to go to Madrid to appear there in cabaret.
Although the military treated her decently, this did not
prevent the Gestapo from looting her castle. In November
1940 Josephine and Jacques arrived in Lisbon, their true
destination. She installed herself at the Hotel Aviz.

Everything had been prepared to make her visit appear
purely professional. She sang in variety and on Radio National. But her real assignment was to find two German spies.
For many months they had been endangering the only escape
route from France to the free world: over the Pyrenees to
Lisbon and on by sea to London. Several Free French agents
and the British intelligence officers Douglas Hay, Fred
Waller, John Benett and Ian Donaldson were in Lisbon in
connection with the same affair. They wanted to extract some
of the French ministers, politicians and generals wishing to
join General de Gaulle.

Josephine has always been rather reluctant to disclose the
details of how she unmasked Heinz Reinert, the burly, six
foot four Gestapo chief who was in charge of stopping the
escapes. Reinert shuttled between the French frontier, Madrid and Lisbon in the guise of a German businessman by the

name of Georg Runke. For many months he remained
undiscovered by the Allied agents. Josephine managed to
unmask him. Into the bargain, she identified another dangerous Gestapo man, Karl Klump, who had, with the assistance of the Franco police, caught several French fugitives
and delivered them to the SS men waiting on the frontier.
They perished in German concentration camps. But many
more fugitives owed their lives and freedom to Josephine.

From Lisbon Abtey-Hebert had established contact with
his former chief, Commandant Palloile of the 'Tourville'.
Palloile had gone to Vichy, where he pretended to support
the Pétain Government while setting up a most efficient De
Gaulle network which covered the whole of unoccupied
France.

Josephine's Lisbon assignment was finished. The Germans never found out who it was that had unmasked Reinert
and Klump. Now she coolly petitioned the Vichy Government for an entry permit to Marseilles, under the pretext that
she had to fulfil an engagement at the opera-house there. At
first she had not wanted to sing in France, declaring: 'I shall
not play again before the last Nazi has been driven out of
France.' But she had to agree with Abtey that she could be
much more useful if she pretended to be friendly with the
Pétain-Laval quislings. In December she sang to full houses
in Offenbach's *La Créole* at Marseilles, while Abtey remained in Lisbon, where an emissary from London, 'Bacon',
met him and brought £1,000 for Josephine. But she refused
to accept the money.

London ordered Abtey and Josephine to North Africa.
The plans for the landing in Algeria were being prepared.
The invasion of Oran and Algiers did not take place until
November 1941, but already Military Intelligence in London
needed all the information available. Josephine arrived in
Algiers in January 1941 and for many months travelled all
over North Africa, singing at night in theatres and cabarets or
over the air, and in her 'spare time' gathering vital bits of
information about coastal defences, deployment of troops
and the complex political situation. In Morocco she had

secret meetings with Bee Bachin, brother of the Sultan, a supporter of the Allies. In Marrakesh she enlisted the help of El Glaoui Pasha, the old Berber warrior chief, who later became a close friend and host to Winston Churchill.

She accomplished many delicate missions, including the distribution of bribes among the Bedouin and Berber sheikhs. Some of this money came from her own pocket. Only Josephine could have enchanted men such as Moulay Larbi el Alaoui, the cunning Vezir of Morocco, into giving her important information. She made friends among the high-ranking officers of the entourage of General Noguès, the Vichyite and pro-German governor-general. They, too, provided her with information, which was promptly passed on to London. It was a risky thing for them to do in those dark days when Rommel's Afrika Korps had pushed the British army almost to the outskirts of Alexandria.

Josephine was everywhere: in Agadir, in Fez, in Tunis. She crossed into Libya and offered to sing for the German and Italian troops in order to contact the Senousi chiefs who harassed the Axis army in the desert. During every moment of this 'entertainment tour' she was running the risk of being unmasked by the Germans as an Allied agent and put before a firing squad.

In the winter 1941–2 Josephine fell suddenly ill in Casablanca. Her illness was officially diagnosed as para-typhoid. But it is almost certain that she was the victim of attempted murder by poison. For some time German Abwehr agents had suspected her of being at least a De Gaulle sympathizer, if not an Allied spy. But because of her great popularity the Nazis and the Italians dared not arrest her because it would have caused an outcry throughout French North Africa, where they were anxious to maintain the goodwill of the Vichy officials and collaborators. For many months Josephine was between life and death. As she lay in hospital Allied aircraft attacked Casablanca almost ceaselessly.

At last the invasion began. For three days and three nights 150,000 American and 140,000 British and Free French troops poured from hundreds of ships and landing boats onto the beaches of North Africa.

When General Patton led the spearhead of his army into Casablanca and heard that Josephine was ill, he sent her a flower arrangement with a card: 'To Josephine Baker who helped us so valiantly.'

While she was still very weak from her illness she insisted on singing at a gala performance of the newly opened Liberty Club. In her audience were many great Allied military leaders: Field-Marshal Alexander, General Clark, General Patton, General Anderson, Admiral Cunningham. For several weeks she entertained American and British troops. Then she was given another secret assignment.

Palloile, Abtey's former intelligence chief, had arrived in North Africa with Colonels Rivet and Du Crest. The situation in the French mandated territories of Syria and Lebanon was disturbing.

The French were facing serious eruptions of Arab nationalism. The Allies now had the upper hand in the Middle East, but this was not having the quieting effect on the Arabs for which some observers had hoped. The agents of Hitler and Mussolini had helped to sow the seed of rebellion which was to grow into a mighty upheaval that to this day envelops the Middle East.

In January 1943 Roosevelt and Churchill met at Casablanca to prepare the second front in Europe. Josephine was sorely tempted by an invitation to the United States consulate at Saadia, where the two statesmen were staying. But she decided that duty came first. She had been told to go to Beirut and to report to the French envoy, M. Helleu. The assignment was of a different kind from those she had been given before. It was not Nazi or Italian spies she had to cover, but Arab nationalists and revolutionaries. Haj Amin, the Mufti of Jerusalem, had fled to Germany. But his disciples were busy undermining British and French rule. In Iraq and Syria supporters of Rashid Ali, whose Nazi-inspired and financed rebellion against the British had been suppressed in 1941, had become troublesome again. There was the Arabic

League of Ibrahimi el Wazzami, intermingled with Nazi agents.

As late as 1943, long after the total defeat of Rommel in North Africa, emissaries despatched by the Germans from Turkey did their utmost to inflame the Arabs' hatred of France and Britain. Josephine, herself a coloured person, was asked to obtain as much detailed evidence of this campaign as she could.

Josephine travelled across Libya and Egypt to Beirut and Bagdad. Through Commandant Brousset of the French secret service she was introduced to officers of British Middle East intelligence. At times she disguised herself as an Arab woman and, accompanied by the Moroccan prince Si Menebhi, helped to run to earth some of the Nazi spies in the area. For instance, she was instrumental in achieving the downfall of two women agents of the Gestapo, Aglaya Neubacher and Paula Kock.

Eventually Josephine returned to Algiers. On her way back she insisted on entertaining the weary troops, resting uneasily after their great victories. In Cairo, Alexandria, Misurata, Tobruk, Benghazi, Tripoli, she sang, riotously greeted, at Ensa concerts. In Algiers she was received by General de Gaulle.

Italy had capitulated, the war was almost over. France was not yet wholly free, but already rising from defeat and subjugation. At last, on 25 August 1944, the French 2nd Armoured Division entered liberated Paris. Josephine sailed for her beloved France. But she did not return to her castle in the Dordogne. Behind the armies which pushed across the Rhine and into Germany 'the darling of Paris' travelled to give comfort and pleasure to the soldiers. She sang at liberated Strasbourg, at Metz, at Colmar, a few hours after the enemy's departure.

After Germany's surrender, Josephine, a 'special agent' in retirement but still the celebrated singer, visited the French troops in occupied Karlsruhe, Stuttgart and Hamburg and was greeted everywhere by the British Tommies and American GIs as enthusiastically as by her own compatriots. In

Germany she was the guest of the United States High Commissioner, Mr Robert Murphy, at the Hohenzollern castle at Sigmaringen. Back in Paris, General de Gaulle bestowed on her the Cross of Lorraine and the Resistance Medal. He also sent her a letter, in which he thanked her for her 'magnificent work and the great services rendered at a time of France's gravest difficulties'.

Josephine Baker, nearing middle age, but still a celebrated star in great demand all over the world, spent her vacations from theatrical engagements dedicated to her nine adopted children. Once these babies of many races, French, Arab, Negro, Jewish, Spanish, were unwanted strays. Instead they enjoyed the love and tender care of their new mother. When, at the beginning of the war, Josephine embarked on her perilous travels, she demanded, perhaps a little frivolously, to be accompanied by her dogs and monkeys. When in 1958 she was performing in Stockholm, she felt lonely without her large young family. So she sent for three of her toddlers: Marianne, who is French; Brahim, a little Algerian boy; and baby Koffi, who was born in Central Africa.

There were women agents who accomplished more spectacular feats of espionage. There are singers and dancers of greater virtuosity. But there was rarely a woman so human, so gracious, so big-hearted as Josephine Baker.

Nancy Wake (1917–)

The Feminine Fury

Nancy Wake was one of many heroines of the Second World War, but she is unique in having been the only female actually to have led men into action. Born in New Zealand, Nancy grew up in Australia, was a nurse and then a freelance journalist. Her job took her to Paris, where she met and married a Frenchman; the couple settled in France just a few years before the outbreak of hostilities. Even then she became involved in the war quite by chance, as Russell Braddon described in his best-selling biography, *Nancy Wake* (1956). But in time such was Nancy's legend that one French Resistance leader said of her, 'She is the most feminine woman I know – until the fighting starts. Then she is like five men!' This adaptation of her remarkable feats as an agent code-named 'The White Mouse', saboteur, bomb-maker and leader of the Maquis d'Auvergne, is by **Paula May** and was originally published in 1971.

When war broke out in 1939 Nancy Wake was living in Marseilles with her husband, Henri Fiocca, a wealthy steel industrialist. When Henri was called up Nancy became an ambulance driver, a dangerous and distressing occupation during the last months before the French collapsed and the British were pushed into the sea. Her ambulance was often full of badly wounded soldiers and civilians and she drove under fire from Stukas, flying low and machine-gunning the roads. In the end there was nothing effective that either she or anybody else in France could do and she returned to Marseilles, in the unoccupied part of France, where she was eventually joined by her husband.

She became involved in the war quite by chance. Waiting in a hotel for a friend with whom she was to dine, her attention was drawn to a tall, fair, good-looking man sitting at the bar quietly reading a book. Somehow he seemed unmistakably English and when the barman whispered to Nancy that the man was reading an English book she was startled. It was quite a risk to take in a hotel in which the German and Italian Missions were staying. Also taking a risk – the man could have been a German agent trying to trap Gaullist agents – Nancy engaged him in conversation and found that he was a British army officer who wanted to get back to England. By making enquiries for him, Nancy introduced herself and her husband to an escape organization. Then by delivering 'packages' for strange people she became a member of the French Resistance. Life was dangerous enough without these activities because, of course, she was British and if the Germans found out she would be taken away.

She made many trips guiding groups of men on their way to Spain and eventually England, and her organization got more than 1,000 men to safety, probably more than any other network managed to extricate.

Early in November 1942 Nancy Wake's activities became even more risky when the Germans decided, after all, to march into unoccupied France. It was no coincidence that at this time the Gestapo began to write reports about a Resistance agent they called 'The White Mouse'. They used this *nom de guerre* because they had no other name for her. The white mouse was Nancy Wake. Her husband also was running appalling risks in helping the Underground's work. In addition, he gave well over £6,000 to the movement, plus an allowance to Nancy of £25 a day, most of which went on her subversive activities.

En route to England, early in 1943, she was arrested in Toulouse, beaten and questioned, but the Resistance managed to get her out of gaol and she continued her trip. Her train to Perpignan, on the Spanish frontier, was searched by the Germans but, warned by a railway official, Nancy and her fellows jumped. German machine-gunners sprayed bullets over the vineyard through which the party fled, but most escaped. Soon after this a Gestapo agent within the Resistance 'blew' much of the organization and in June 1943, after an adventurous journey, Nancy Wake reached England.

Her war experience to date had been a prelude; she was not yet a soldier, though she had been under fire. But soon after arriving in England she was asked by Colonel Buckmaster, one of the most famous spymasters in history, to join his group. Enlisting under her maiden name, she signed up for service at the headquarters of an organization known as the First Aid Nursing Yeomanry. This unit had been created in 1907 to give an opportunity to wealthy, upperclass women to serve their country, under attractive conditions – pleasant company, very mild discipline and in fashionable uniform. Rank hardly mattered at all in the FANY, for all the women were of the same social class. But not all were connected with first aid. Not by a long way. For the group had also become a cover to train women as saboteurs and military leaders to be dropped into France. Nancy Wake was appointed an ensign, and with others climbed trees and walls, jumped gaps, slid down long ropes. Transferring to the Special Operations Executive, she was the only woman on a tough course which included demolitions. She learned how to make her own explosives from ingredients which could be bought innocently and openly from a chemist or an ironmonger.

She acquired the reputation of a crack shot with a sten-gun because her bullets never flew high – a frequent failing with many men. Nancy did not mention that as she had weak wrists the barrel tended to drop anyway and so could not fire high.

She was taught how to kill silently, how to use a compass by night, how to operate a radio. But it is pleasing to report that she did *not* outshine the male students and that she was *not* a natural-born warrior. She was often incompetent with grenades, she capsized a rowing-boat in a simple exercise. After all this the group learned how to parachute-jump, but training did not end there. In the New Forest in Hampshire they attended another school, basically dealing in security, where Nancy learned how to identify German badges of rank, aircraft and regiments. There were interrogation exercises, too, but she had been through these before – the real thing.

Nancy was the first of her group to be posted and on 29 February or 1 March 1944, with a male agent, she parachuted into France, near Montluçon, to begin a career under the name of Madame Andrée. (Among her other names she was Hélène to her superiors in London, and Gertie to her intimates in France.) She set up her headquarters at Chaudes-Aigues, and soon found herself in virtual control of more than 7,000 men. The whole of the Maquis d'Auvergne, in fact, for they had been left leaderless after a German raid. When she met the group leaders of these men she laid down the conditions under which, in future, the region would be militarily operated. It was no small feat to become, in a month, a strong and respected leader. The men she controlled were tough, rebellious, difficult, and they resented, initially at least, having a woman give them orders. But she always bested them, even at drinking and swearing, and they soon found that in these masculine fields she was more of a man than they were.

Life was hard for innocent civilians in areas in which the Maquis was active, for they caught the full fury of the Nazis' spite. Farmhouses were burned down and the occupants murdered. Hostages were taken and shot or hanged from trees as a warning to the Maquis. There was much of this terrorism in the Auvergne, for it was a notable Maquis stronghold and one which the Germans were determined to crush. Knowing that the Resistance men were on the plateau above Chaudes-Aigues they, on 20 June, launched a full-scale military attack; 22,000 SS troops, equipped with artillery and supported by aircraft, moved in to encircle the 7,000 Maquis.

Nancy Wake probably worked harder than anybody that day as she loaded weapons, ammunition and supplies onto her truck and distributed them to the Maquis posts. She came under direct artillery fire during these excursions and the house in which she took a short sleep was hit. Later in the day, having taken an urgent order to a Maquis leader, she was driving along a difficult road when two planes machine-gunned and riddled her car from the rear; then one turned and roared back down the road. This time the burst of fire ended just short of the car. The plane kept after Nancy and when she had to shelter in a ditch the pilot succeeded in blowing up the vehicle. Then developed the remarkable sight of Nancy Wake and a lone young Maquis member alternately dodging and running as the German plane alternately circled and dived after them, machine-gunning each time.

That night Nancy and the surviving Resistance men, nearly all of them in fact, stole away from the plateau, which 1,500 Germans had died to capture. Nancy carried with her, among more martial equipment, some cosmetics and a red satin cushion. Later, pushing her physical resources to the limit, she rode a bike for more than 500 kilometres, covering the distance and completing a frustrating and dangerous mission all in seventy-two hours. The war-women of old had never been called upon to display such a variety of talents or so much compressed fortitude.

By July 1944 Nancy had moved her headquarters and sphere of operations to the Allier district where she led a force of 2,000 Maquis. Cooperating with a Maquis leader, Tardivat, she took to preparing ambushes for German convoys moving troops and supplies to the Normandy front. Stopping or delaying these convoys was major war work. The ambushes were simple; the waiting Resistance men would wreck the first two or three vehicles and the last two or three on the convoy, throw their high-explosive and fire bombs, fire furiously for a minute and then vanish. Paul Brickhill quotes Tardivat as saying of Nancy, 'She is the most feminine woman I know – until the fighting starts. Then she is like five men!' Feminine she managed to remain; she always slept in a nightdress, no matter how hard the going might be.

With her men, she disappeared from her headquarters when the Germans attacked and then moved her camp to another forest, but here again the Germans attacked – at least 6,000 of them against 200 Maquis. Nancy took twenty men and two American weapons-training officers, who had arrived during the action, to attack enemy armoured cars and machine-guns, a tall order. Seven Frenchmen refused to take cover when ordered and were shot down, whereupon the other thirteen, who were only youths, panicked and ran. Nancy screamed black-foul French at them. 'Wholly feminine, transformed by the catalyst of her own anger into an astonishingly erect and fine-drawn beauty she stood there, feet apart, hands on hips . . .' wrote Russell Braddon. '. . . like a whip, her voice pursued them.'

Some stopped and did as she ordered, while Nancy and the American officers closed in to fire bazooka rockets at the German armoured cars and machine-guns. In what would probably have been a Victoria Cross action in the regular army, this one woman and the two men wiped out the direct threat to the Maquis camp. But the danger was still acute and with only one man Nancy crawled and ran two miles for help, under fire much of the distance. With the help of Tardivat's group she managed to extricate her own group.

Being commander of a Maquis force was unlike any other military command; Nancy had to be her own chief-of-staff, adjutant, quartermaster, paymaster, and, most importantly, *chef du parachutage* – organizer of the drops. And all this among men who were not accustomed to military organization. Her multifarious duties kept Nancy out of some fighting, but now life was so dangerous that she had to use a personal bodyguard, while Spanish maquisards volunteered as a standing escort. She and they had to shoot their way out of German traps, and once a French communist threw a grenade at her.

In between times there was opportunity for kindness, such as the time Nancy rescued two French girls, falsely accused of being traitors, from the clutches of the Maquis. The men had kept secret their possession of these women and had foully misused and continually raped them: Nancy ordered their release and the younger girl became her maid.

Then there was the incident of Montluçon Gestapo headquarters. After careful planning, one day at lunch-hour Nancy, Tardivat and fourteen others raided the headquarters with grenades – despite the presence in the town of hundreds of enemy troops – and in a classic action left thirty-eight dead Germans. Excitement like this had become a way of life for Nancy Wake.

She was by now a captain, but not until late in August was she able to wear her regular uniform and badges of rank. In that month the Maquis actually took Montluçon and held it until the Germans sent in a strong force to counter-attack. At this the Maquis vanished into the forest again, though there was a scare when a long German convoy rumbled up the drive of the château in which Nancy had comfortably established her headquarters. But it passed by without stopping, while Nancy's own calmness prevented the men from opening fire and betraying themselves.

Every soldier has lived through experiences which have made him regret his trade. One such episode came to Nancy Wake one night in a raid on a factory making machinery for the Germans. Her part, with three men, was to disable German sentries. Her particular victim had his back to her as she crept up and had he kept it that way he would have suffered nothing more than a fractured skull. But he turned, thus forcing Nancy's hand. She had been trained to kill silently and now she did just this, breaking the German's neck with a Commando-movement that is best not described here. It was the only time she killed a man with her own hands, and she did not like it.

When, finally, the Allied troops appeared and the Germans moved out, violent action was over for Nancy Wake. In Vichy, very soon after Nancy and the Maquis moved in, in September 1944, the Swiss ambassador gave a party in her honour. But next day, at another public ceremony, a woman told her that Henri, her husband, had been executed by the Gestapo. He had, in fact, been betrayed and cruelly tortured before the Germans shot him on October 16, 1943. What they had most wanted to know was the whereabouts of Nancy; he told them nothing.

Britain awarded Nancy Wake the George Medal. The citation read:

This officer was parachuted into France as assistant to an organizer who was taking over the direction of an important circuit in Central France. The day after their arrival she and her chief found themselves stranded and without directions, through the arrest of their contact, but ultimately reached their rendezvous by their own initiative.

Ensign Wake worked for several months helping to train and instruct Maquis groups. She took part in several engagements with the enemy and showed the utmost bravery under fire. During a German attack, due to the arrival by parachute of two American officers to help the Maquis, Ensign Wake personally took command of a section of men whose leader was demoralized. She led them to within point-blank range of the enemy, directed their fire, rescued two American officers and withdrew in good order. She showed exceptional courage and coolness in the face of enemy fire.

When the Maquis group with which she was working was broken up by large-scale German attacks, and W/T contact was lost, Ensign Wake went alone to find a wireless operator through whom she could contact London. She covered some 200 kms on foot, and by remarkable steadfastness and perseverance succeeded in getting a message through to London. . . .

Ensign Wake's organizing ability, endurance, courage and complete disregard for her own safety earned her the respect and admiration of all with whom she came in contact. The Maquis troop, most of them rough and difficult to handle, accepted orders from her, and treated her as one of their own male officers. Ensign Wake contributed in a large degree to the success of the groups with which she worked . . .

She won more than the 'respect and admiration' of the men she worked with and led – she won their devotion. She did nothing to buy popularity – she was sometimes very tough – but most of the men would have done anything for her. They showed their feelings on several occasions, notably when they gave her a birthday feast at the château, presented her with flowers and gifts and marched past her as she stood on the château steps. It must have been one of the most remarkable functions ever held in Occupied France.

America awarded her the Medal of Freedom with Bronze Palm.

Ensign Nancy Wake, British National, FANY, for exceptionally meritorious achievement which aided the United States in the prosecution of the war against the enemy in Continental Europe, from March 1944 to October 1944. After having been parachuted into the Allier Department for the purpose of co-ordinating Resistance activities, she immediately assumed her duties . . . Despite numerous difficulties and personal danger she, through her remarkable courage, initiative and coolness, succeeded in accomplishing her objective. Her daring conduct in the course of an enemy engagement safeguarded the lives of two American officers under her command. Her inspiring leadership, bravery and exemplary devotion to duty contributed materially to the success of the war effort and merit the praise and recognition of the United States.

France awarded her two Croix de Guerre with Palm, a third Croix de Guerre with Star and the Resistance Medal. No citations were appended but the award of no fewer than four decorations speaks for itself. Few women have such an array of awards.

ACKNOWLEDGMENTS

Introduction and prefaces to individual accounts © 1999 by Gemma Alexander. The contributions to this collection are reprinted with the permission of the following newspapers and publishers:

'Lady Godiva – The Naked Heroine' by Marina Warner © 1982 by *Times* Newspapers Ltd.

'Ursula Sontheil – The Mother of Fortune-Tellers' by Josephine Gibney © 1973 by *This England* Publications Ltd.

'Princess Pocahontas – The Defender of Love' by Christine Baker-Carr © 1954 by the *Liverpool Echo*.

'Aphra Behn – The Notorious Mrs Behn' by Dorothy Hobman © 1957 by Watts & Co Ltd.

'Mary Anne Talbot – The Adventurous Life of "John Taylor"' by Margaret Dowie © 1934 Harrap & Co Ltd.

'Miranda Stuart – The Bizarre Career of "Dr James Barry"' by Reginald Hargreaves © 1958 by The Bodley Head.

'Lola Montez – The Most Outrageous Woman in the World' by Kendall McDonald © 1955 by Associated Newspapers Ltd.

'Jane Digby – The Queen of the Desert' by Alexander Allen © 1986 by Jupiter Books Ltd.

'Martha Jane Canary – "Calamity Jane": Frontierswoman' by James D. Horan © 1954 by Hamlyn Books Ltd.

'Emmeline Pankhurst – The Militant Suffragette' by Sylvia Pankhurst © 1935 by Constable & Co.

'Lucrezia Borgia – The World's Wickedest Woman?' by Margaret Nicholas © 1953 by Cassell & Co.

'Elizabeth Báthory – The Bloody Countess' by Peter Haining © 1994 by Boxtree Publishers Ltd.

'Mary Frith – Moll Cutpurse, The First Highwaywoman' by Philippa Waring © 1989 by Robert Hale Publishers Ltd.

'Mary Read & Anne Bonney – The Unique Pirate Duo' by Stephanie Brush © 1976 by *Viva* Publications Ltd.

'Charlotte Corday – The Angel of the Assassination' by Margaret Goldsmith © 1935 by Methuen Publishers Ltd.

'Ethel Le Neve – The Woman Who Loved Crippen' by Alfred Draper © 1977 by Associated Newspapers Ltd.

'Mata Hari – Mystery of the Exotic Dancer' by Ronald Seth © 1954 by Peter Owen Ltd.

'Ulrika Meinhof – The Urban Terrorist' by Margaret Nicholas © 1978 by Cassell & Co Ltd.

'Phoolan Devi – Law of the Bandit Queen' by Phoolan Devi © 1984 by *India Today*.

'Nell Gwynne – The Irresistible Sweet Nell' by Andrew Ewart © 1973 by IPC Magazines Ltd.

'Madame de Pompadour – The Power behind the Throne' by Nancy Mitford © 1954 by Hamis Hamilton Ltd.

'Lady Emma Hamilton – The Beguiling Lady Hamilton' by George Ryley Scott © 1929 by The Harleian Press.

'Catherine Walters – "Skittles": The Darling of London' by Donald MacAndrew © 1948 by Hutchinson & Co Ltd.

'Sarah Bernhardt – The Star Called "The Bernhardt"' by Lysiana Bernhardt © 1949 by Hurst & Blackett.

'Mae West – The Bad Girl of Broadway' by Mae West © 1960 by W. H. Allen & Co Ltd.

'Clara Bow – The "It" Girl in Hollywood' by David Stenn © 1989 by Ebury Press.

'Tallulah Bankhead – The Outrageous Tallulah' by Tallulah Bankhead © 1952 by Victor Gollancz Ltd.

'Madonna – The Natural-Born Exhibitionist' by Andrea Stuart © 1996 by Jonathan Cape Ltd.

'Queen Boadicea – The Revenge of the Warrior Queen' by Jean Thorley © 1949 by *East Anglian Magazine*.

'Countess Agnes Dunbar – "Black Agnes": The Scottish Amazon' by Harry Graham © 1936 by Methuen & Co Ltd.

'Christian "Kit" Cavanagh – "Mother Ross": The Bold Dragoon' by Charles Thompson © 1938 by Hutchinson & Co Ltd.

'Hannah Snell – The Brave Marine of Pondicherry' by John Laffin © 1967 by Abelard-Schuman Ltd.

'Charlotte Walpole – Mrs Pimpernel Atkyns' by Howard Swales © 1971 by *Norfolk Fair* Magazine Ltd.

'Sarah Emma Edmonds – Heroine of the American Civil War' by Julie Wheelright © 1989 Pandora Books.

'Constance Markievicz – On the Run with "The Red Countess"' by Constance Markievicz © 1927 by The Talbot Press.

'Dorothy Lawrence – The Sapper at the Front Line' by John Laffin © 1967 by Abelard-Schuman Ltd.

'Josephine Baker – The Secret Life of "Nefertiti"' by E. H. Cookridge © 1959 by Oldbourne Press Ltd.

'Nancy Wake – The Feminine Fury' by Paula May © 1956 by Associated Newspapers Ltd.